PANORAMA OF THE HUDSON RIVER

By Greg Miller

A photographic documentary of both sides of the river from
New York Harbor to Albany, updating and reprinting the classic 1910 *Panorama of the Hudson*

Published on the occasion of the exhibition *Panorama of the Hudson River: Greg Miller*, curated by Brian Wallace, held from July 11, 2009, through March 28, 2010, in the Sara Bedrick Gallery of the Samuel Dorsky Museum of Art.

Cover and Inside Photos:
Greg Miller, ***Panorama of the Hudson River***, 2009, digital photograph, dimensions variable, courtesy of the artist; Hudson River Day Line and Wallace Bruce, ***Panorama of the Hudson Showing Both Sides of the River from New York to Albany,*** before 1910, scanned page from souvenir book, 7 in. x 11 in., courtesy of the Samuel Dorsky Museum of Art.

Major support for this publication was provided by:
Congressman Maurice Hinchey
New York State Senator Vincent L. Leibell
Furthermore: a program of the J. M. Kaplan Fund
Hudson River Valley National Heritage Area
Barnabas McHenry
National Park Service
Open Space Institute, Inc.
Samuel Dorsky Museum of Art at SUNY New Paltz
The State University of New York Press

With additional involvement and support from:
Greg Miller
Ralph Brill
Christine Davitt
J. Gilbert Plantinga
Reed Sparling
Bert Butlin — *Serenity*
Greg Porteus — *Launch 5*
Rick Scarano — *Adirondack*

This publication is a joint undertaking of the Samuel Dorsky Museum of Art and Open Space Institute, Inc.:
Sara Pasti, The Neil C. Trager Director, and Brian Wallace, Curator, Samuel Dorsky Museum of Art; Joe Martens, President, and Tally Blumberg, Vice President External Affairs, Open Space Institute, Inc.

Published by the Samuel Dorsky Museum of Art
State University of New York at New Paltz
One Hawk Drive
New Paltz, New York 12561

Designed by Jeffrey Jenkins

Map Illustration courtesy of Connie Brown and Duncan Milne of Redstone Studios,
commissioned by Beacon Institute for Rivers and Estuaries

Printed by Maar Printing Company, Inc., Poughkeepsie, NY, a Forest Stewardship Council (FSC) certified printer.

Distributed by the State University of New York Press (www.sunypress.edu)

ISBN No. 978-0-615-29285-4

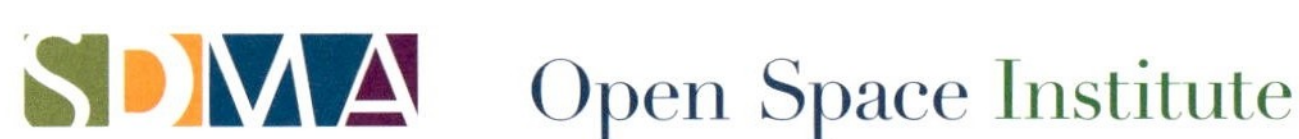

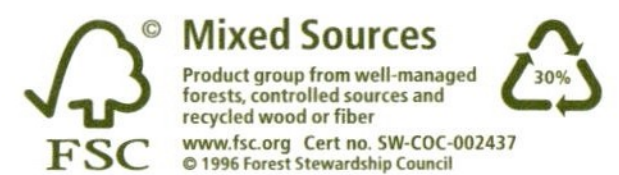

In honor of the 400th anniversary of Henry Hudson's voyage of discovery on the river that now bears his name, we are delighted to present this new edition of *Panorama of the Hudson*. It offers a 21st-century updating of a long-cherished 1910 photographic survey of every inch of the river's shorelines, tracing the *Half Moon*'s 1609 route from New York Harbor to present-day Albany. It also reprints the earlier edition, making it readily available for the first time in decades.

This book — and a concurrent exhibition at the Samuel Dorsky Museum of Art at the State University of New York at New Paltz — not only combines two extraordinary feats of photographic artistry, but provides an important record of changes that have occurred along the river since the Hudson Tricentennial celebrations of 1909. It should interest anyone enchanted by the Hudson River's beautiful and varied landscapes. At the same time, it could provide an excellent tool for those involved in continuing efforts to protect treasured but threatened places along its banks. We also hope it spurs future generations to create similar visual documentation.

With the maiden voyage of Robert Fulton's steamboat in 1807, a trip up the Hudson River became de rigueur on any itinerary of the United States. Satisfying a need for a keepsake of this journey whose sights inspired some of the purplest prose in 19th-century diaries, William Wade created the first panorama of the river's banks from Manhattan to the state capital in 1845. His 10-foot-long engraving, sold both in color and black and white, is a fascinating, masterful work.

The original photographic panoramas were sold as souvenirs aboard Hudson River Day Liners, grand steamships that plied the river between 1863 and 1948, offering the most fashionable (and enjoyable) mode of travel between New York City and upriver ports. The first panorama was published in 1888. The photographer of that and subsequent editions was G. Willard Shear. Except for a brief residency in Florida, where he was co-owner of a studio in the 1880s, little is known of Shear's career. Equally obscure is the equipment he utilized on this project — one of the most ambitious of its time. Panoramic cameras were invented in the 1840s; by 1910 Shear had myriad products at his disposal.

According to text in the 1910 edition, Shear's east- and west-bank panoramas are comprised of 800 photos. Despite strides in technology since then, Greg Miller took considerably more shots — as many as 2,500 — for this updated edition. And even with the aid of a computer, he probably spent more time matching up his prints than Shear did in constructing the original panoramas. Blame for that can be laid, in part, on the plethora and size of new buildings along the shore, primarily in and around Manhattan, which played havoc with angles while shooting from the deck of a moving boat.

Shear had the benefit of the Day Liners, which maintained a regular schedule and more or less constant speed. Miller was at the mercy, and generosity, of boat owners who were intrigued by the project. In the end, the variety of craft on which he made the 140-mile journey — the 80-foot schooner *Adirondack; Launch 5*, a former New York City Police Department harbor patrol boat; and the *Serenity*, an electric-powered vessel — says much about the Hudson's continued vitality.

Since the last panorama was produced, the river has made a remarkable comeback. In the first half of the 20th century, heavy industry came to dominate its banks, contaminating the land and wantonly polluting its waters. Beginning in the 1960s, the Hudson Valley became the cradle of a new environmental ethic that challenged this march of "progress." Organizations such as Clearwater, Scenic Hudson, Riverkeeper and the Open Space Institute were founded to improve the river's water quality, protect endangered species, clean up shorelines for the people's enjoyment and protect some of the very landmarks that captivated Hudson and his crew. Thanks to the conservation-minded spirit of these groups and countless individuals, the contemporary panorama bears a striking resemblance to its 1910 predecessor. We must remain vigilant that future images never again diverge.

Wallace Bruce, the poet, diplomat and Hudson Valley native who spearheaded the earlier panorama projects, wrote that "the Hudson, more than any other river, has a distinct personality — an absolute soul-quality." Above all, Greg Miller's panorama proves that nothing has diminished its power to cast a mighty spell.

Steven G. Poskanzer
President,
State University of New York at New Paltz

Joe Martens
President,
Open Space Institute

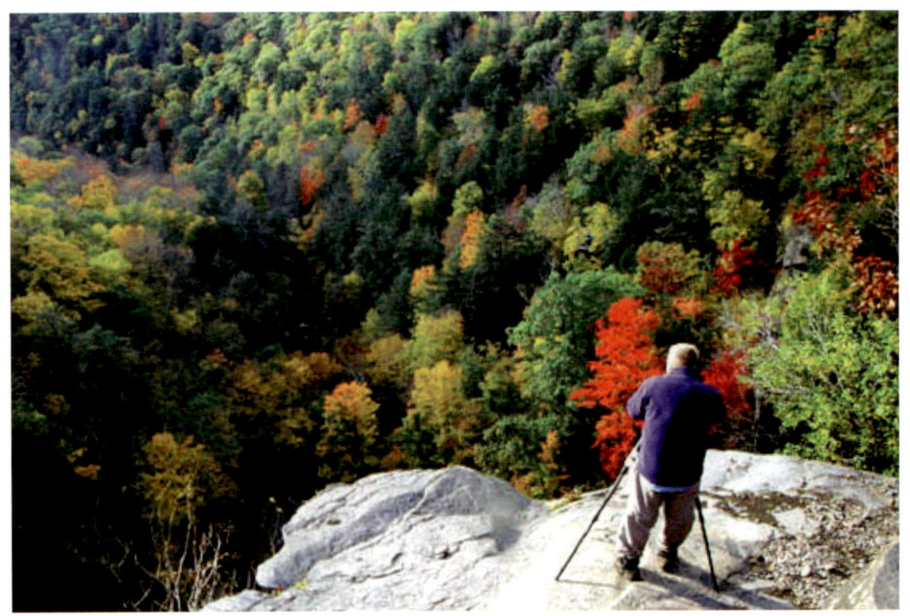

Photographer's Note

A project of this magnitude requires compromise. Some variable factors — such as the weather and boat captains' busy schedules — were relatively easy to manage. A thornier challenge was lining my photographs up with the 1910 images. This task was made more difficult by the fact that no information was available about techniques G. Willard Shear employed to create his panorama. It's also obvious Shear took some liberties with "cutting and pasting" (especially around the Catskills) to make his work appear more dramatic.

My primary intent was to create an updated and complete record of the Hudson's banks — a documentary as opposed to a work of art. In some instances, I had to digitally compress images so that natural and manmade features would coincide more closely with Shear's panorama. This is most evident along the river's northern stretches, where dredging to create a deeper shipping channel in the 1920s significantly altered the shorelines' appearance. Around Storm King Mountain, I felt compression would create too much distortion of one of the river's great landmarks. Here I opted to reduce the panorama's height, allowing me to replicate this iconic vista. Throughout you'll also notice occasional changes in lighting, the result of having to shoot at different hours over the course of several days.

In the end, creating these 80-foot-long photographs — certainly the most complex undertaking of my career — has left me with profound admiration for Shear's ingenuity and, especially, a deeper appreciation for the Hudson's beauty and breathtaking sweep. I hope my own panorama incites similar feelings in you.

Greg Miller
Monroe, N.Y.

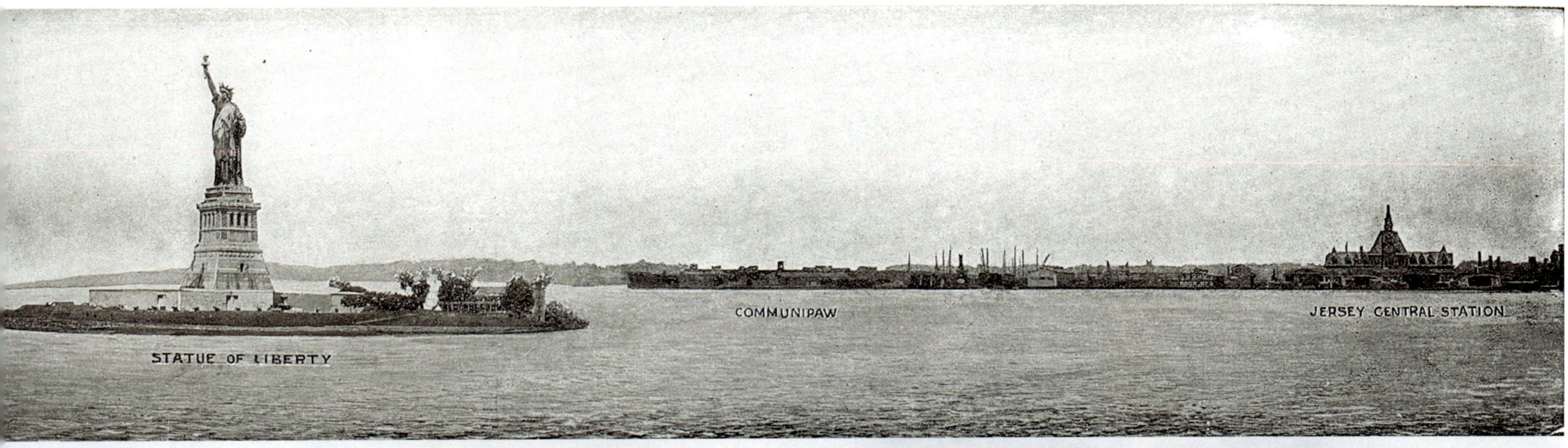

STATUE OF LIBERTY

COMMUNIPAW

JERSEY CENTRAL STATION

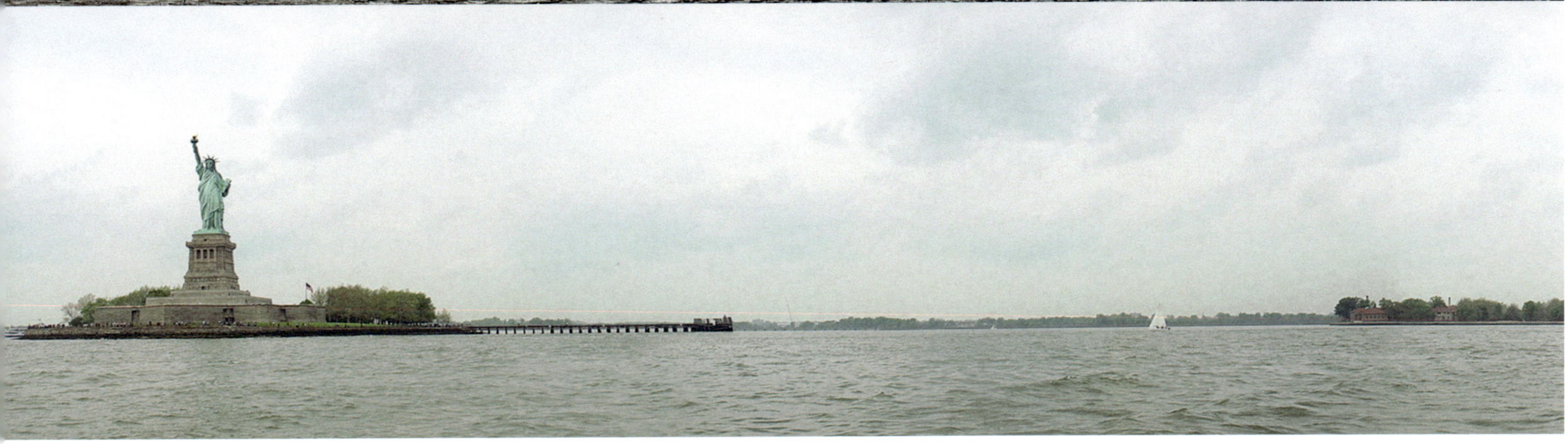

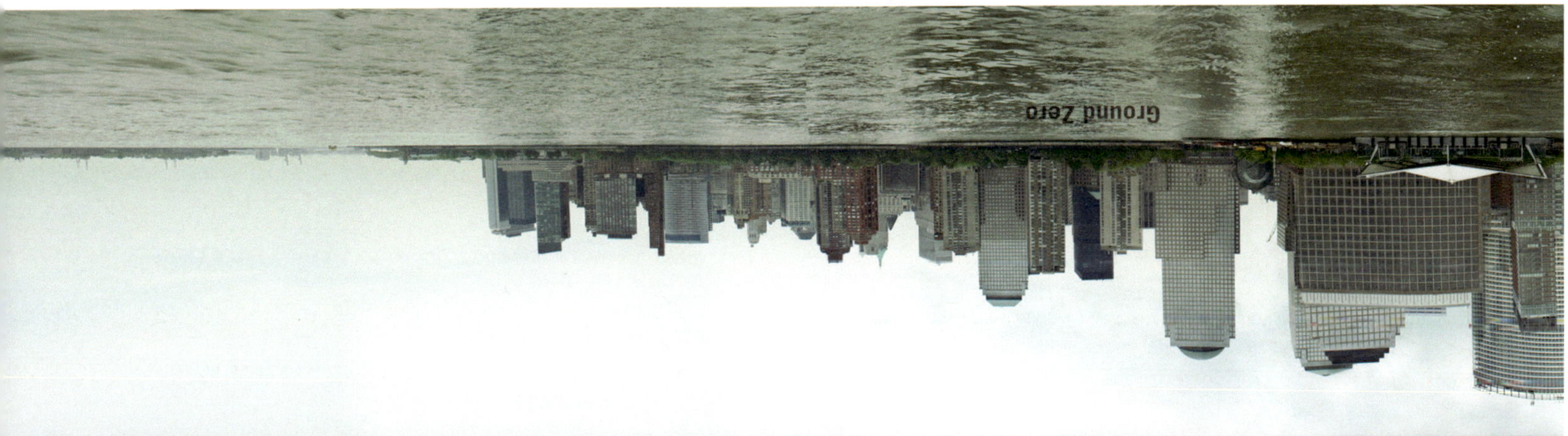

Ground Zero

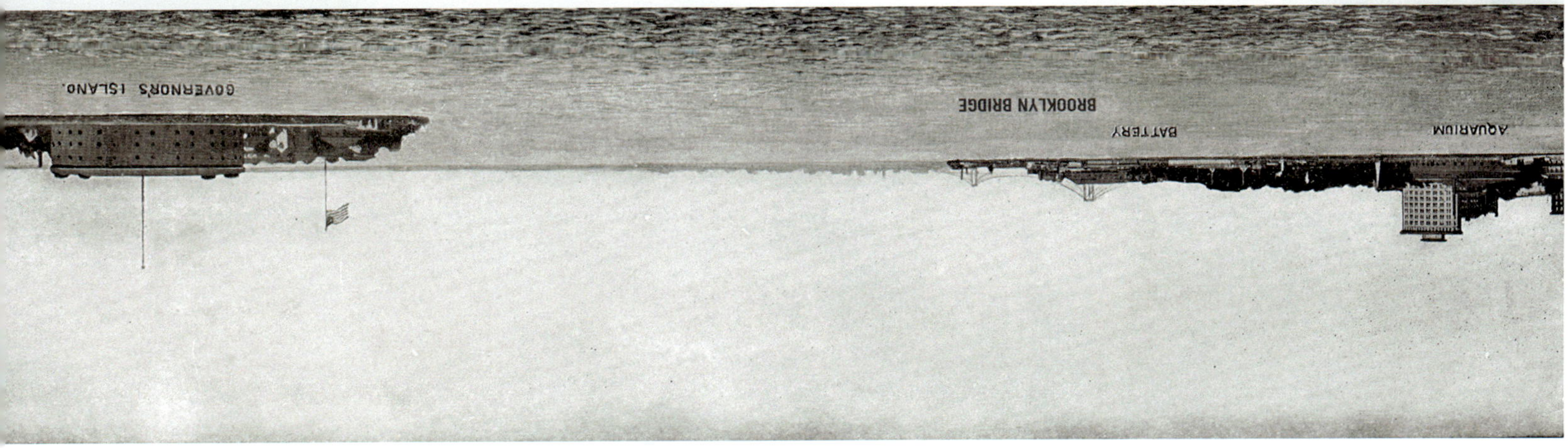

AQUARIUM

BATTERY

BROOKLYN BRIDGE

GOVERNOR'S ISLAND

JERSEY CITY

PENNSYLVANIA R.R. STATION

P.R.R. ELEVAT

Ellis Island

Exchange Pla

Colgate Clock

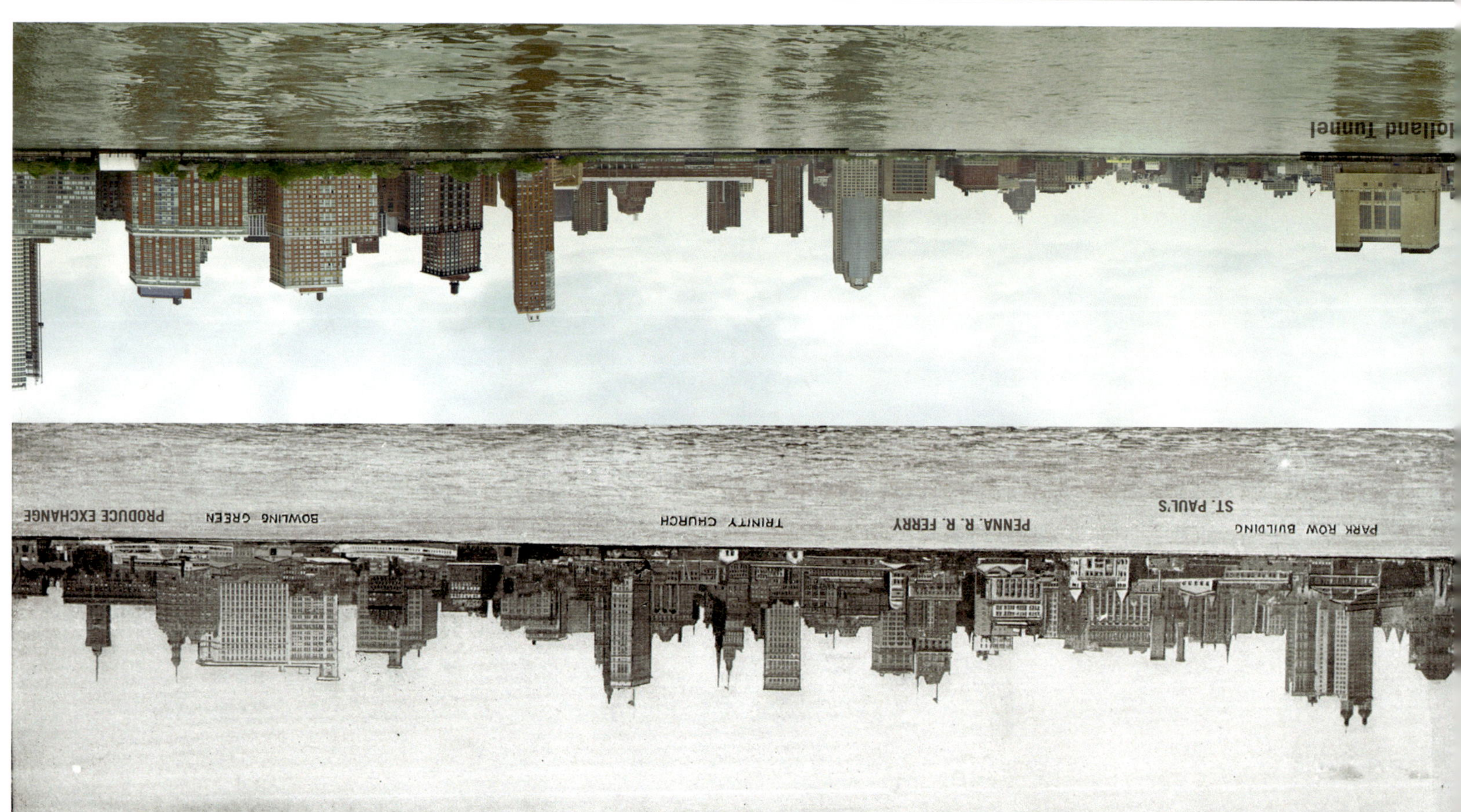

East Bank

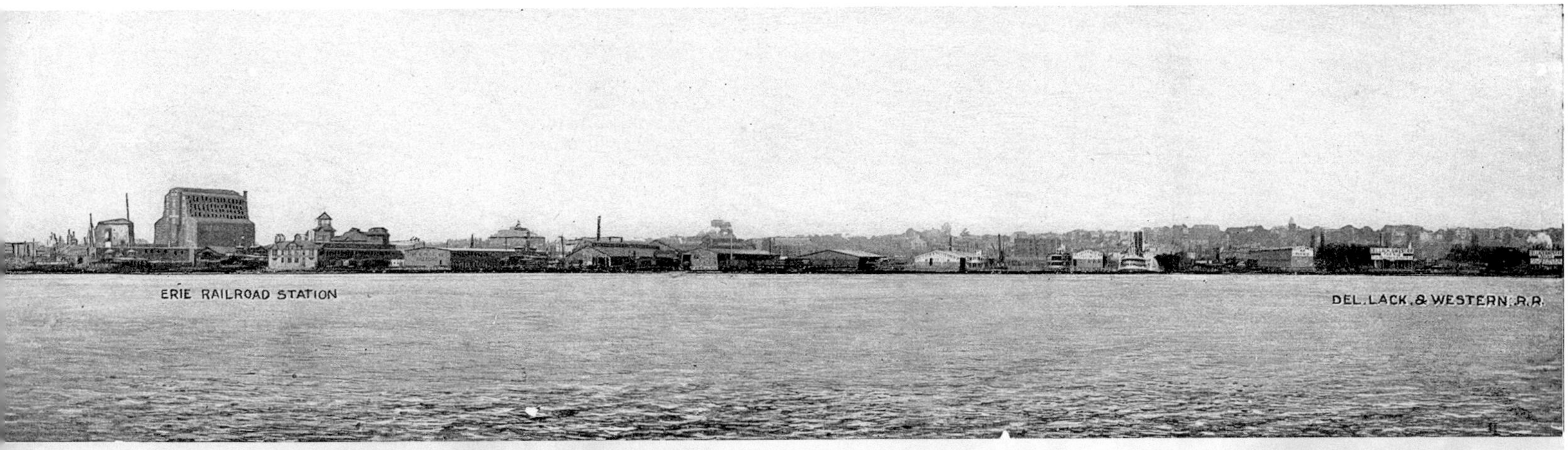

ERIE RAILROAD STATION

DEL. LACK. & WESTERN. R.R.

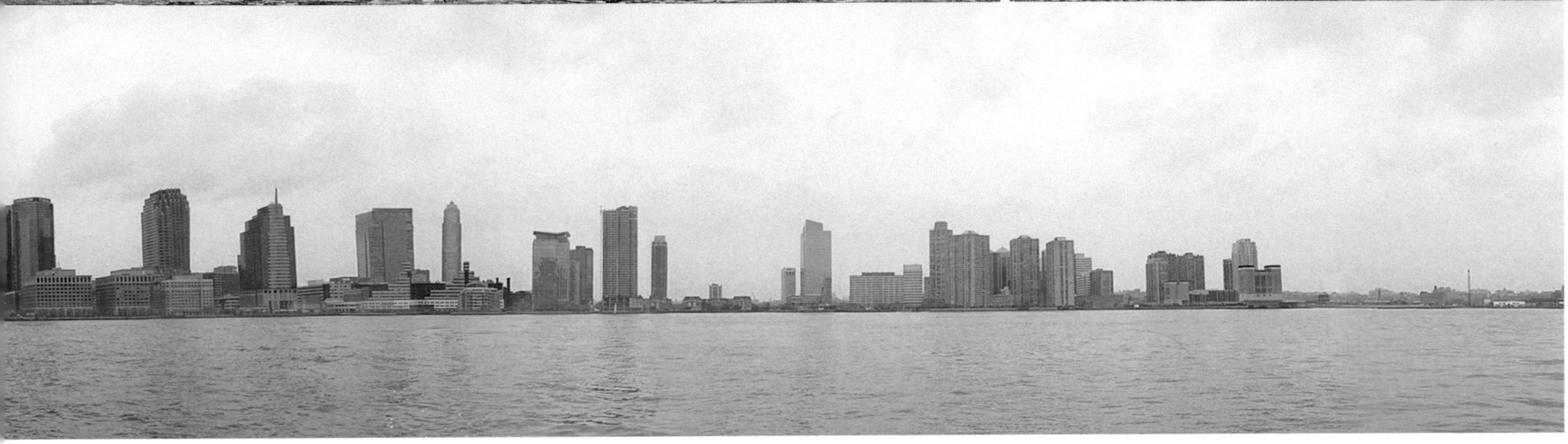

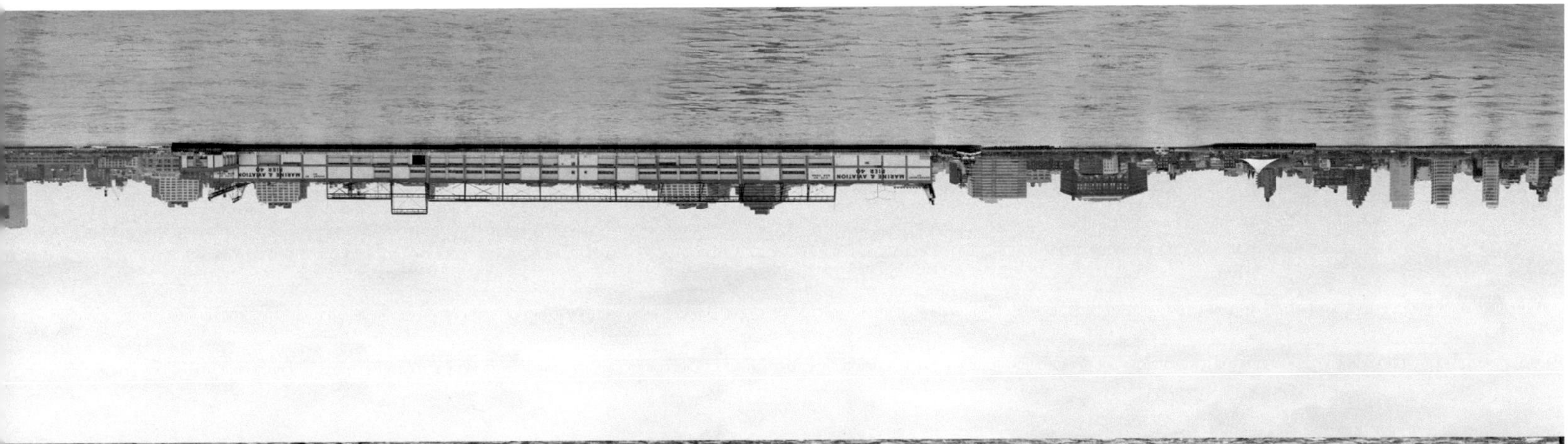

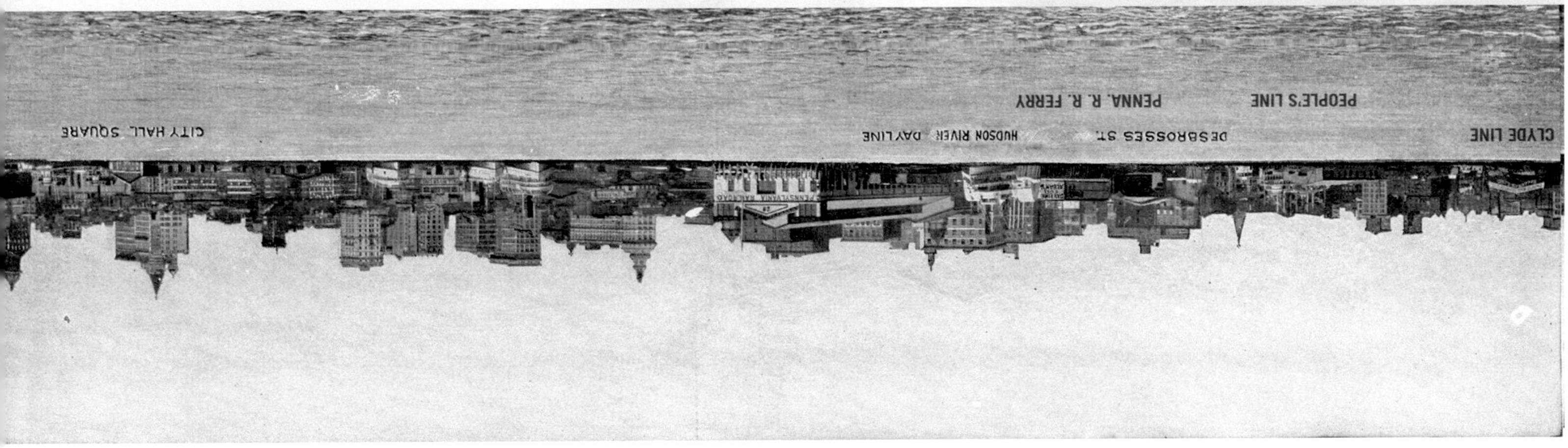

CLYDE LINE

PEOPLE'S LINE

DESBROSSES ST.

PENNA. R. R. FERRY

HUDSON RIVER DAY LINE

CITY HALL SQUARE

HOBOKEN

STEAMSHIP PIERS

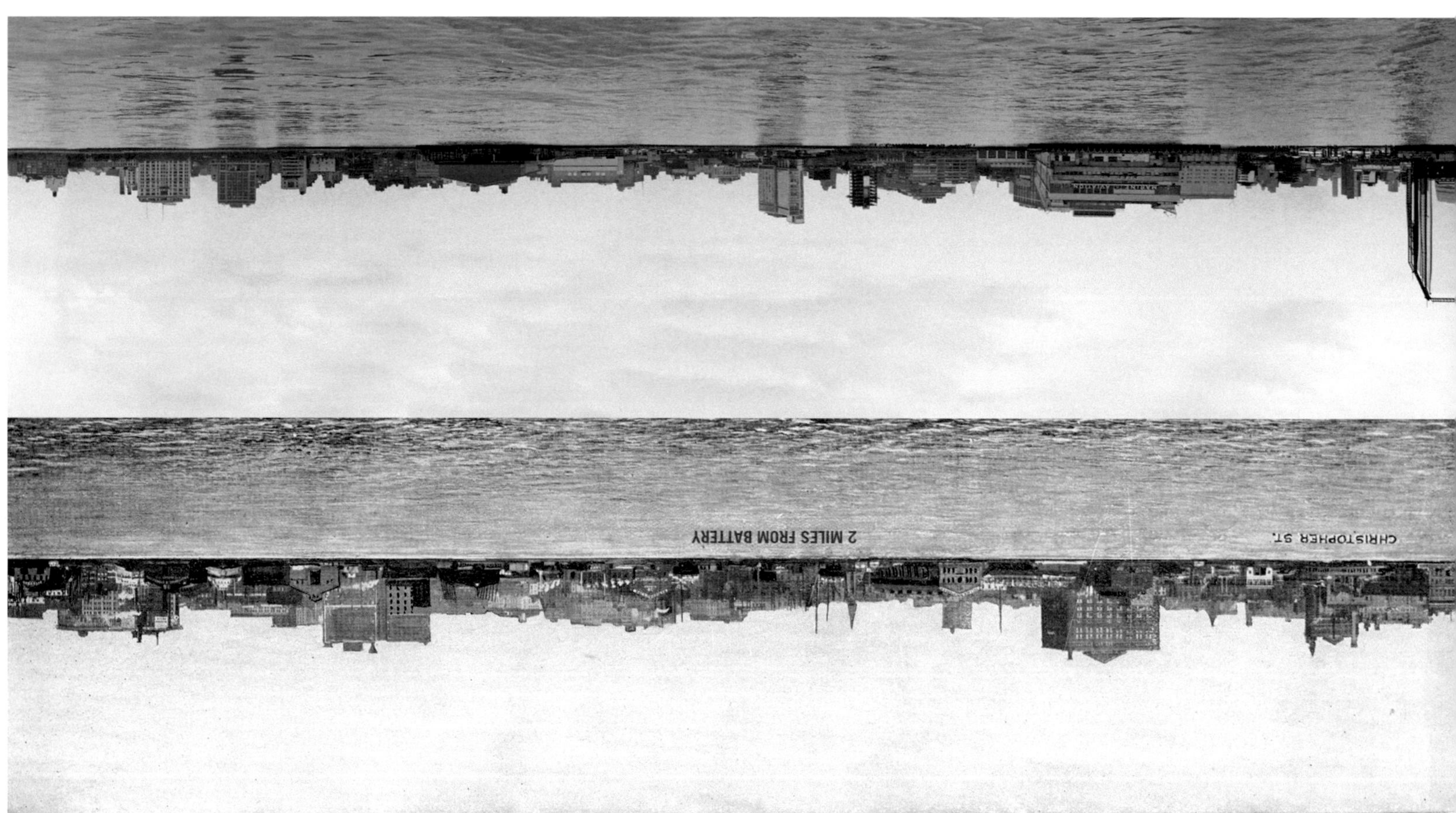

East Bank

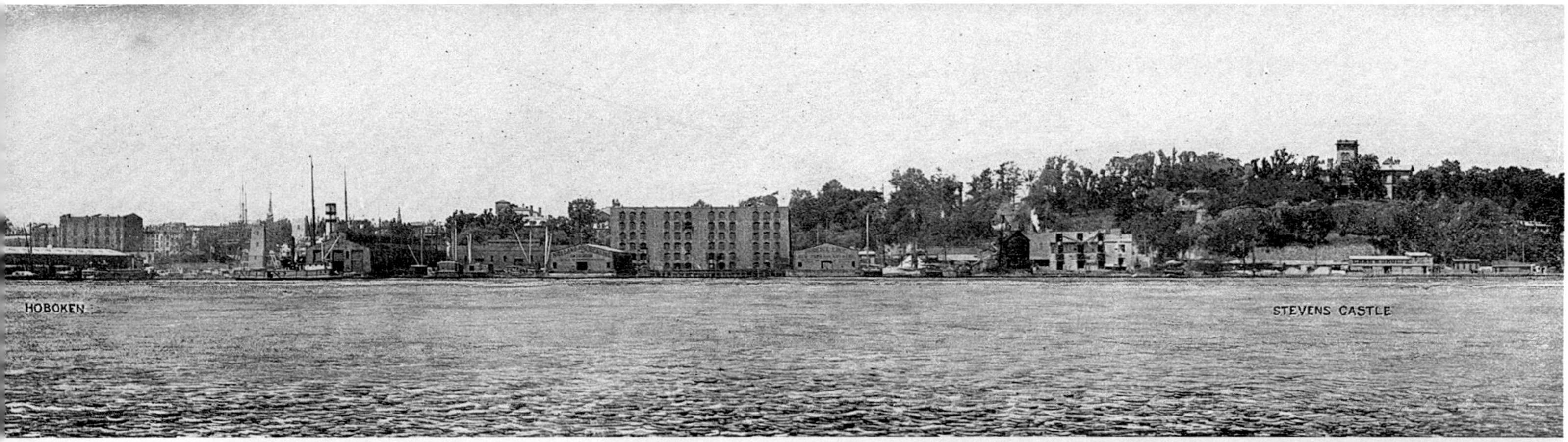

HOBOKEN

STEVENS CASTLE

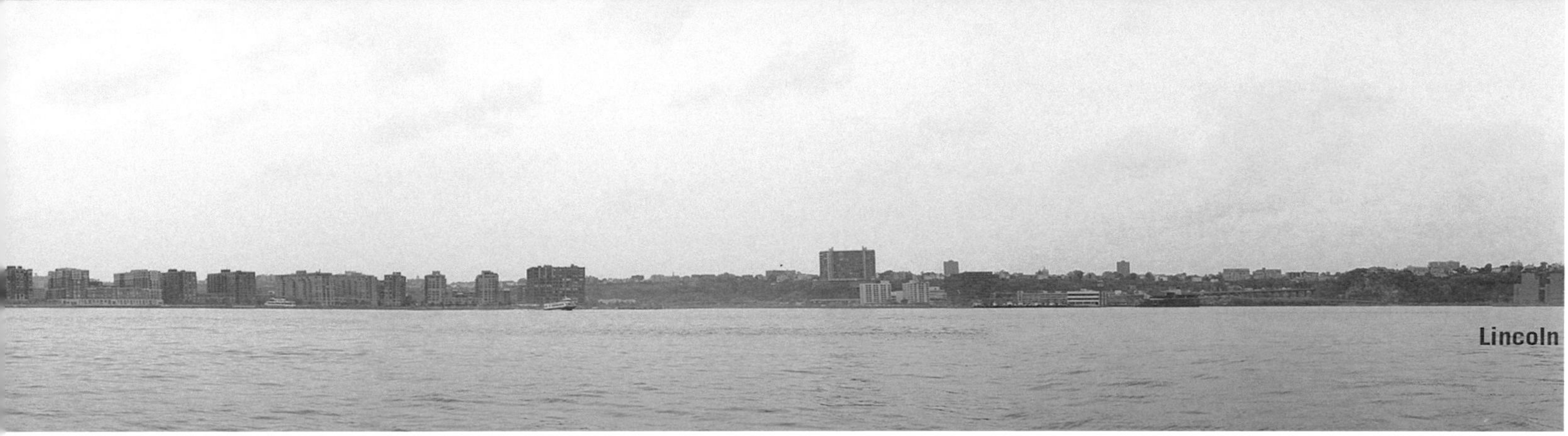

Lincoln

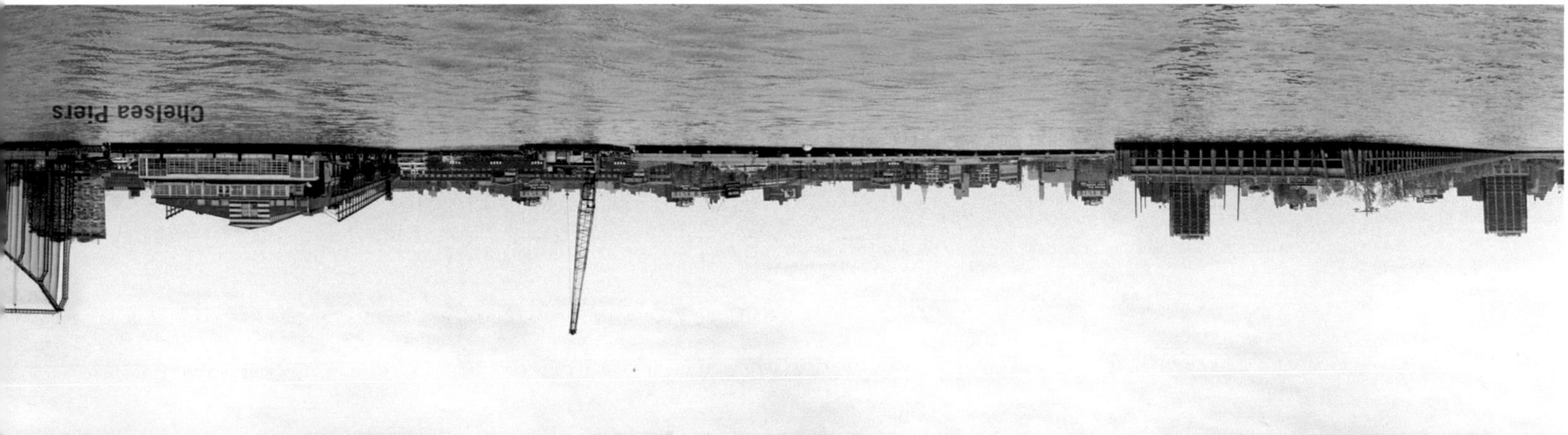

Chelsea Piers

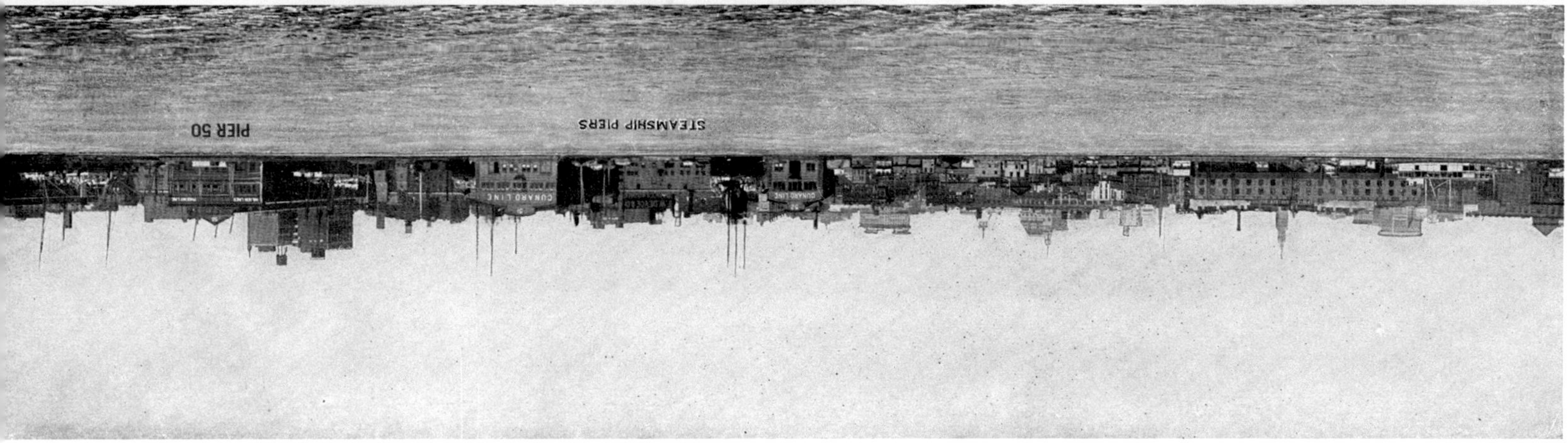

PIER 50

STEAMSHIP PIERS

ELYSIAN FIELDS

Tunnel

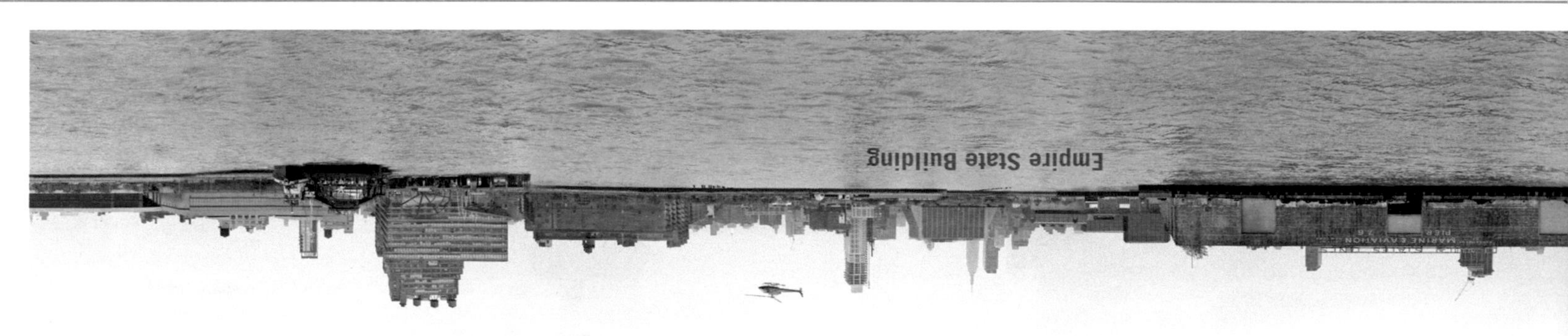

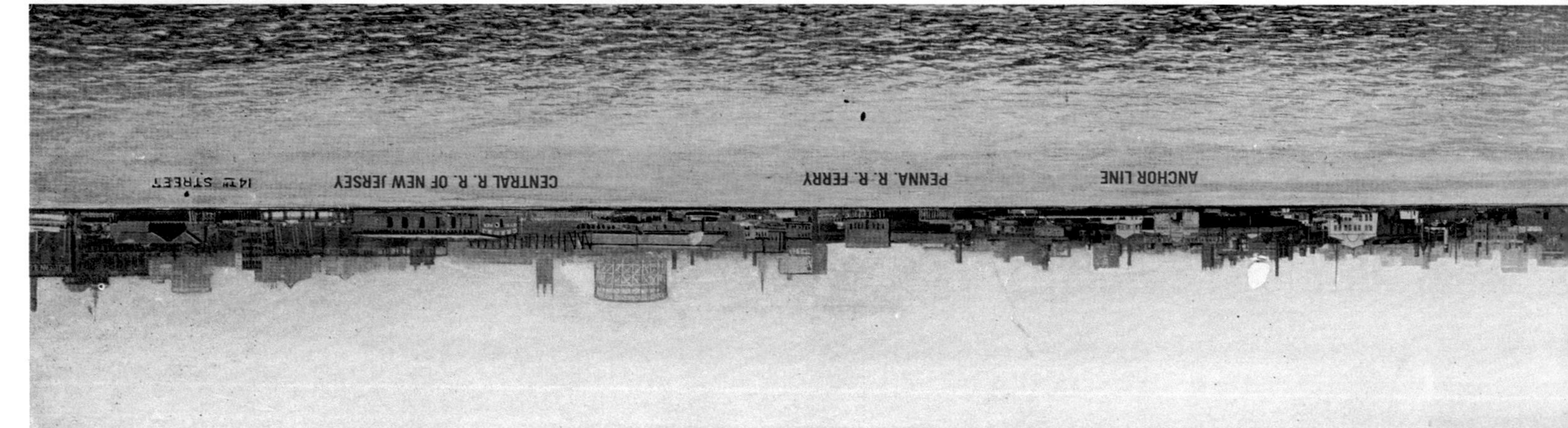

East Bank

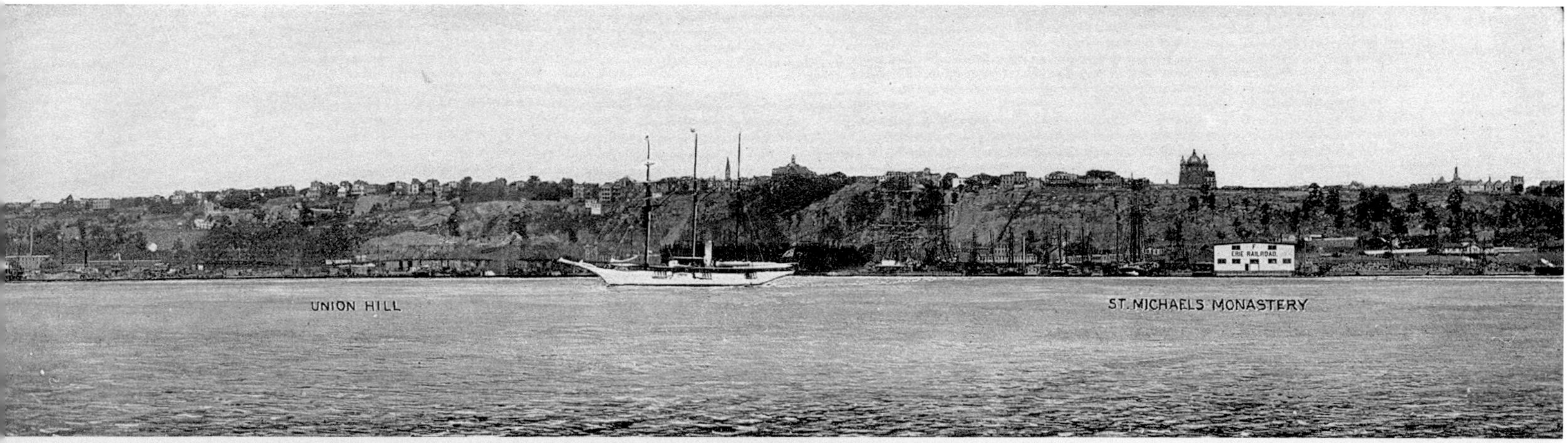

UNION HILL

ERIE RAILROAD

ST. MICHAELS MONASTERY

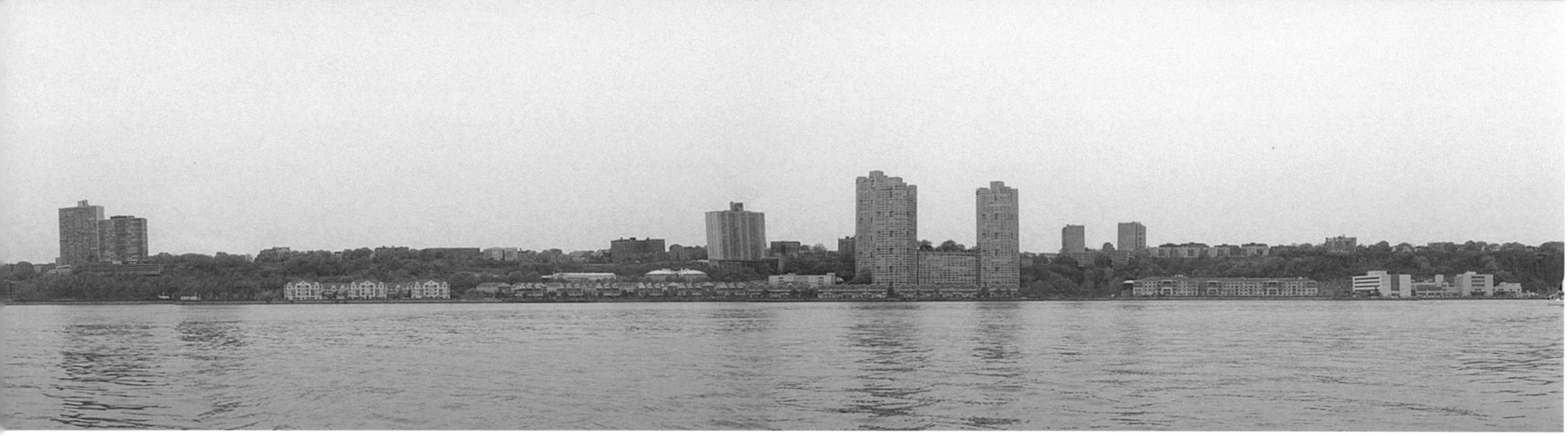

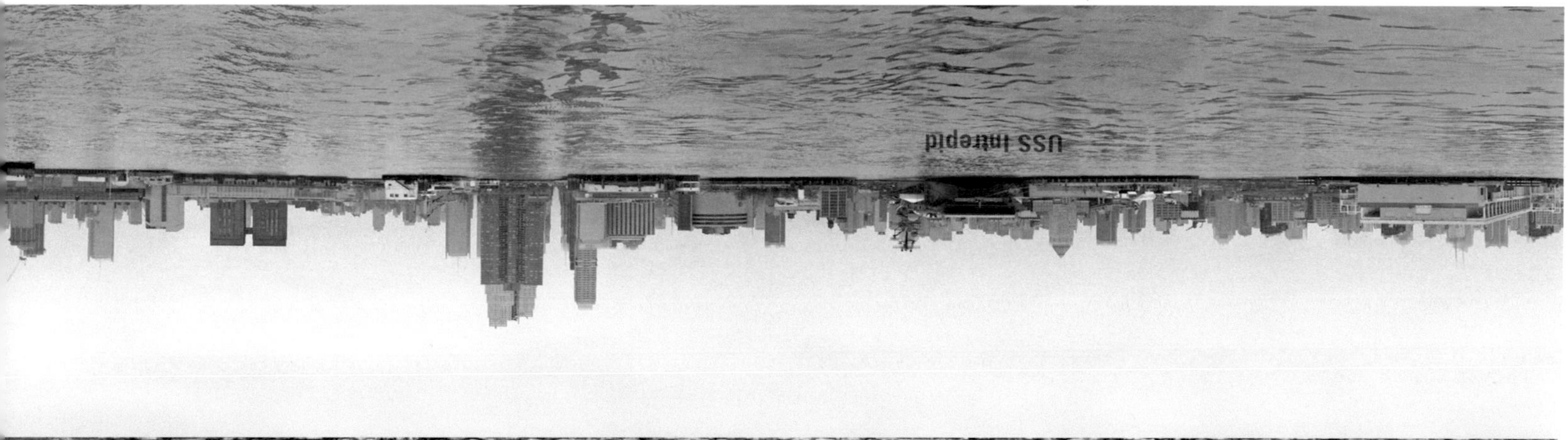

USS Intrepid

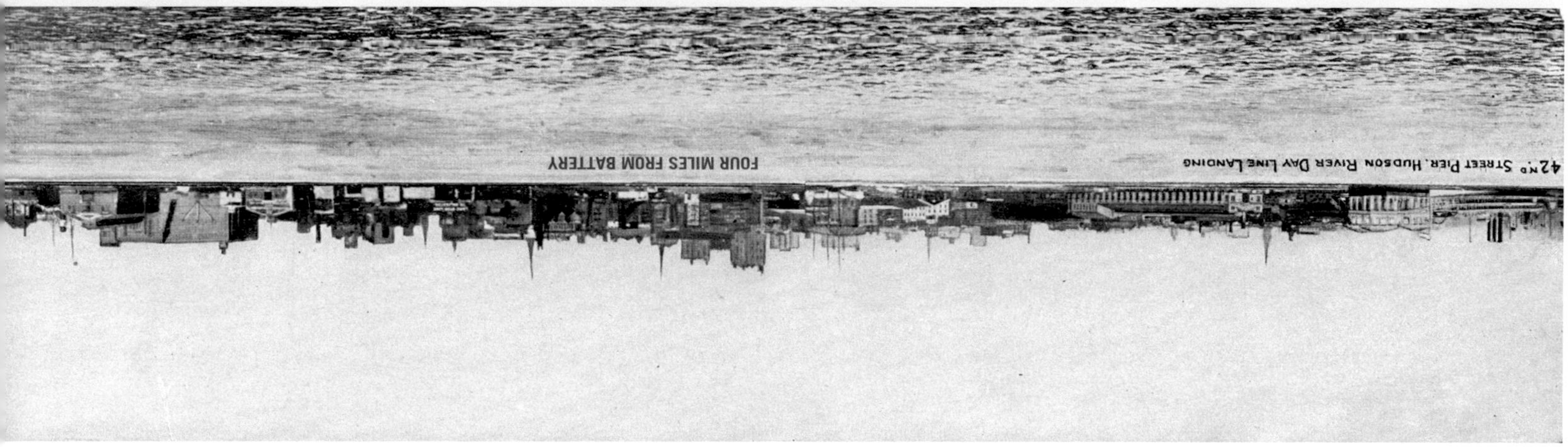

42ND STREET PIER, HUDSON RIVER DAY LINE LANDING

FOUR MILES FROM BATTERY

ERIE R.R. PIERS

WEEHAWKEN

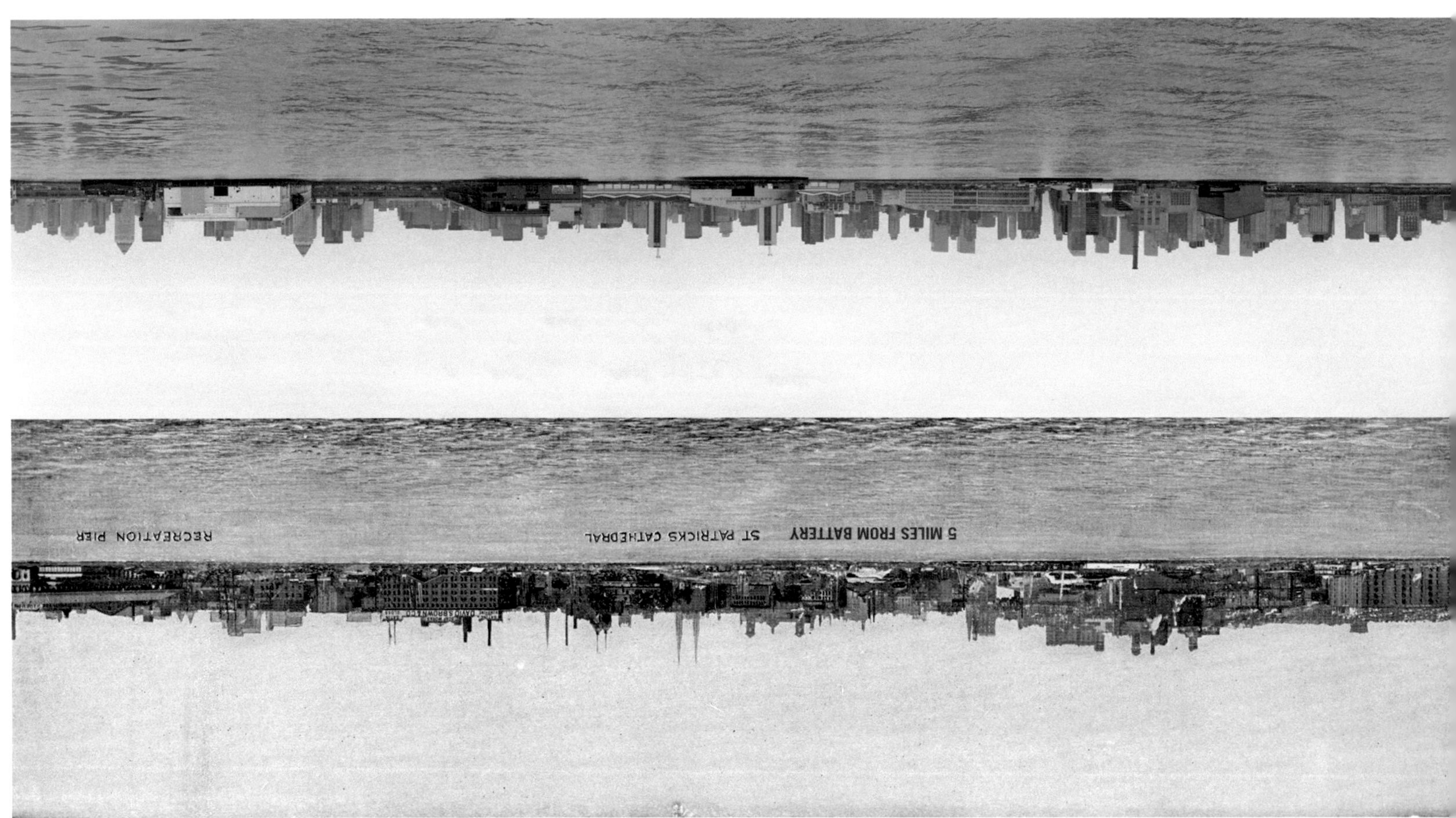

East Bank

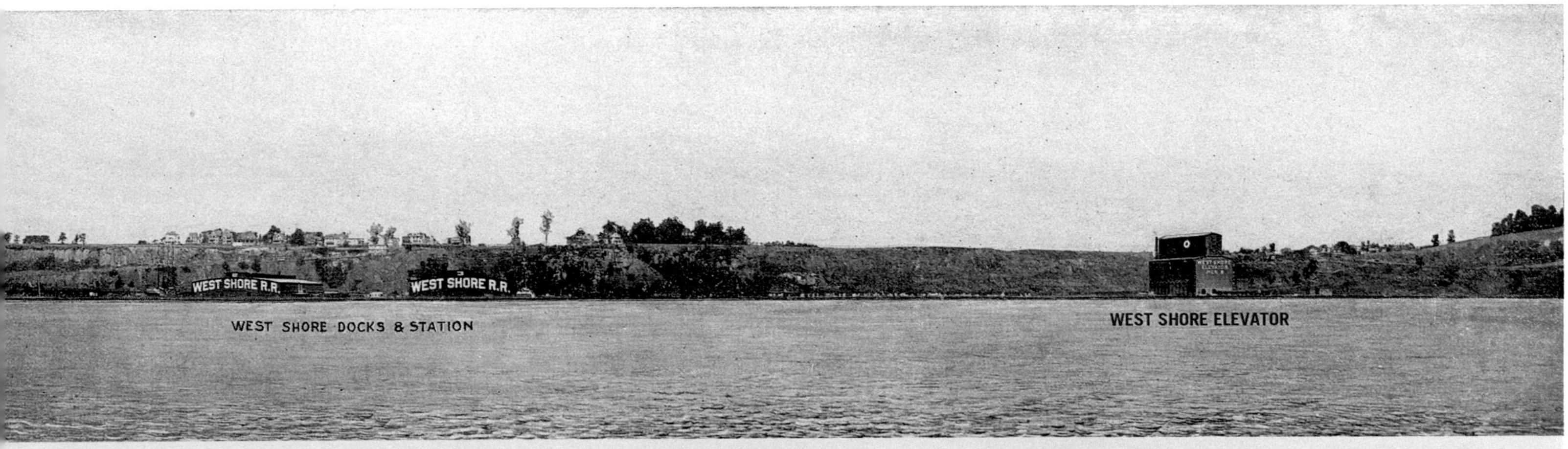

WEST SHORE R.R.

WEST SHORE R.R.

WEST SHORE DOCKS & STATION

WEST SHORE ELEVATOR

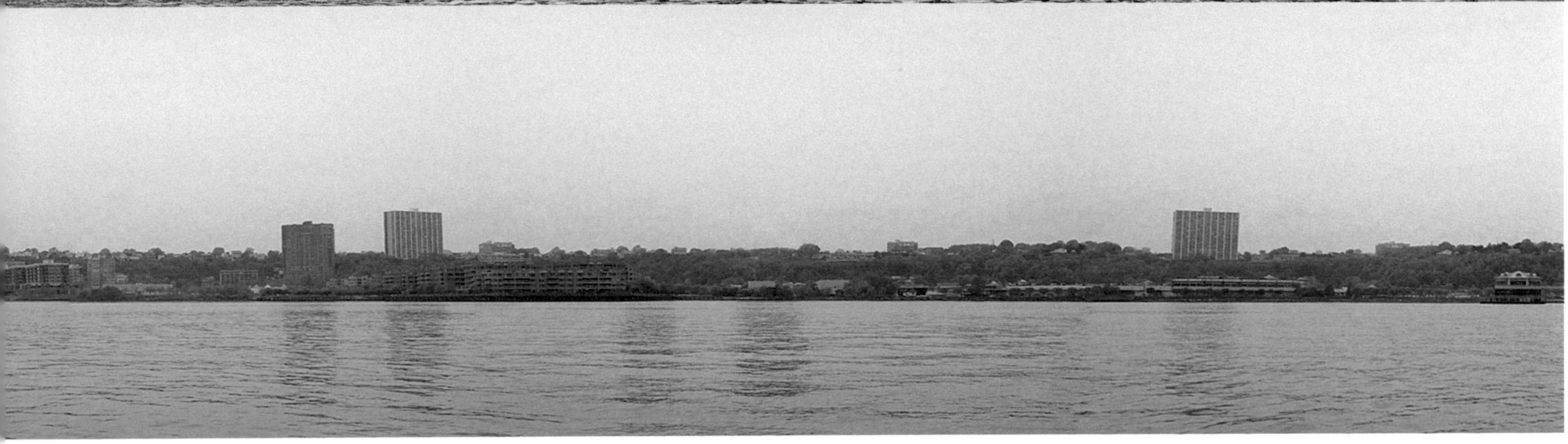

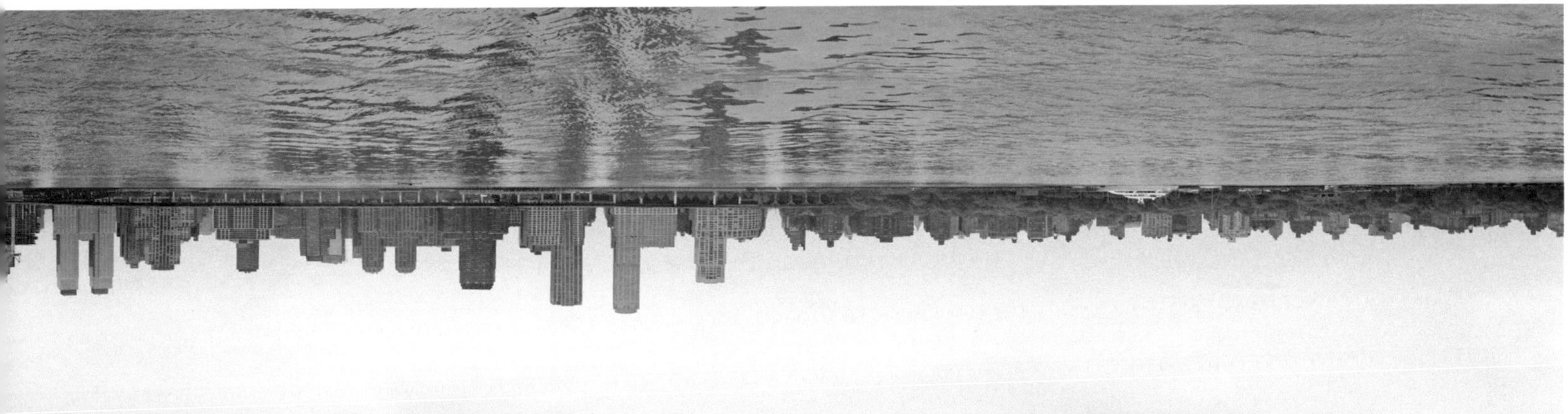

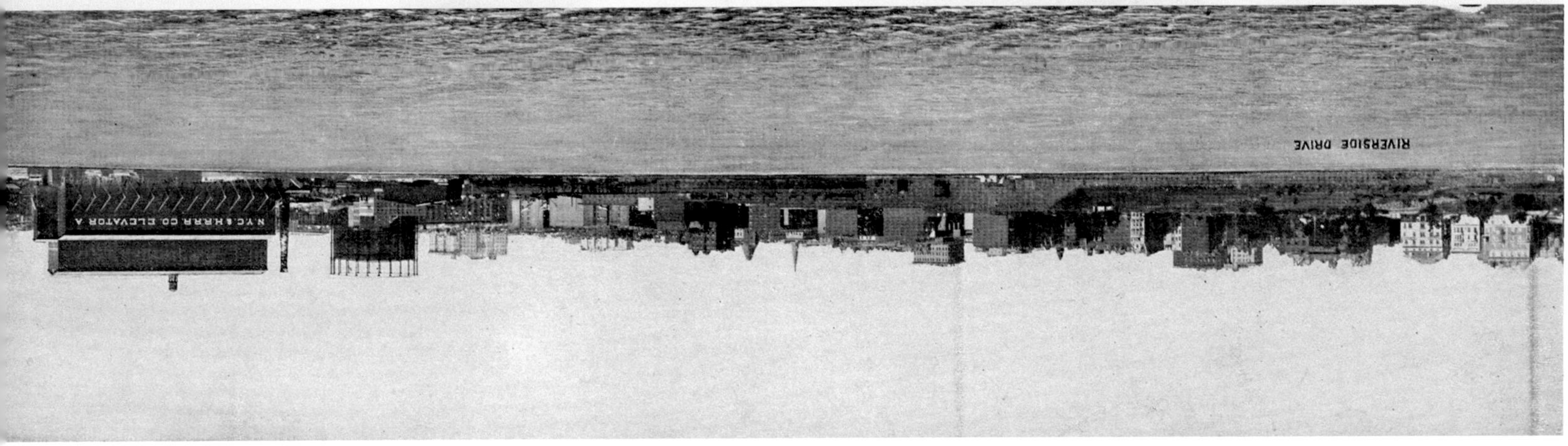

RIVERSIDE DRIVE

N.Y.C.&H.R.R.R. CO. ELEVATOR A

WOODCLIFF

WEEHAWKEN

HESS

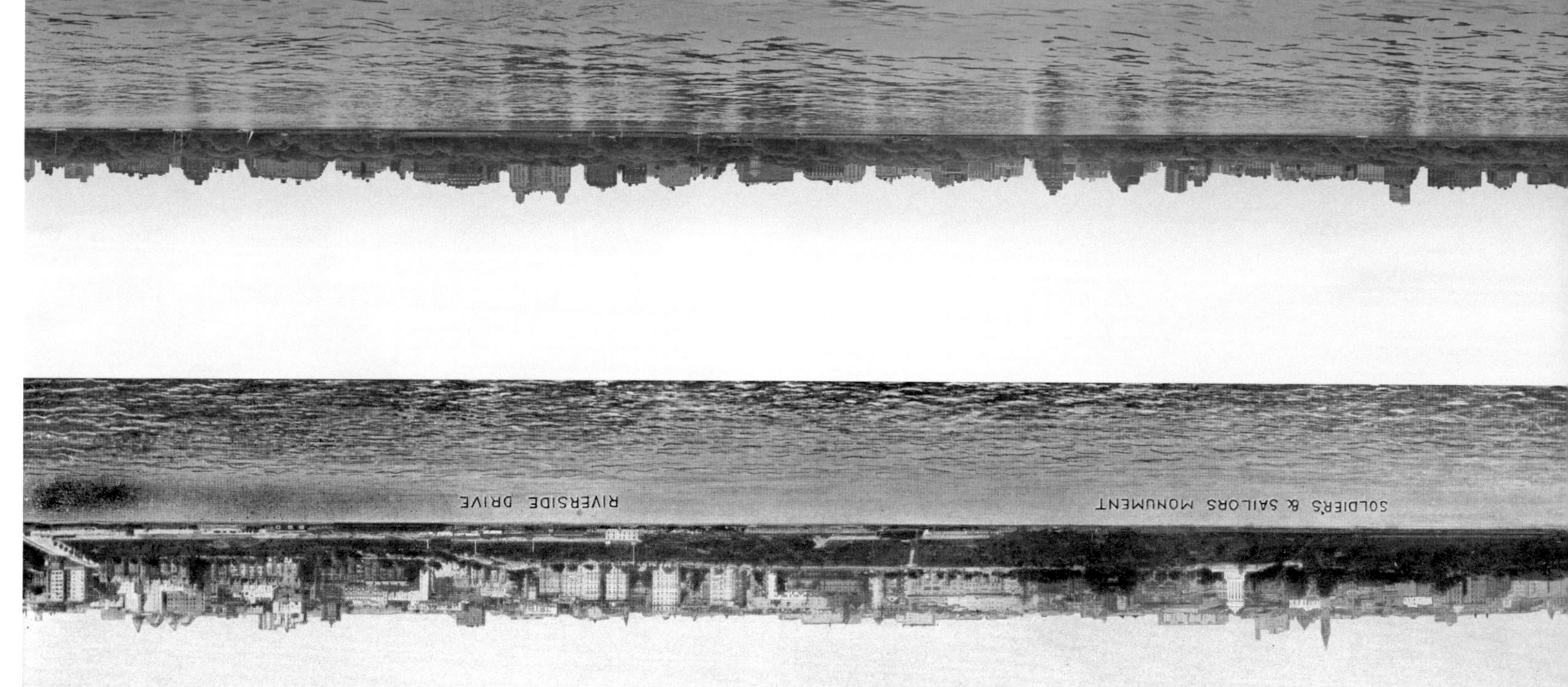

East Bank

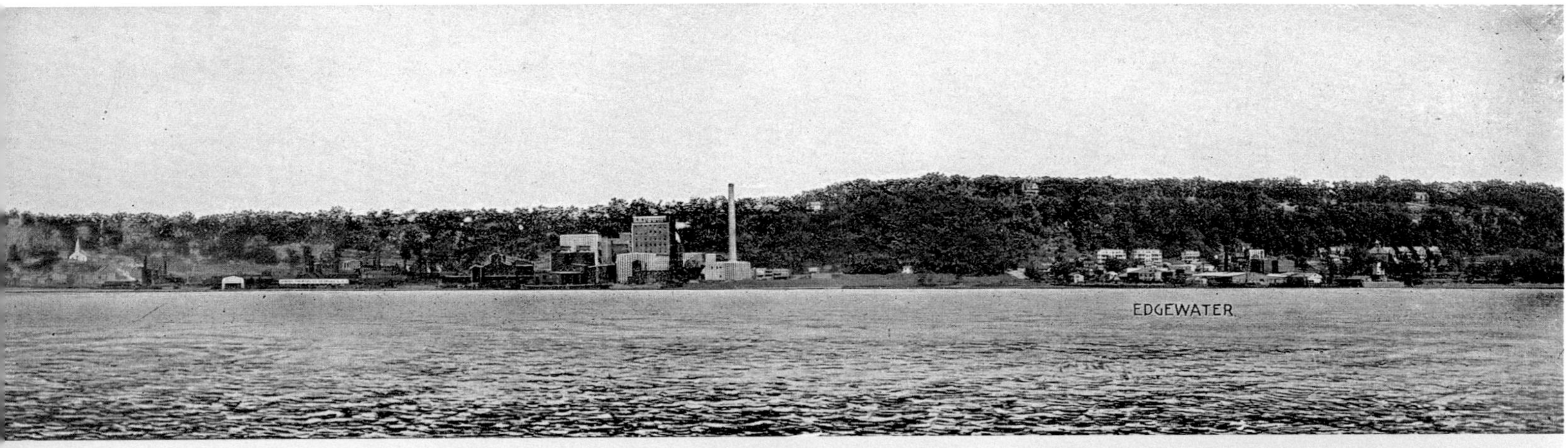

EDGEWATER

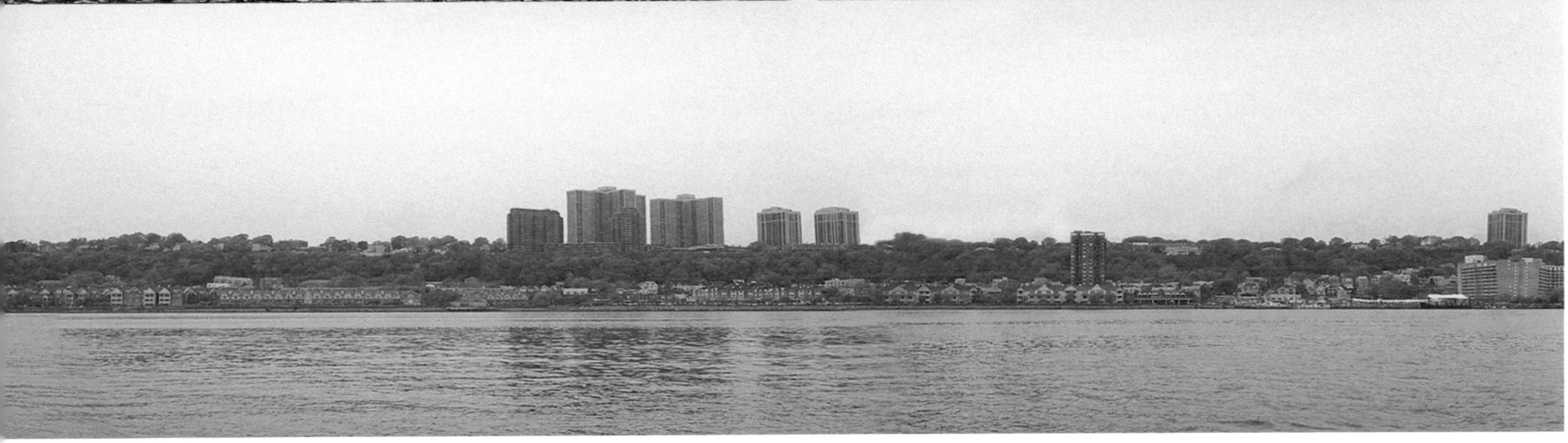

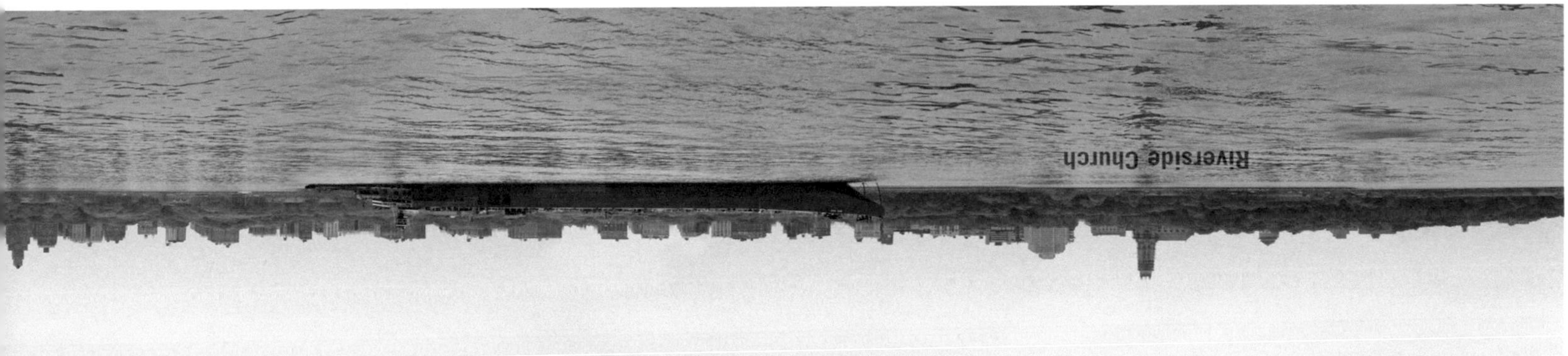

Riverside Church

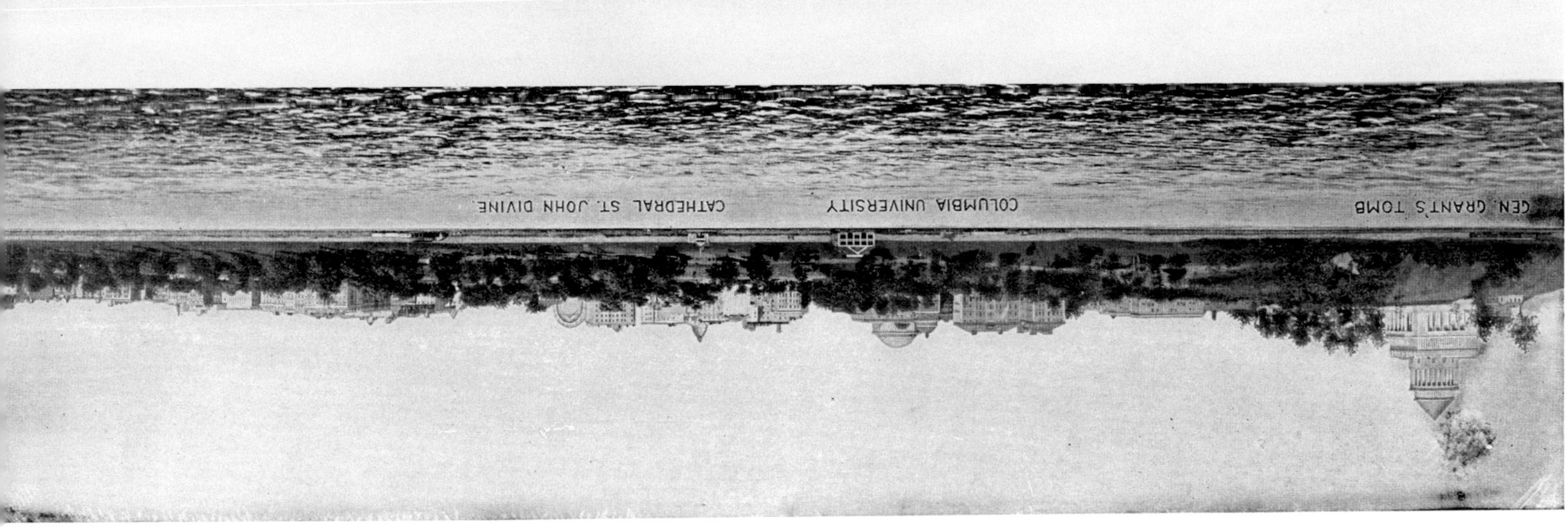

GEN. GRANT'S TOMB

COLUMBIA UNIVERSITY

CATHEDRAL ST. JOHN DIVINE

UNDERCLIFF

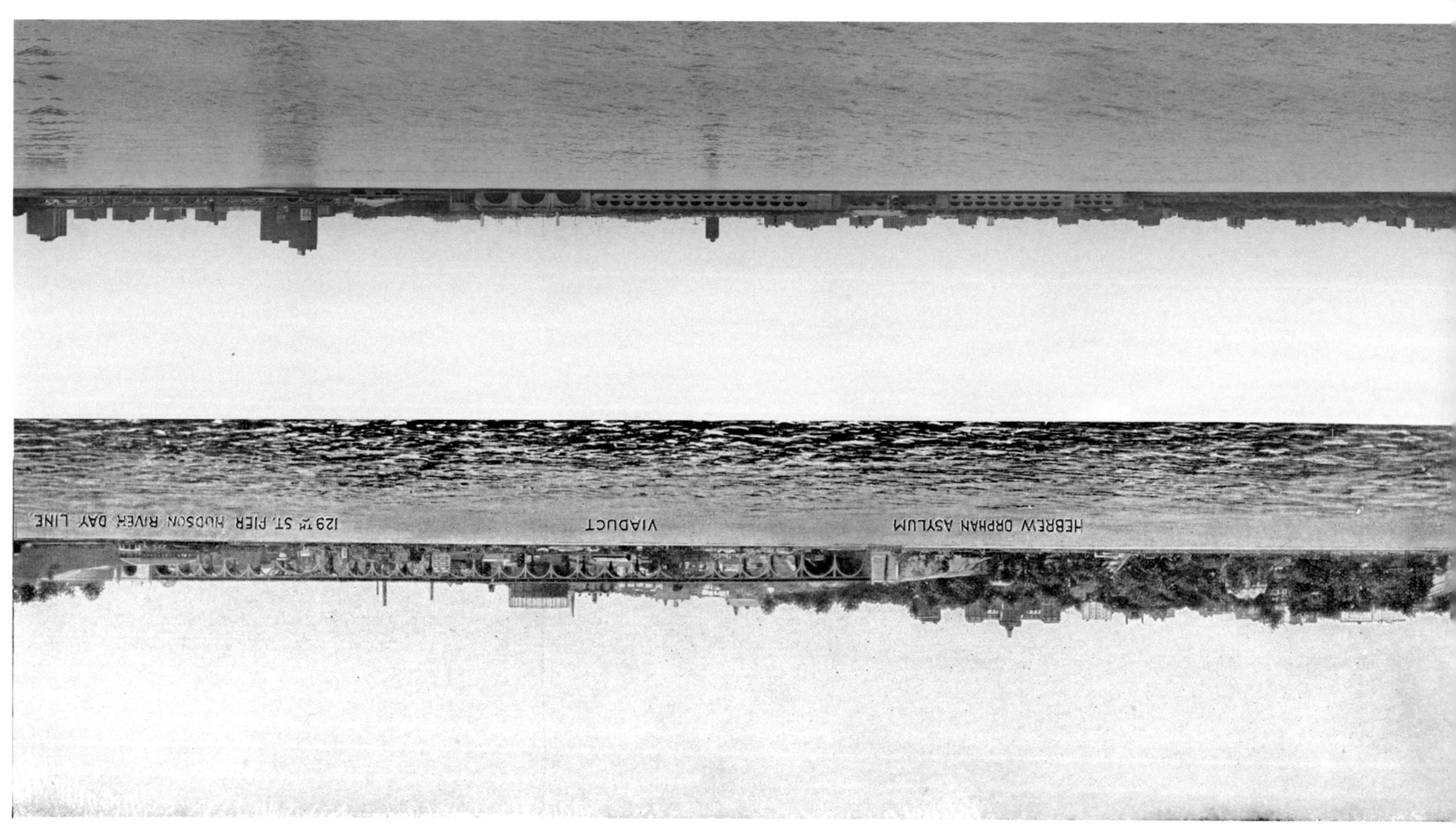

East Bank

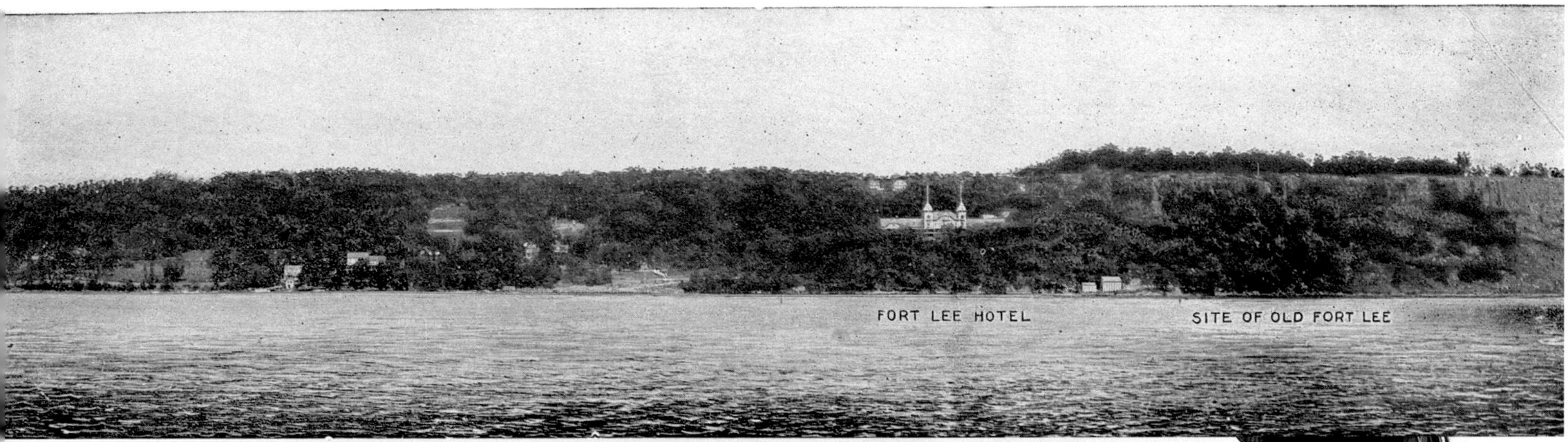

FORT LEE HOTEL

SITE OF OLD FORT LEE

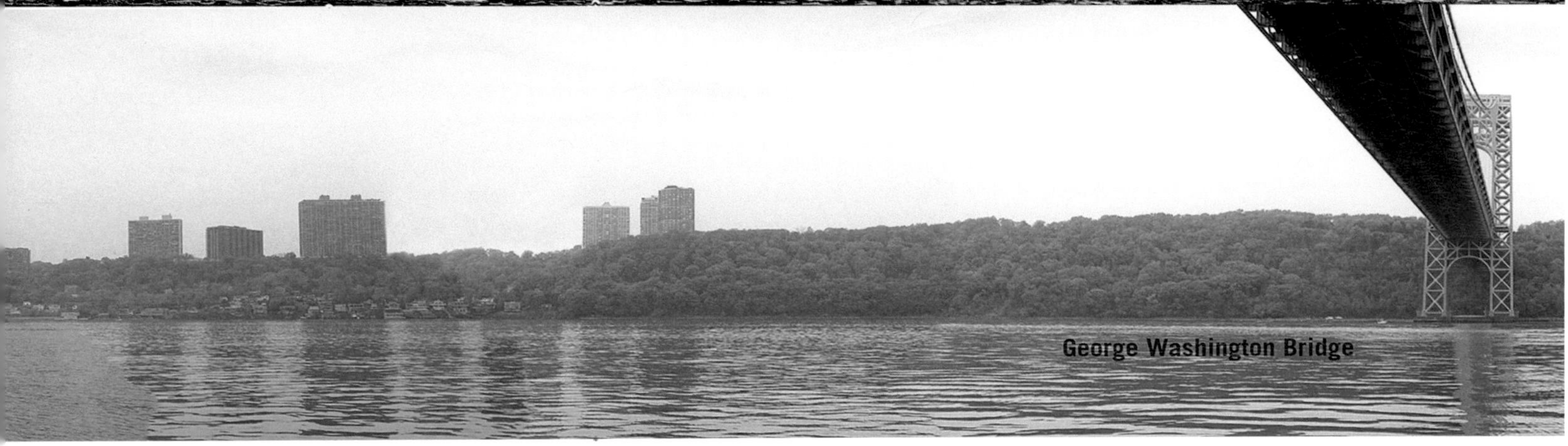

George Washington Bridge

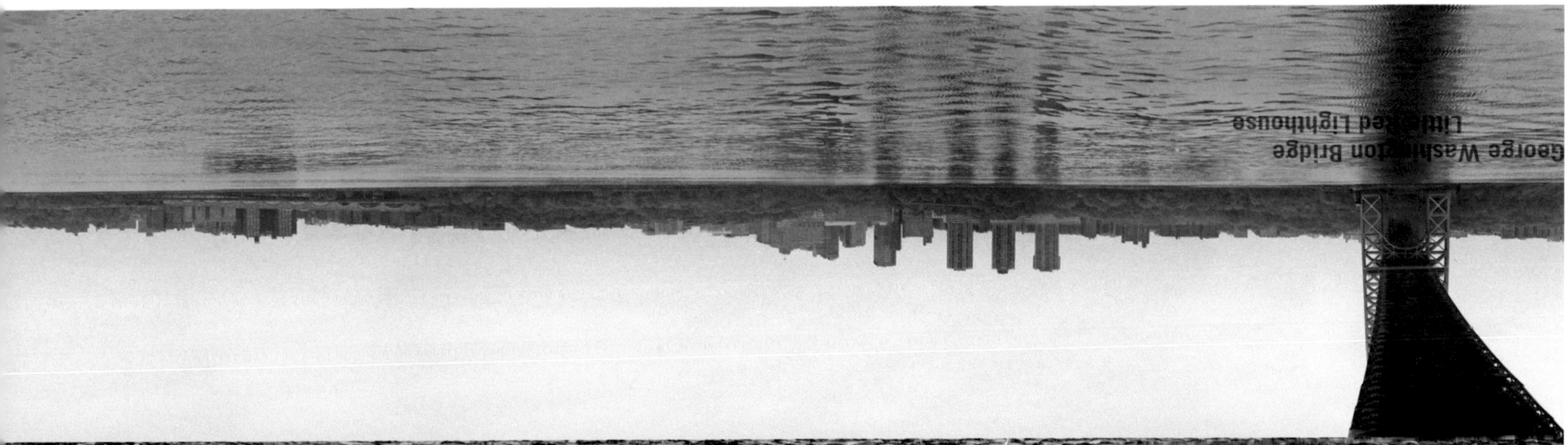

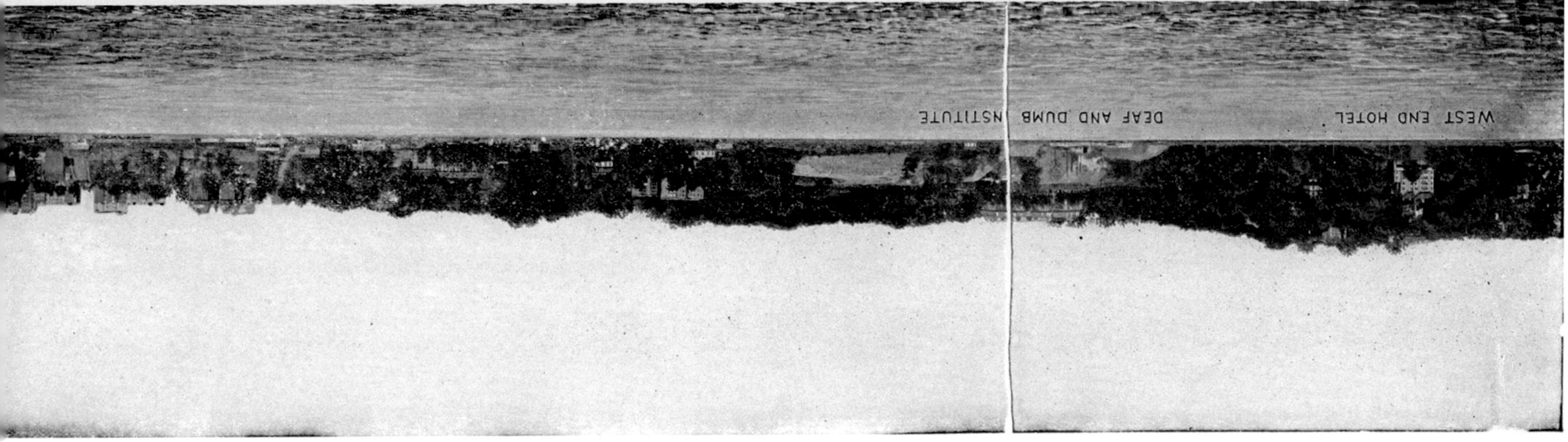

George Washi ton Bridge

Litt ed Lighthouse

WEST END HOTEL

DEAF AND DUMB NSTITUTE

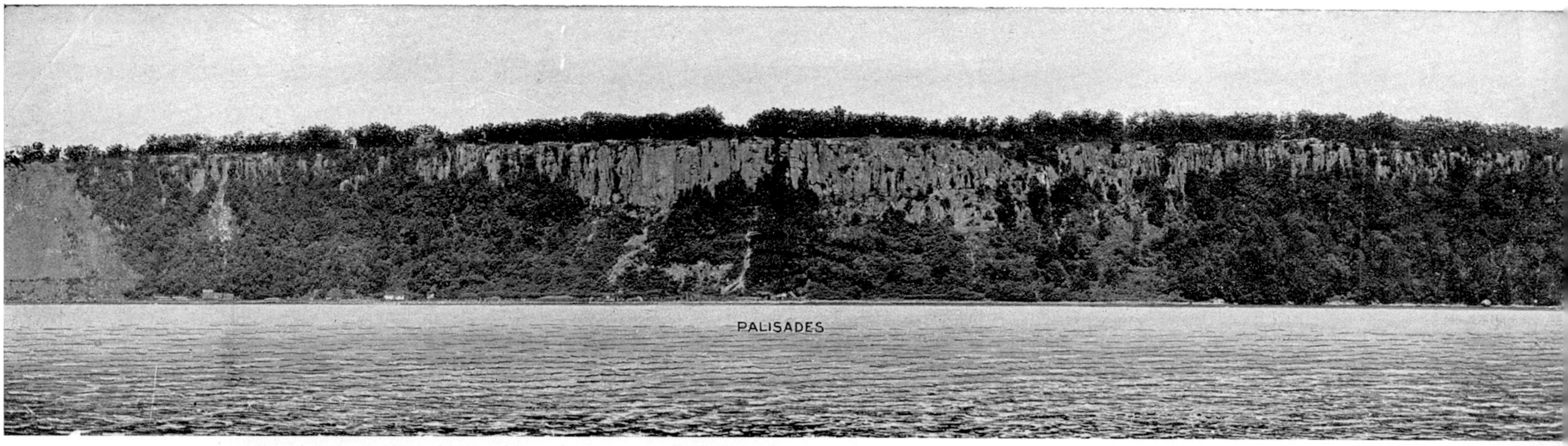

STEWART CASTLE

FORT WASHINGTON POINT

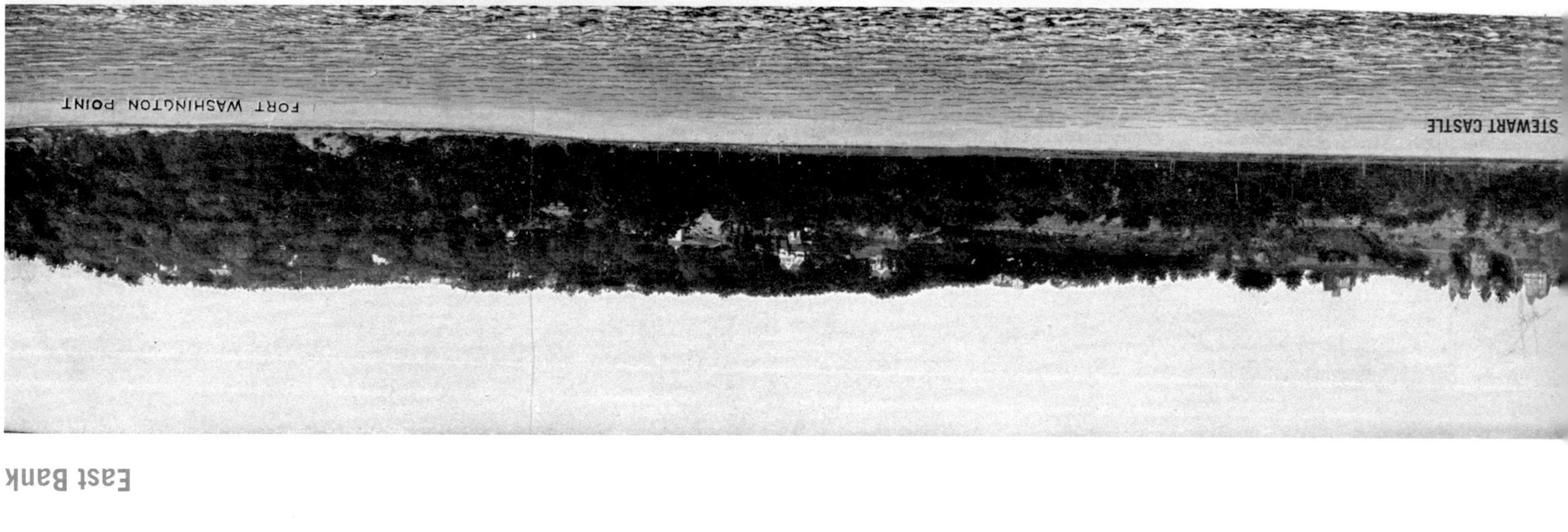

The Cloisters

PALISADES

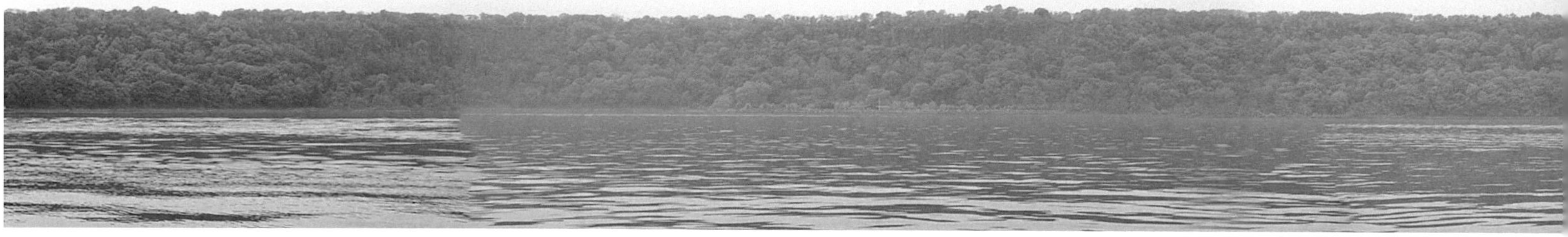

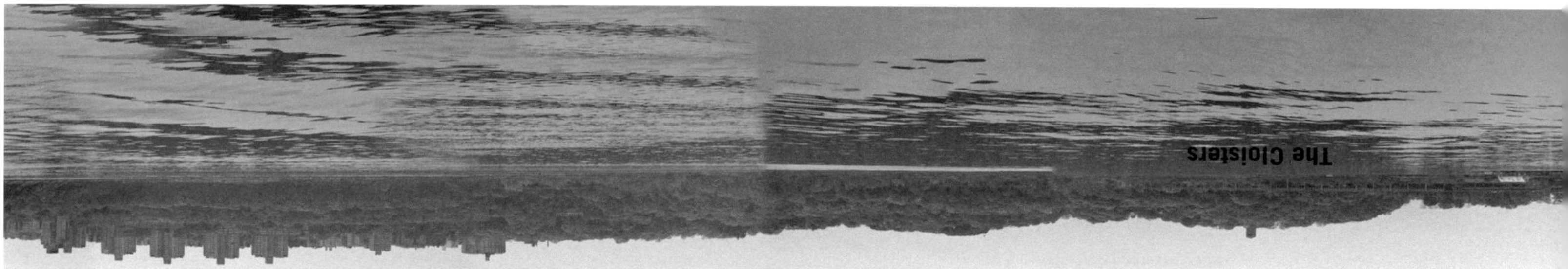

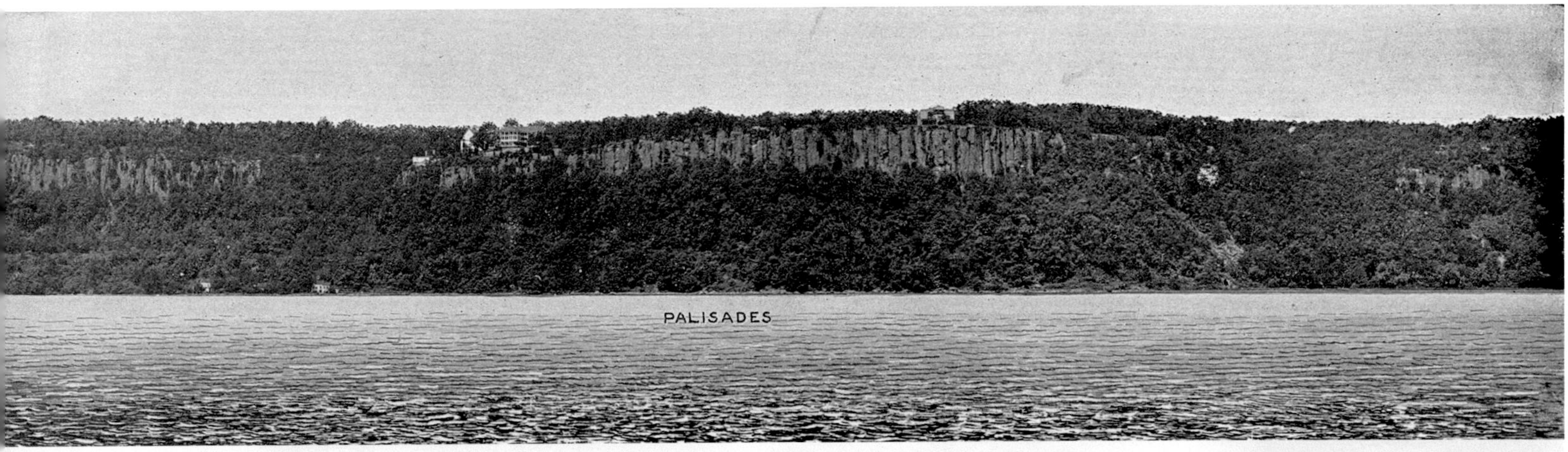

PALISADES

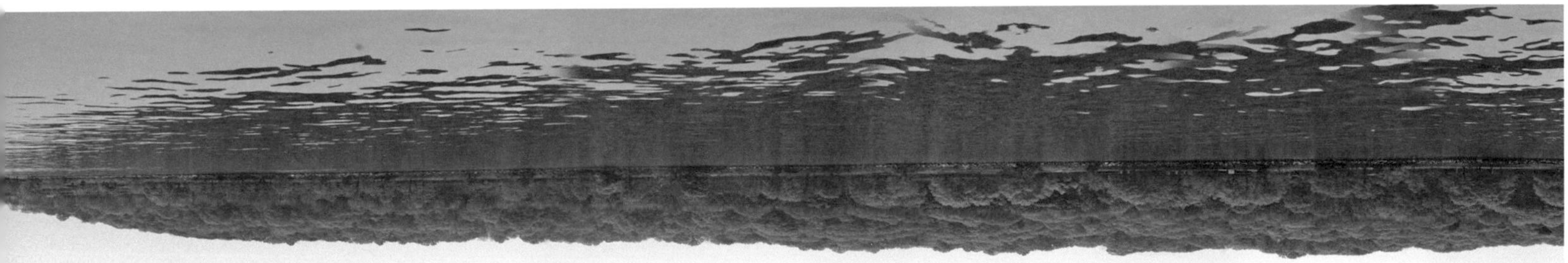

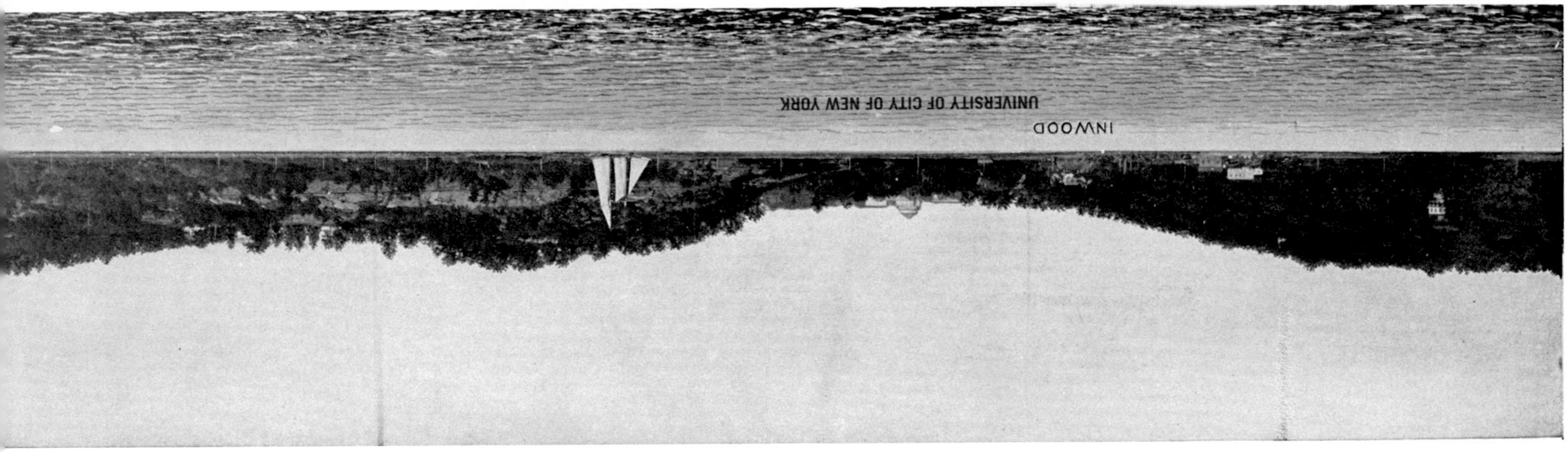

UNIVERSITY OF CITY OF NEW YORK

INWOOD

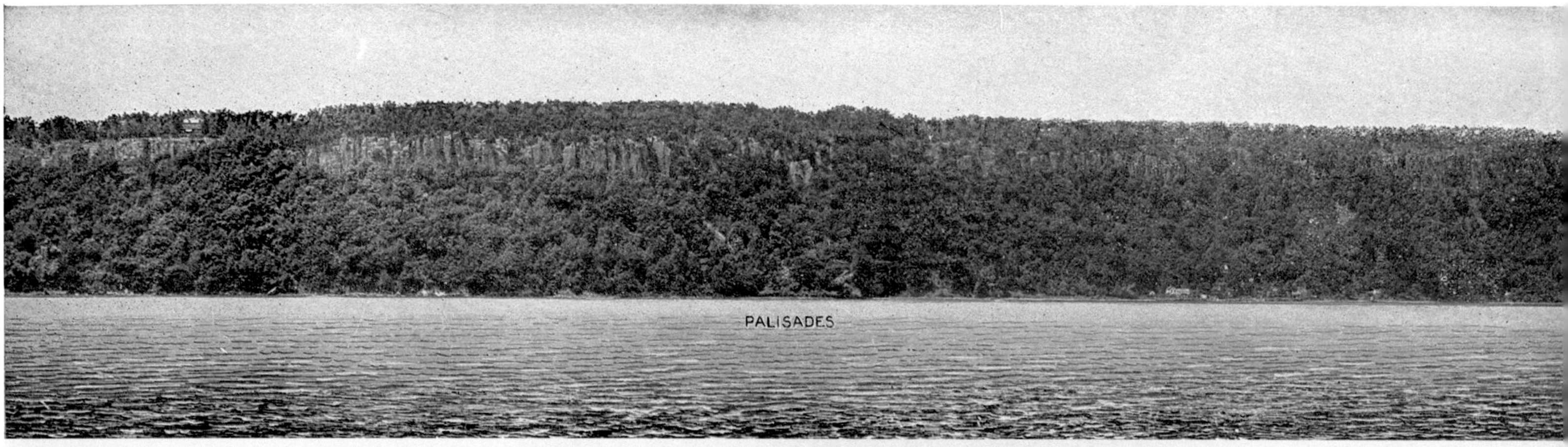

PALISADES

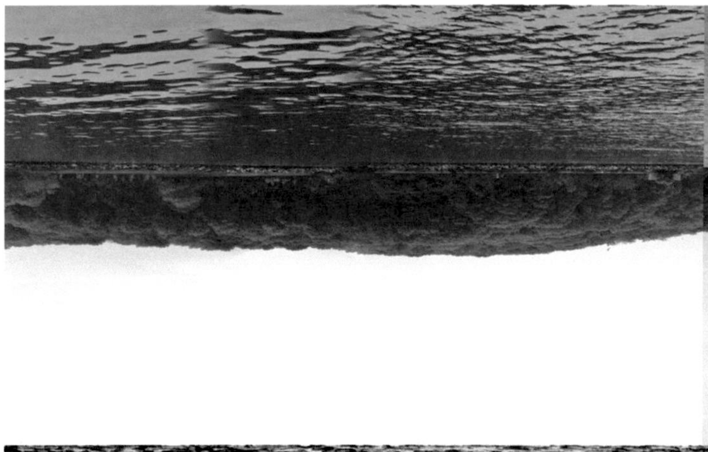

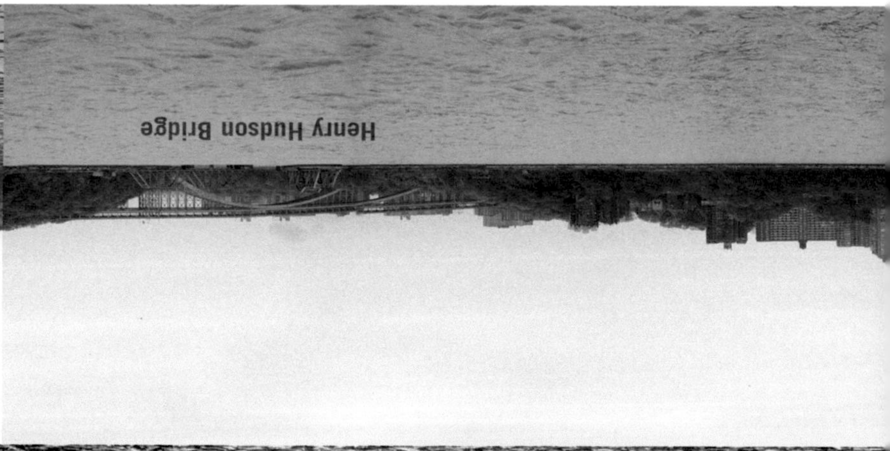

Henry Hudson Bridge

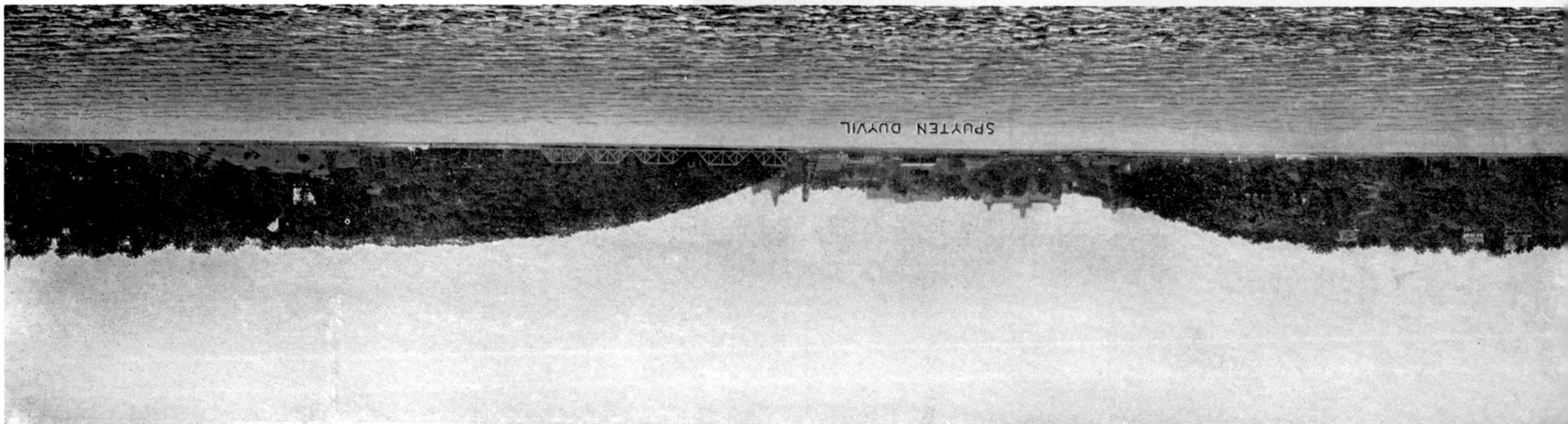

SPUYTEN DUYVIL

East Bank

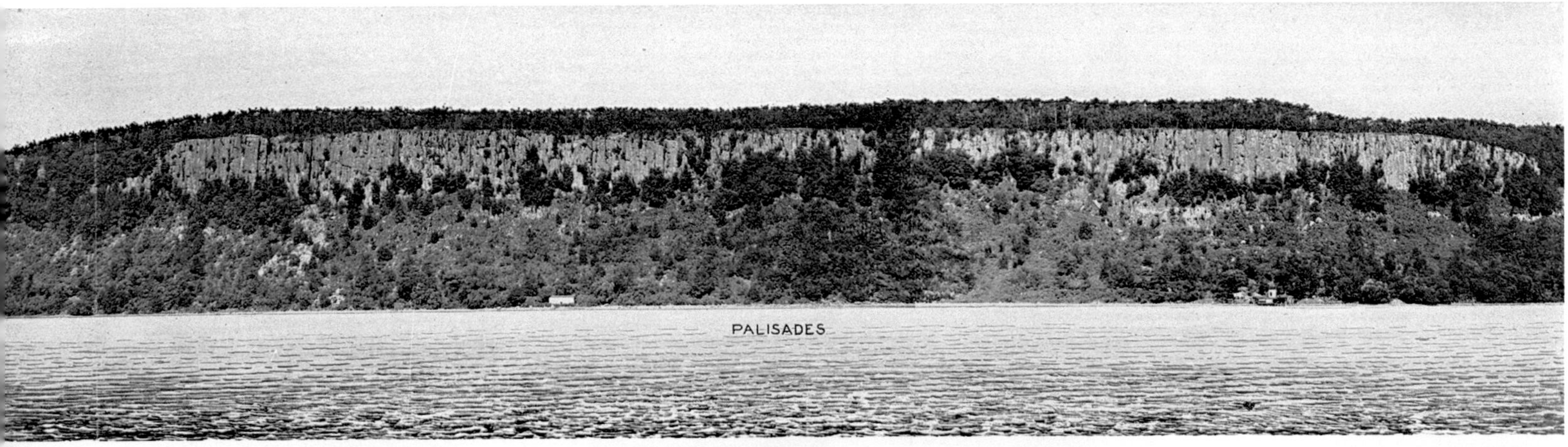

PALISADES

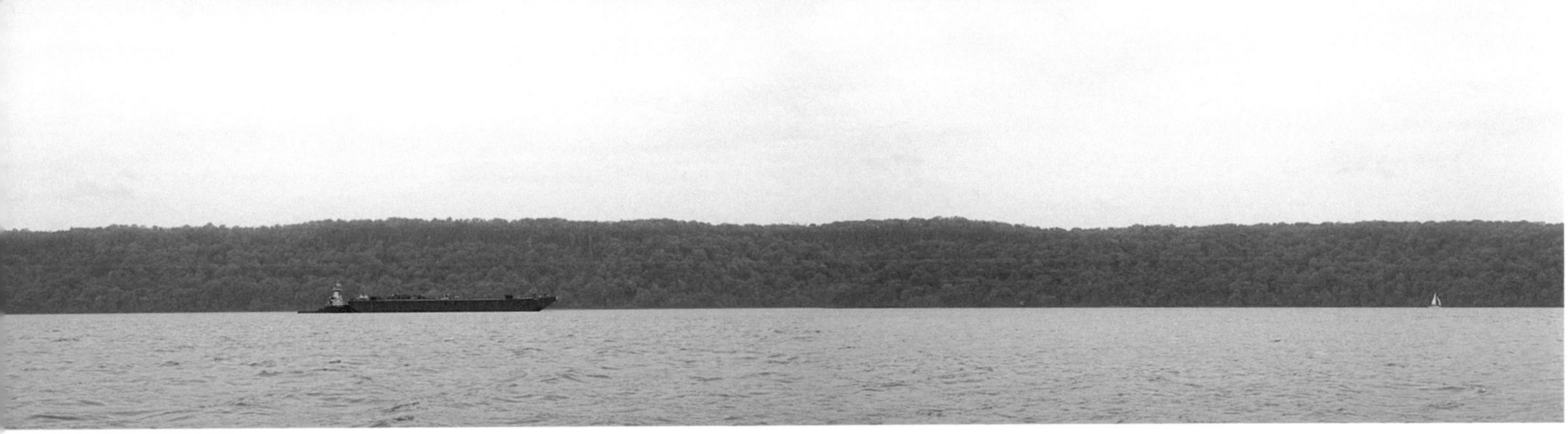

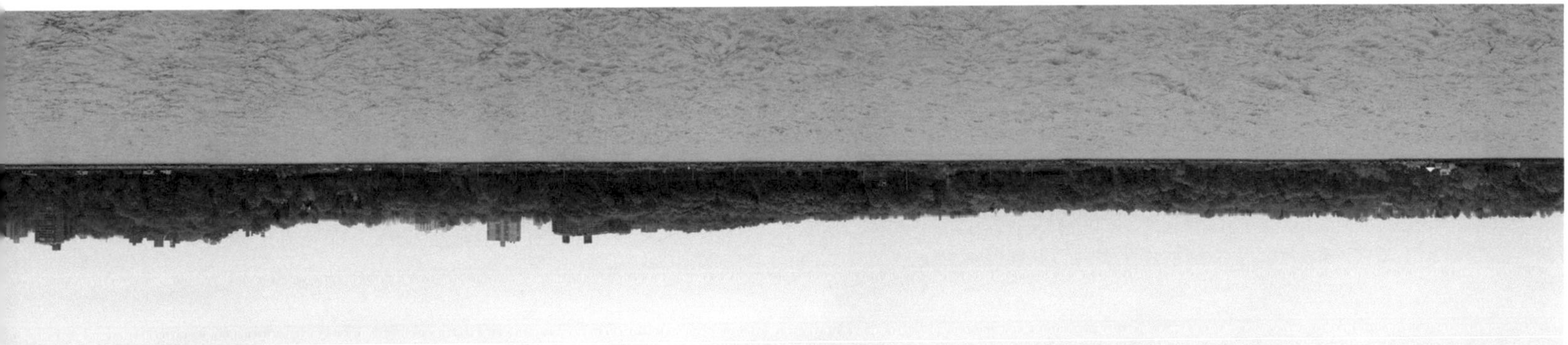

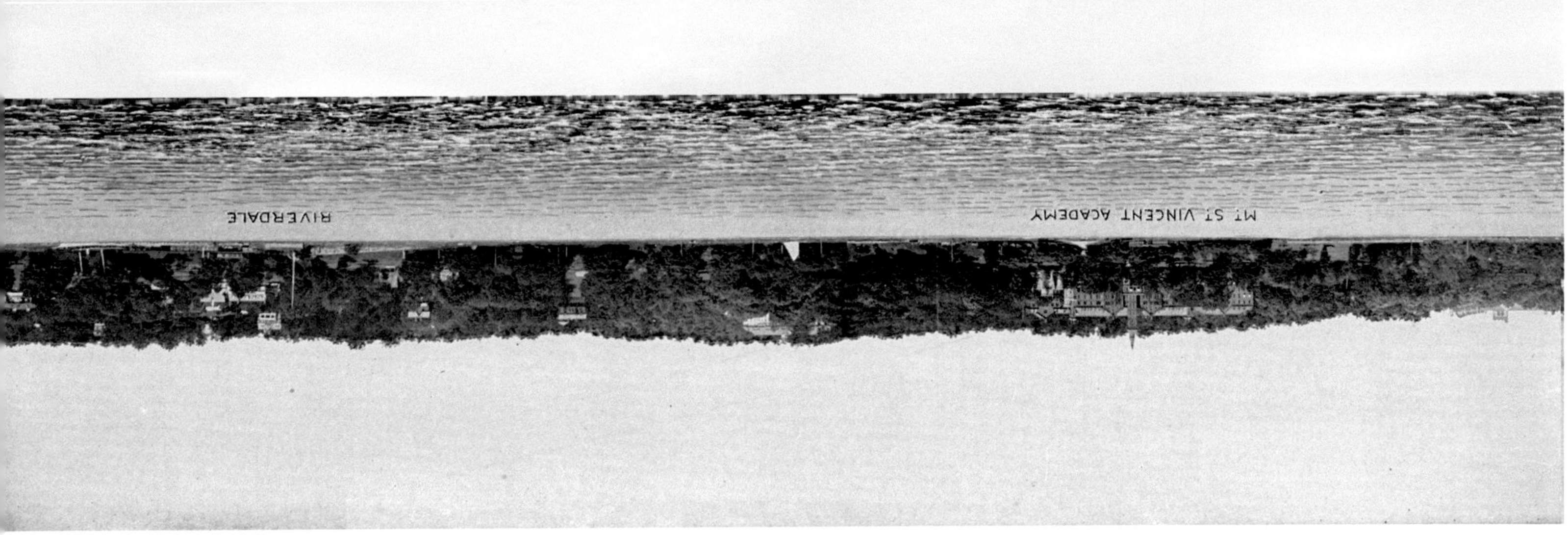

MT ST VINCENT ACADEMY

RIVERDALE

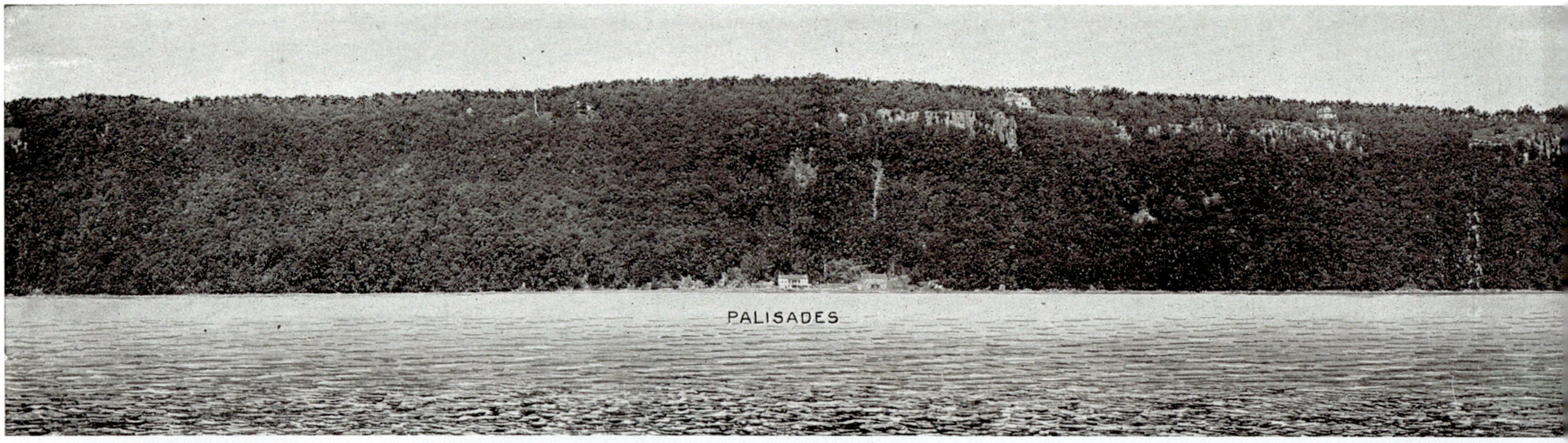

PALISADES

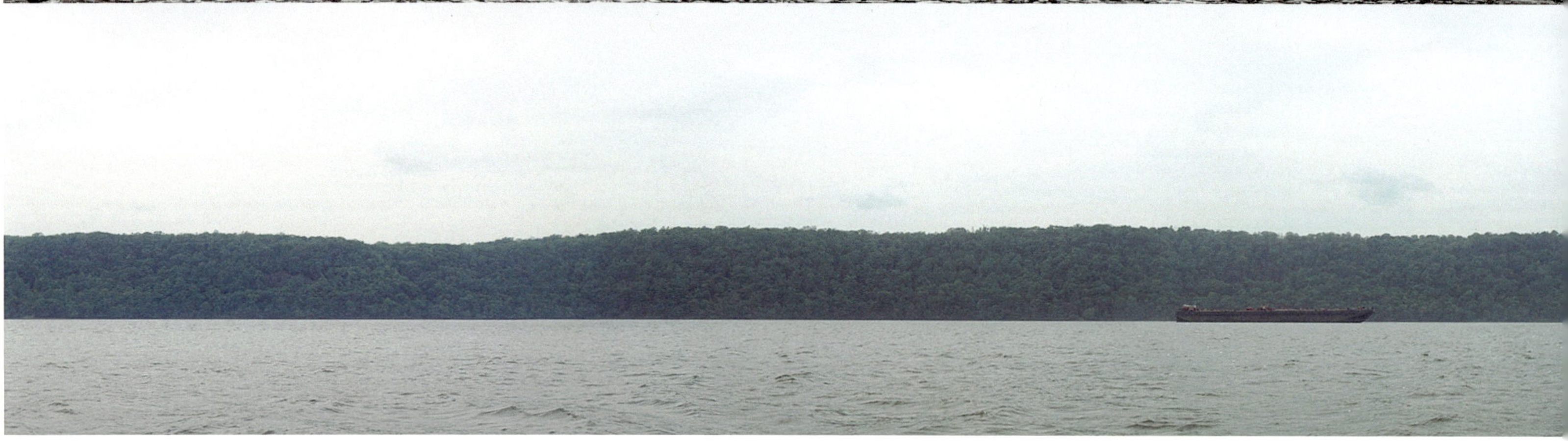

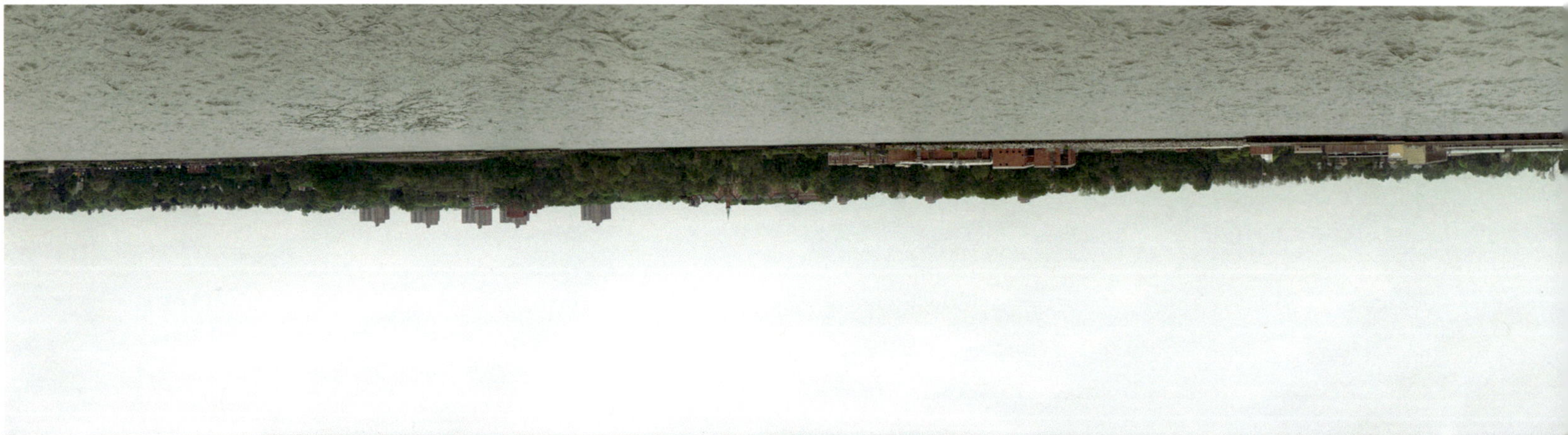

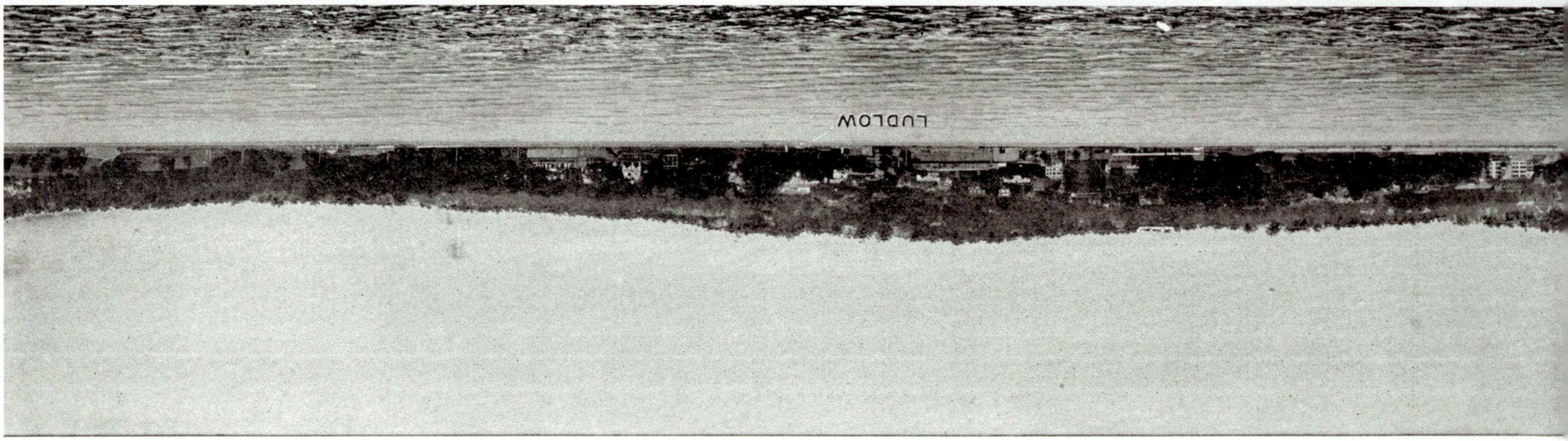

LUDLOW

East Bank

PALISADES

Alpine Landing

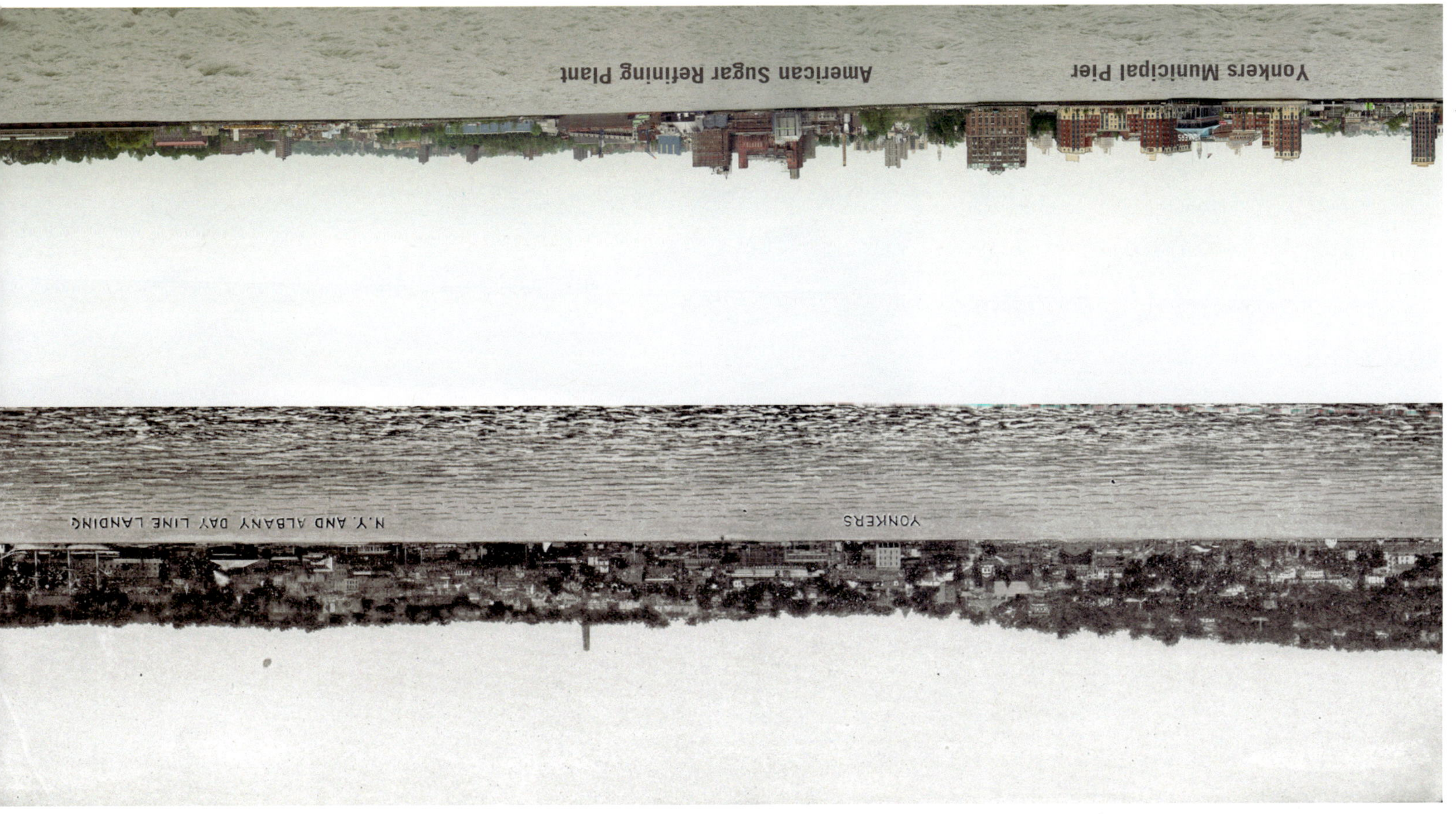

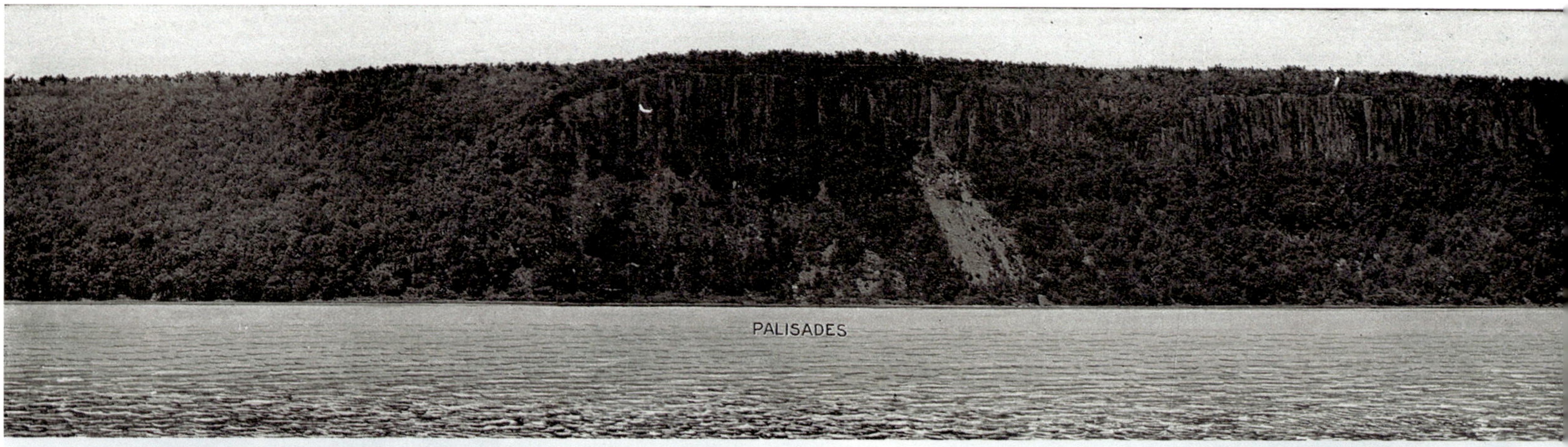

PALISADES

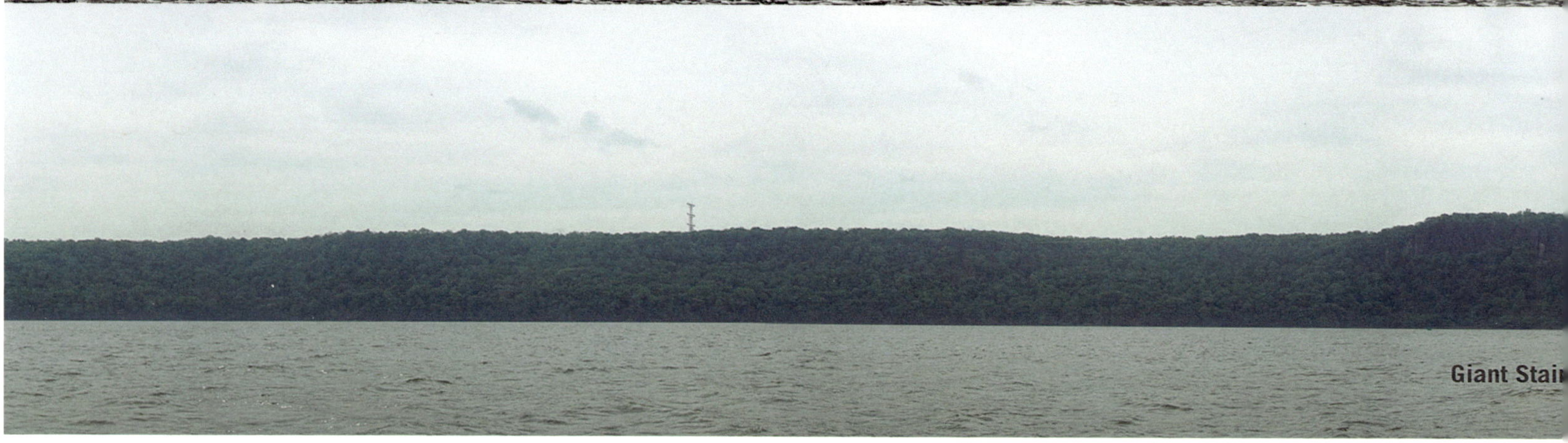

Giant Stair

YONKERS (GLENWOOD)

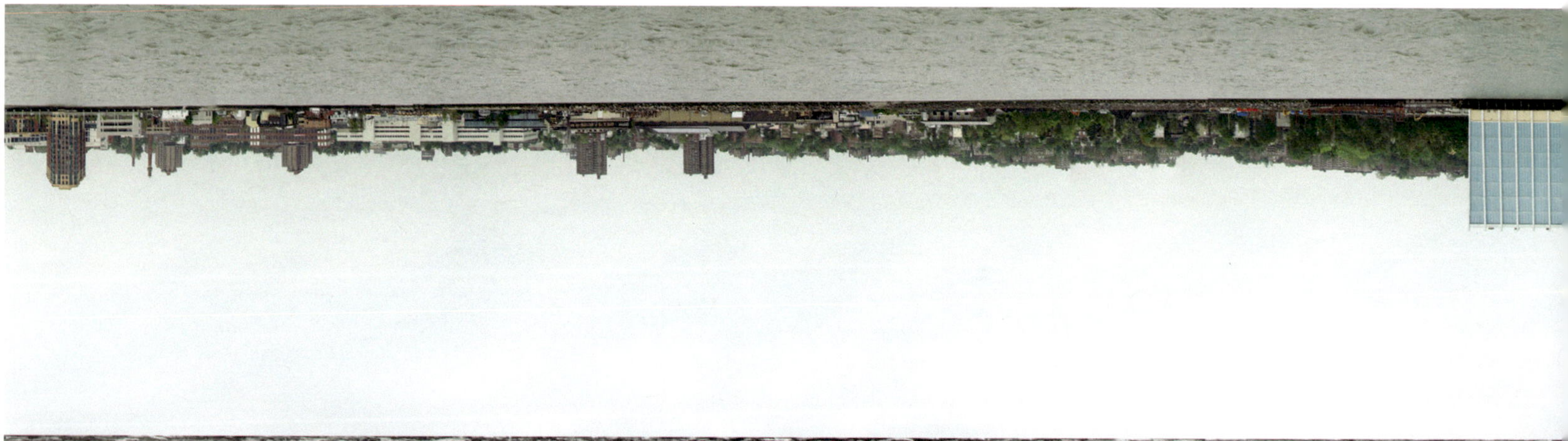

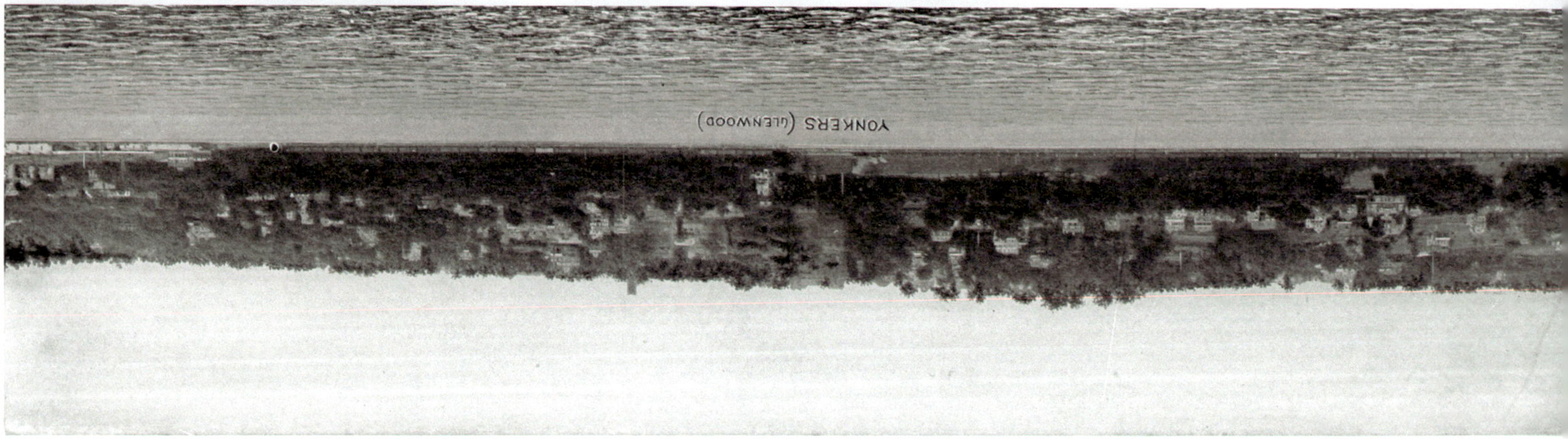

East Bank

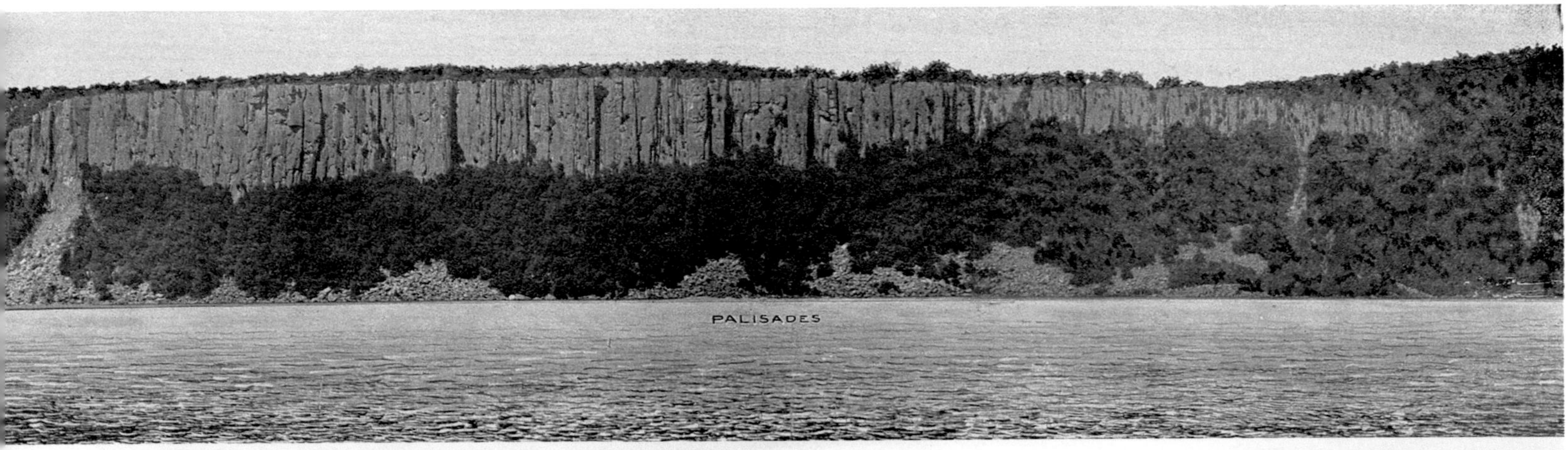

PALISADES

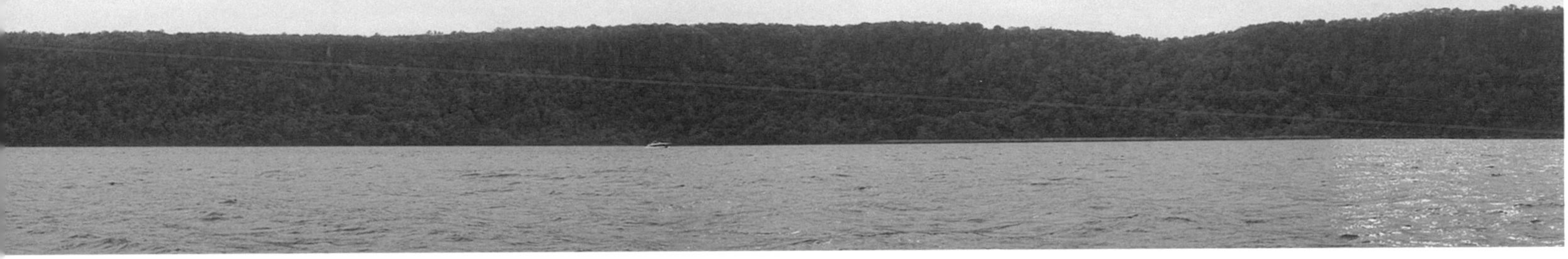

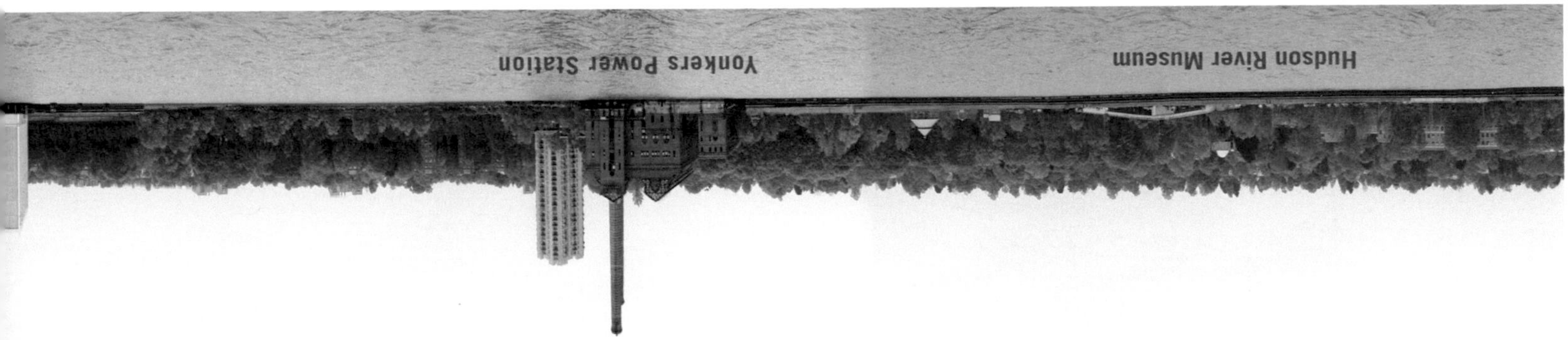

Hudson River Museum

Yonkers Power Station

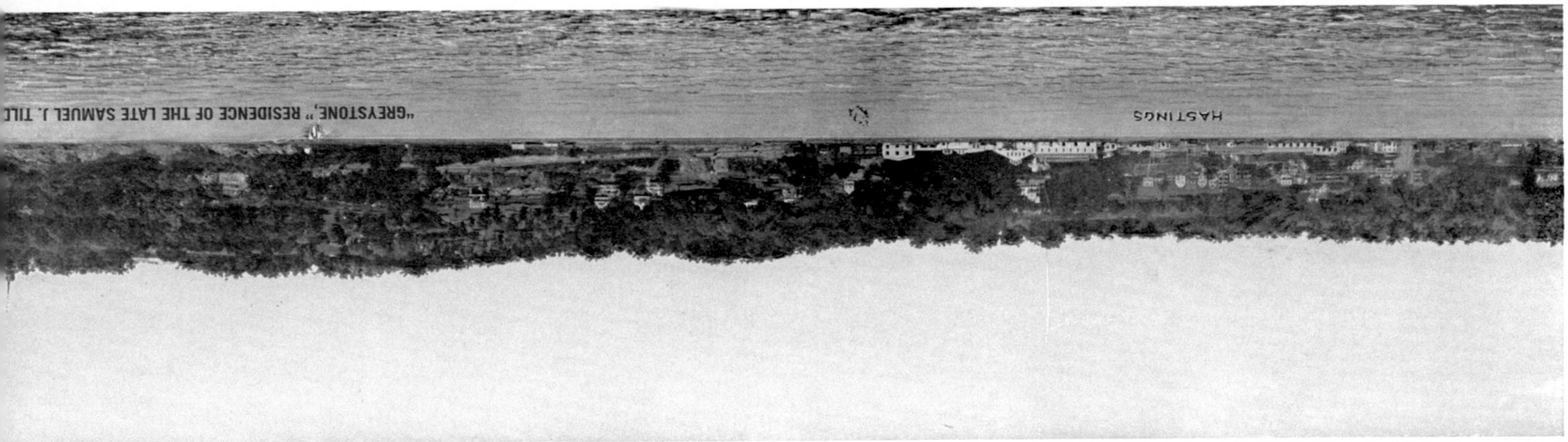

HASTINGS

"GREYSTONE," RESIDENCE OF THE LATE SAMUEL J. TIL

PALISADES

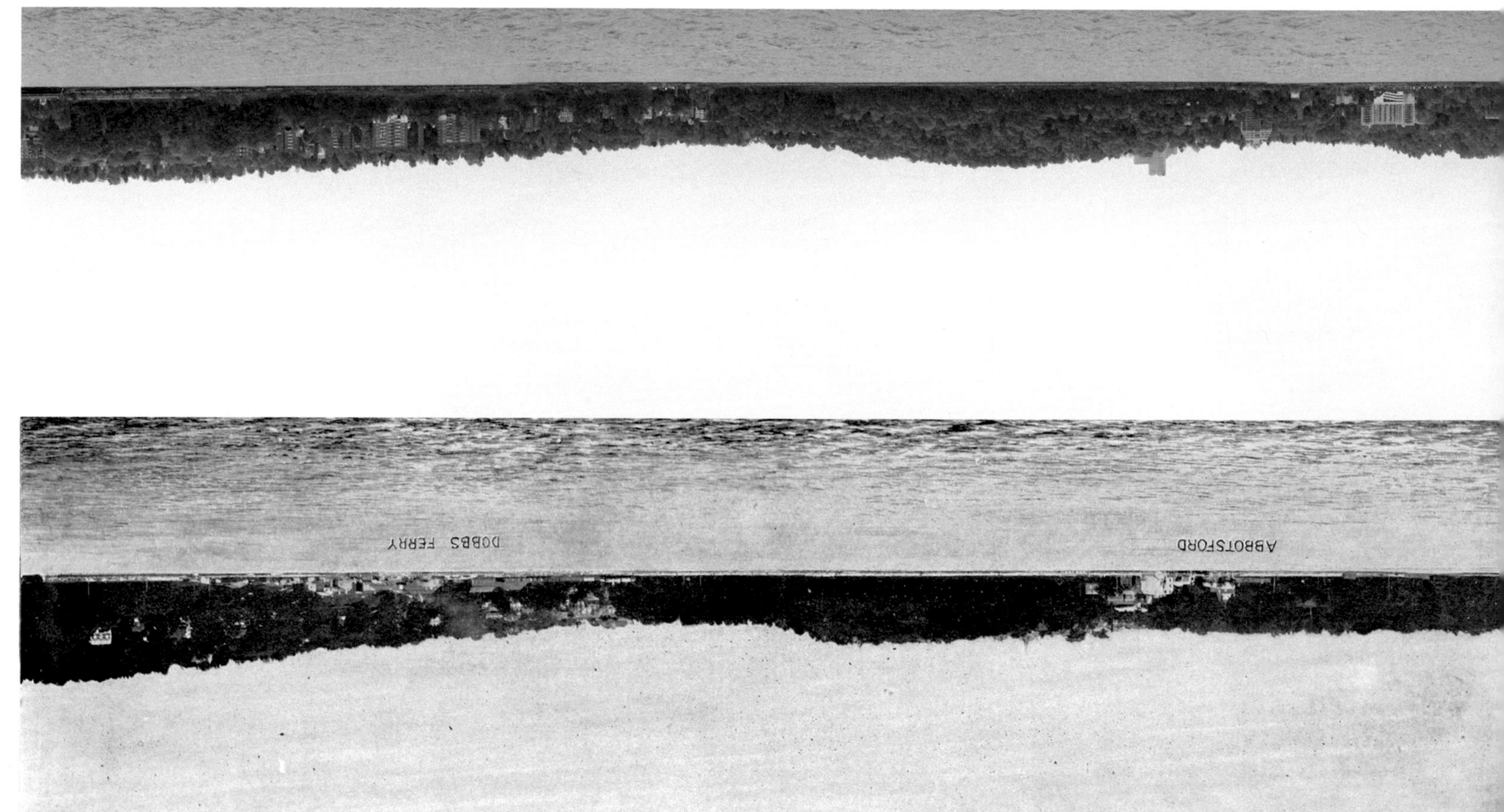

East Bank

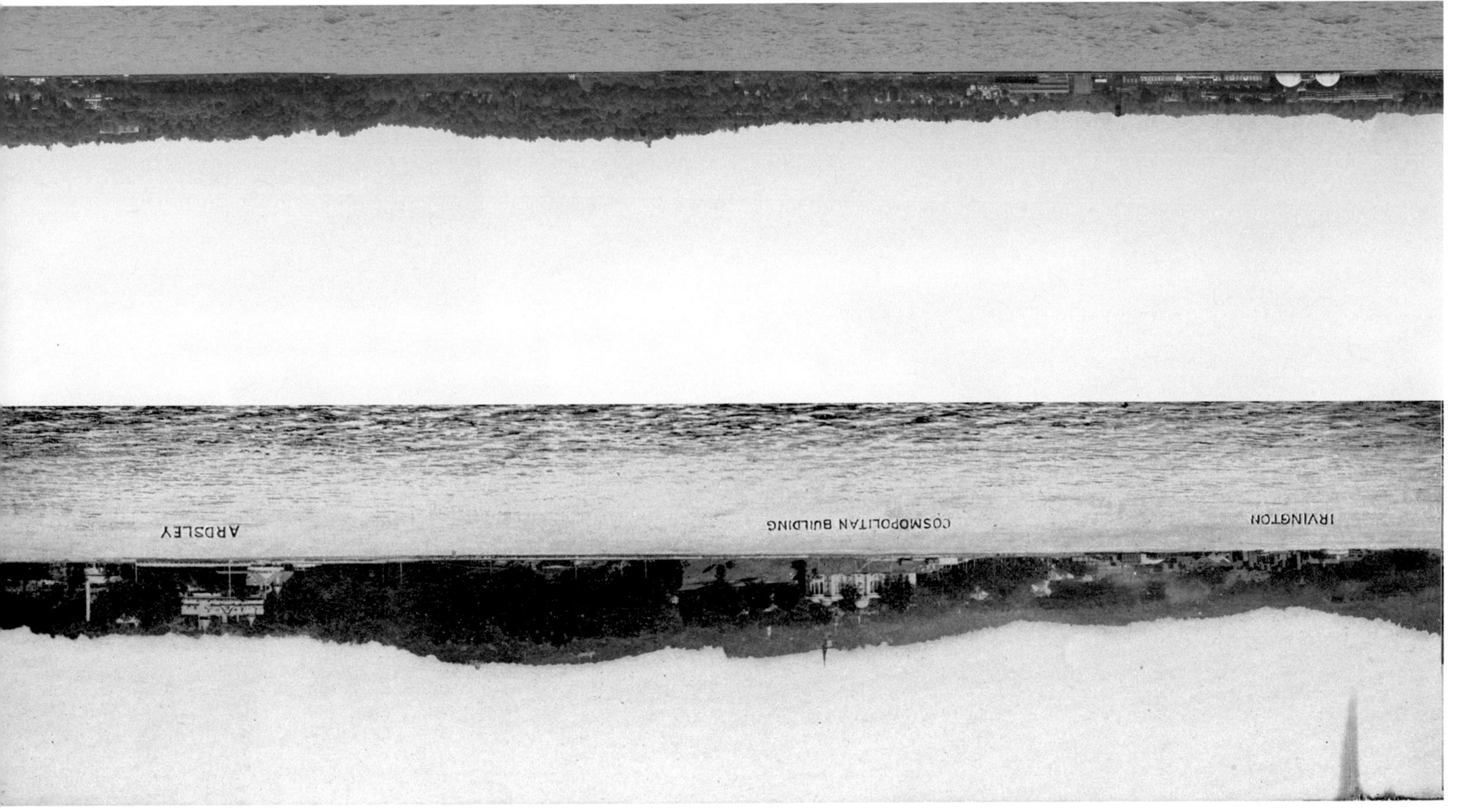
IRVINGTON
COSMOPOLITAN BUILDING
ARDSLEY

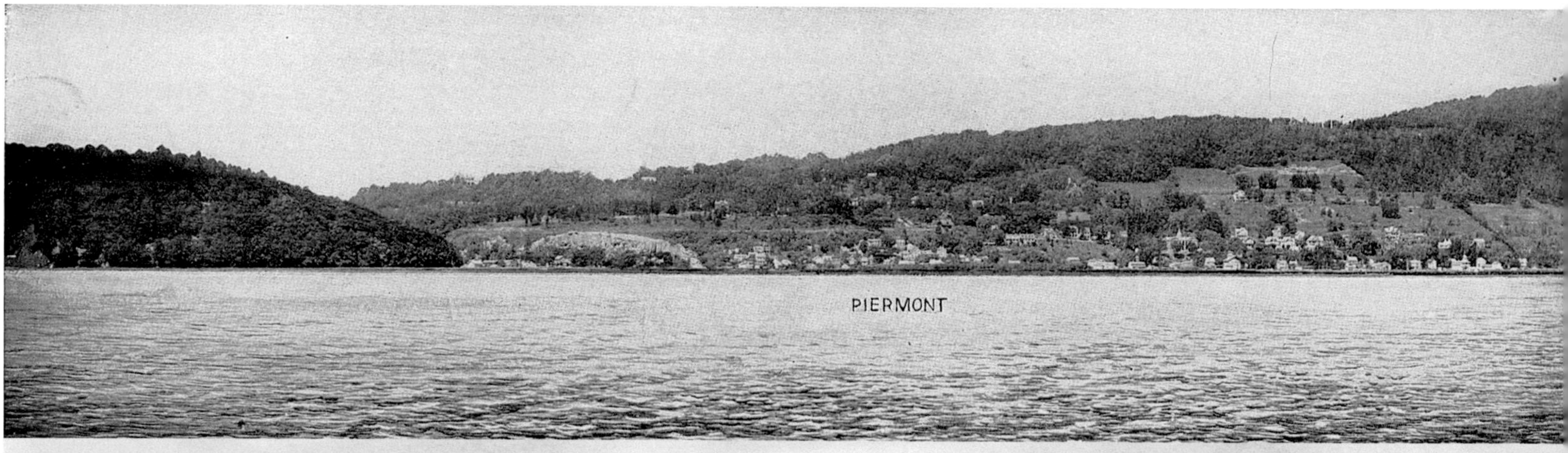

PIERMONT

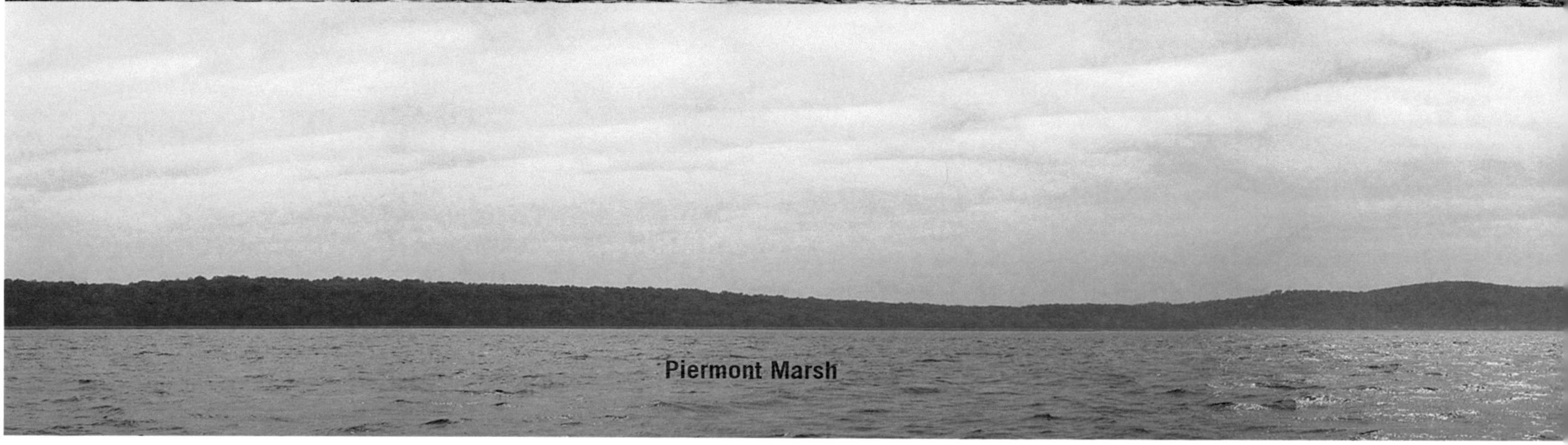

Piermont Marsh

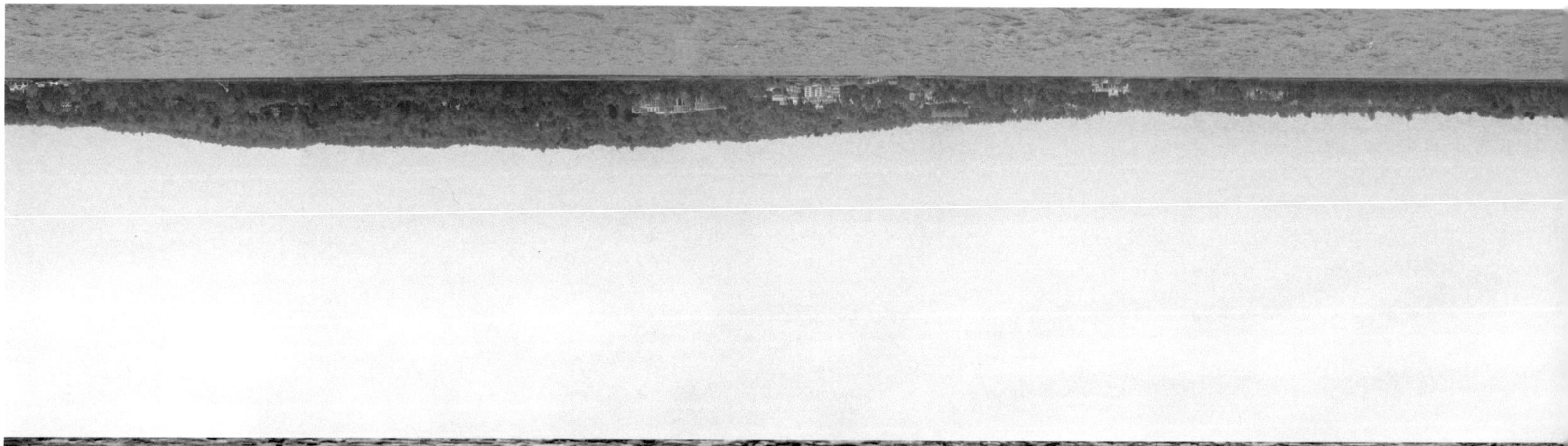

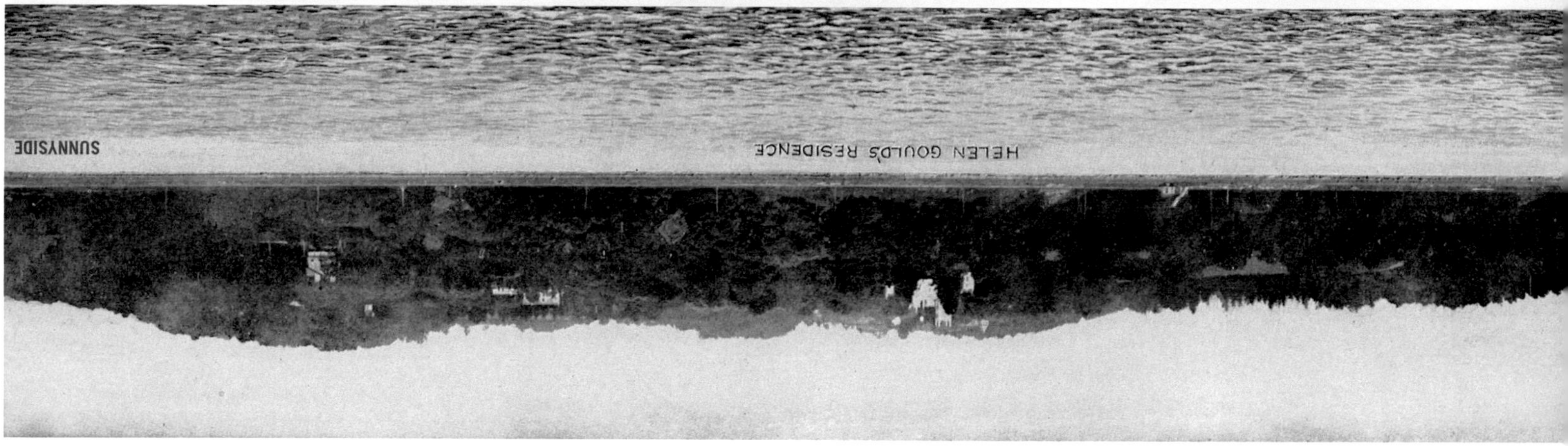

SUNNYSIDE

HELEN GOULD'S RESIDENCE

East Bank

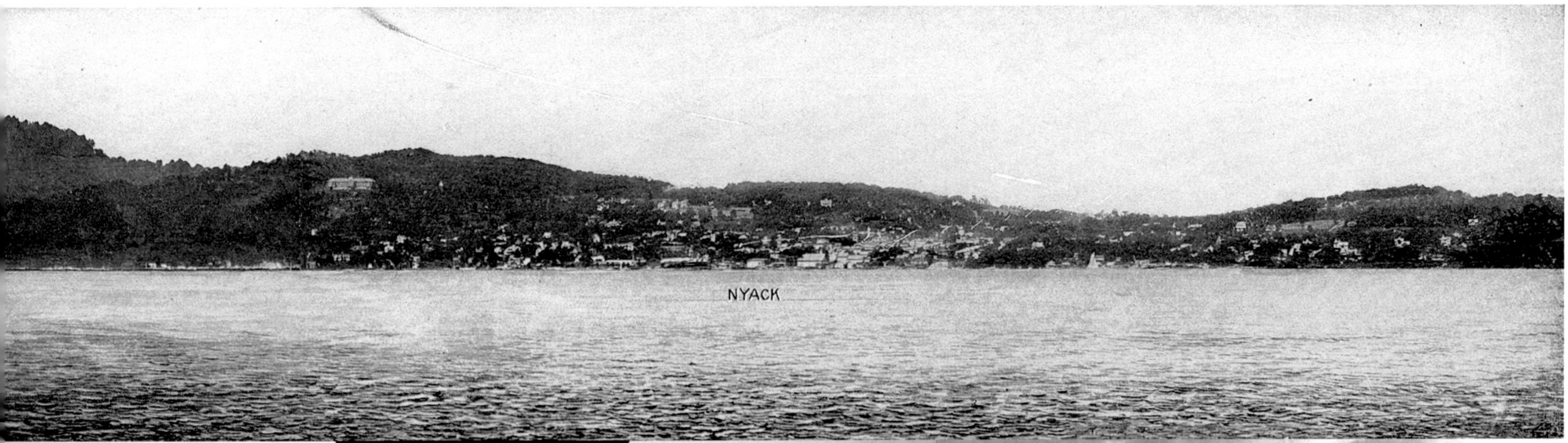

NYACK

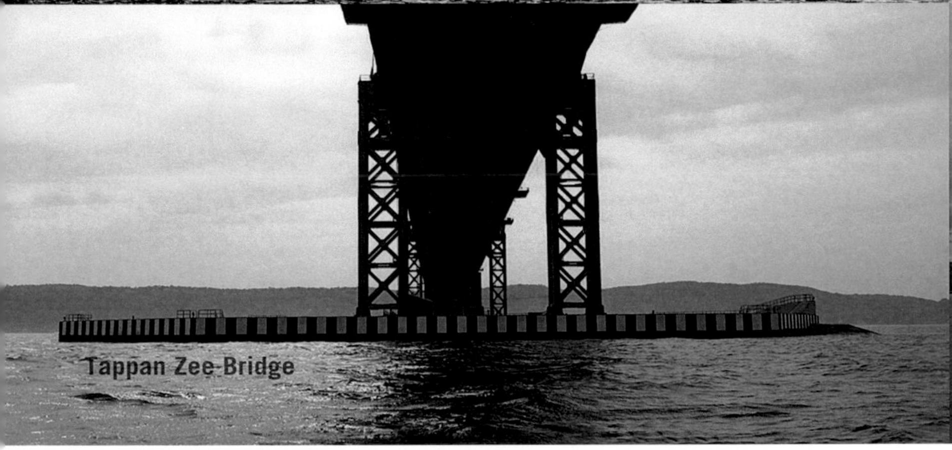

Tappan Zee-Bridge

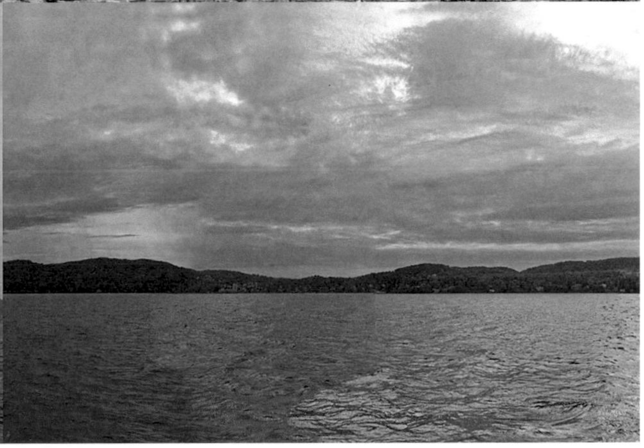

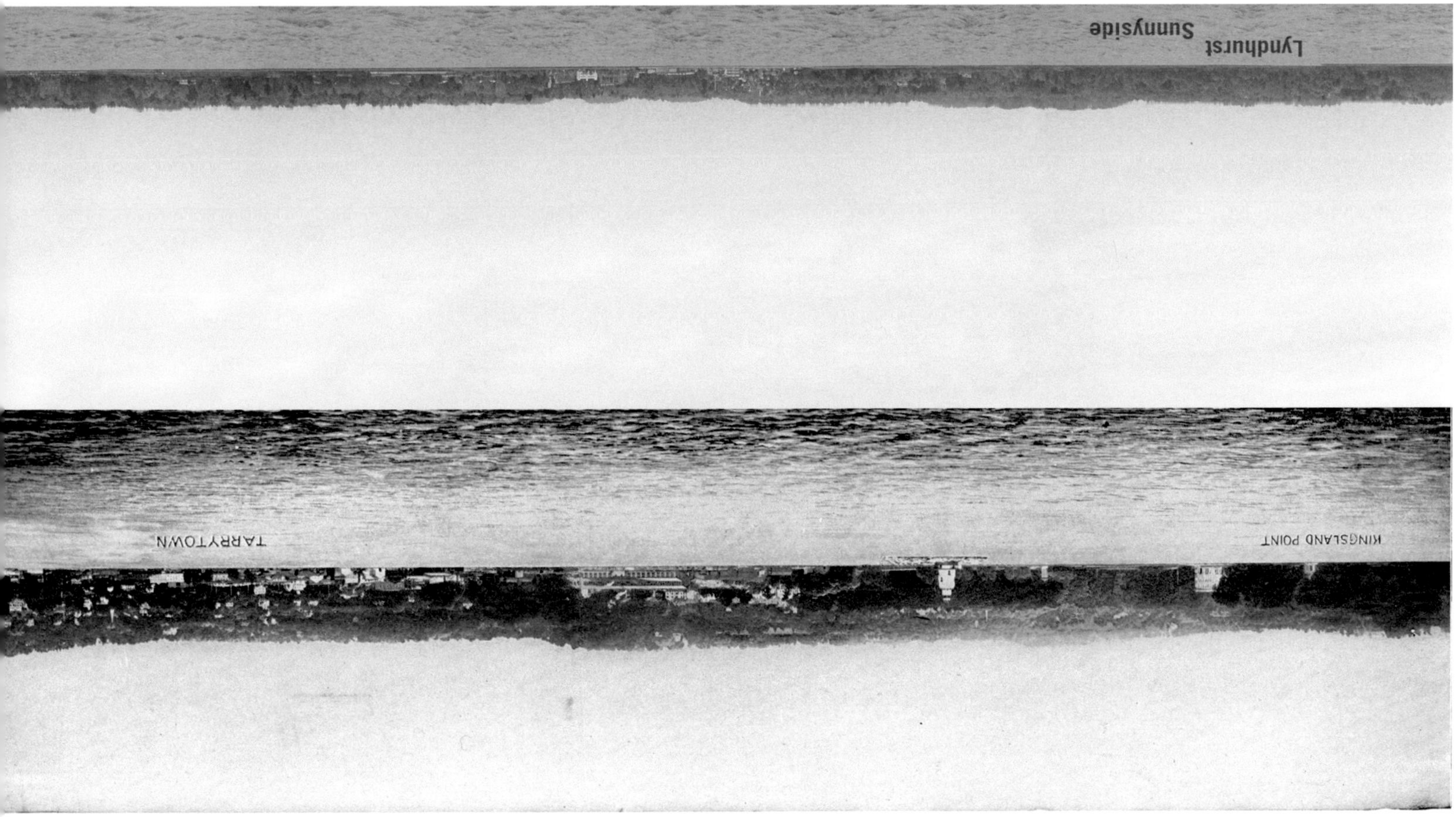

Lyndhurst
Sunnyside

KINGSLAND POINT

TARRYTOWN

HOOK MOUNTAINS

Tappan Zee Bridge
Sleepy Hollow Lighthouse
SCARBOROUGH
MRS ELLIOTT F. SHEPPARD'S RESIDENCE
"ROCKWOOD" WILLIAM ROCKEFELLER'S RESIDENCE

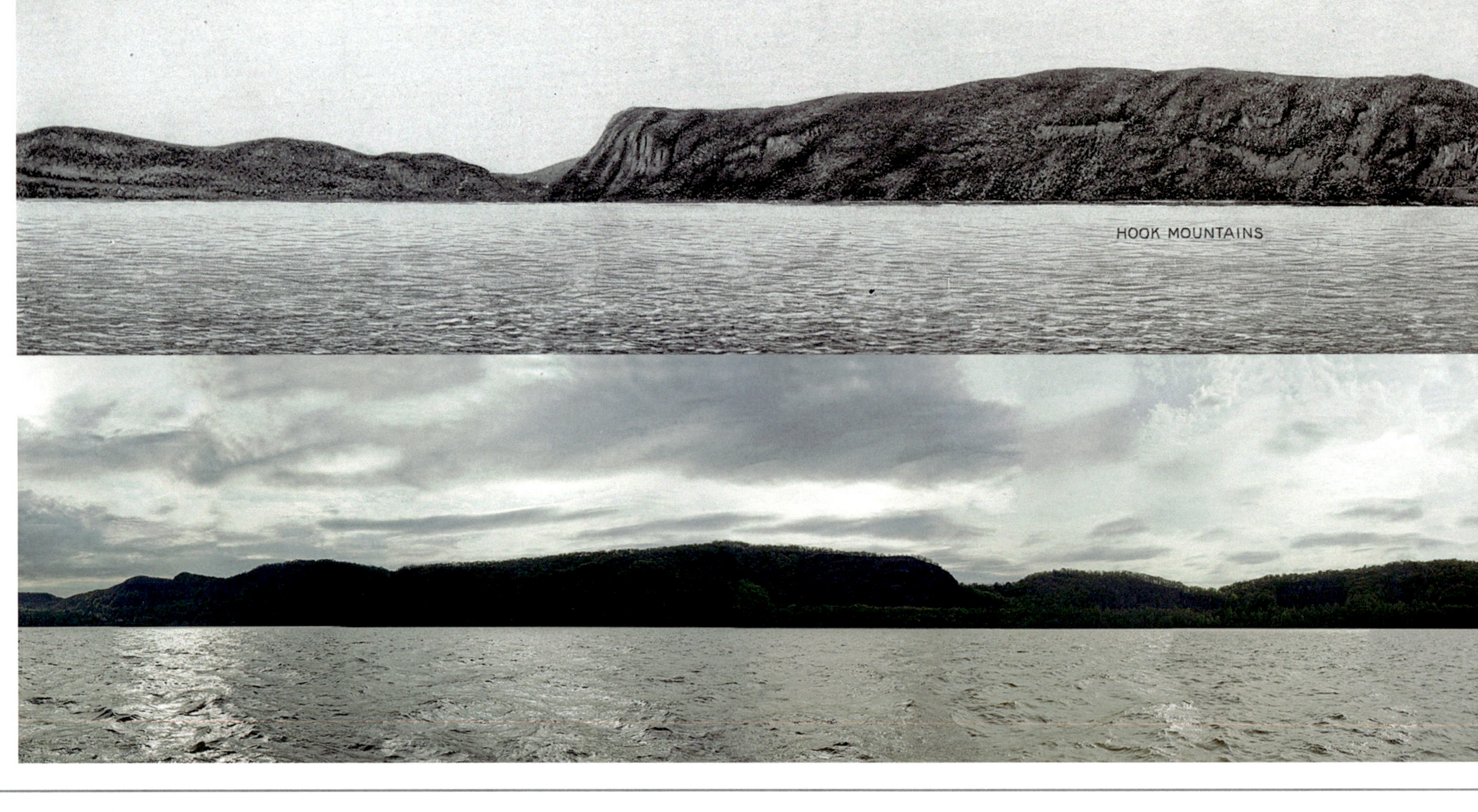

East Bank

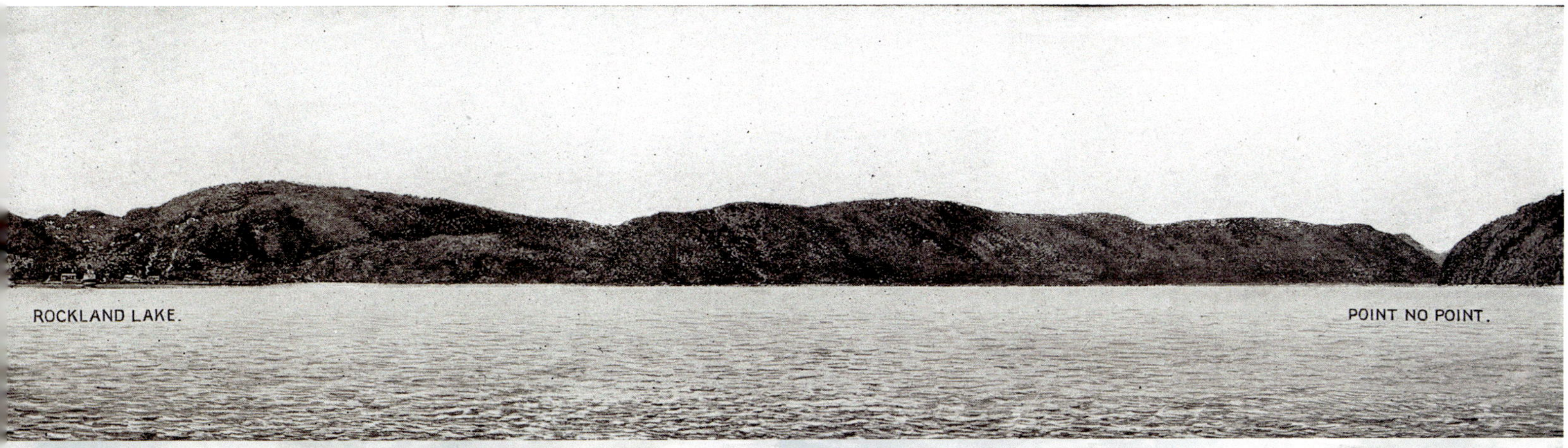

ROCKLAND LAKE.

POINT NO POINT.

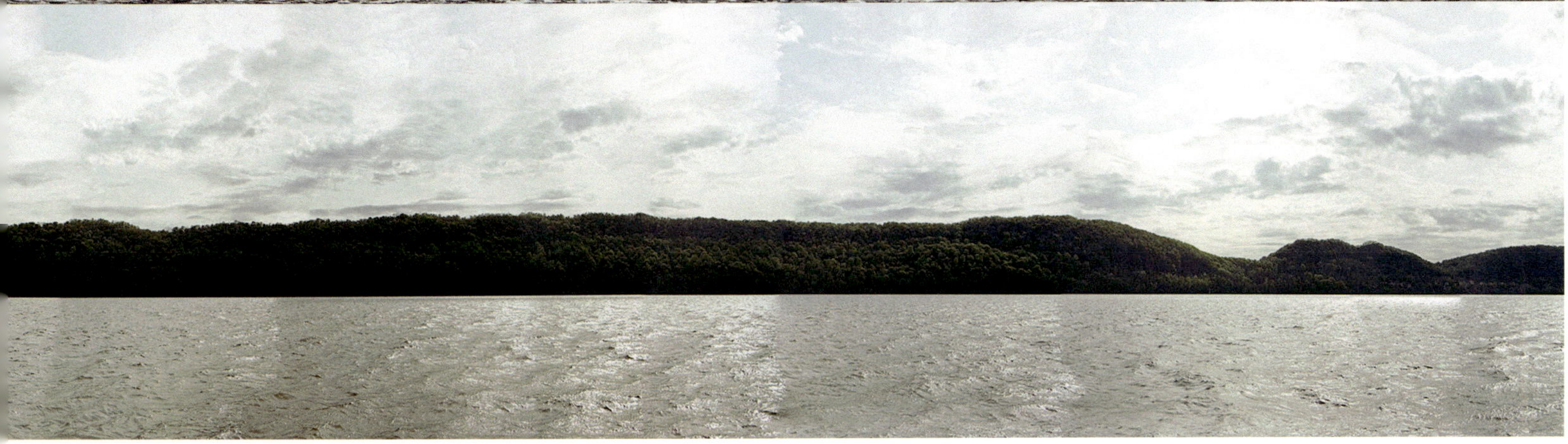

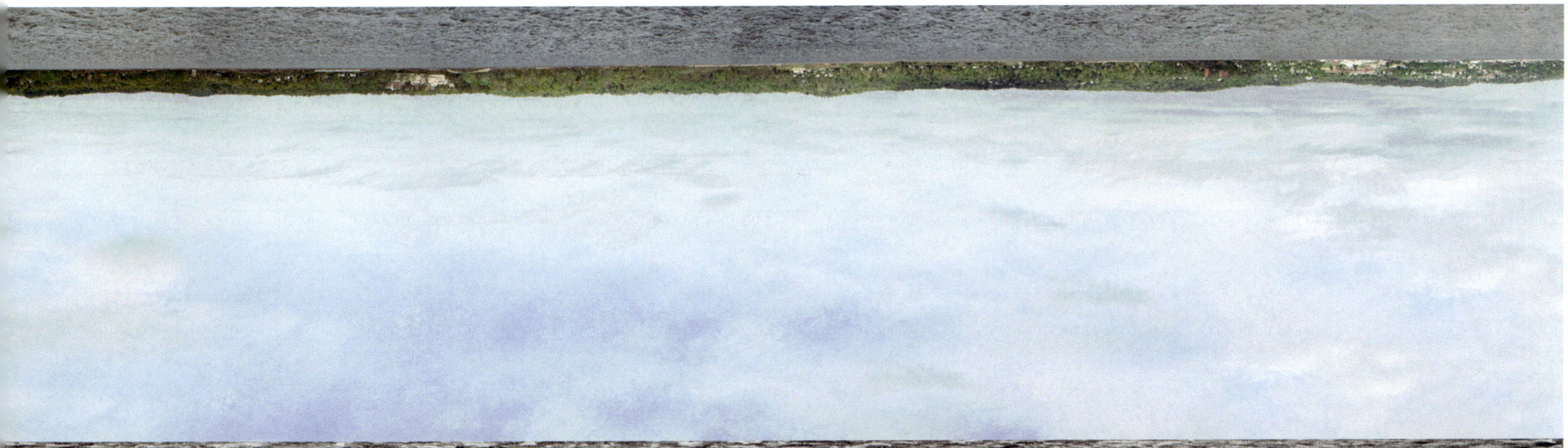

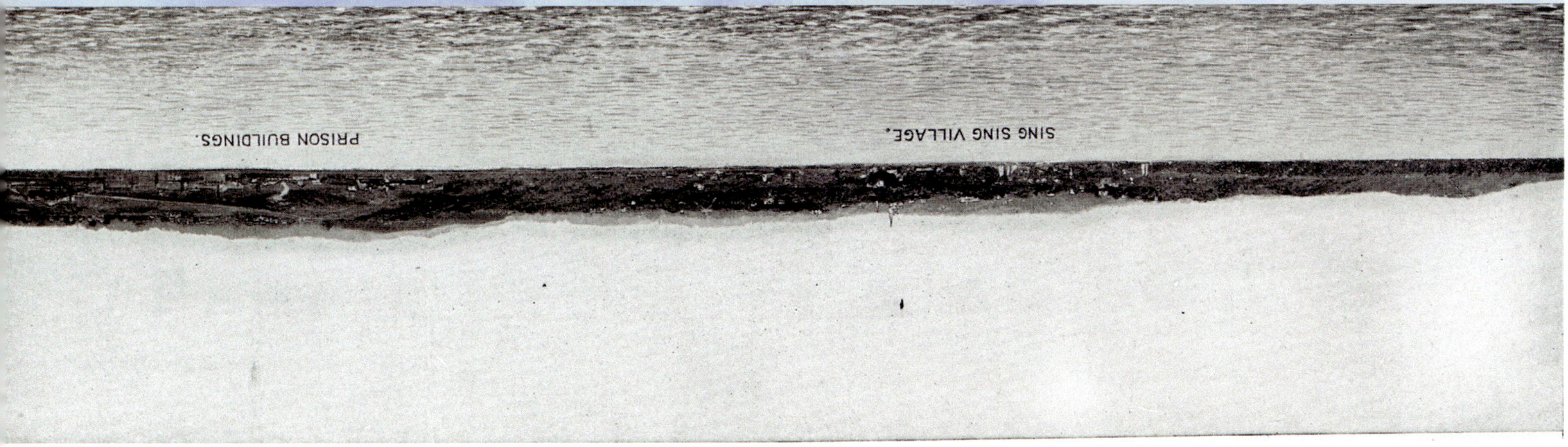

SING SING VILLAGE.

PRISON BUILDINGS.

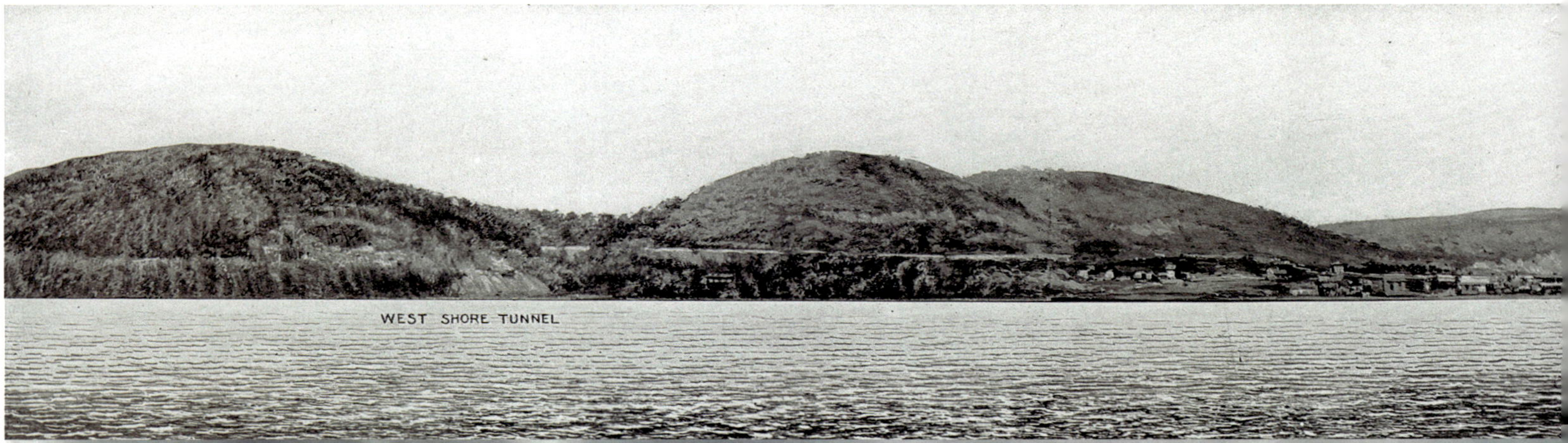

WEST SHORE TUNNEL

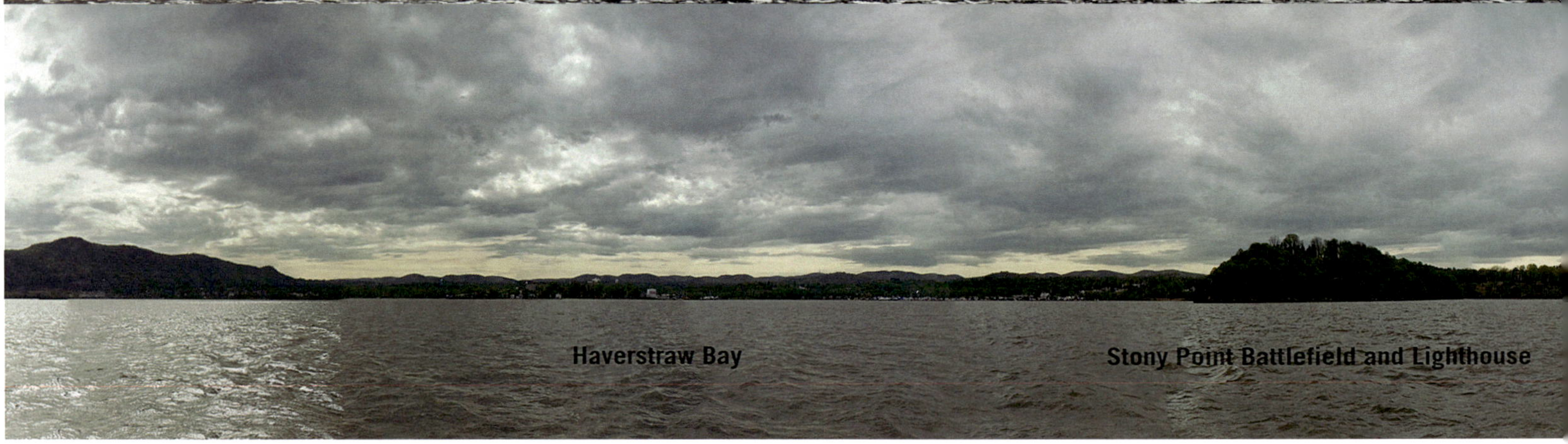

Haverstraw Bay

Stony Point Battlefield and Lighthouse

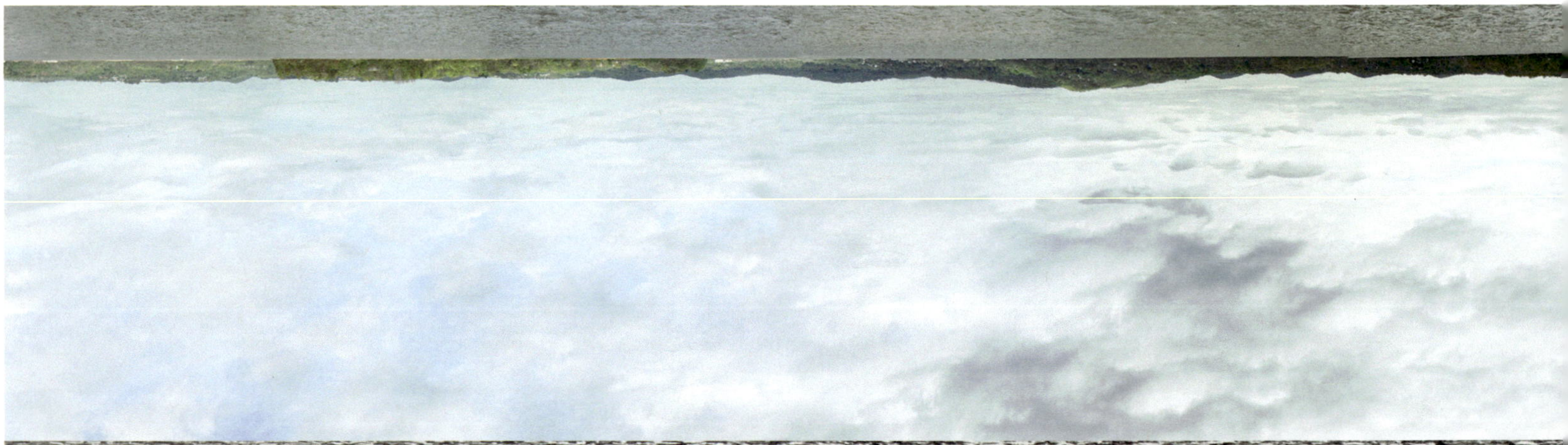

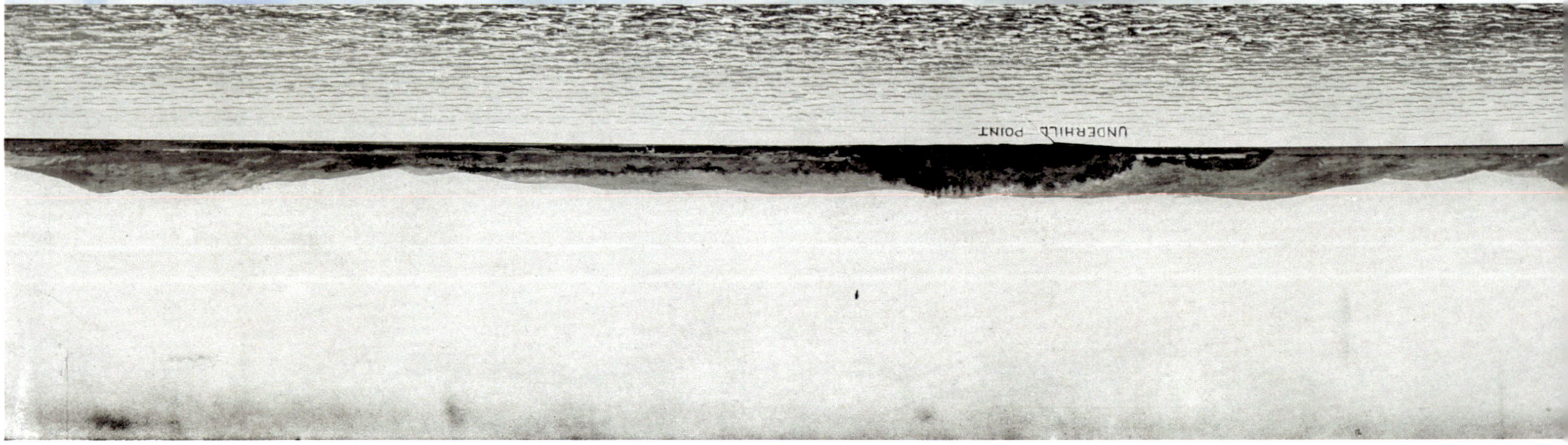

UNDERHILL POINT

East Bank

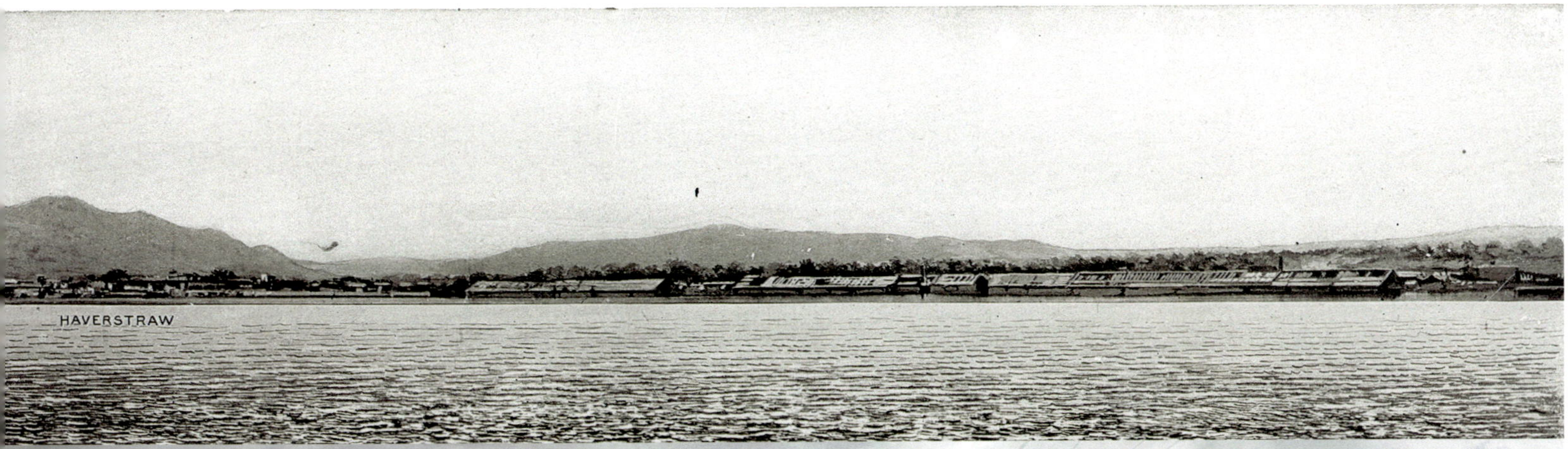

HAVERSTRAW

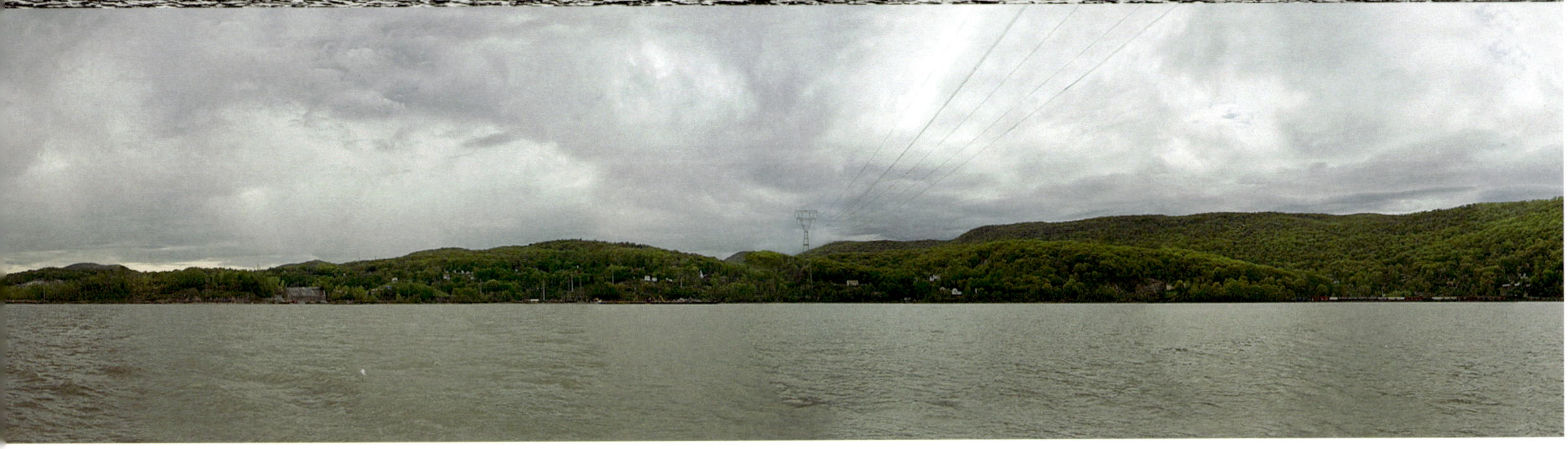

Croton Point Park

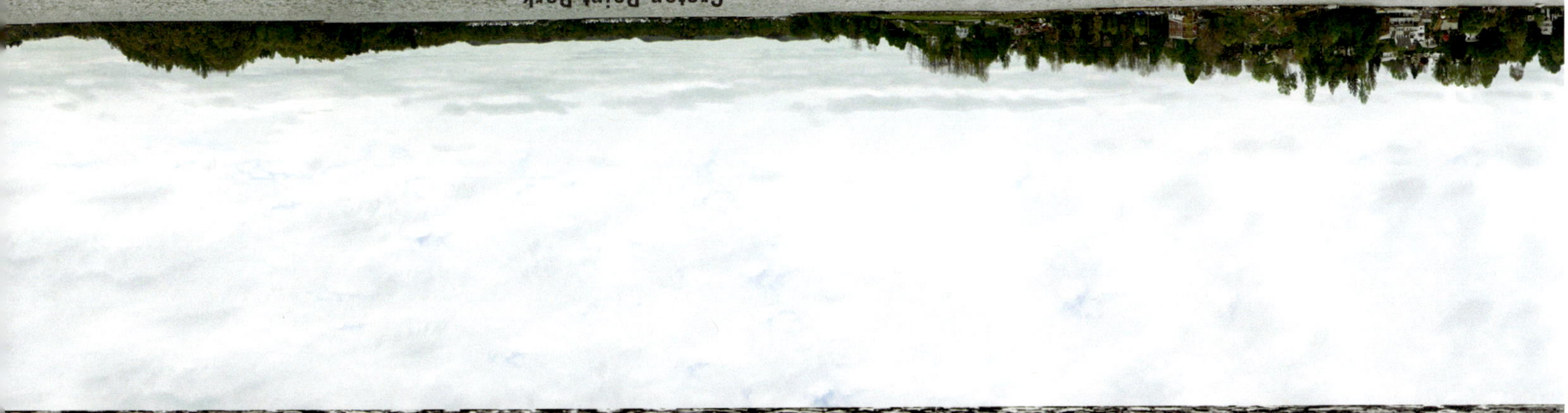

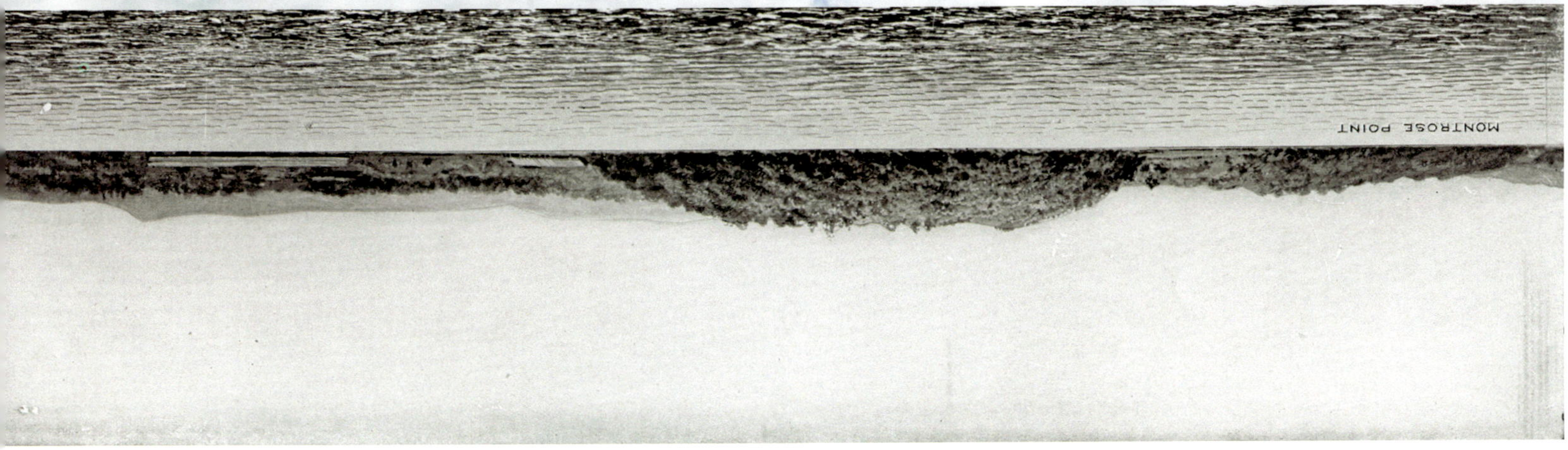

MONTROSE POINT

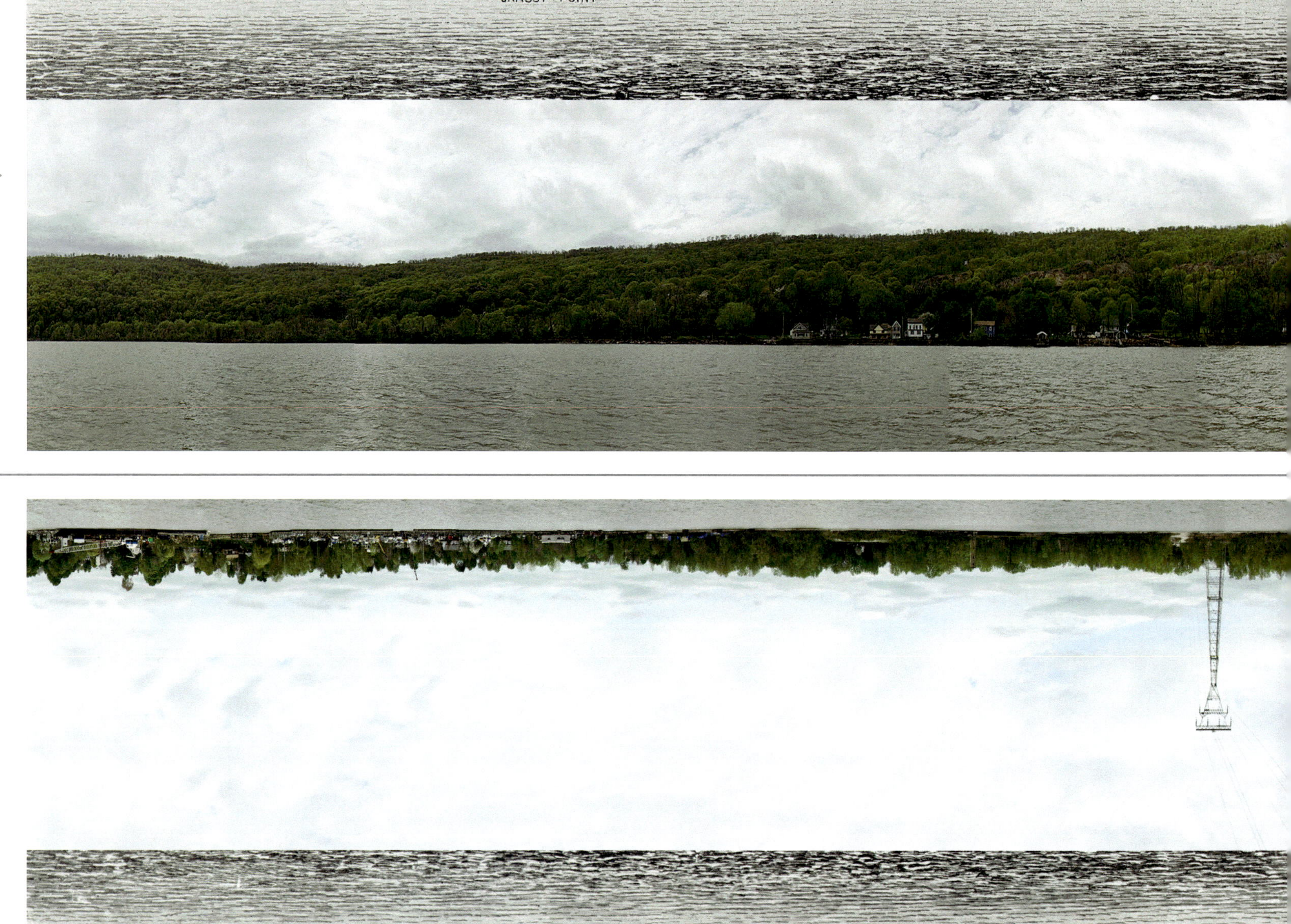

East Bank

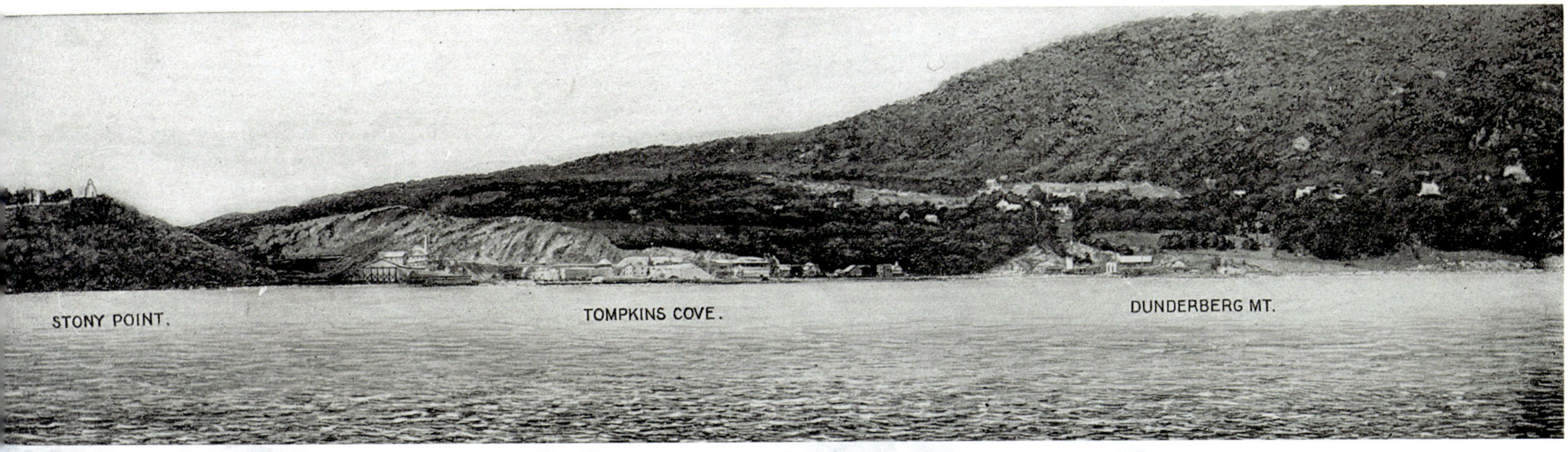

STONY POINT.

TOMPKINS COVE.

DUNDERBERG MT.

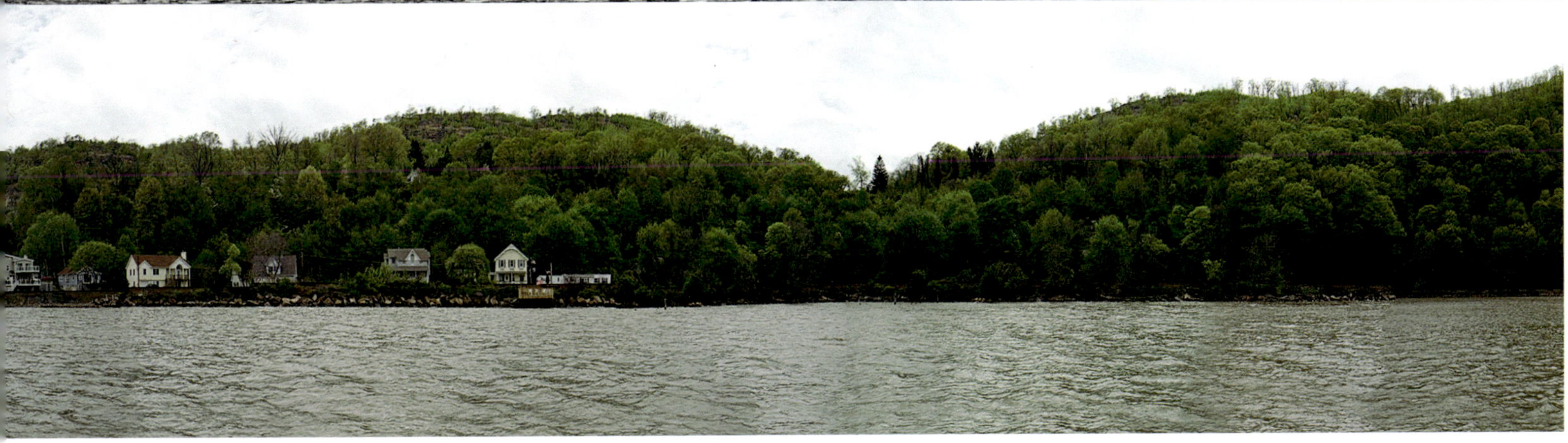

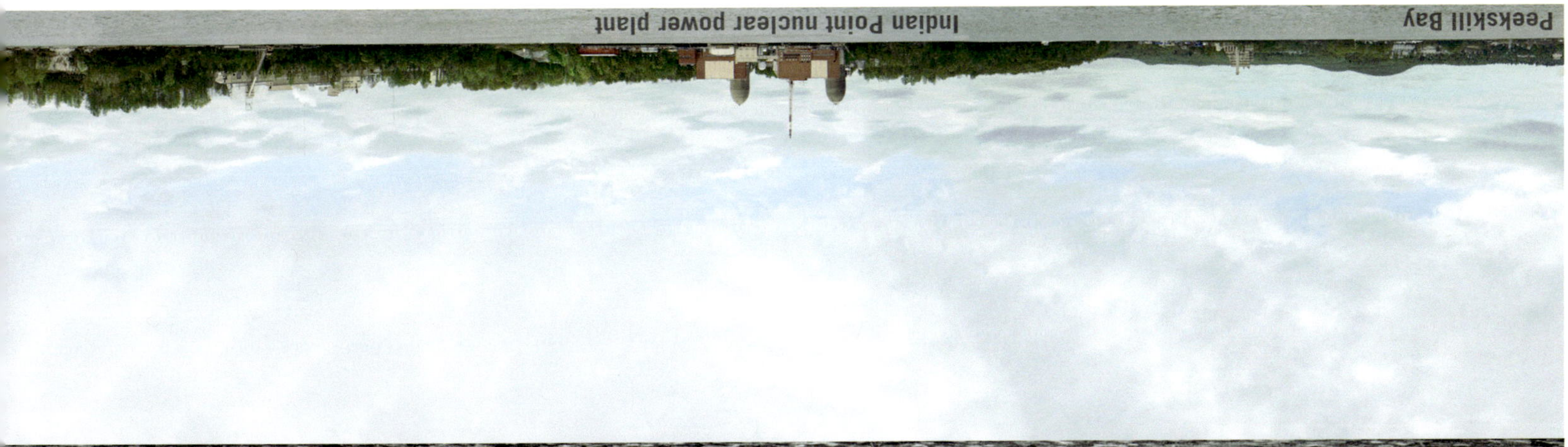

Peekskill Bay

Indian Point nuclear power plant

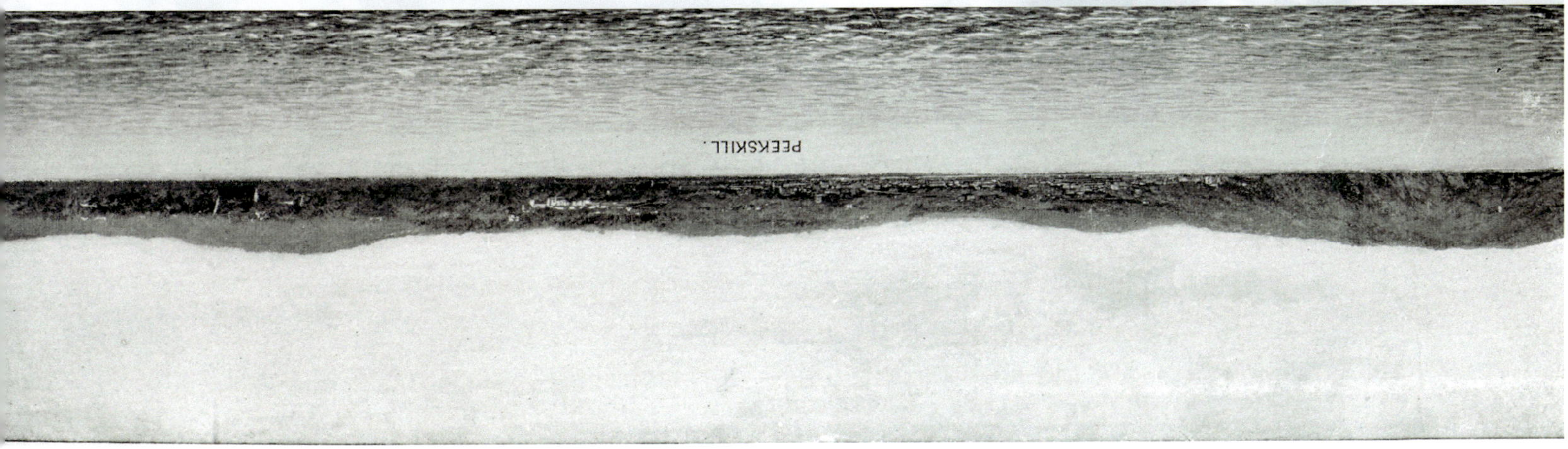

PEEKSKILL.

KIDD'S POINT.

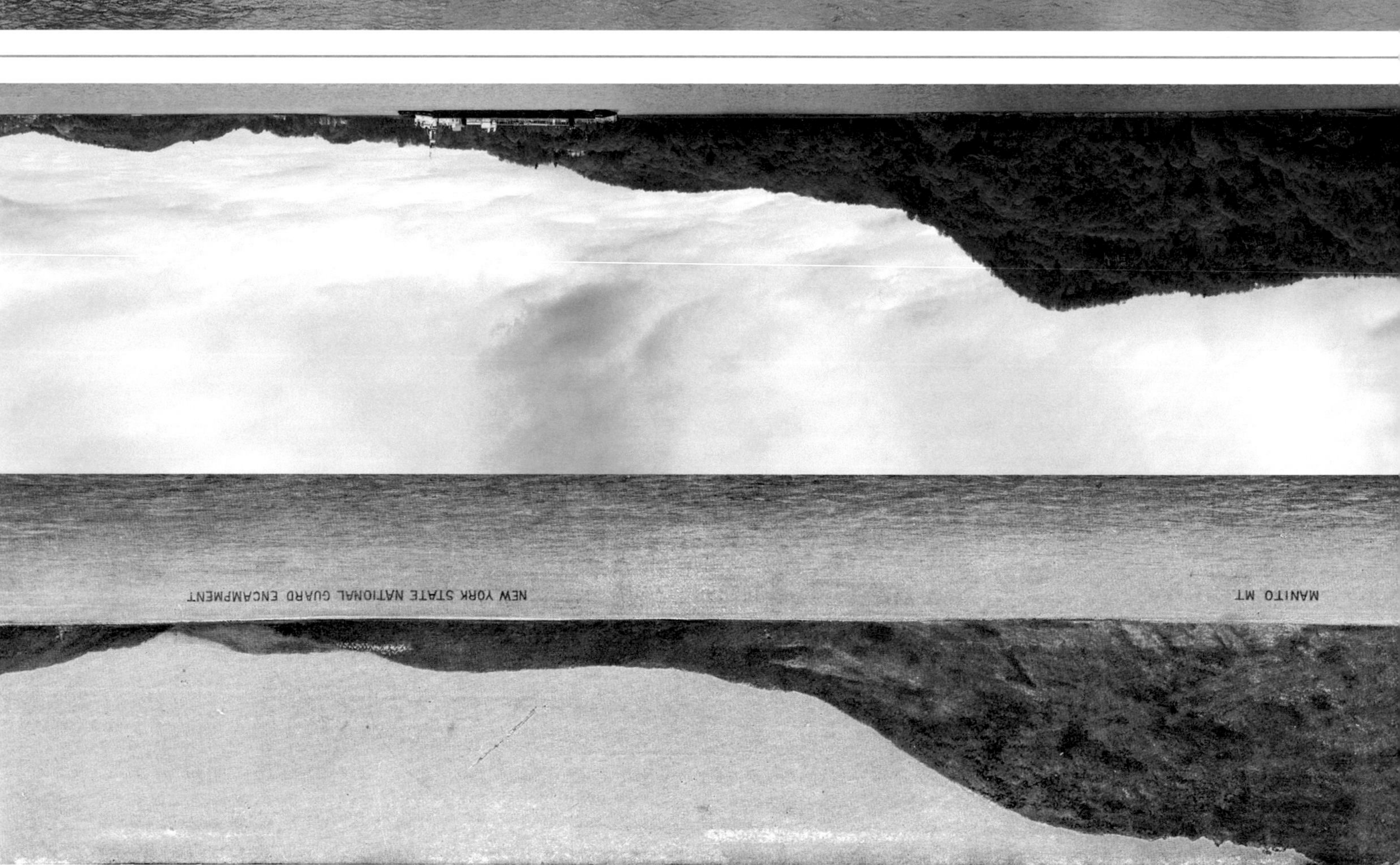

East Bank

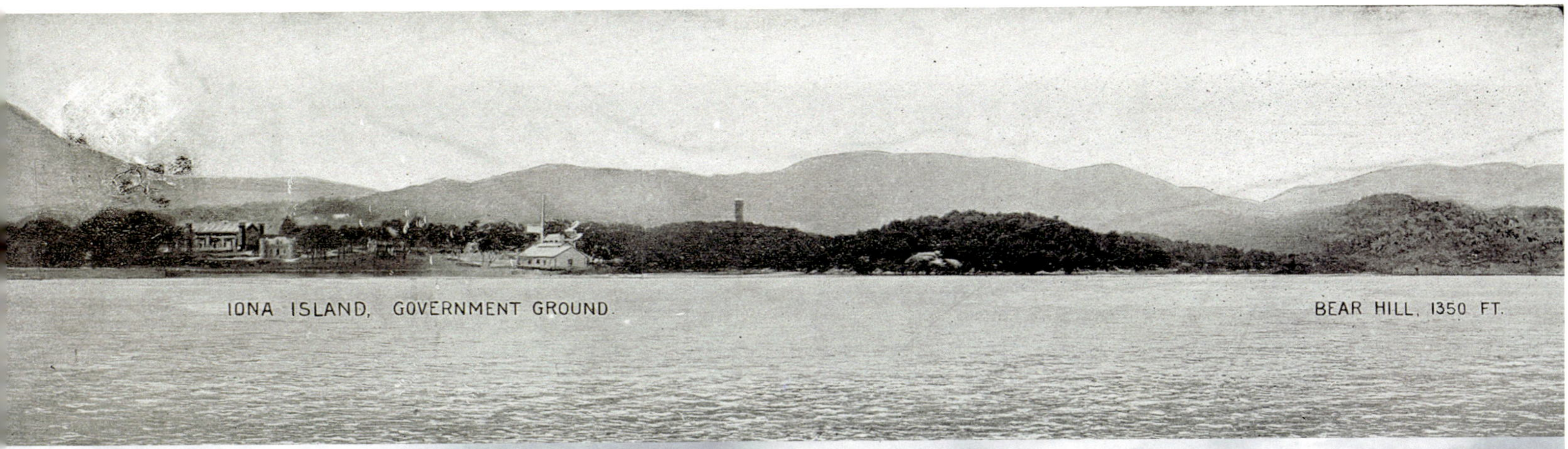

IONA ISLAND, GOVERNMENT GROUND.

BEAR HILL, 1350 FT.

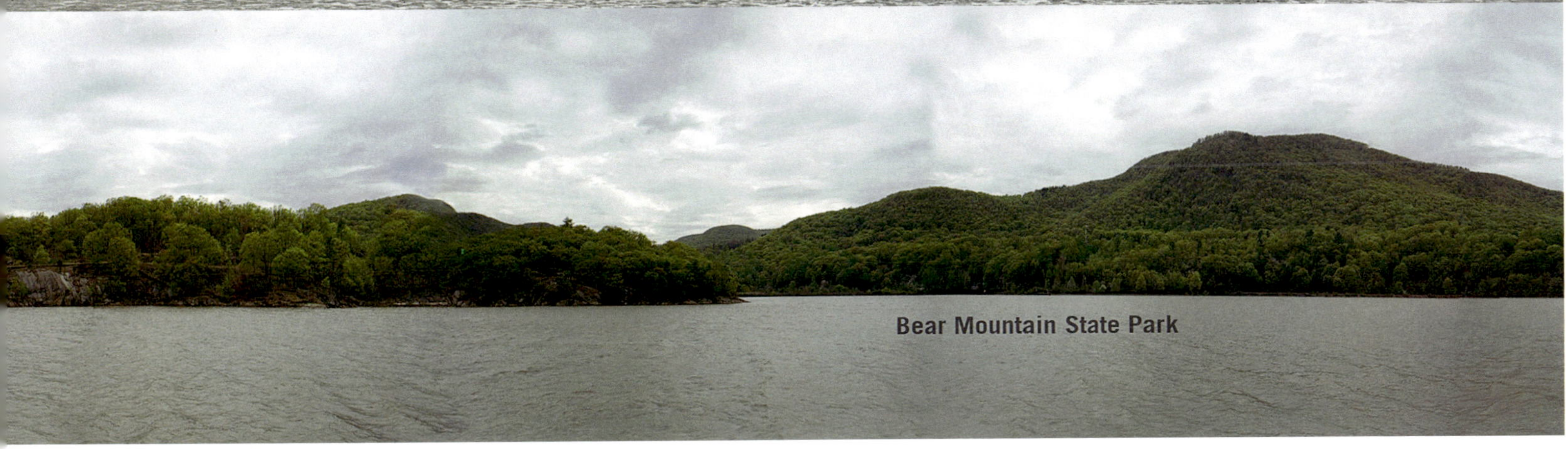

Bear Mountain State Park

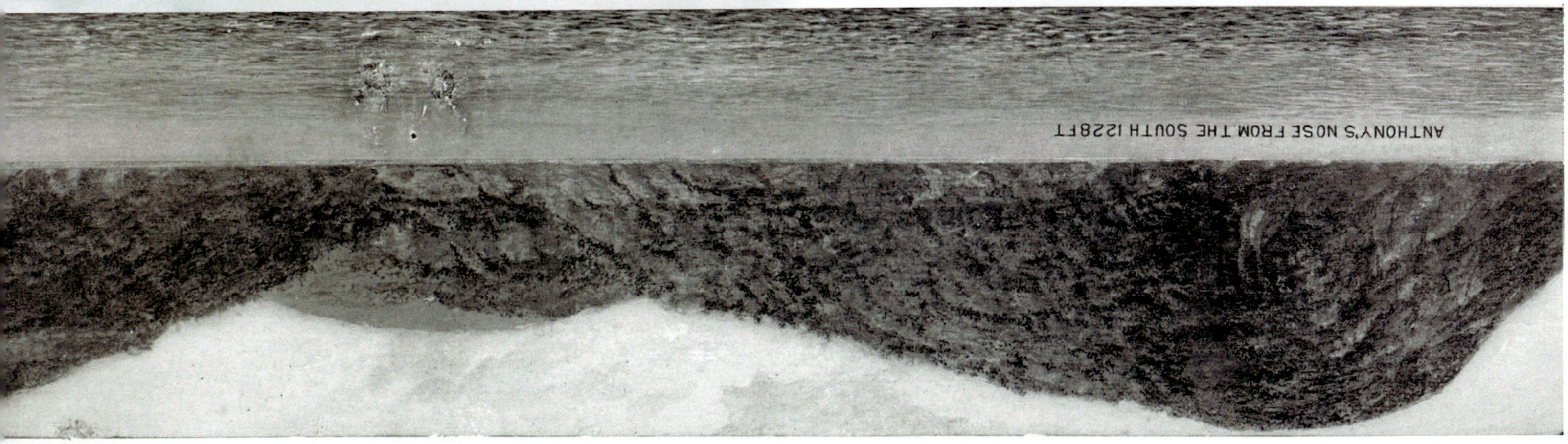

ANTHONY'S NOSE FROM THE SOUTH 1228FT

FORT MONTGOMERY

Bear Mountain Bridge

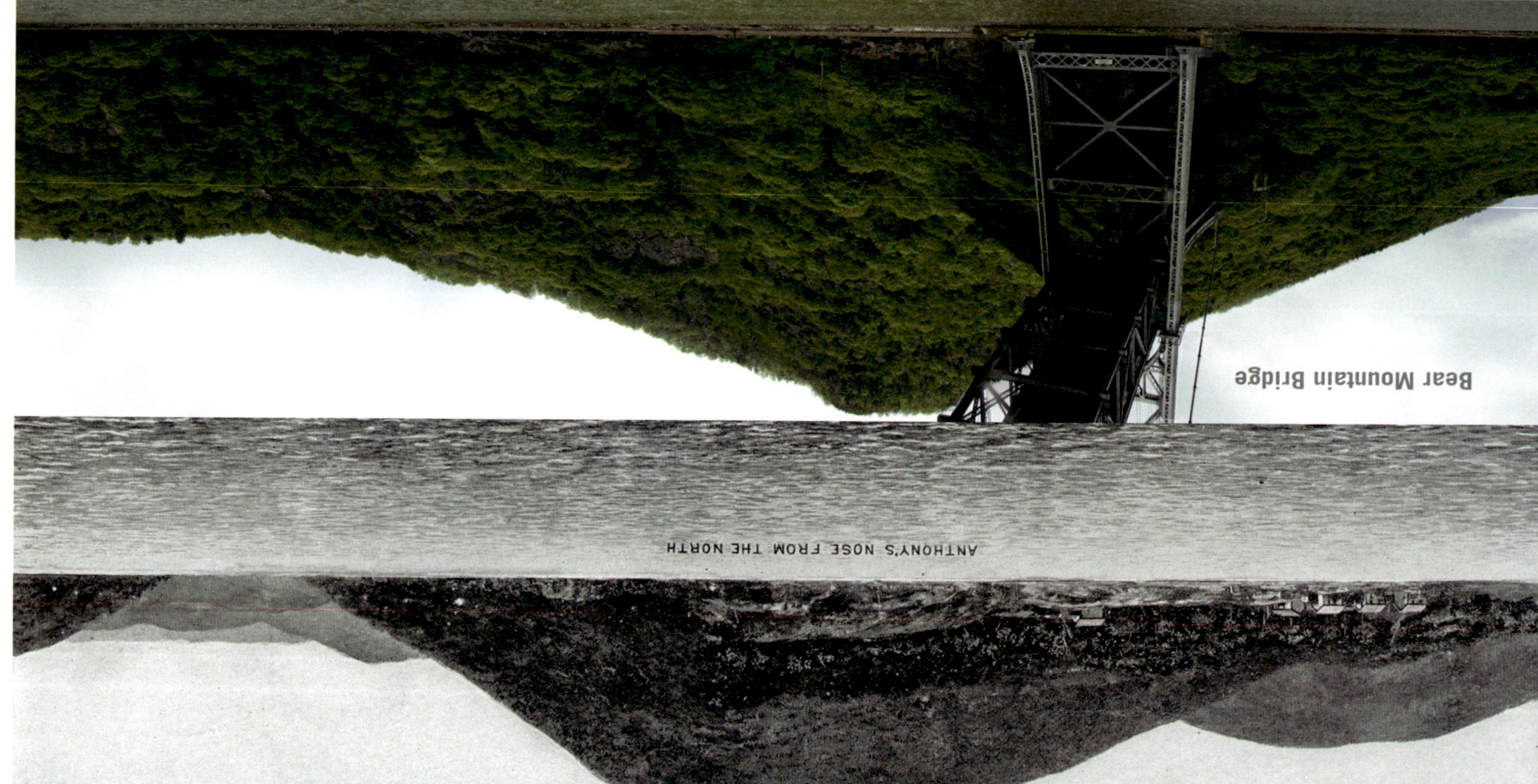

East Bank

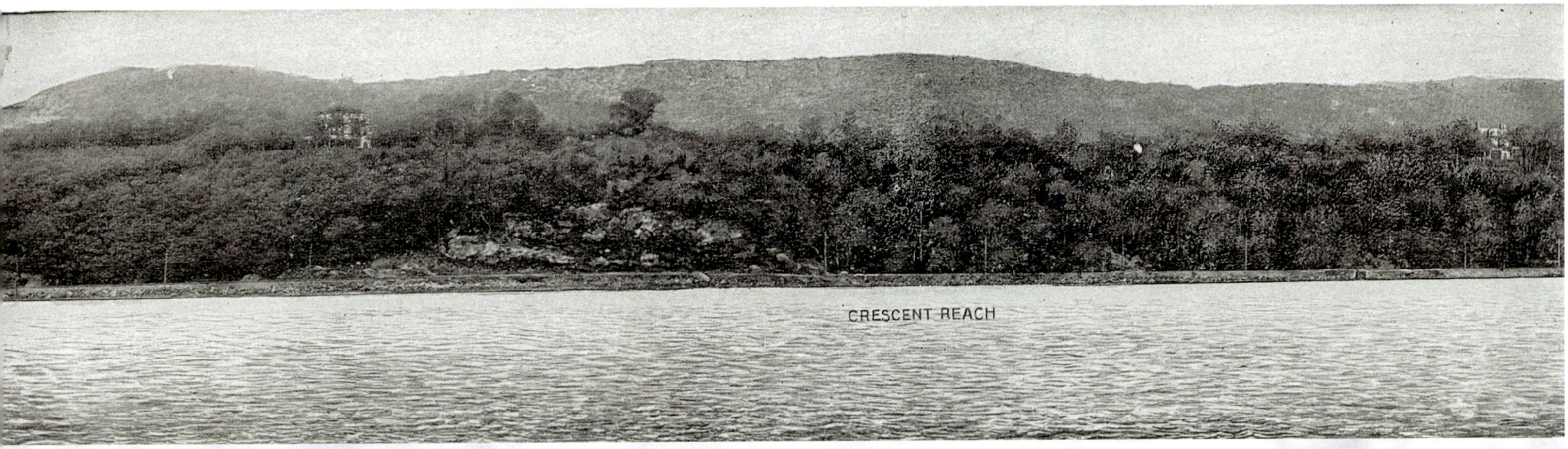

CRESCENT REACH

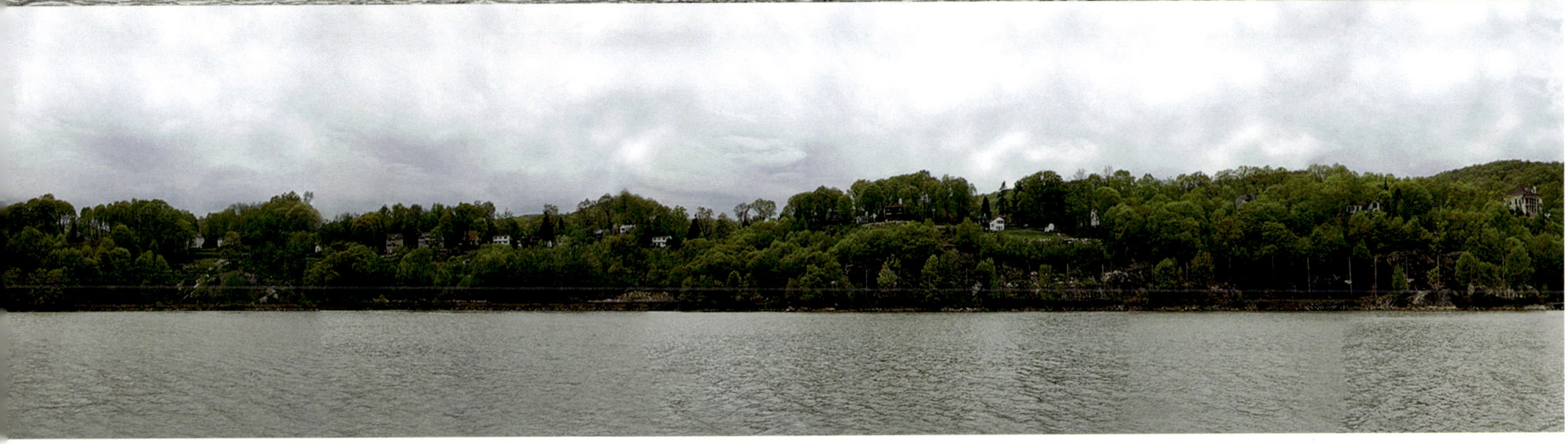

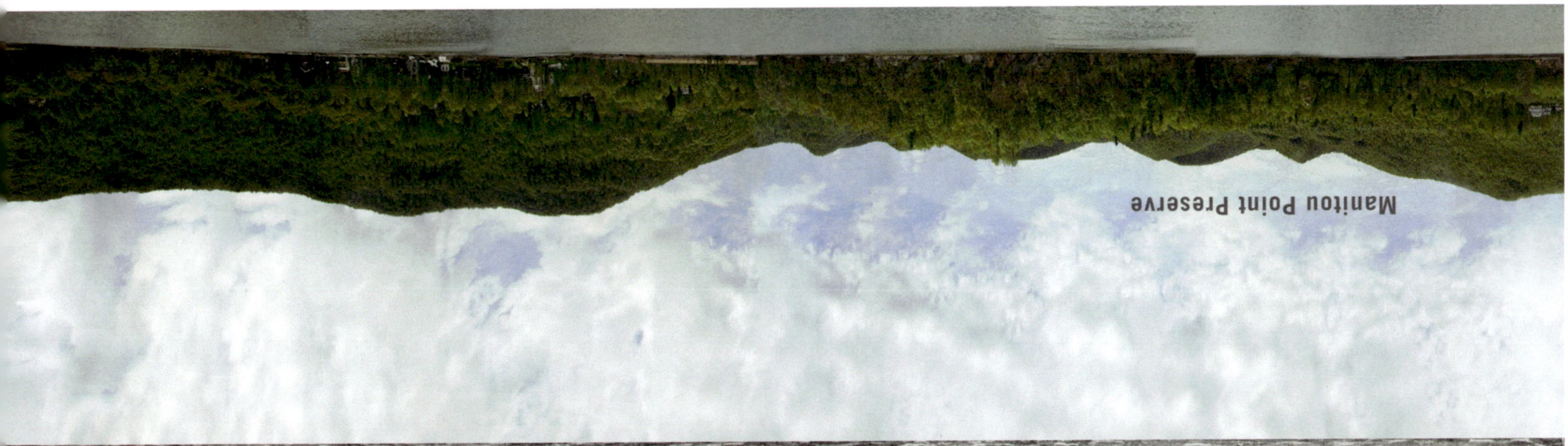

Manitou Point Preserve
EDWARD LIVINGSTON'S RESIDENCE 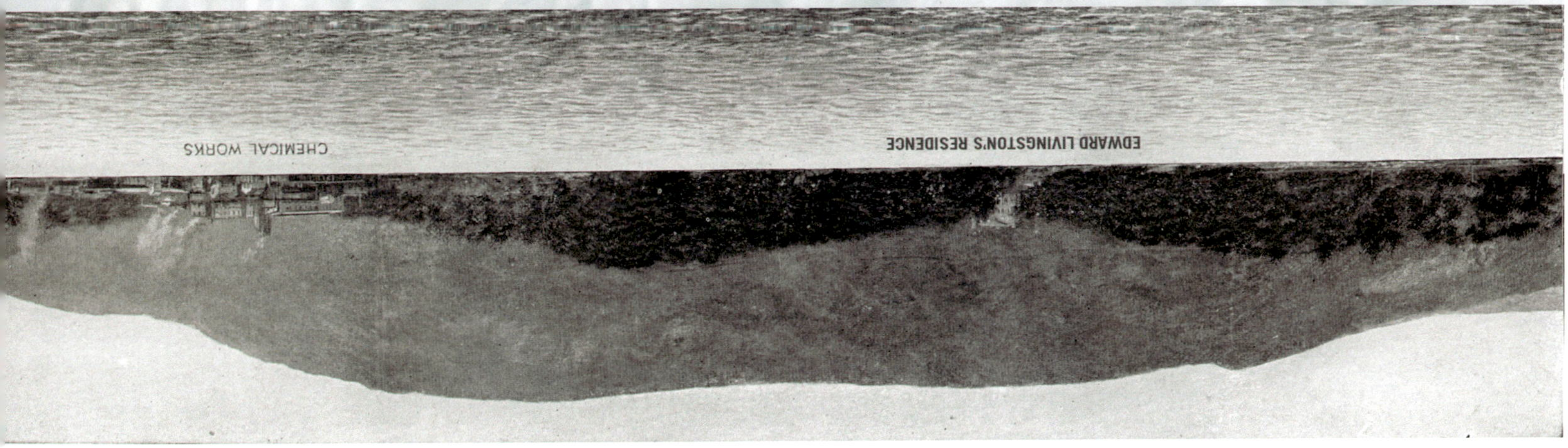
CHEMICAL WORKS

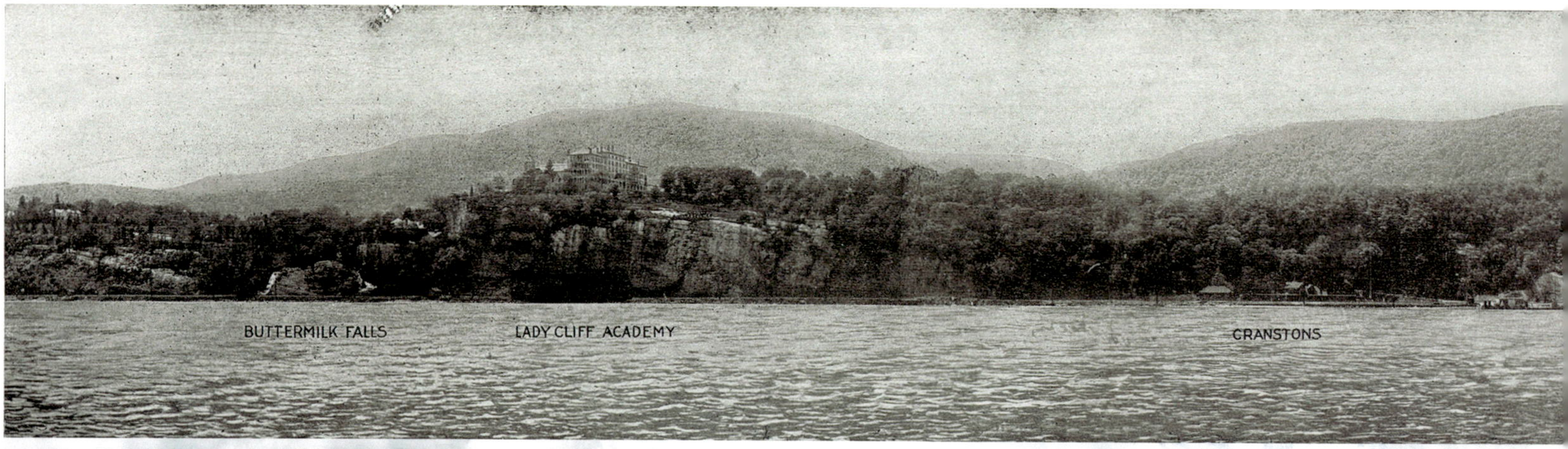

BUTTERMILK FALLS

LADY CLIFF ACADEMY

CRANSTONS

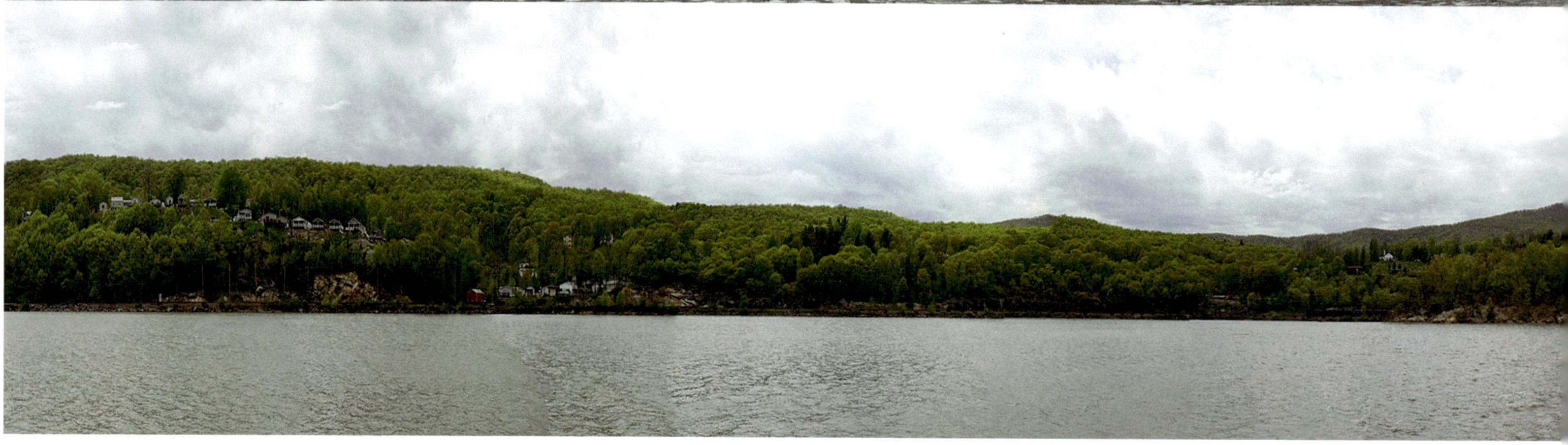

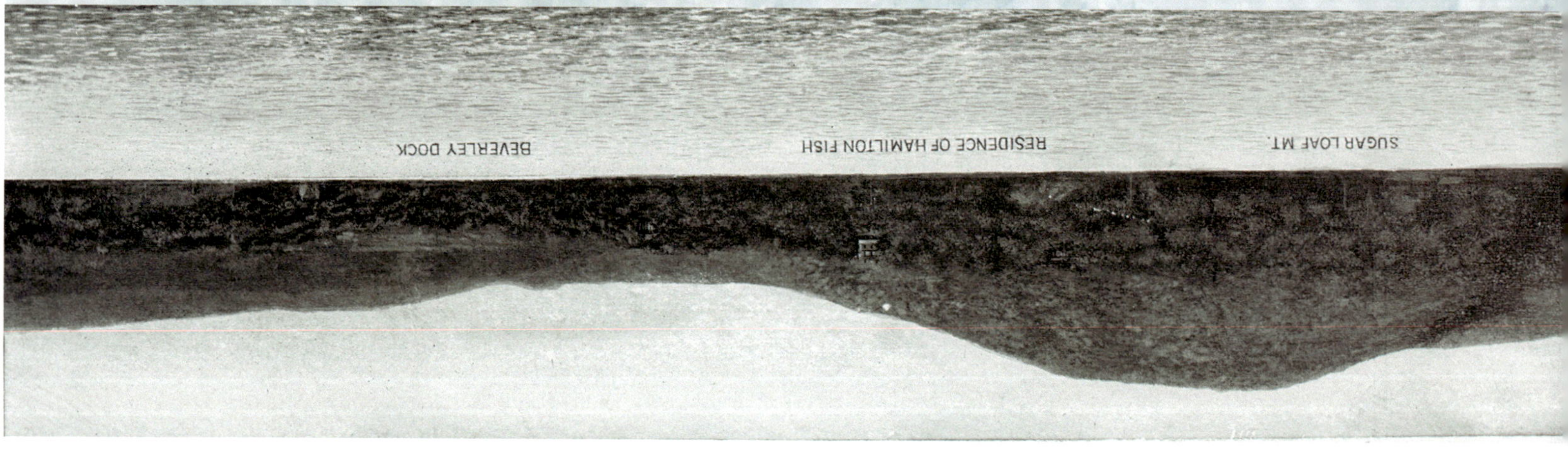

SUGAR LOAF MT.

RESIDENCE OF HAMILTON FISH

BEVERLEY DOCK

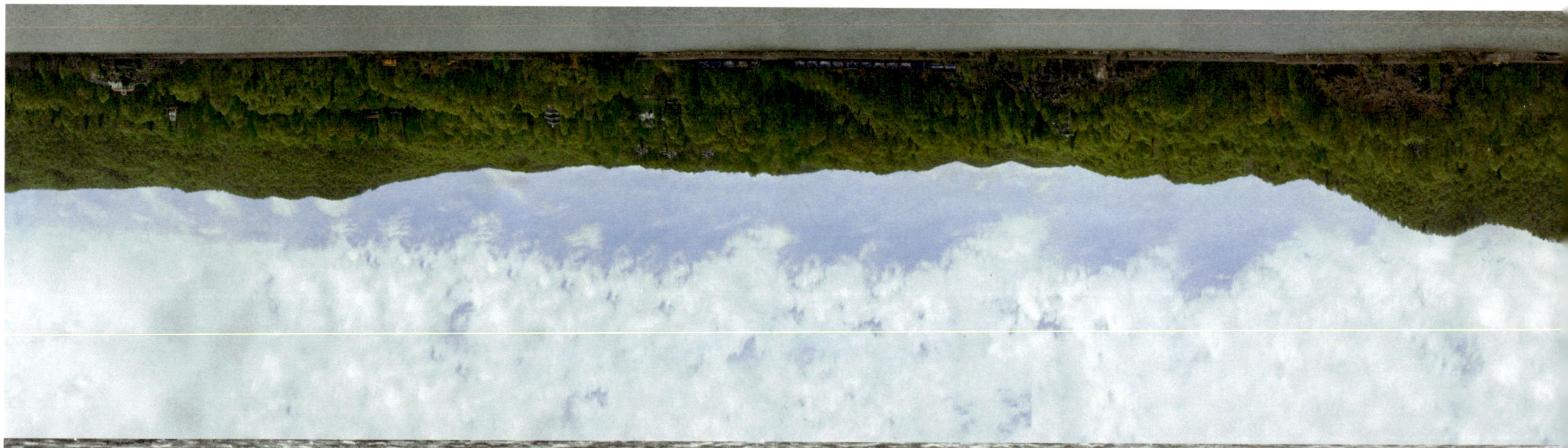

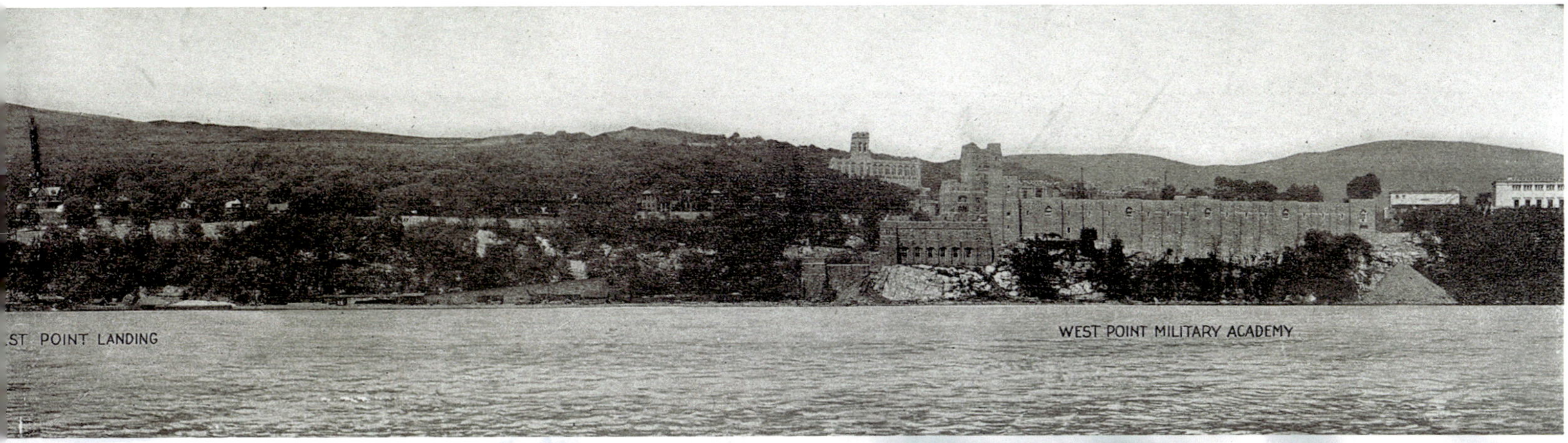

ST POINT LANDING
WEST POINT MILITARY ACADEMY

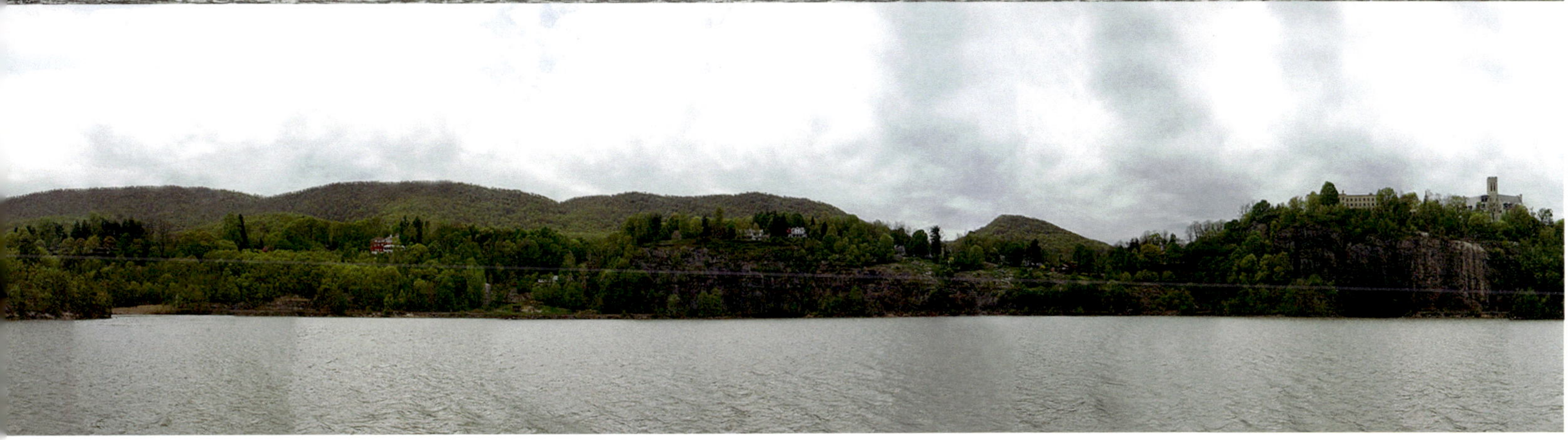

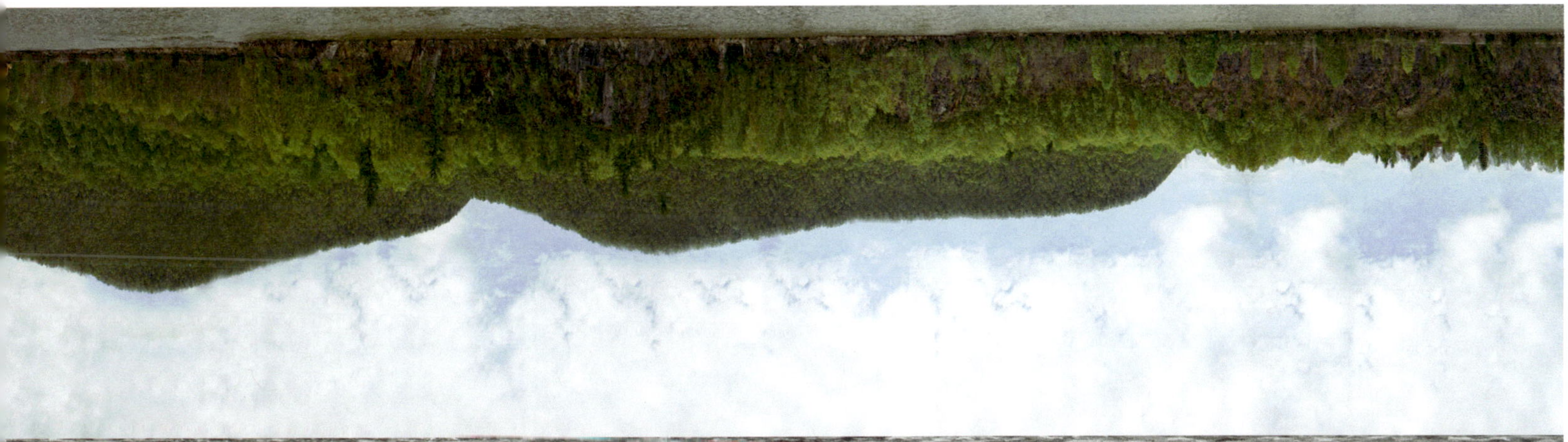

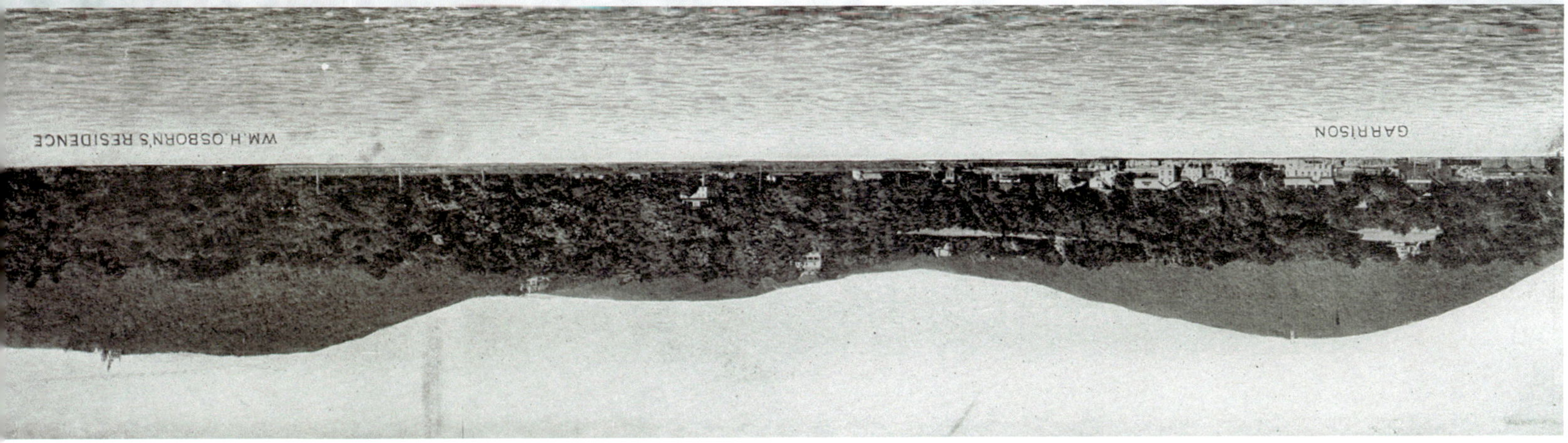

GARRISON
WM. H. OSBORN'S RESIDENCE

WEST POINT LIGHT HOUSE

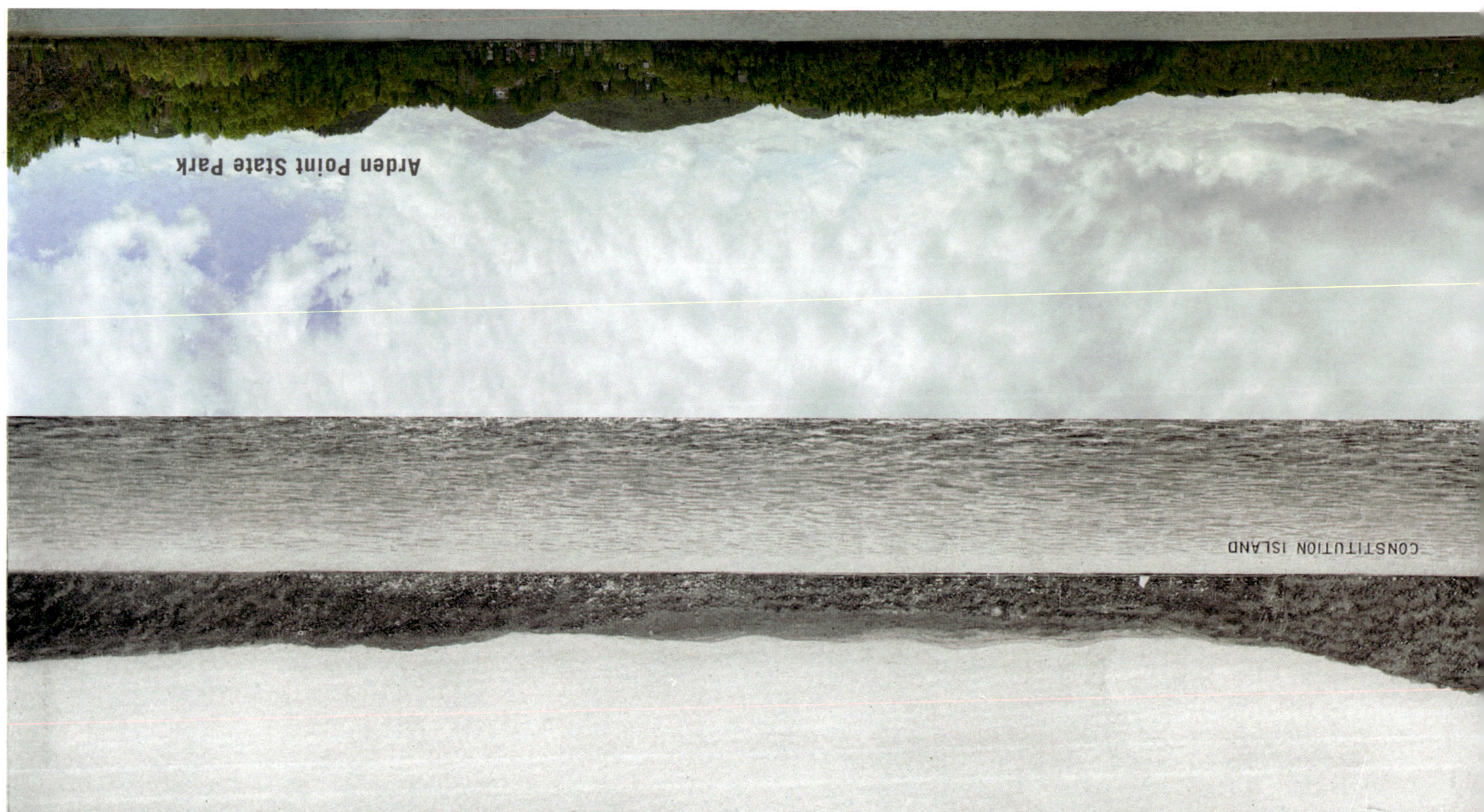

East Bank

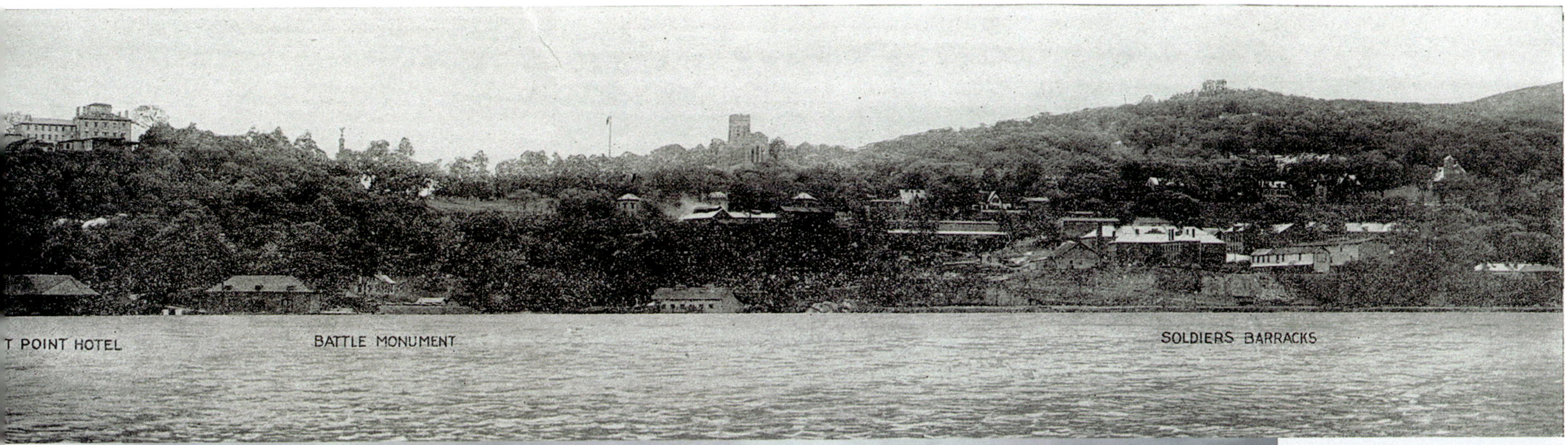

T POINT HOTEL

BATTLE MONUMENT

SOLDIERS BARRACKS

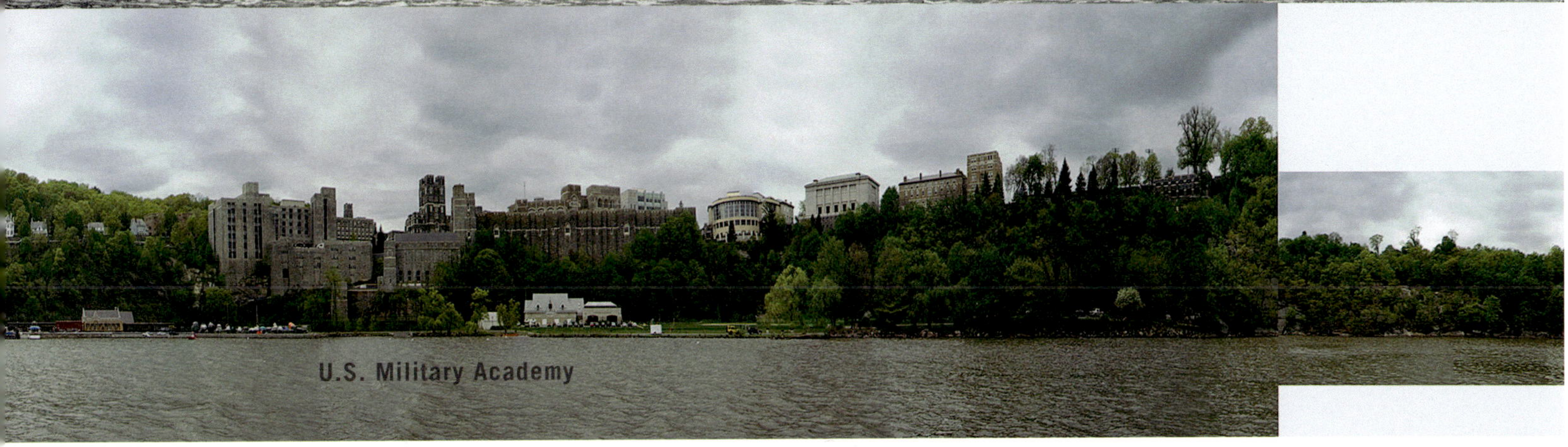

U.S. Military Academy

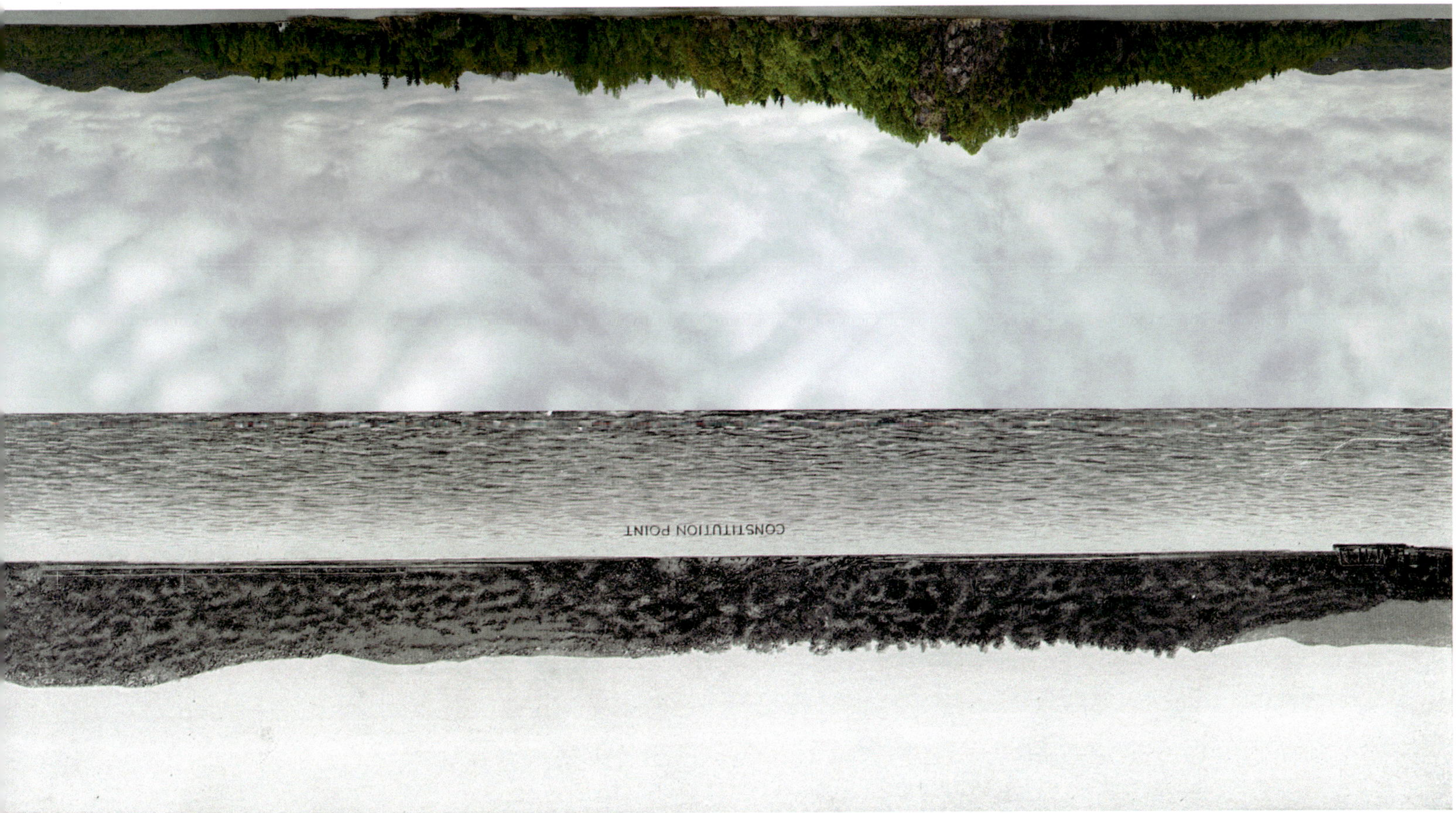

CONSTITUTION POINT

OLD CRO NEST 1410 FT

World's End

Boscobel

Dockside State Park

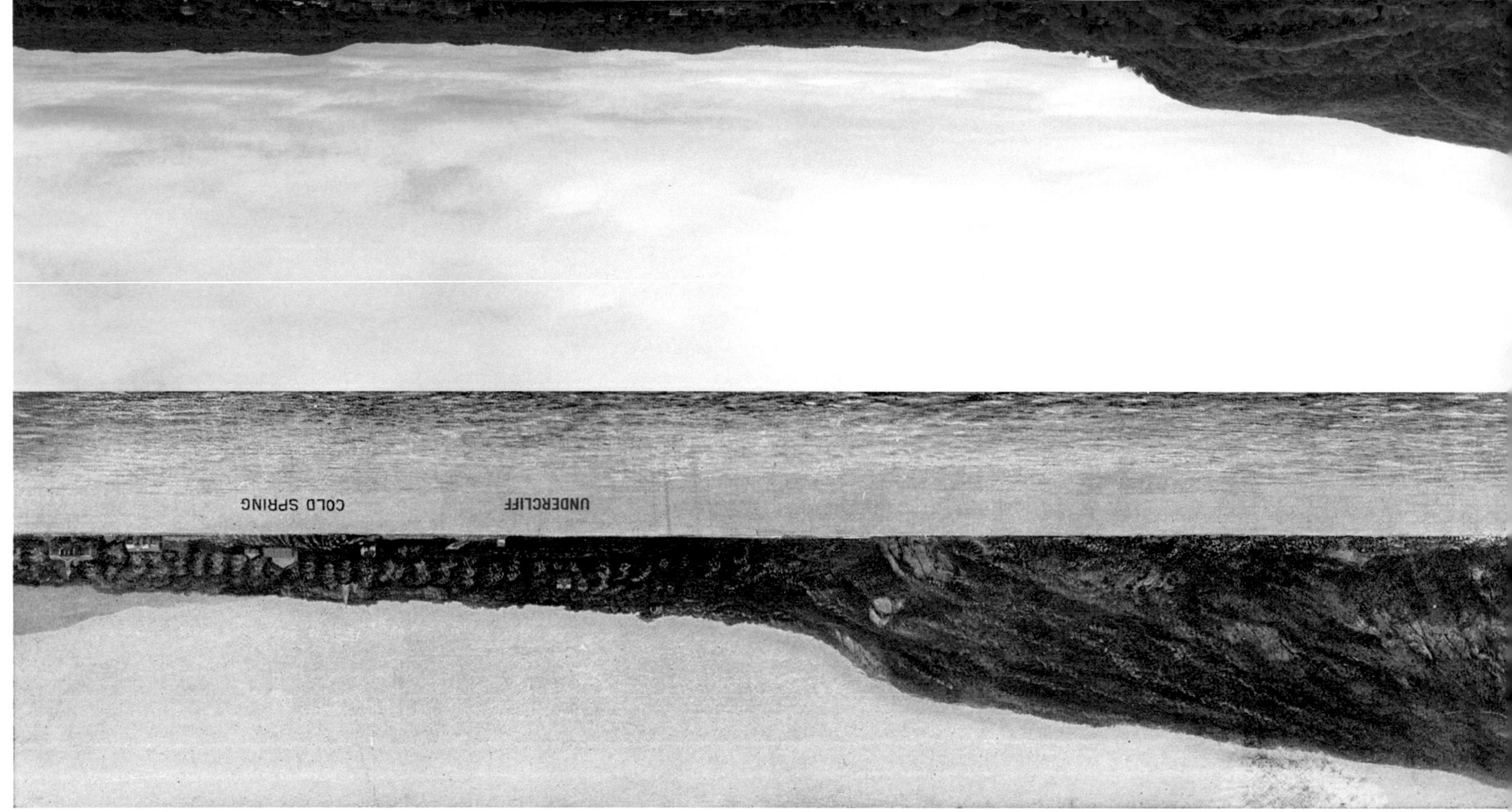

East Bank

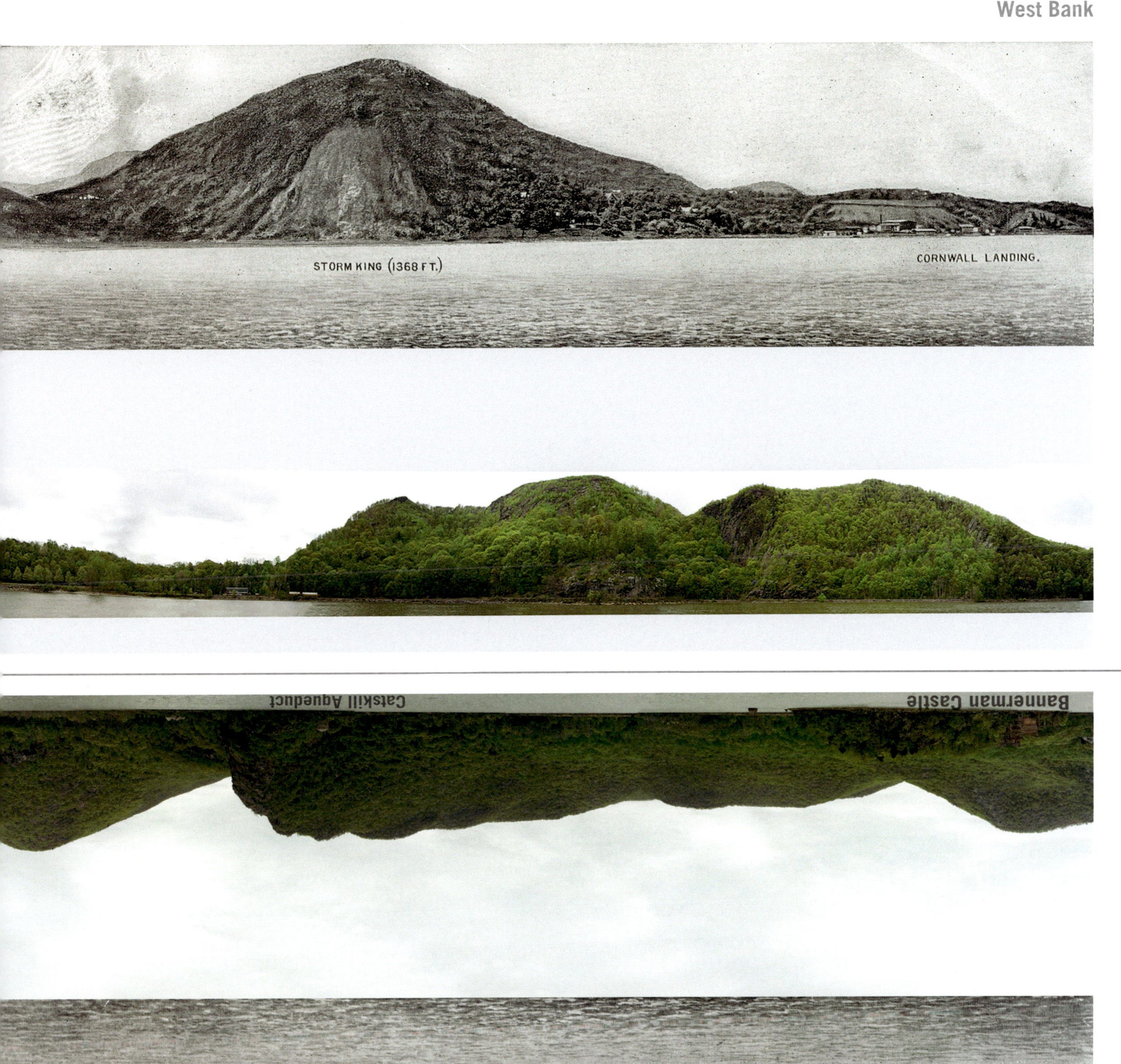
STORM KING (1368 FT.)
CORNWALL LANDING.
Bannerman Castle
Catskill Aqueduct
BEACON MTS.
BREAKNECK MT.

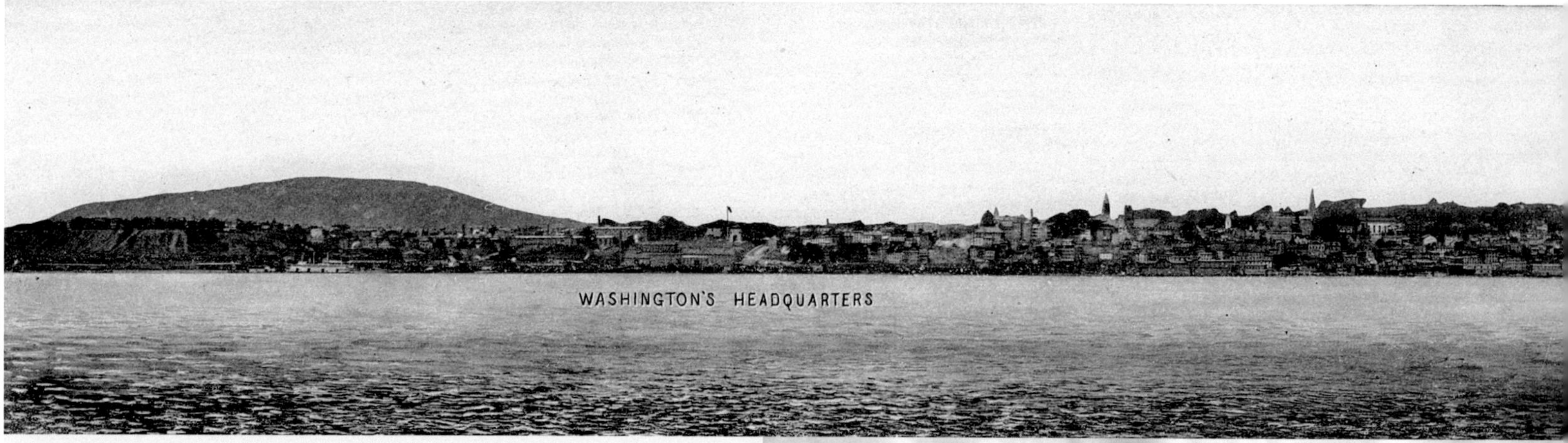

WASHINGTON'S HEADQUARTERS

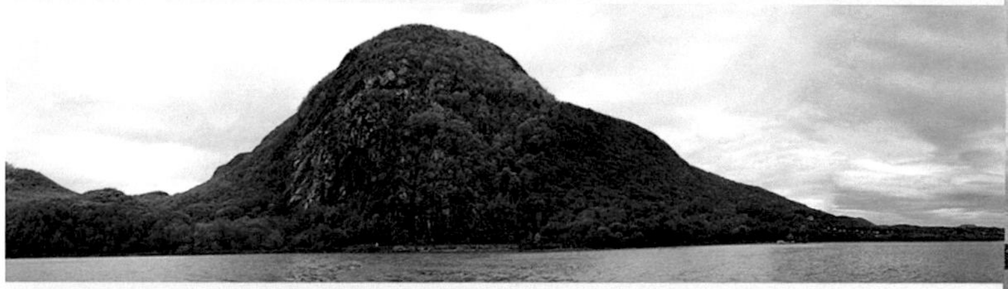

Storm King Highway

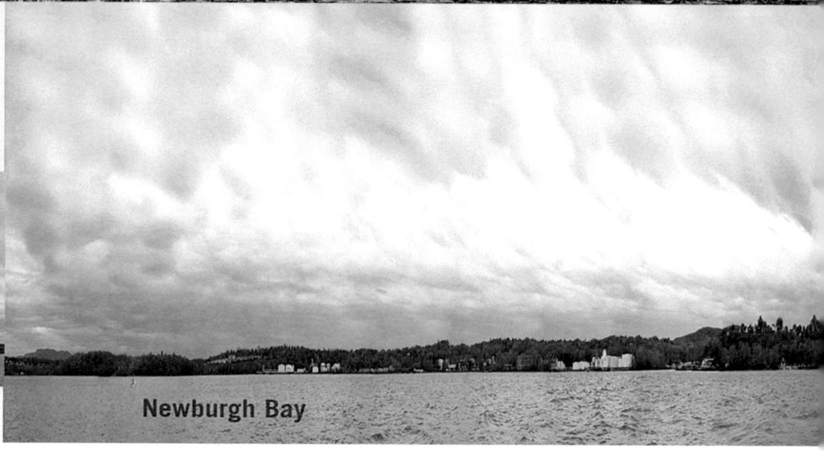

Newburgh Bay

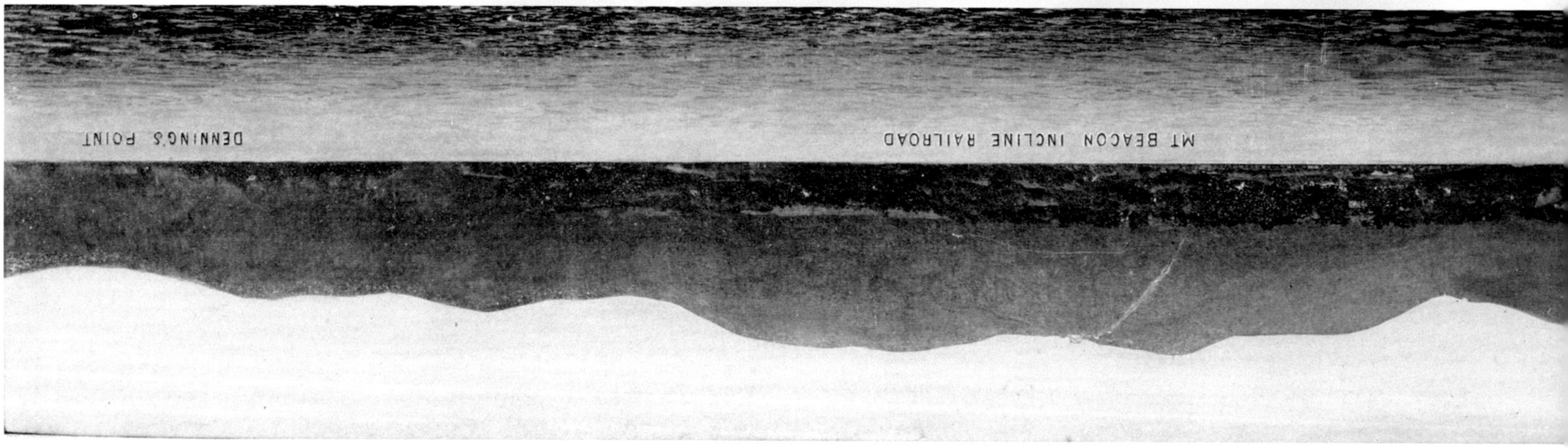

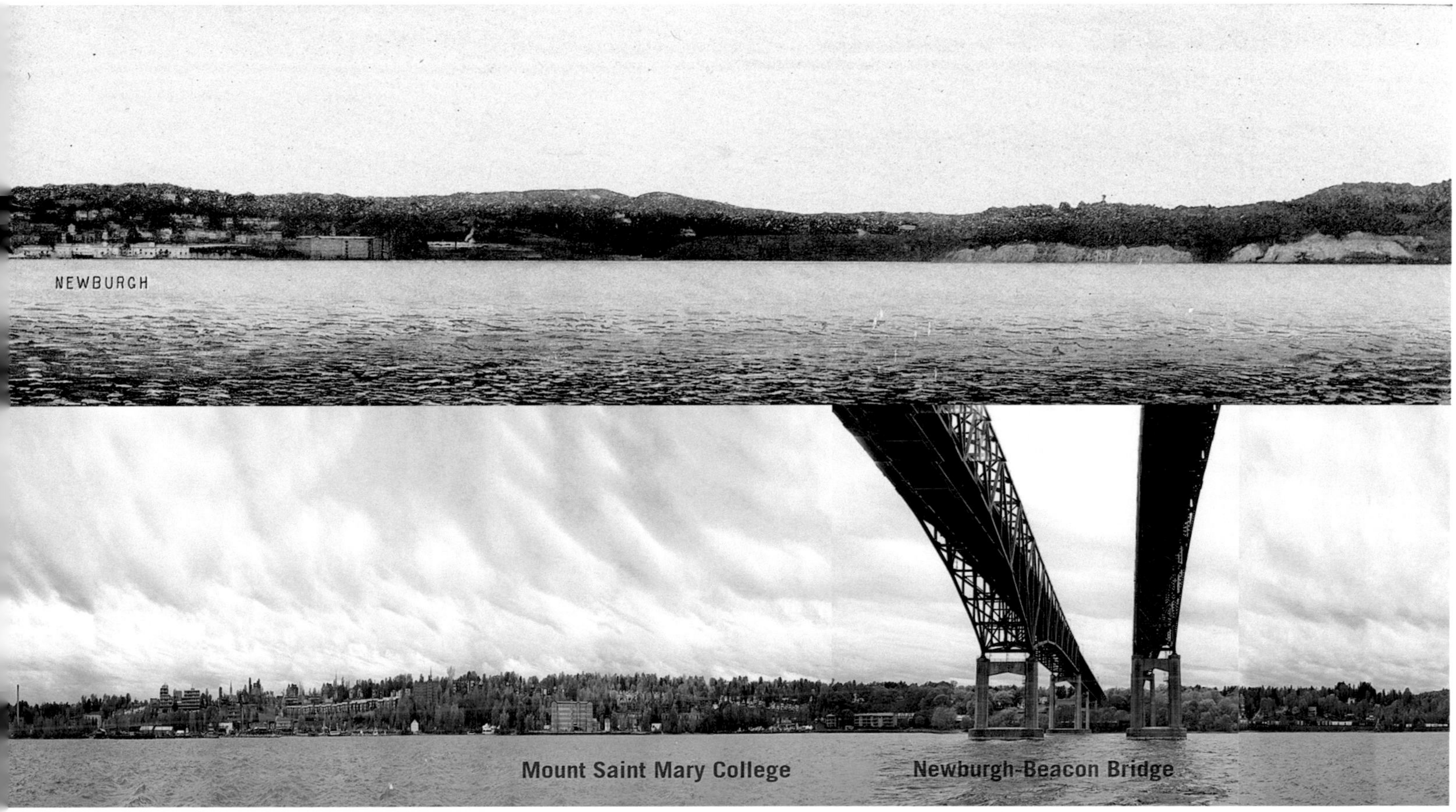

NEWBURGH

Mount Saint Mary College

Newburgh-Beacon Bridge

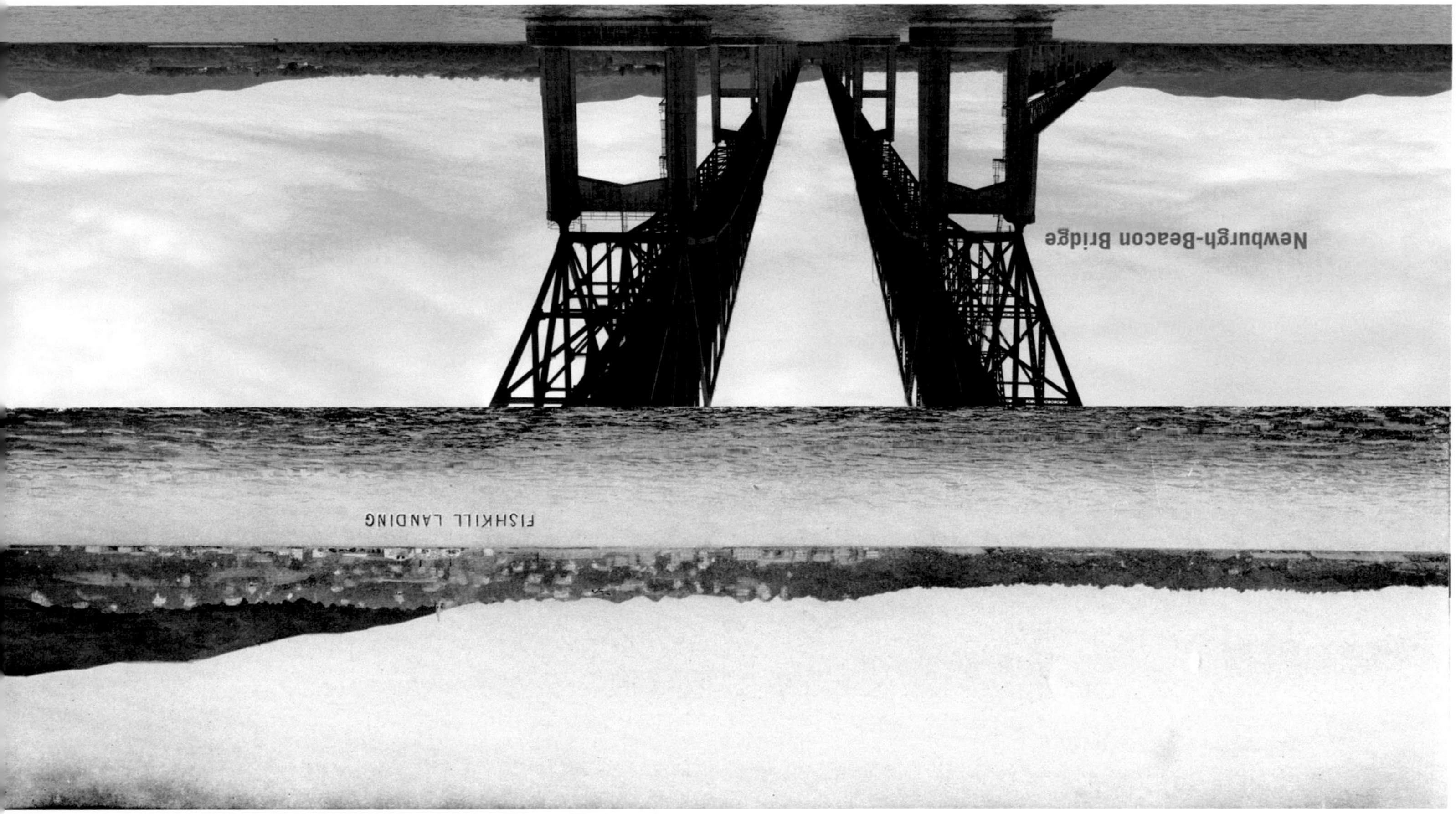

Newburgh-Beacon Bridge

FISHKILL LANDING

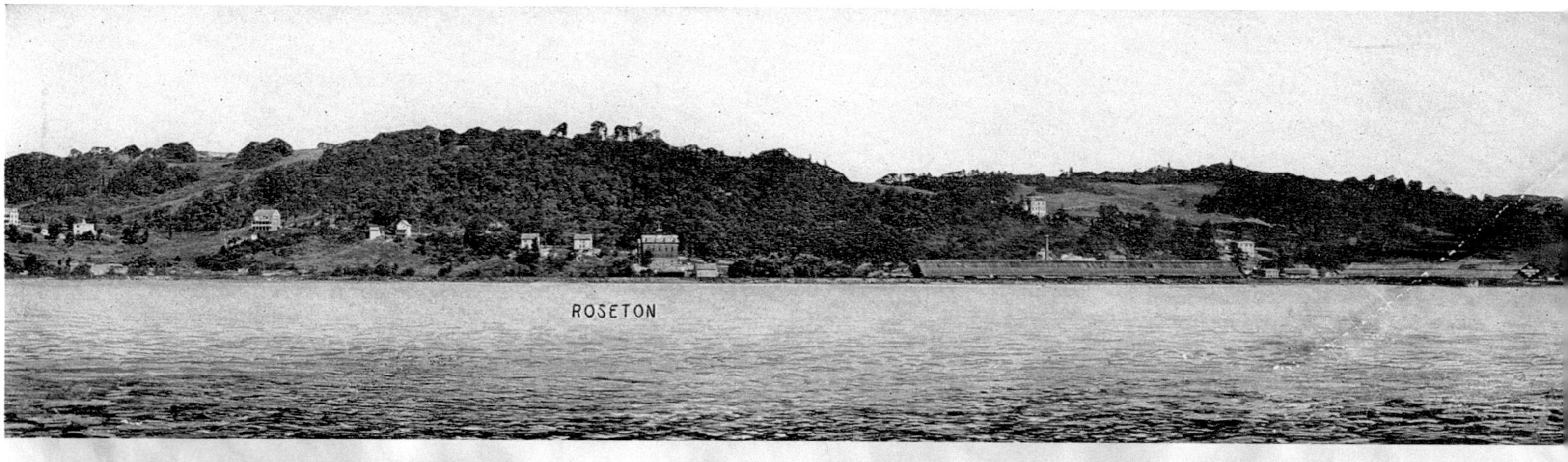

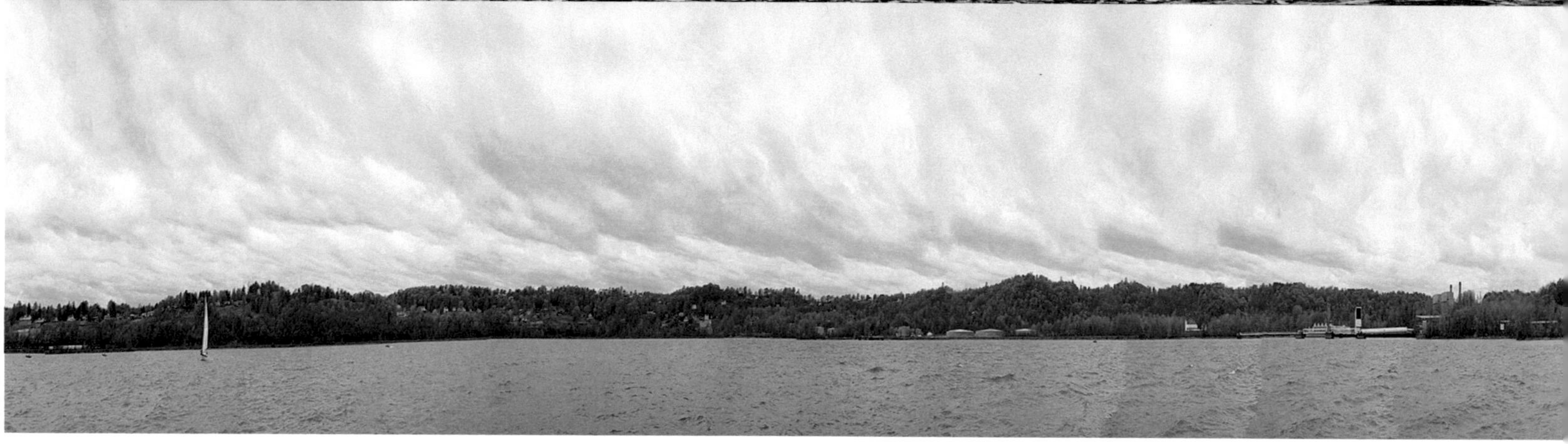

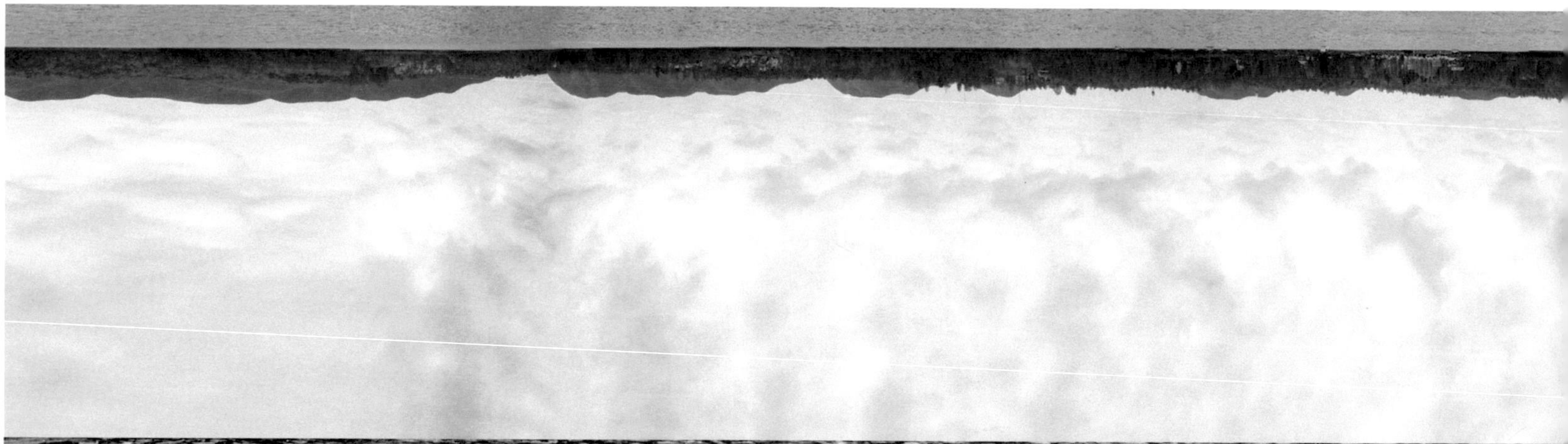

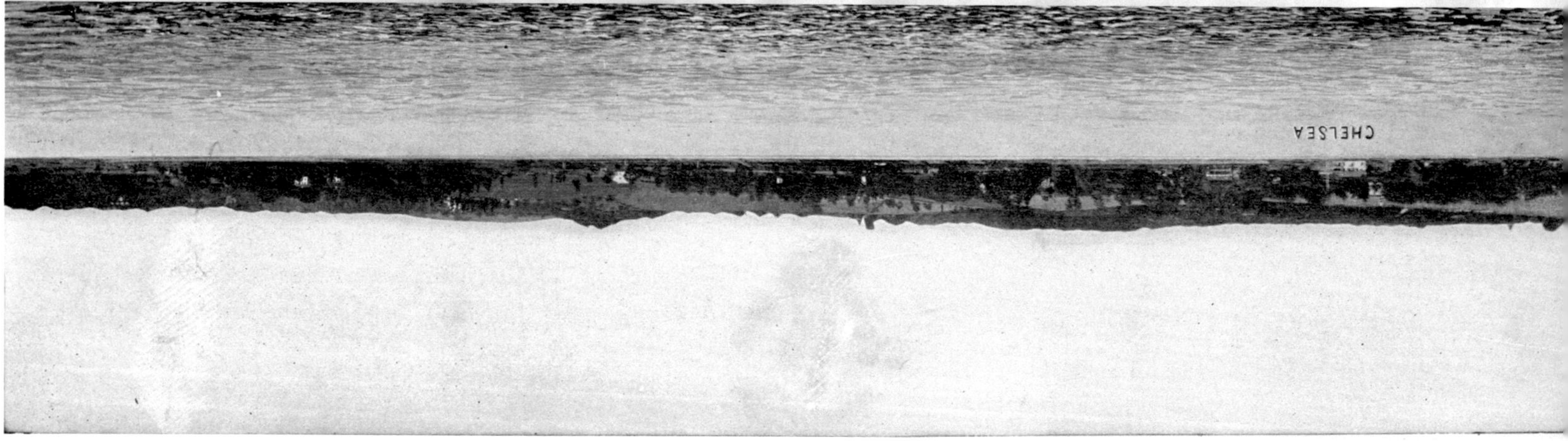

East Bank

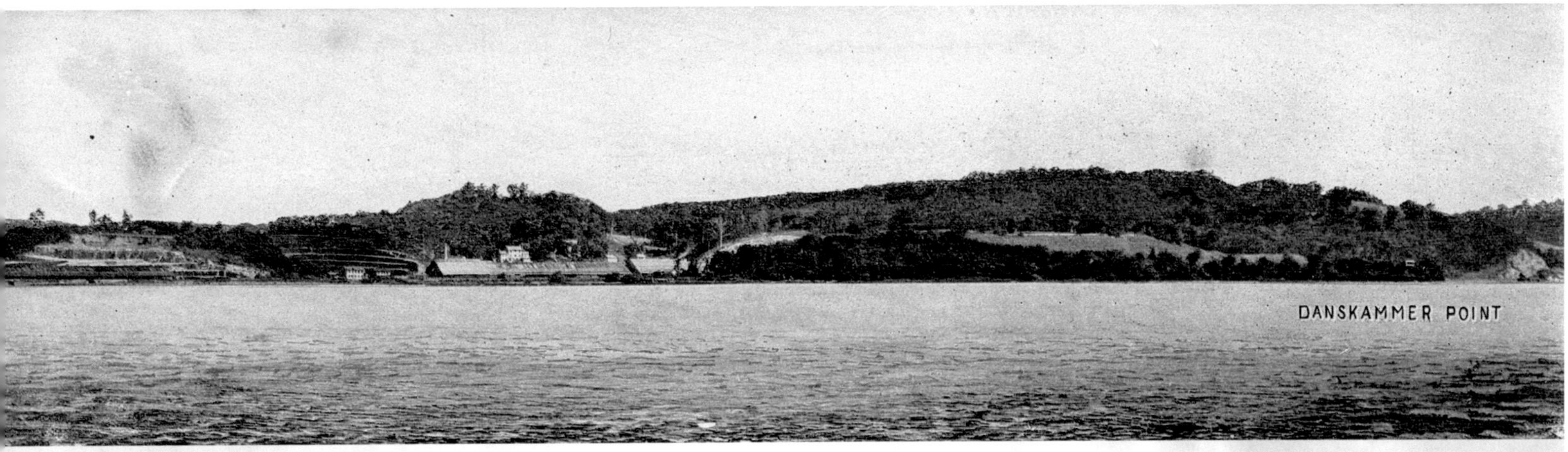

DANSKAMMER POINT

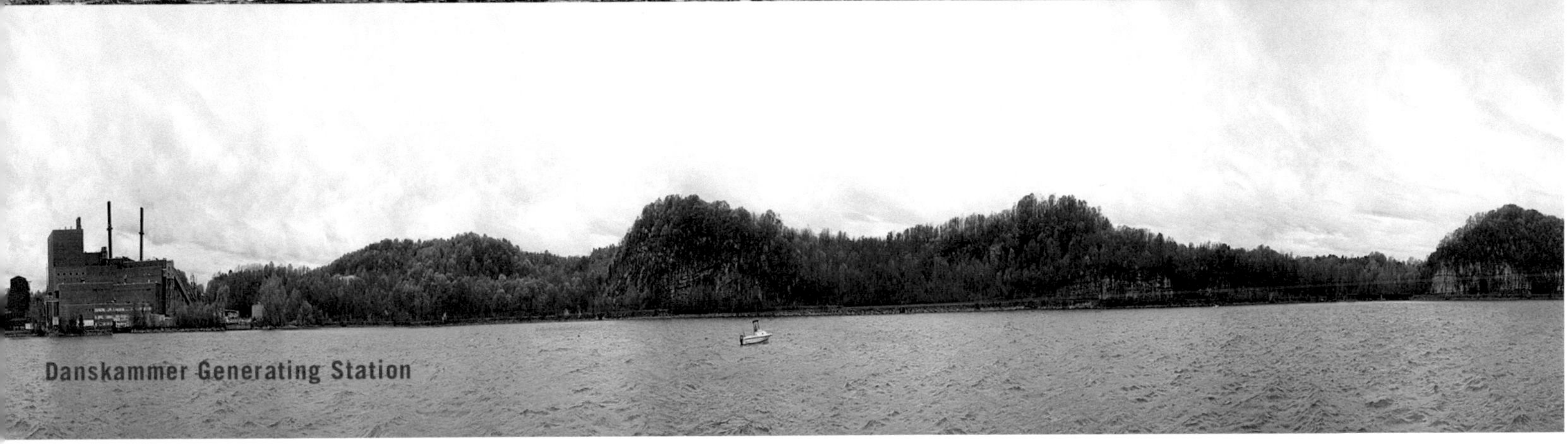

Danskammer Generating Station

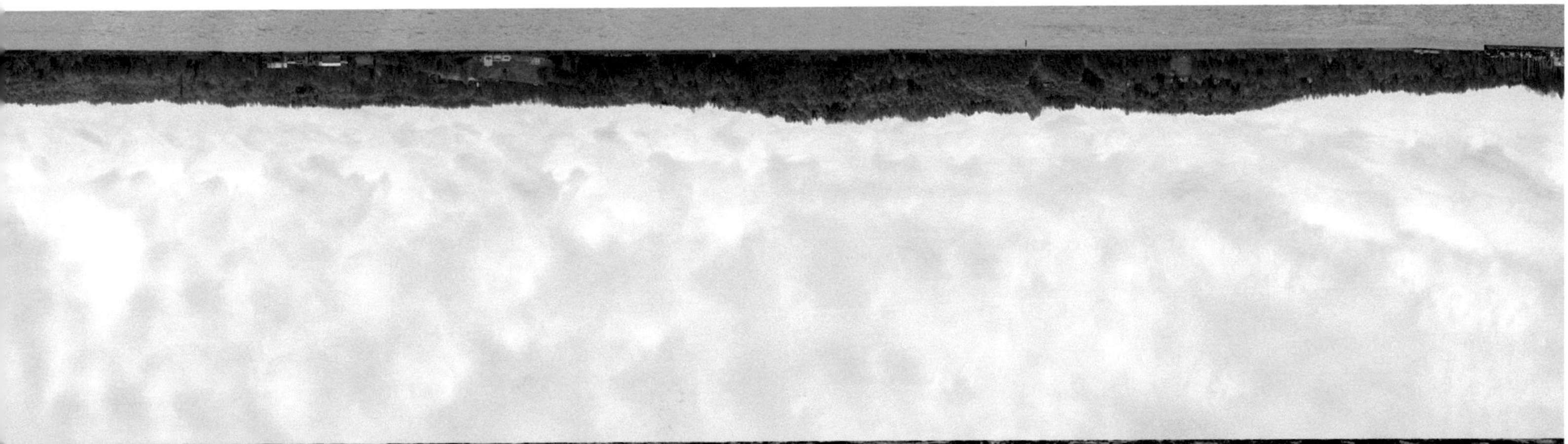

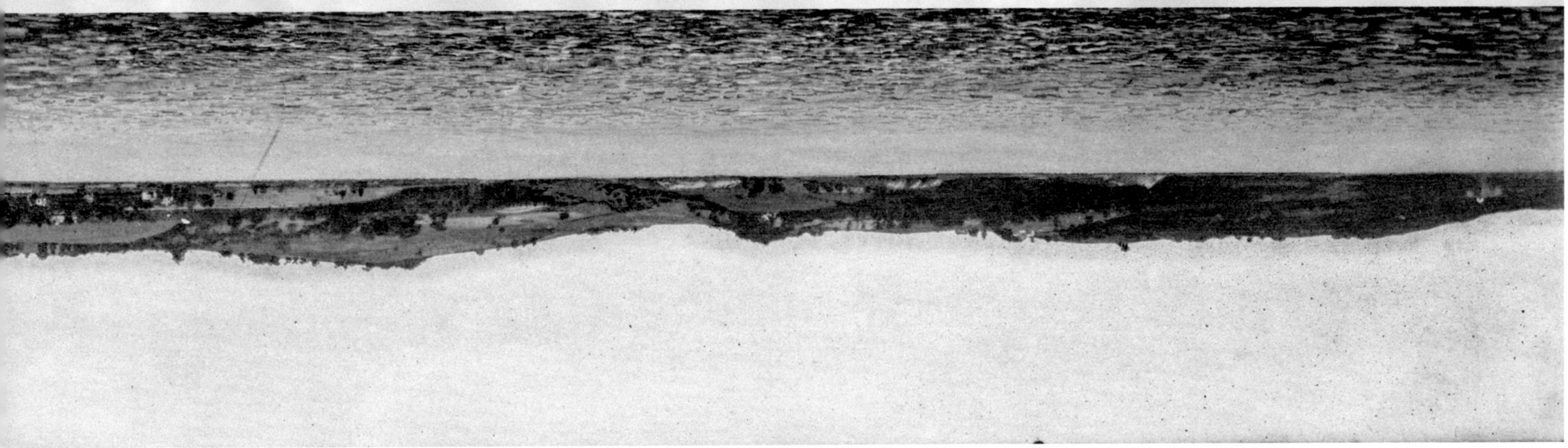

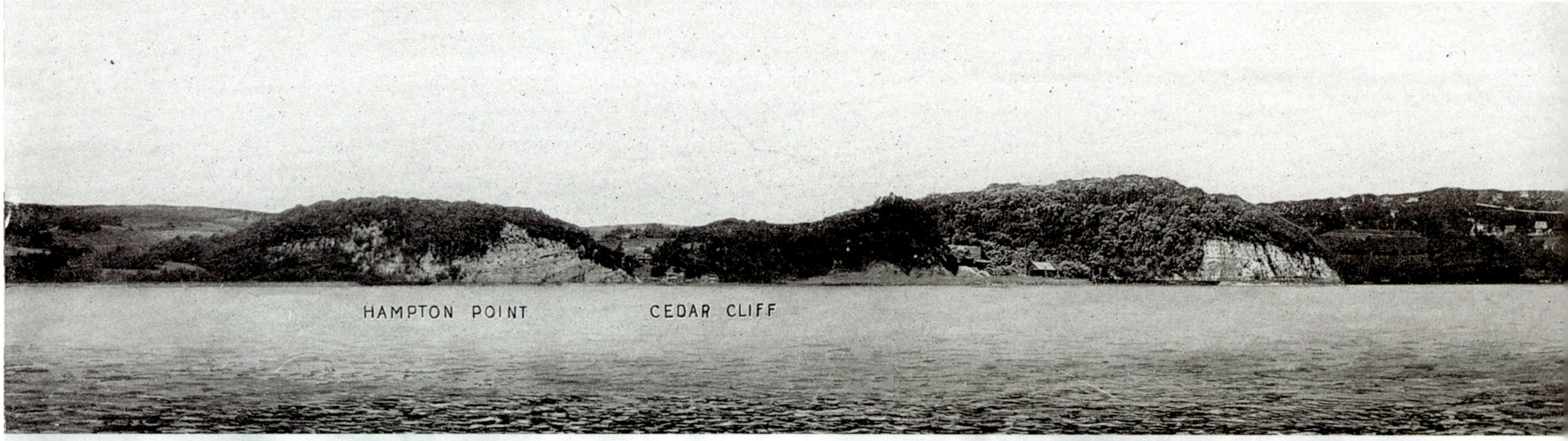

HAMPTON POINT CEDAR CLIFF

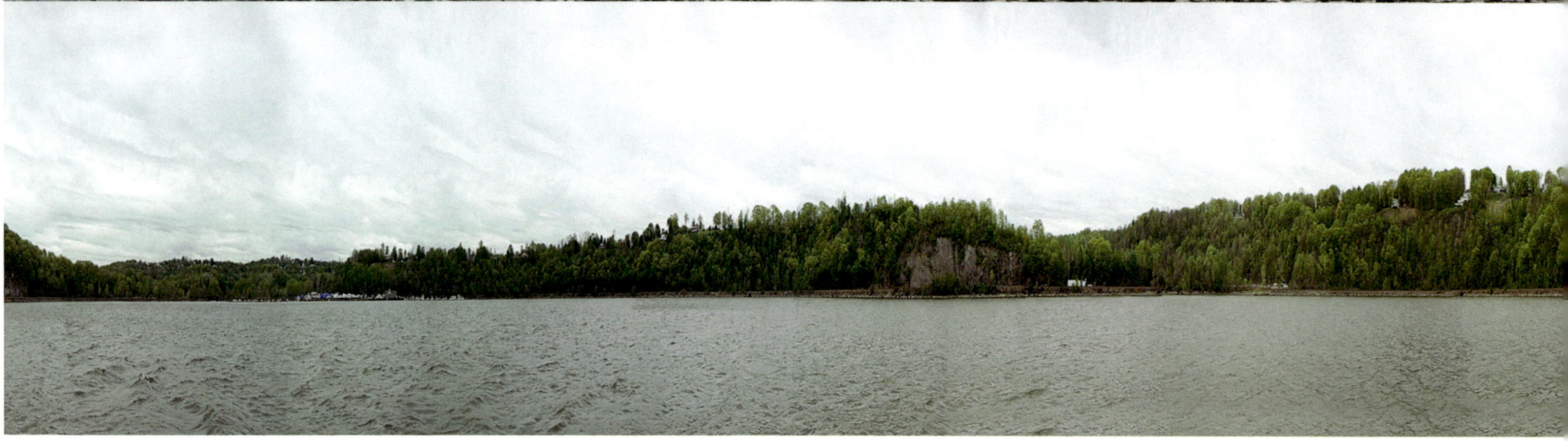

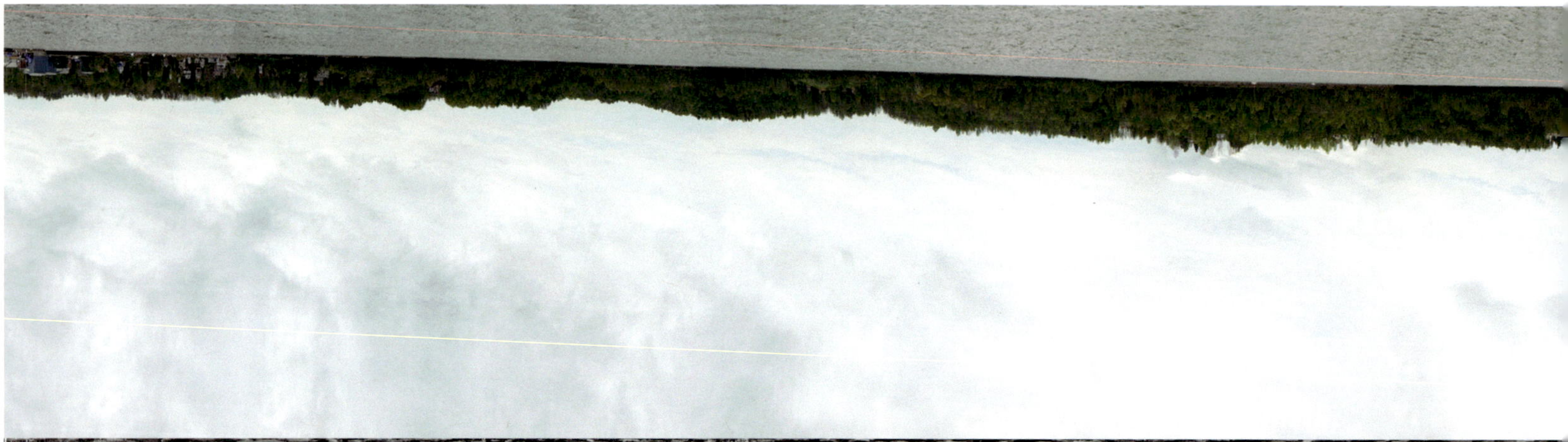

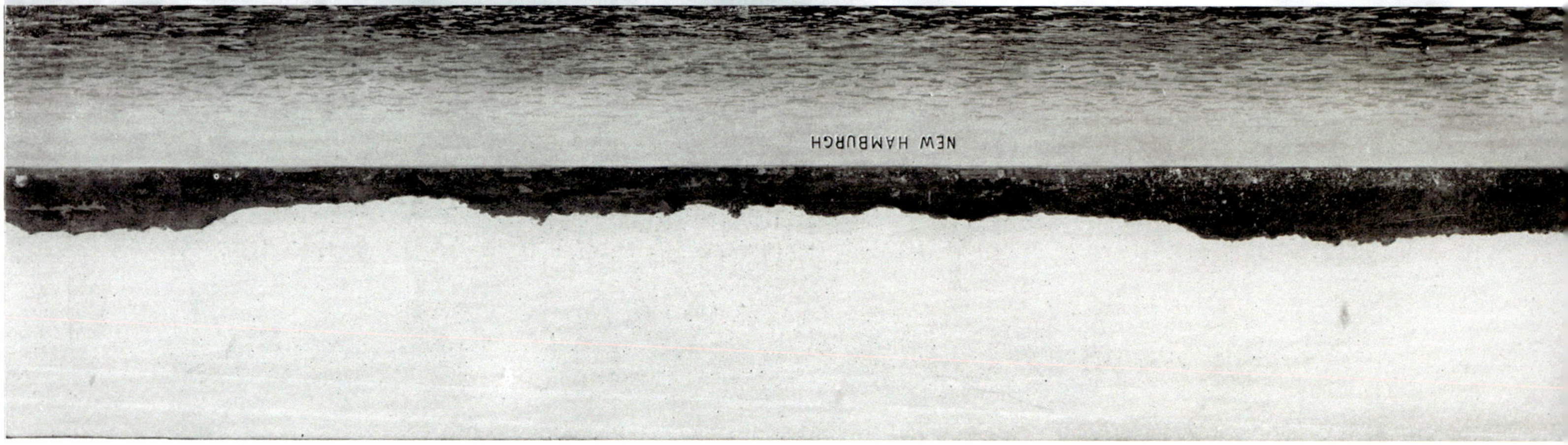

NEW HAMBURGH

East Bank

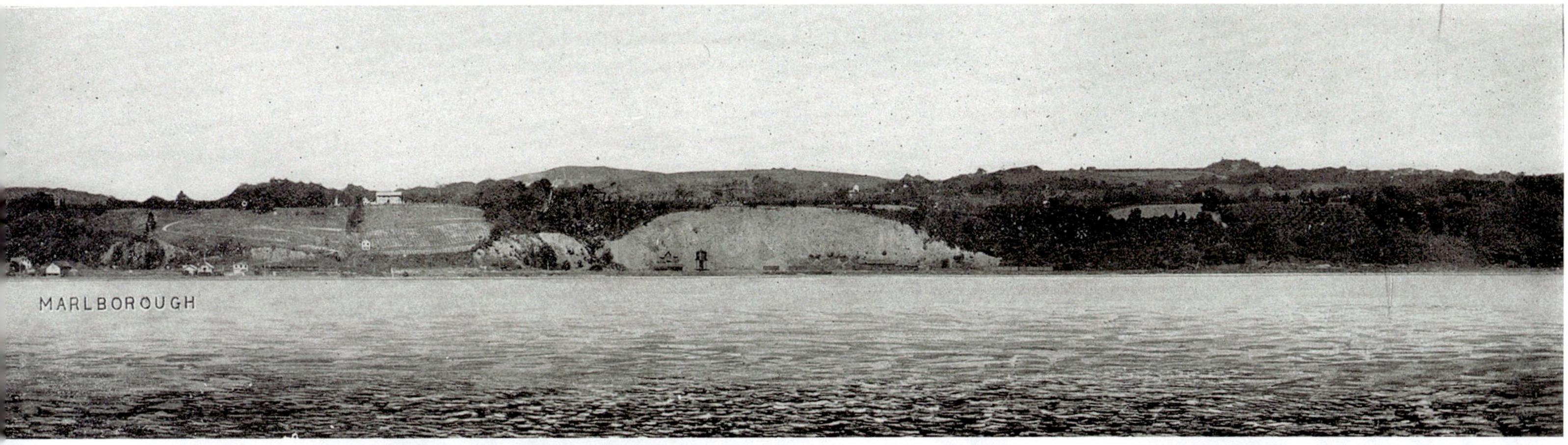

MARLBOROUGH

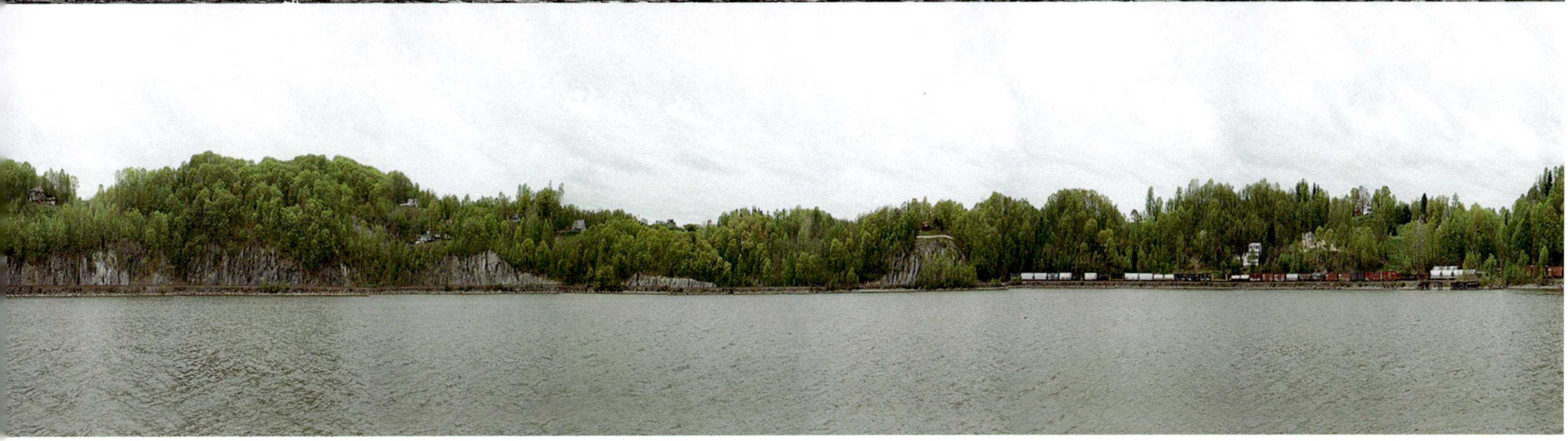

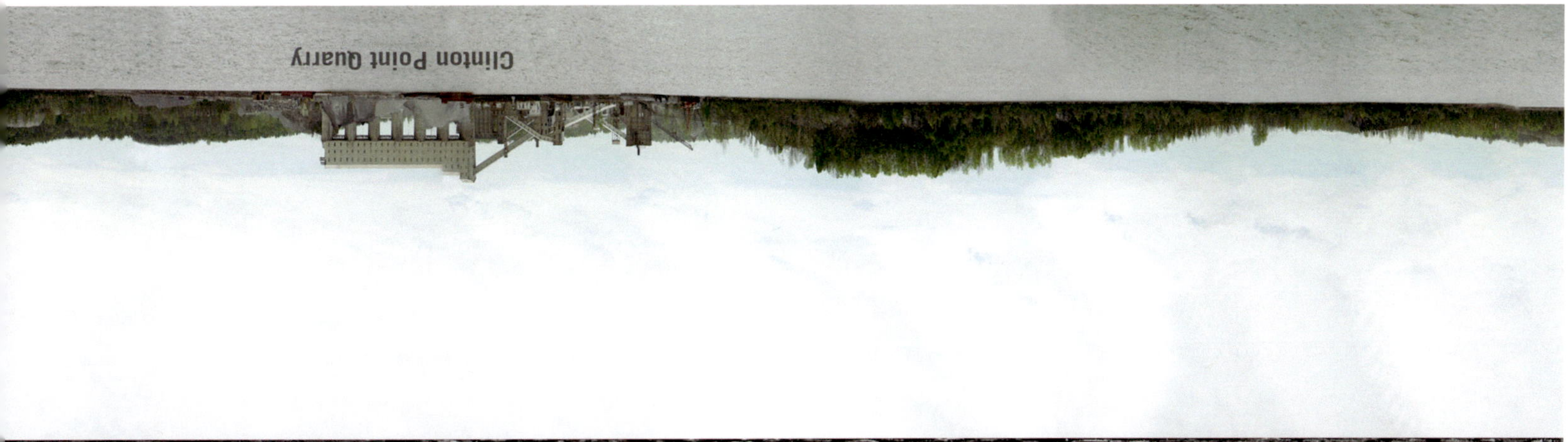

Clinton Point Quarry

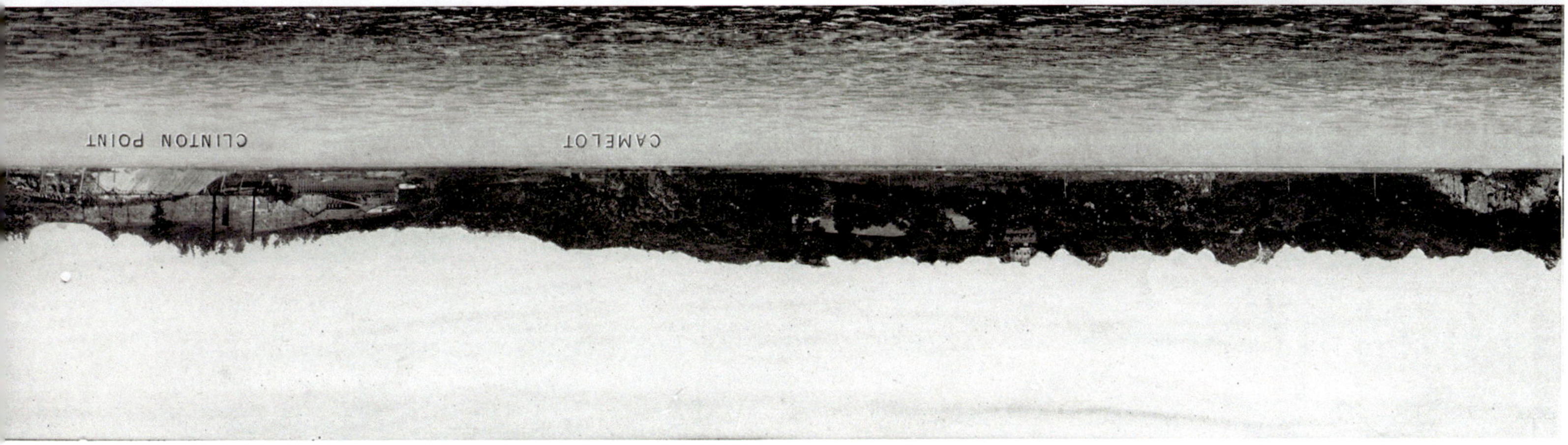

CAMELOT

CLINTON POINT

MILTON

RESIDENCE OF THE LATE PROF. S. F. B. MORSE
SPRING BROOK MILL

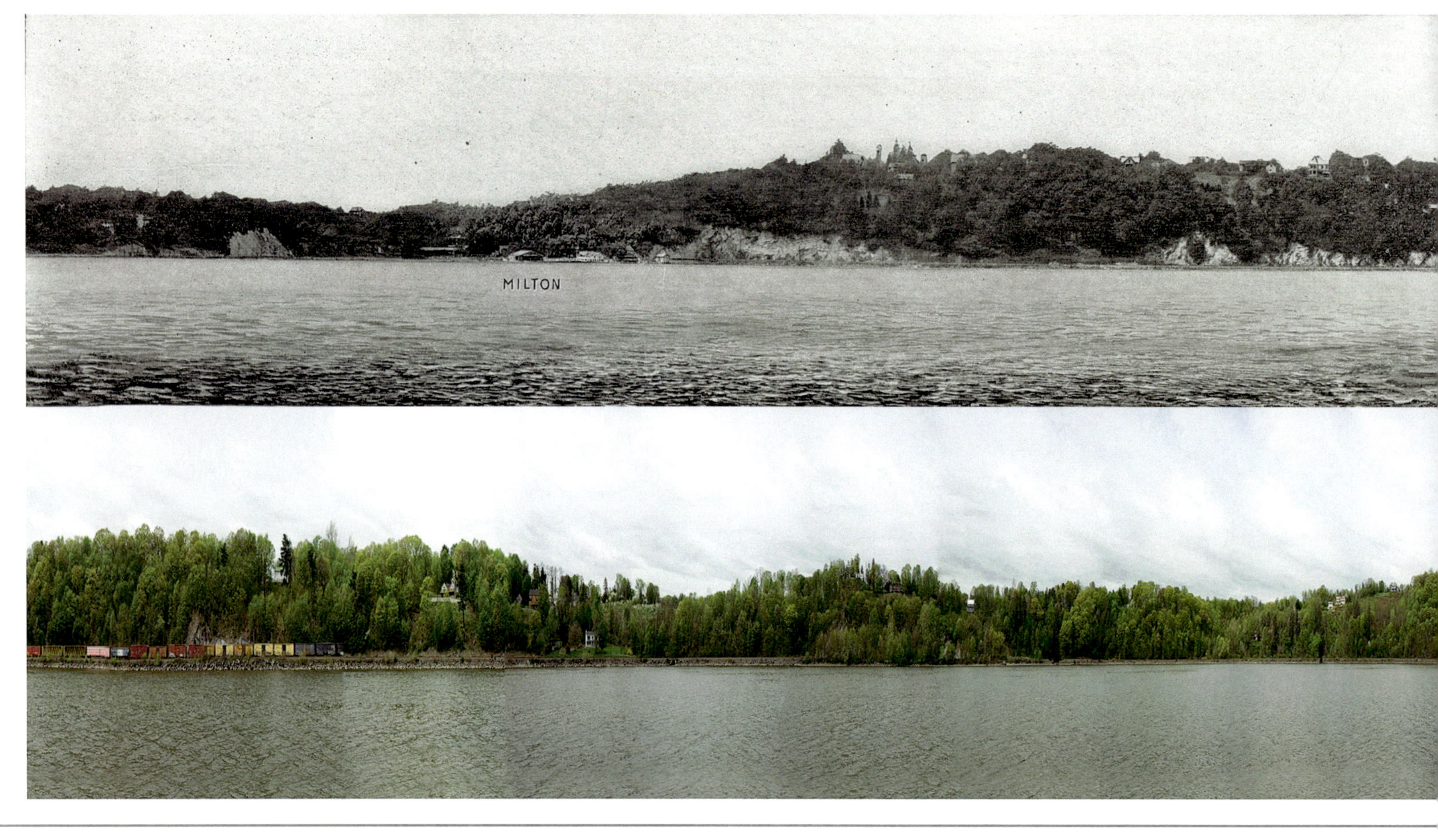

East Bank

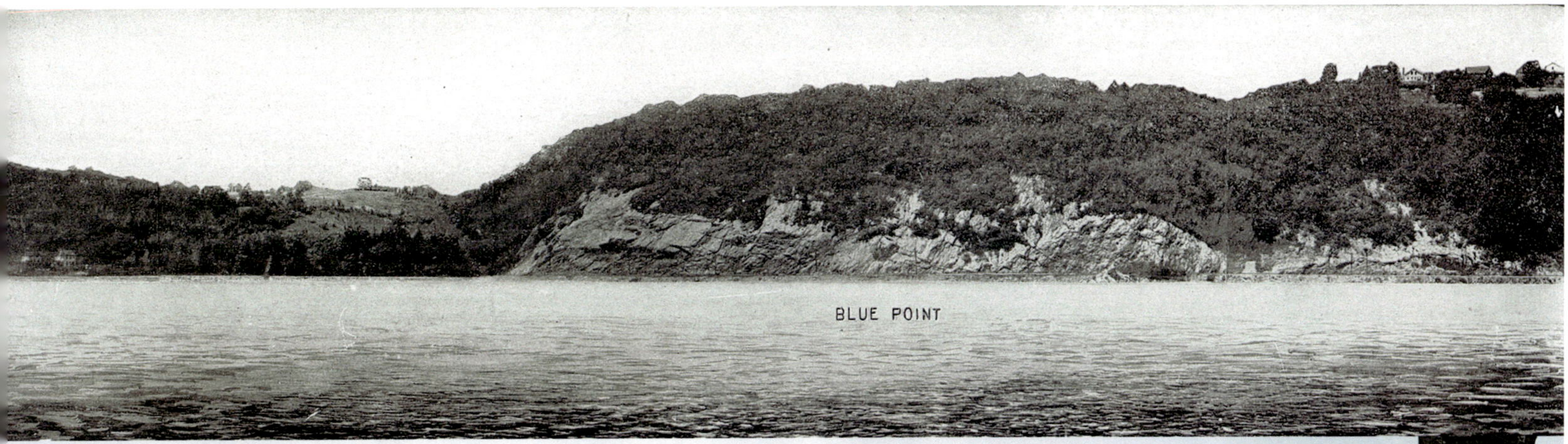

BLUE POINT

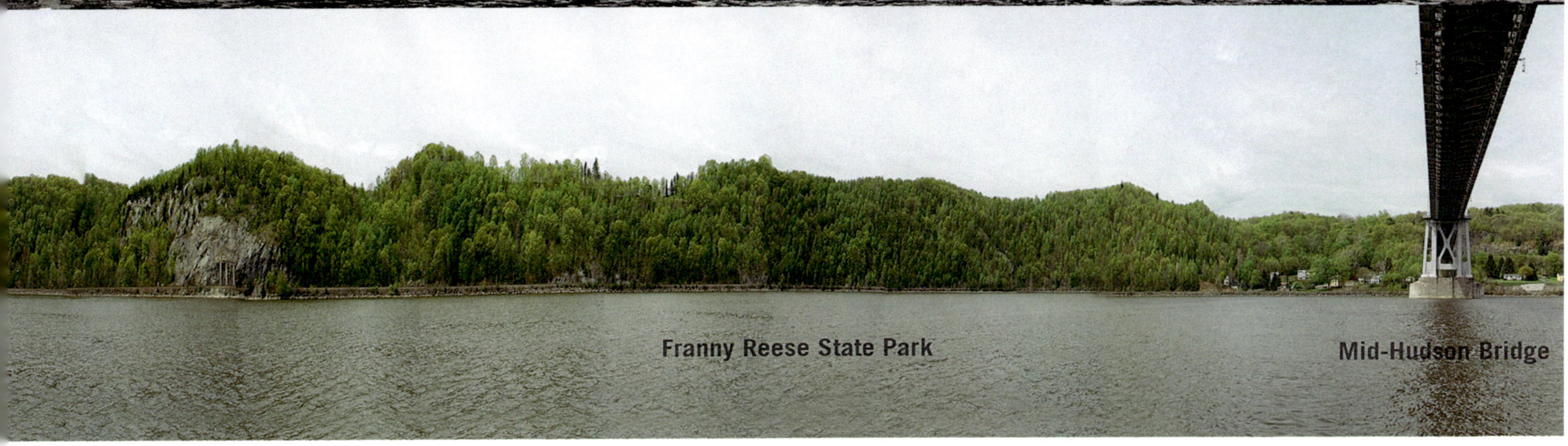

Franny Reese State Park

Mid-Hudson Bridge

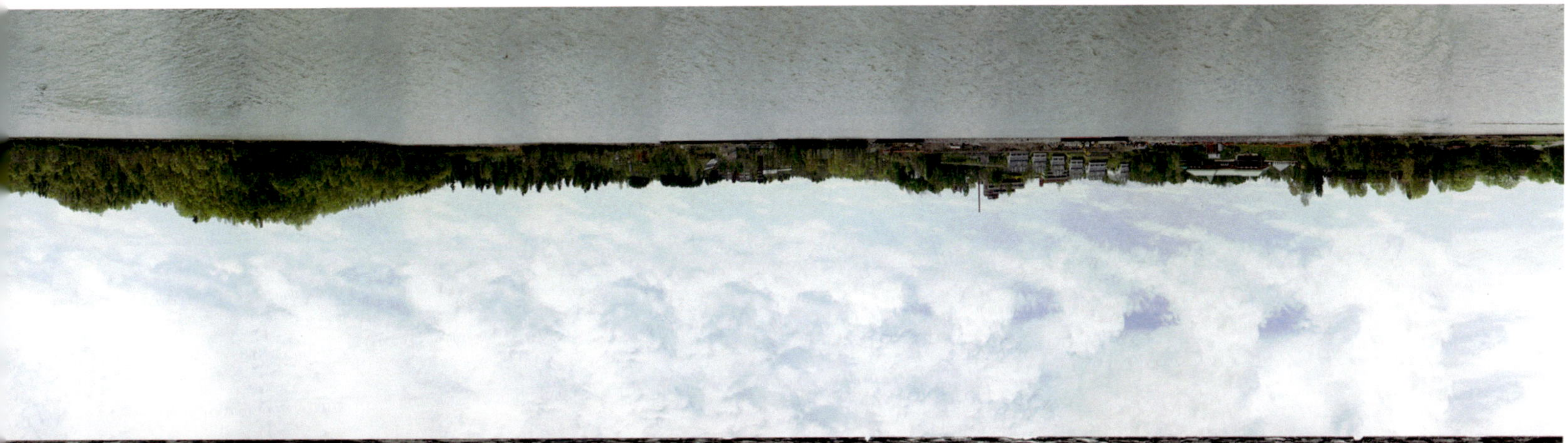

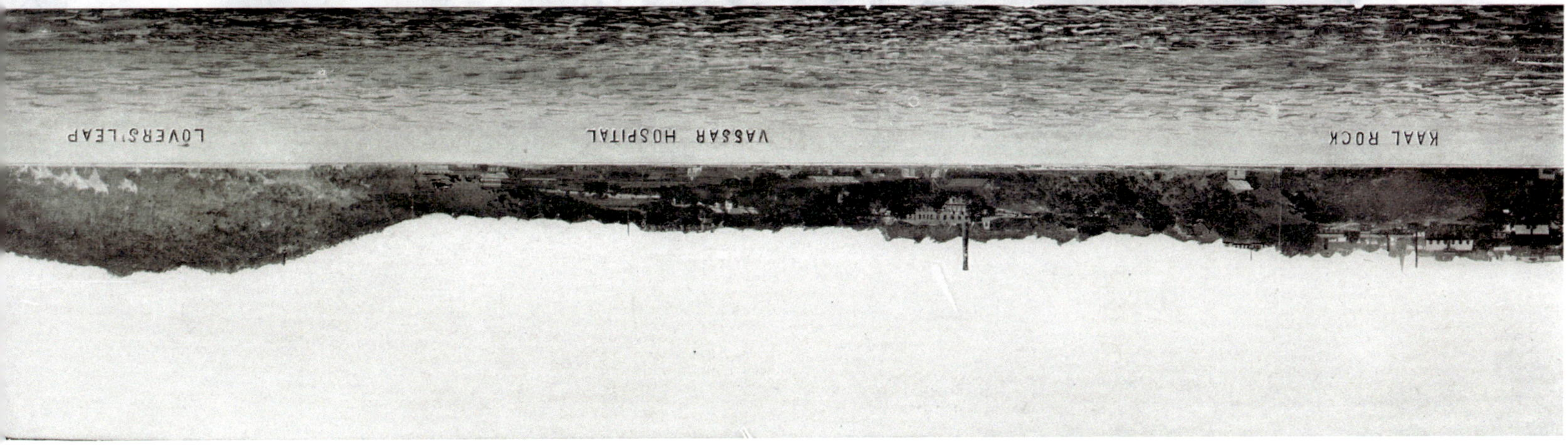

KAAL ROCK

VASSAR HOSPITAL

LOVERS' LEAP

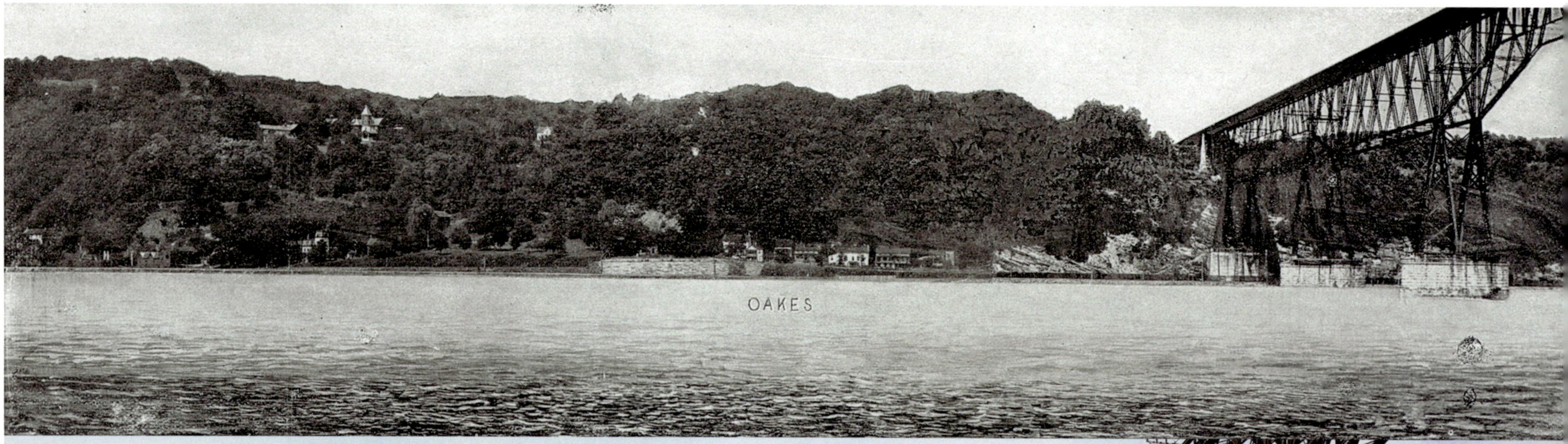

OAKES

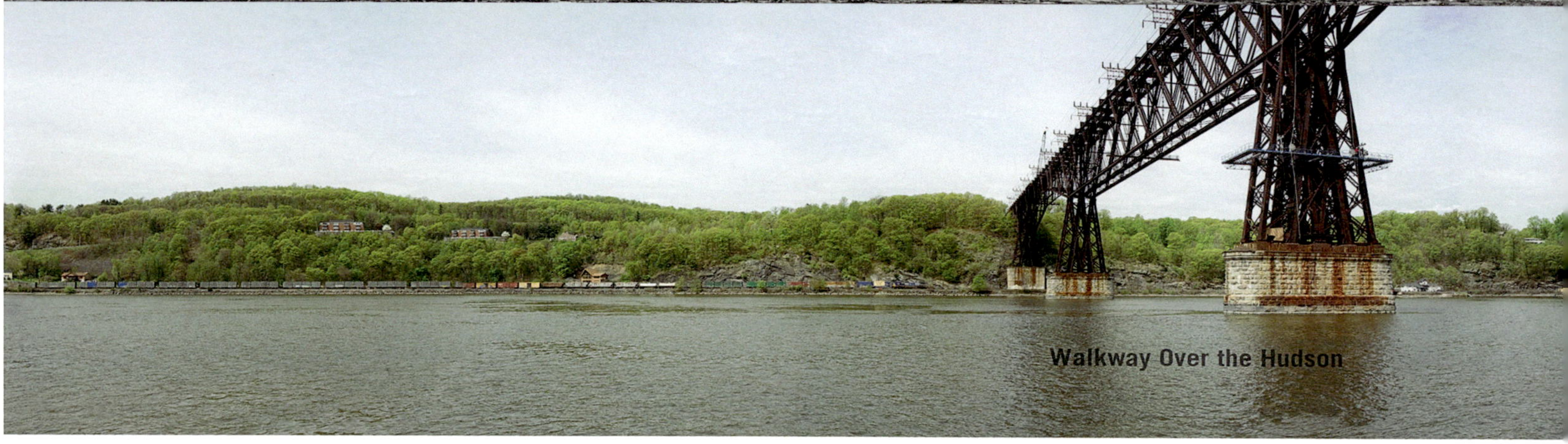

Walkway Over the Hudson

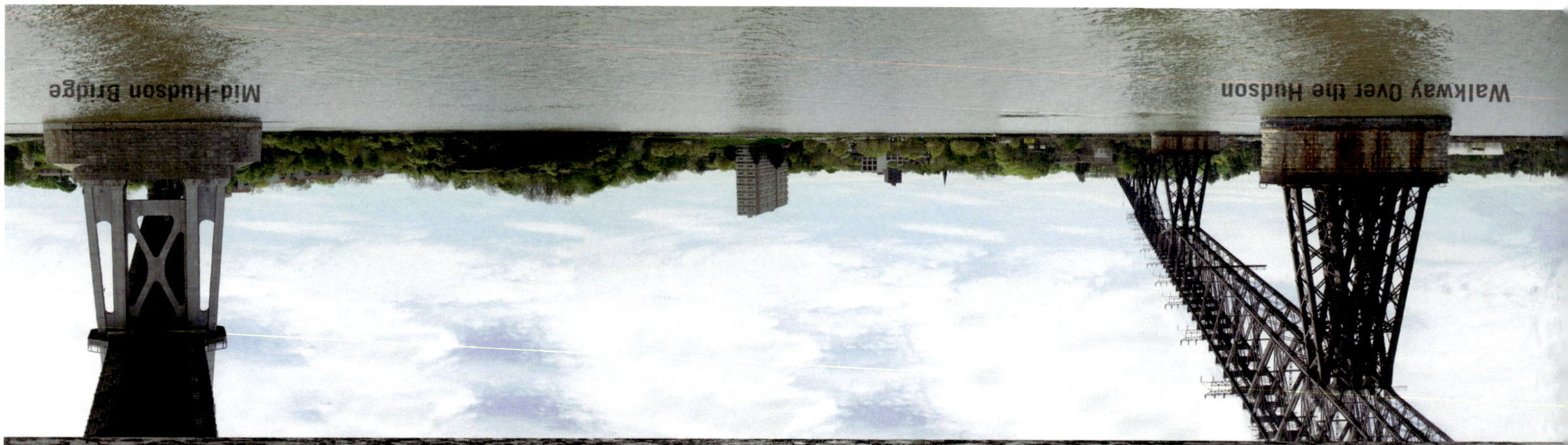

Walkway Over the Hudson

Mid-Hudson Bridge

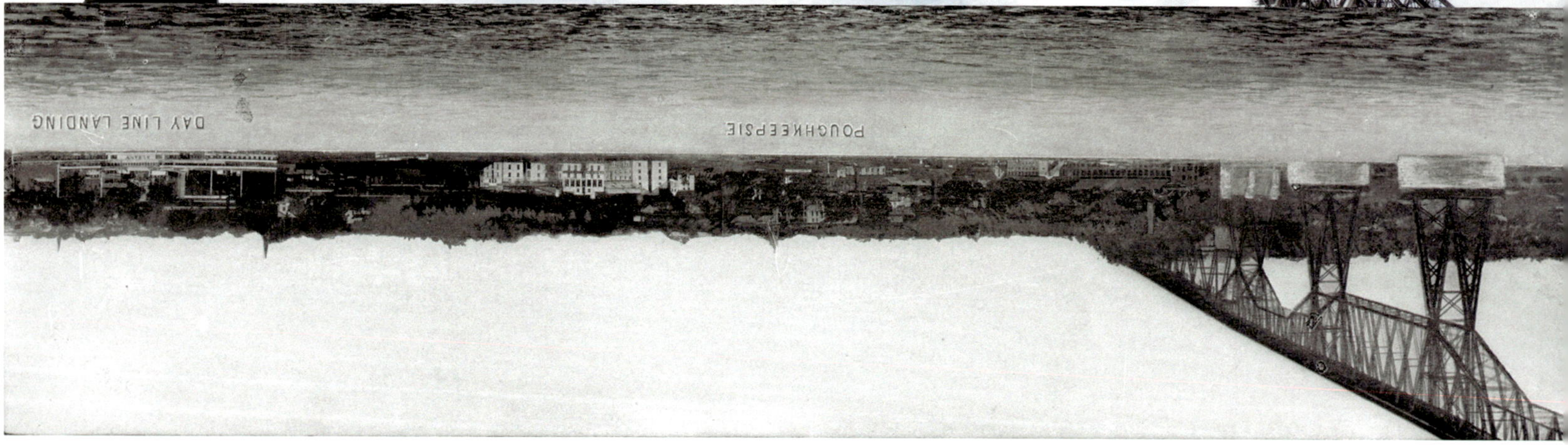

POUGHKEEPSIE

DAY LINE LANDING

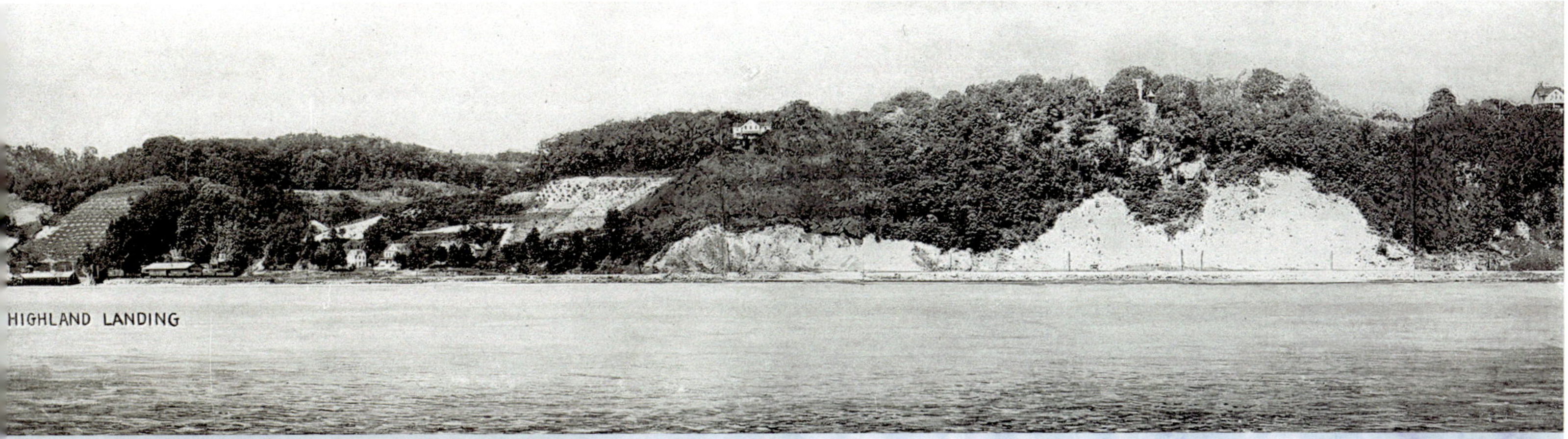

HIGHLAND LANDING

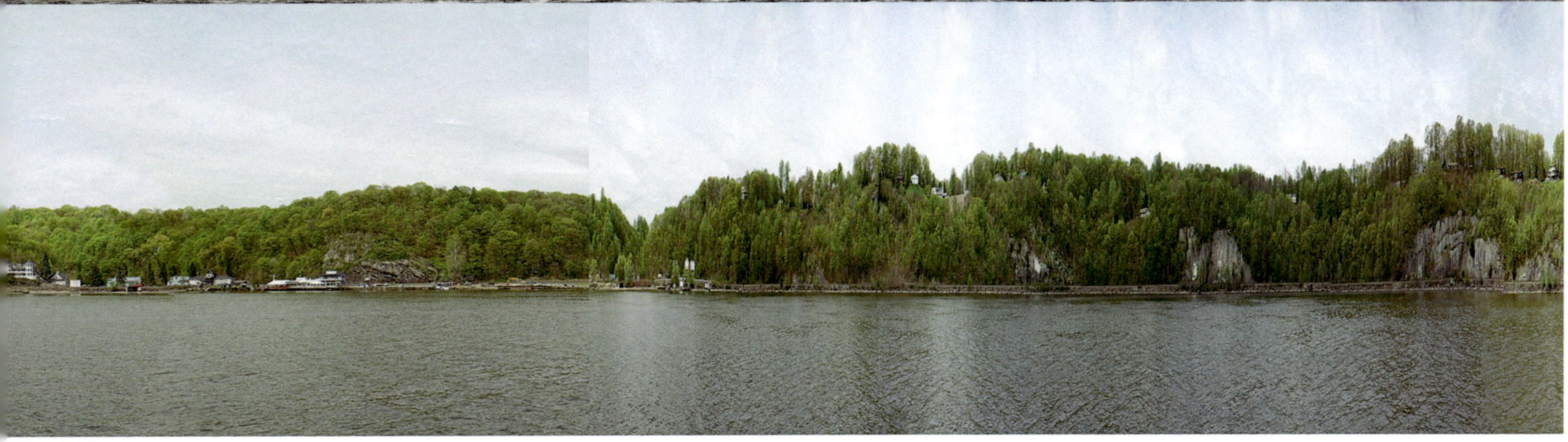

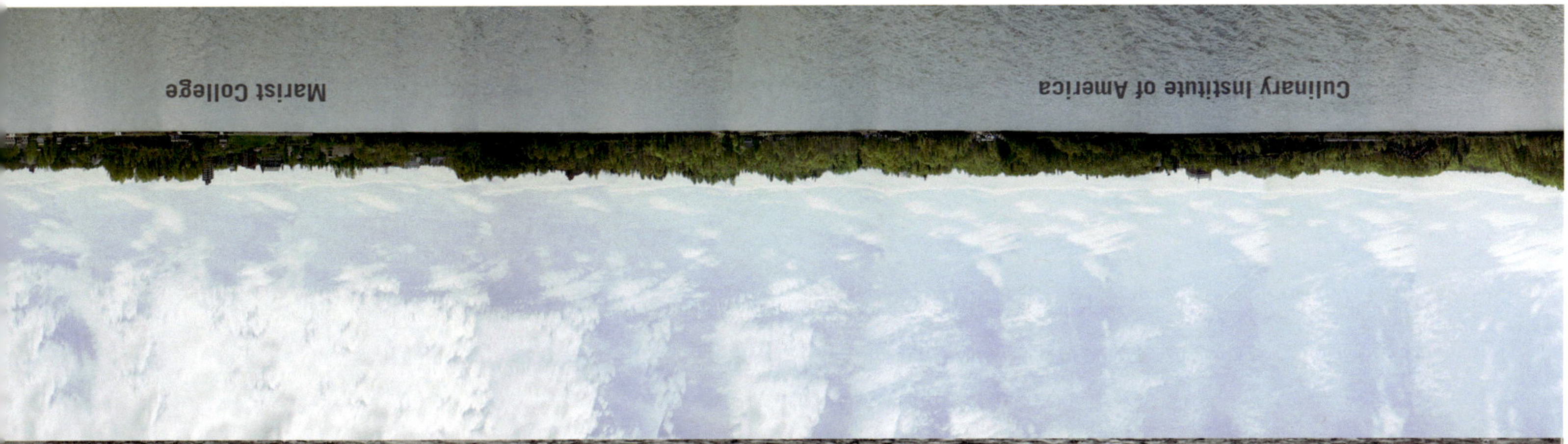

Culinary Institute of America

Marist College

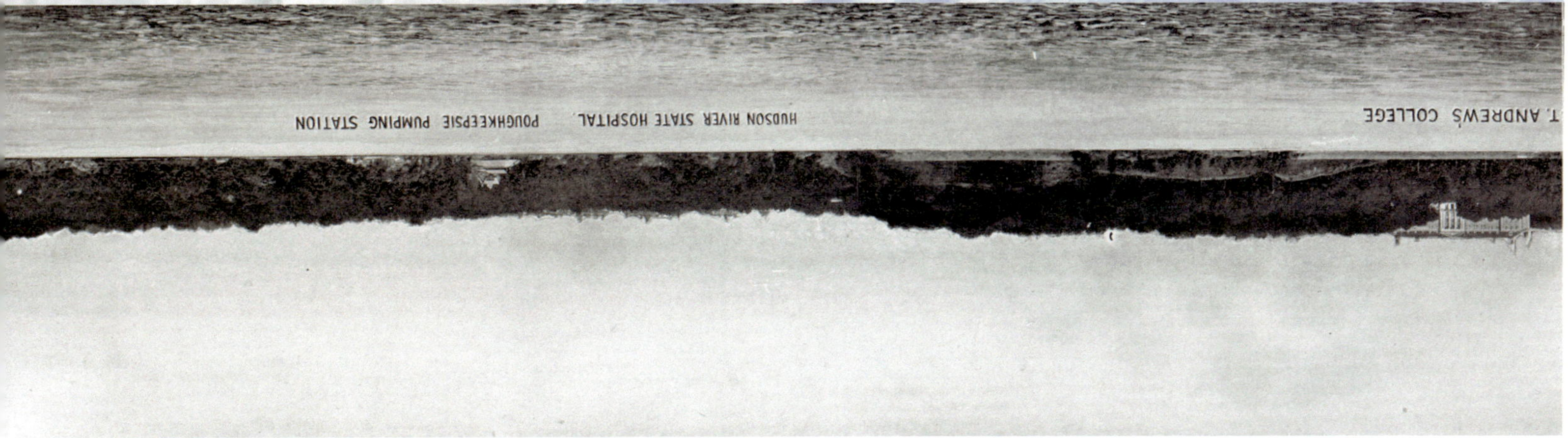

T. ANDREW'S COLLEGE

HUDSON RIVER STATE HOSPITAL

POUGHKEEPSIE PUMPING STATION

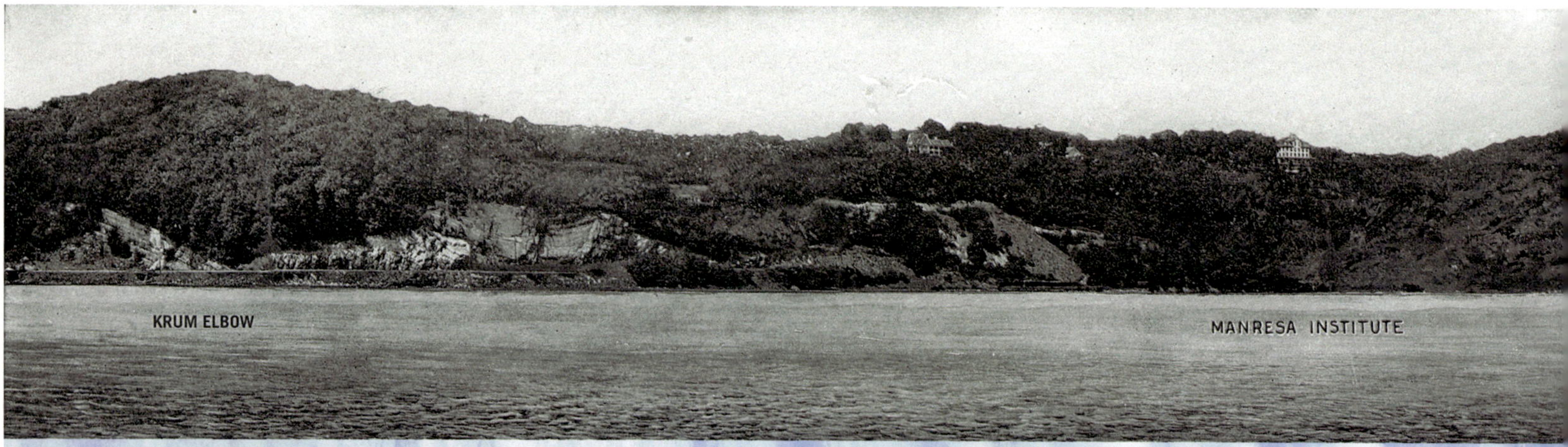

KRUM ELBOW
MANRESA INSTITUTE

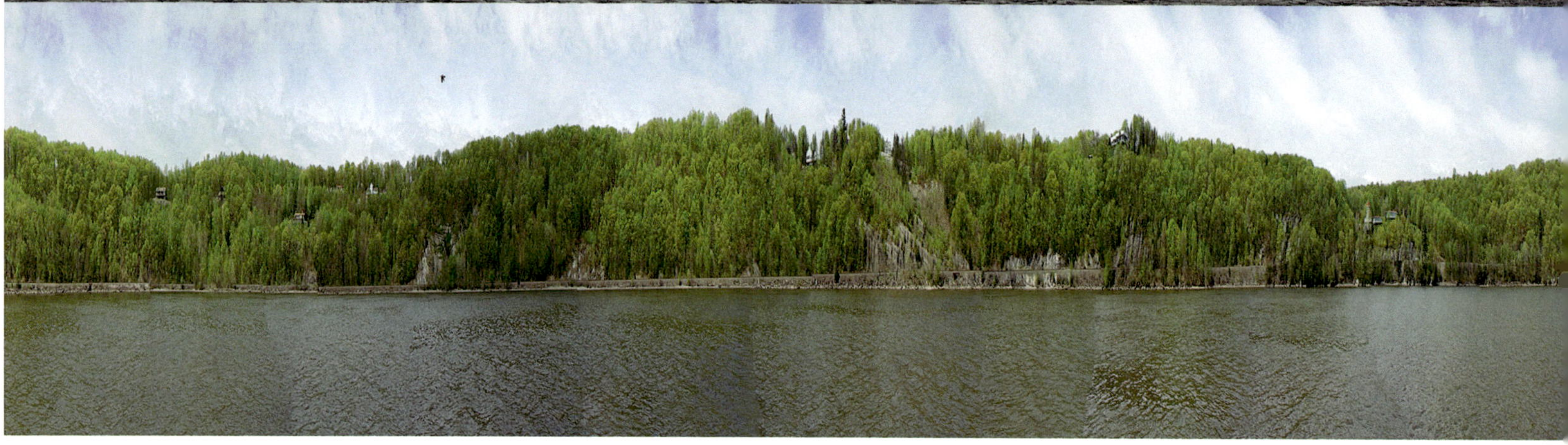

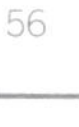

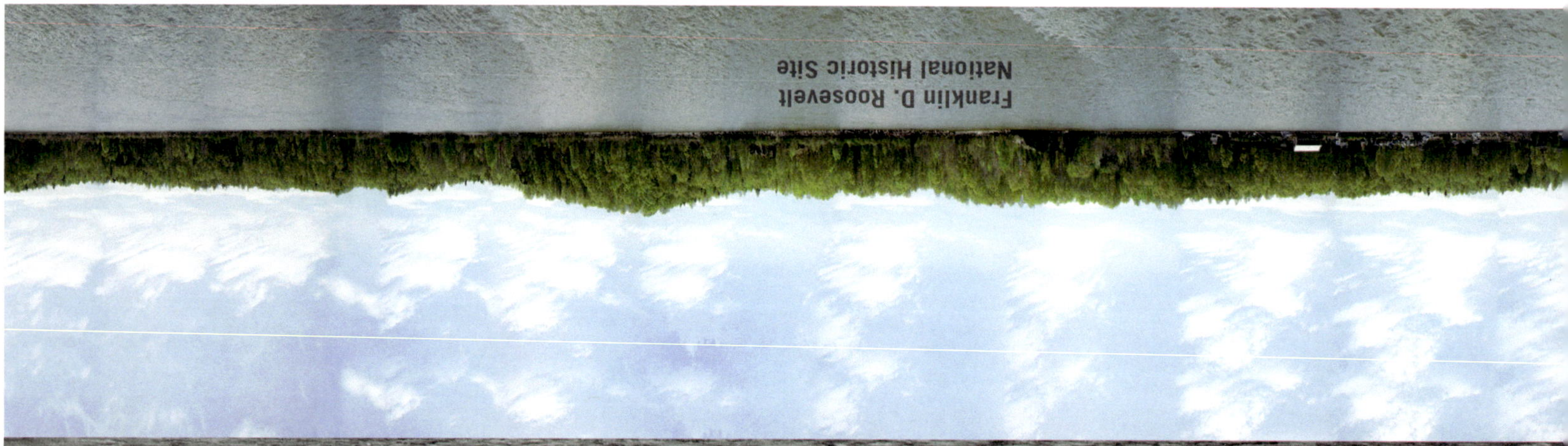

Franklin D. Roosevelt
National Historic Site
A.ROGERS

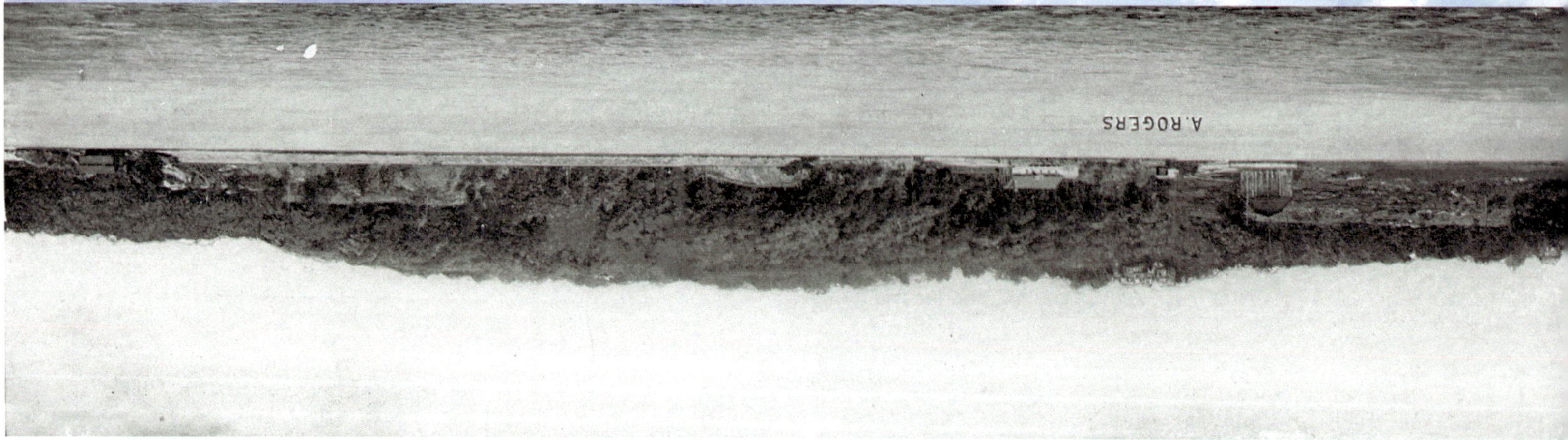

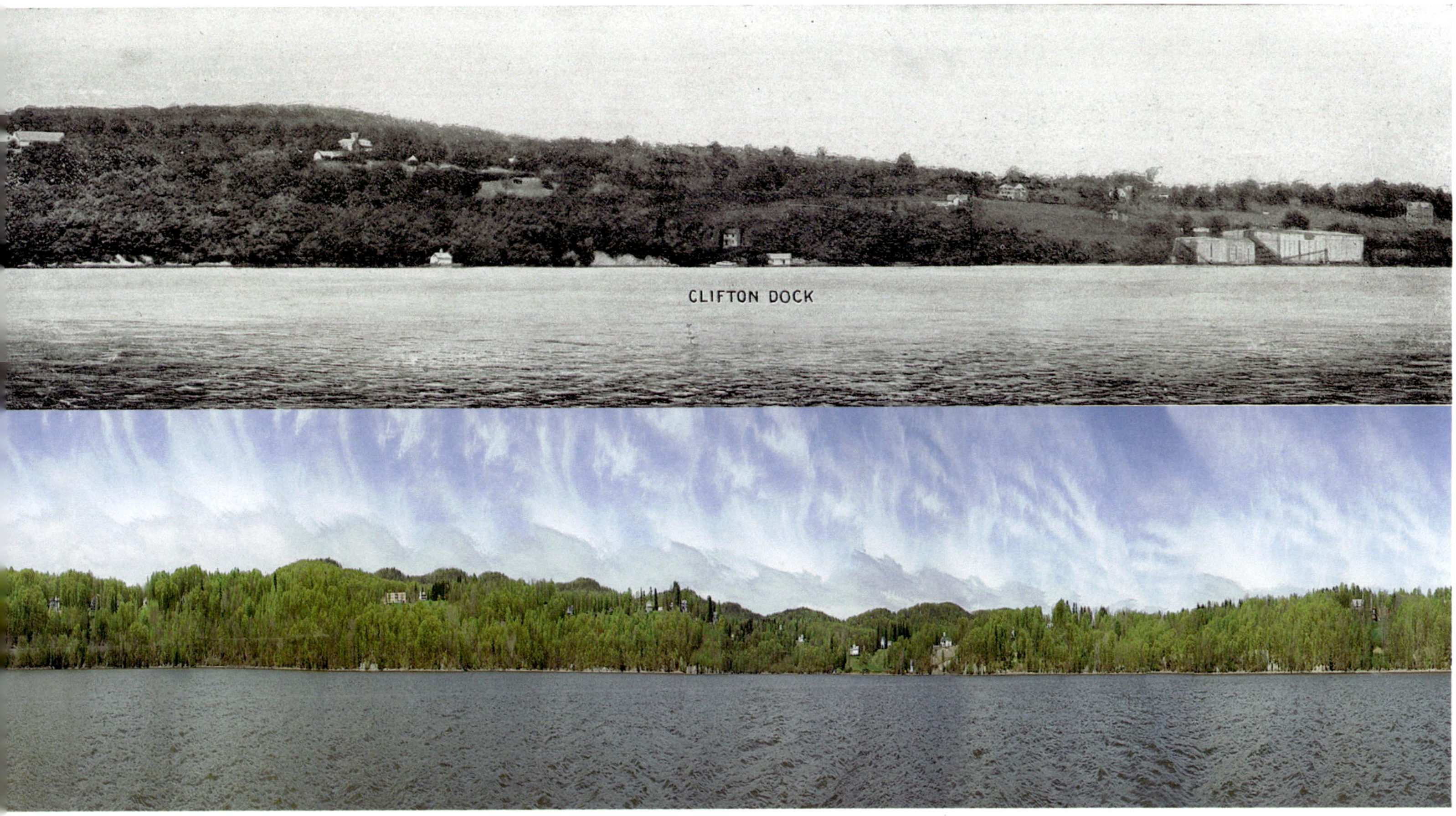

CLIFTON DOCK

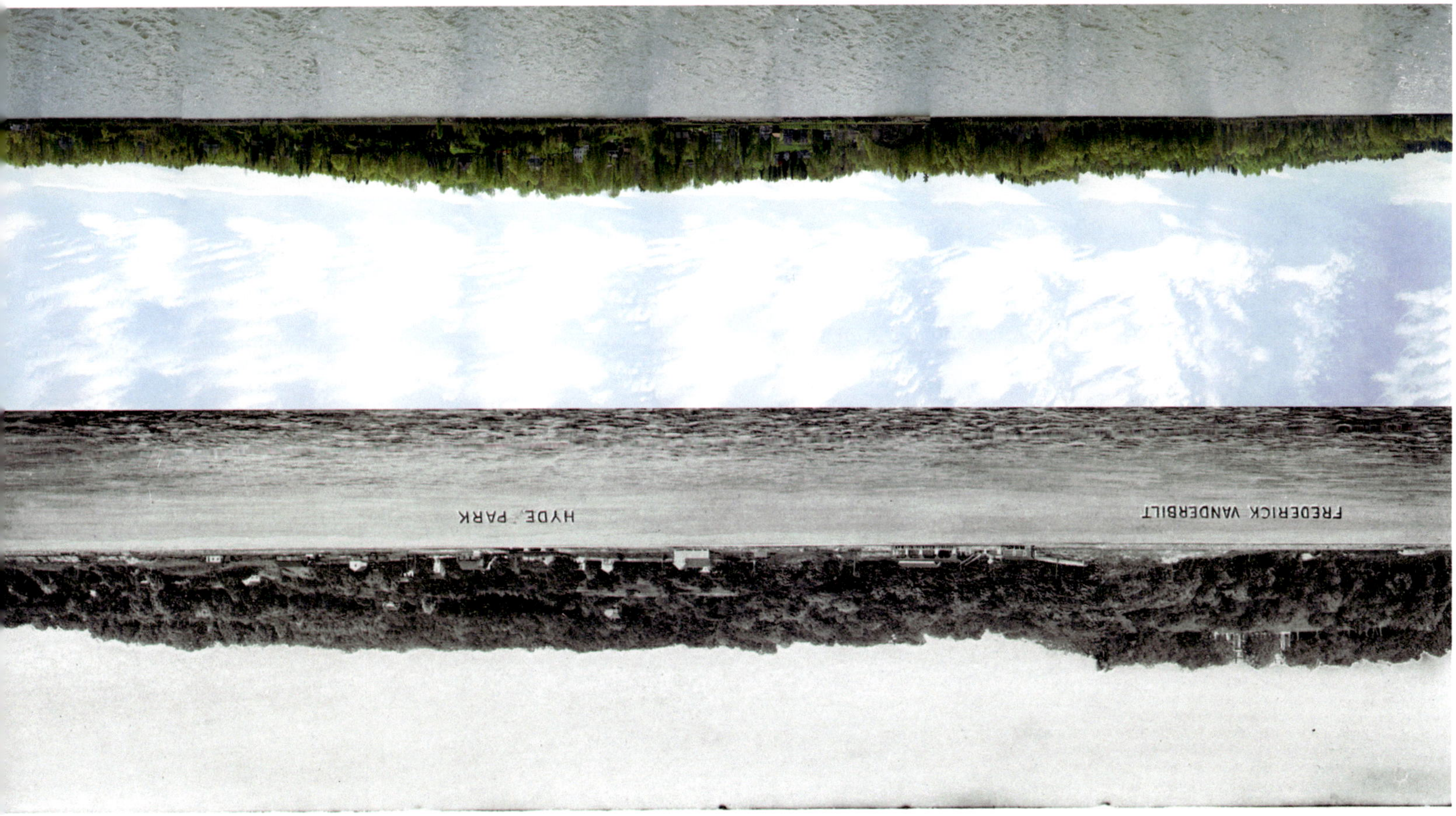

HYDE PARK

FREDERICK VANDERBILT

WALDORF PLACE
ALTON B. PARKER

Mount St. Alphons

Mills-Norrie State Parks
Esopus Island

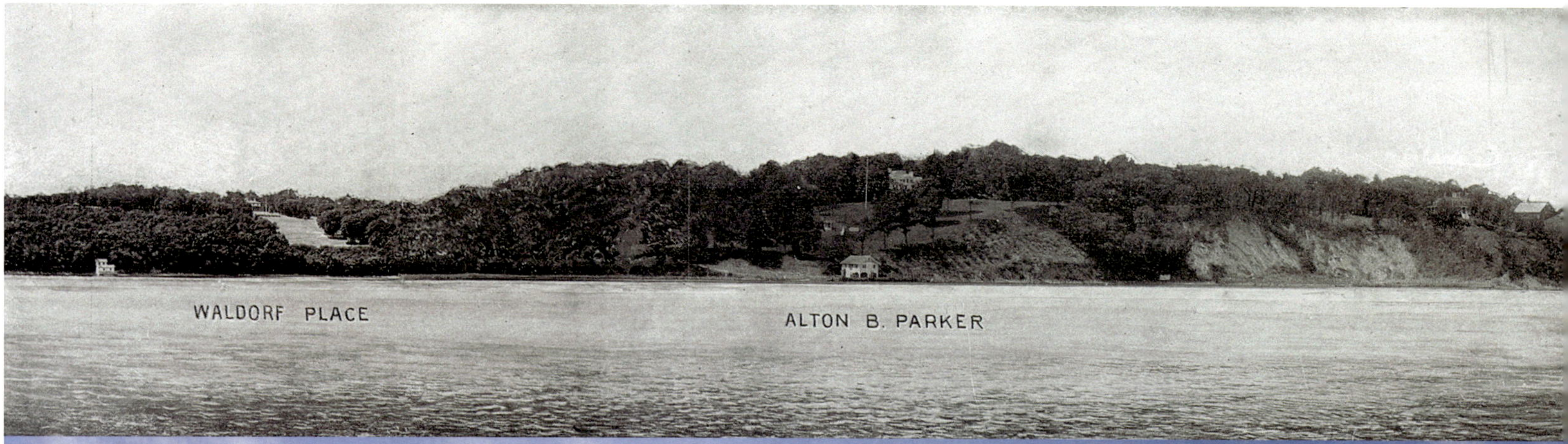

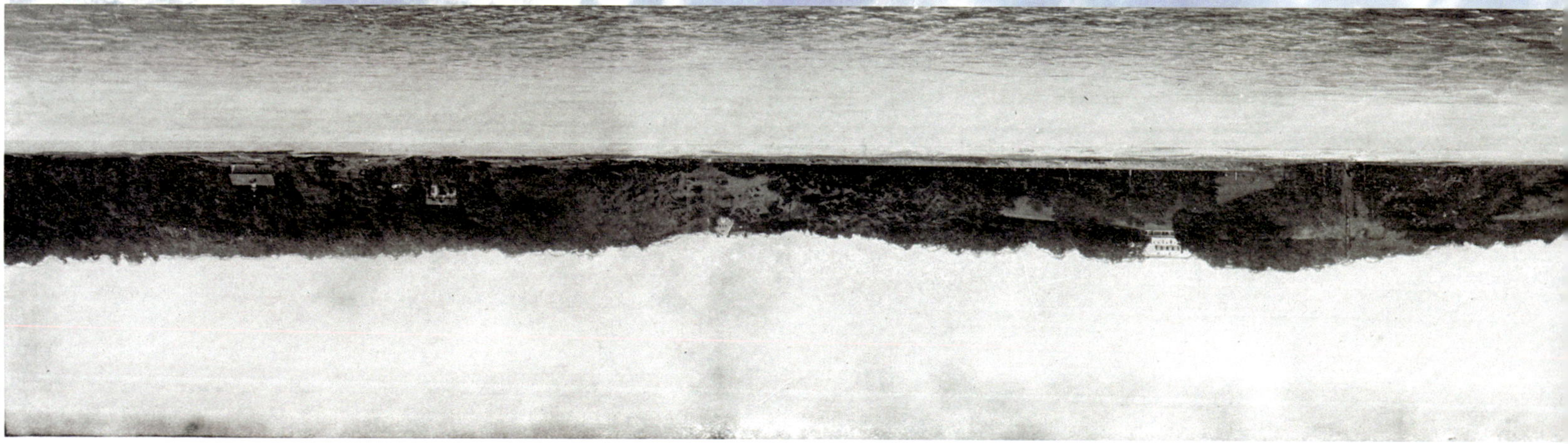

East Bank

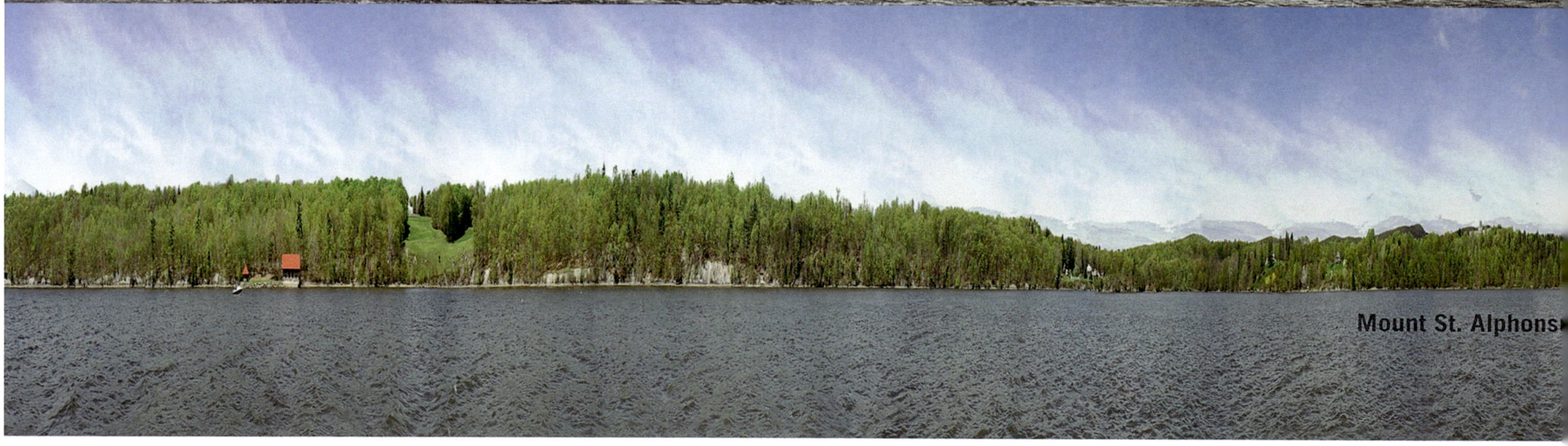

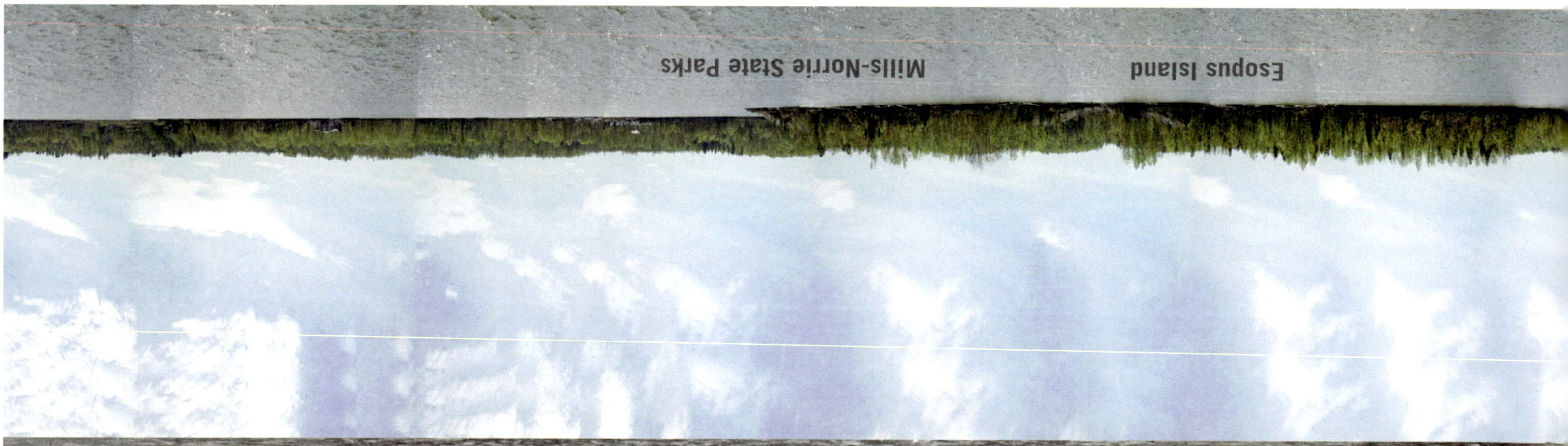

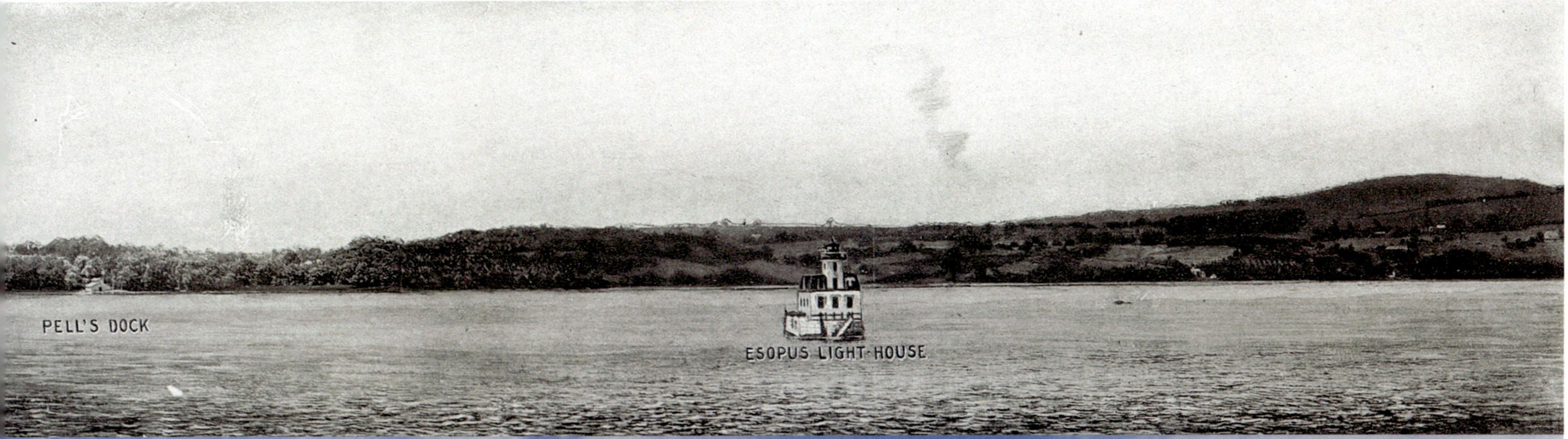

PELL'S DOCK

ESOPUS LIGHT-HOUSE

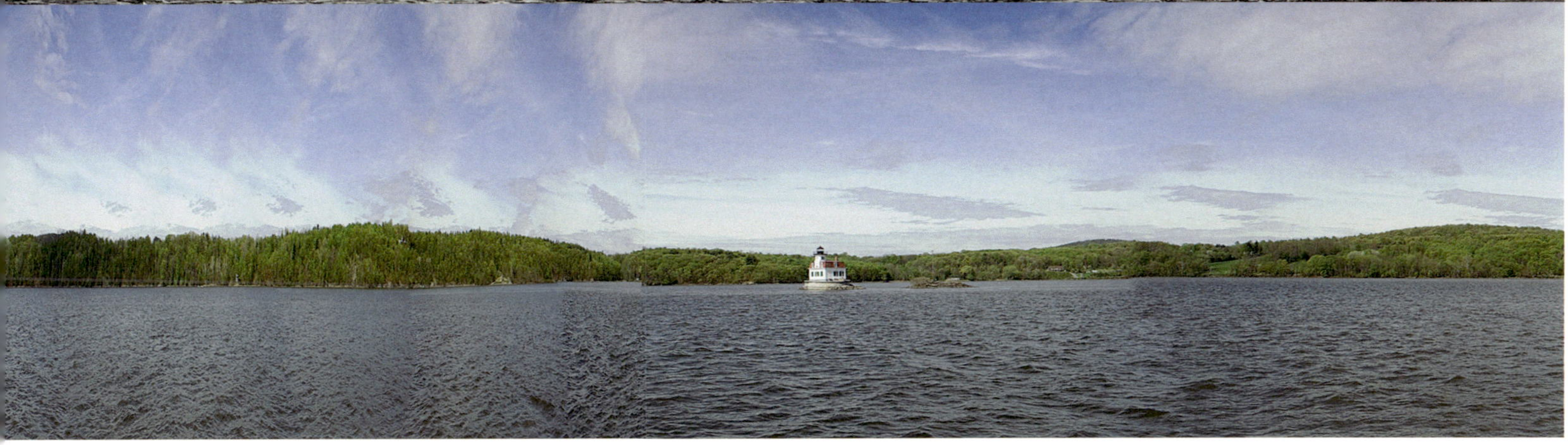

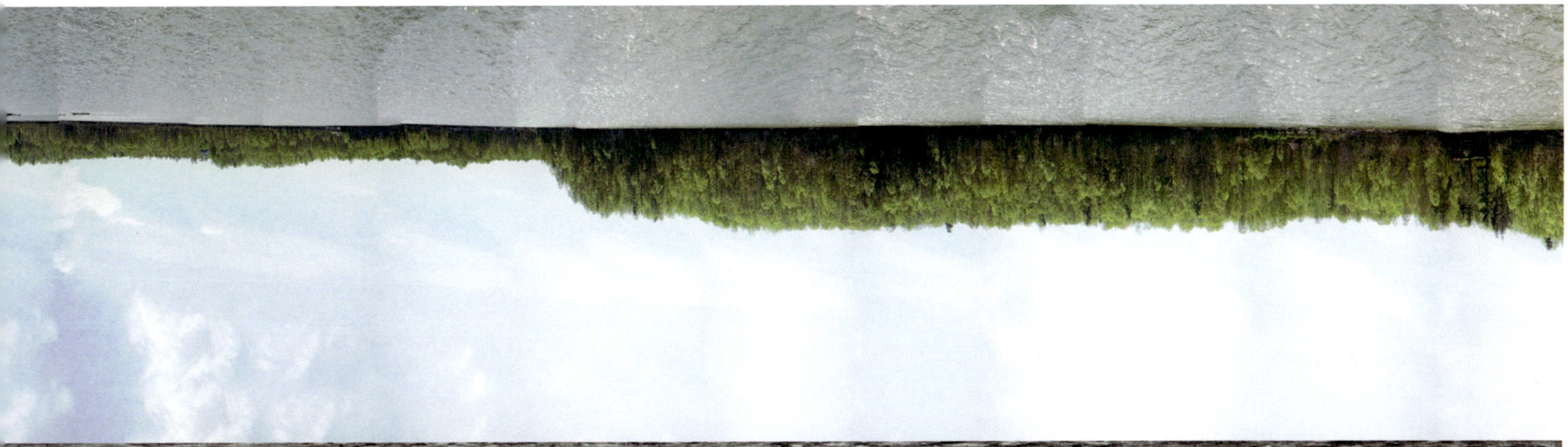

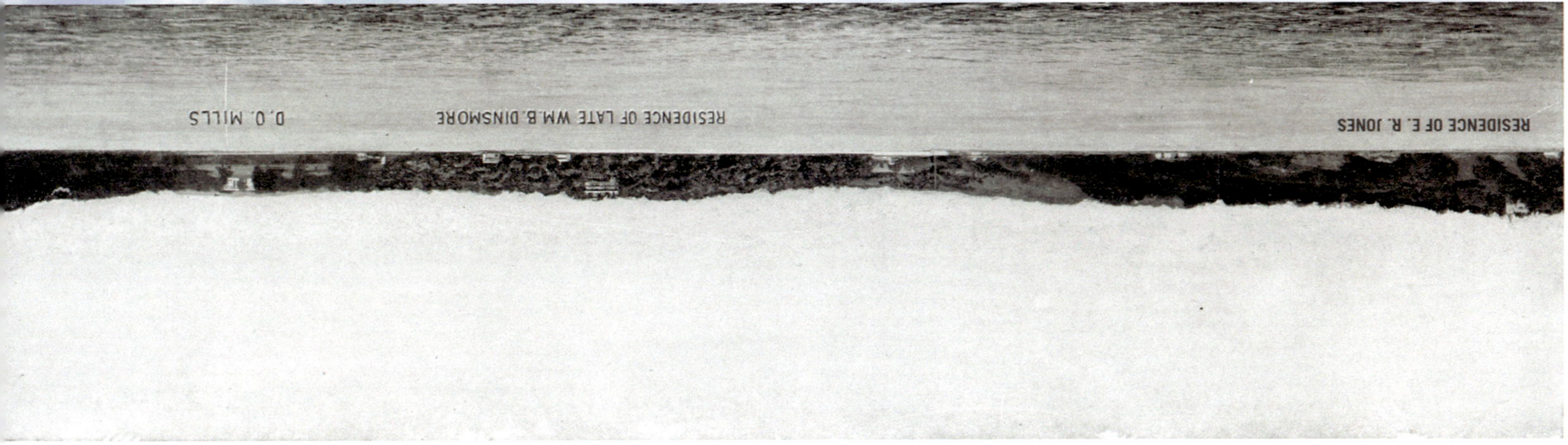

RESIDENCE OF E. R. JONES

RESIDENCE OF LATE WM. B. DINSMORE

D. O. MILLS

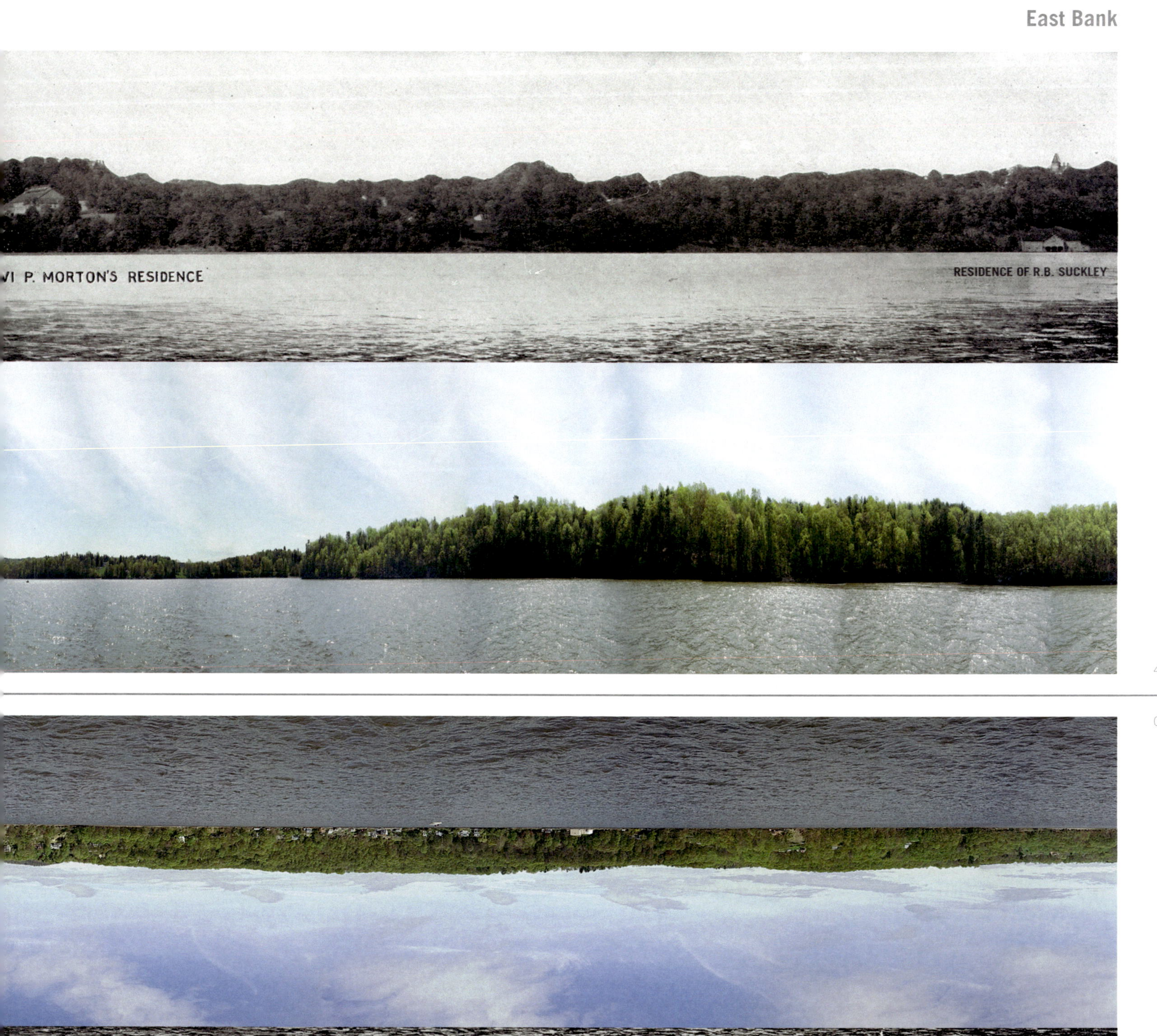

VI P. MORTON'S RESIDENCE
RESIDENCE OF R.B. SUCKLEY

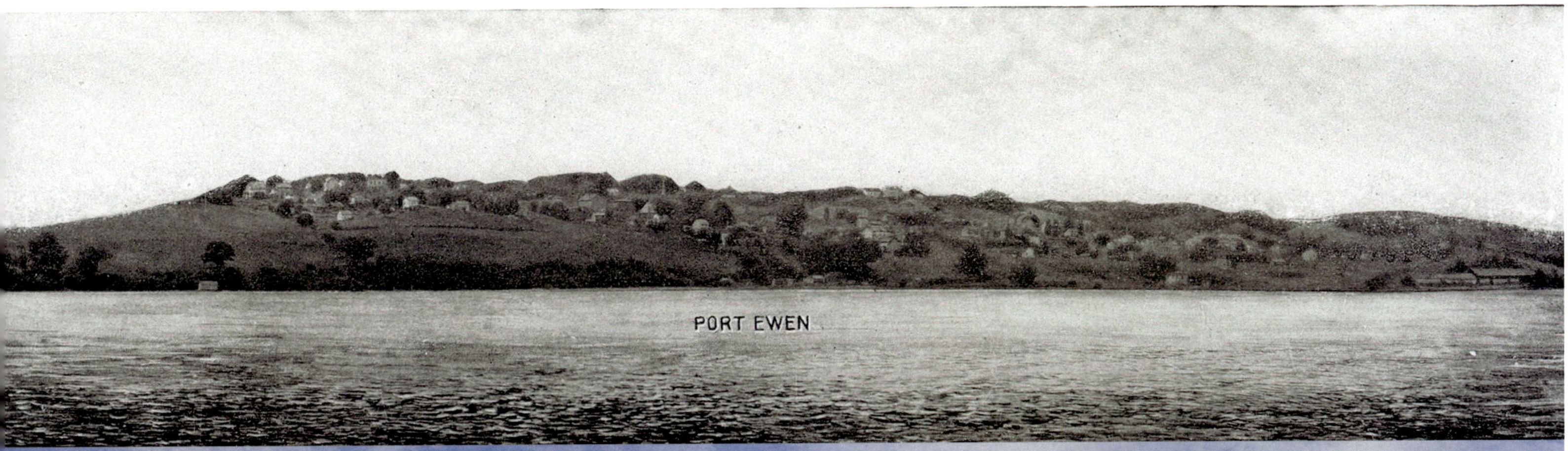

PORT EWEN

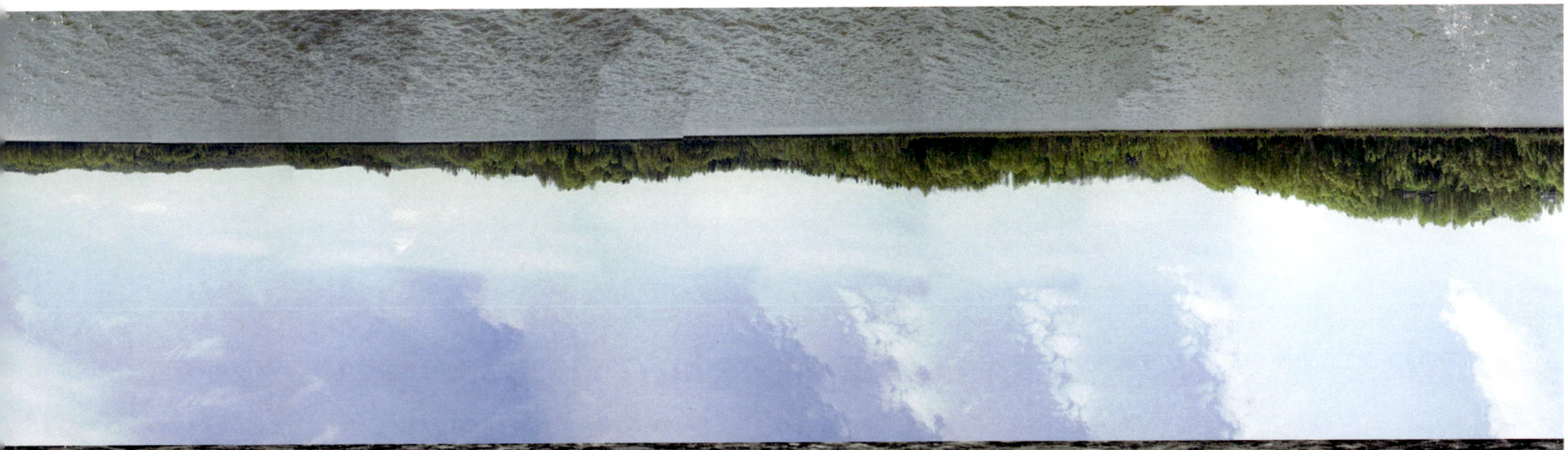

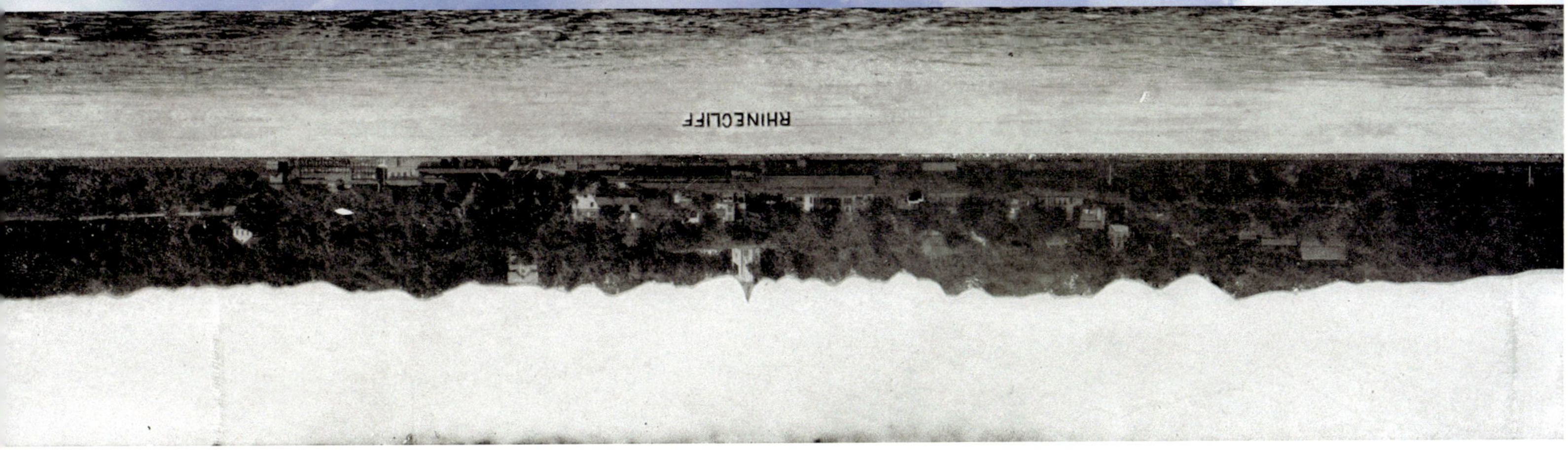

RHINECLIFF

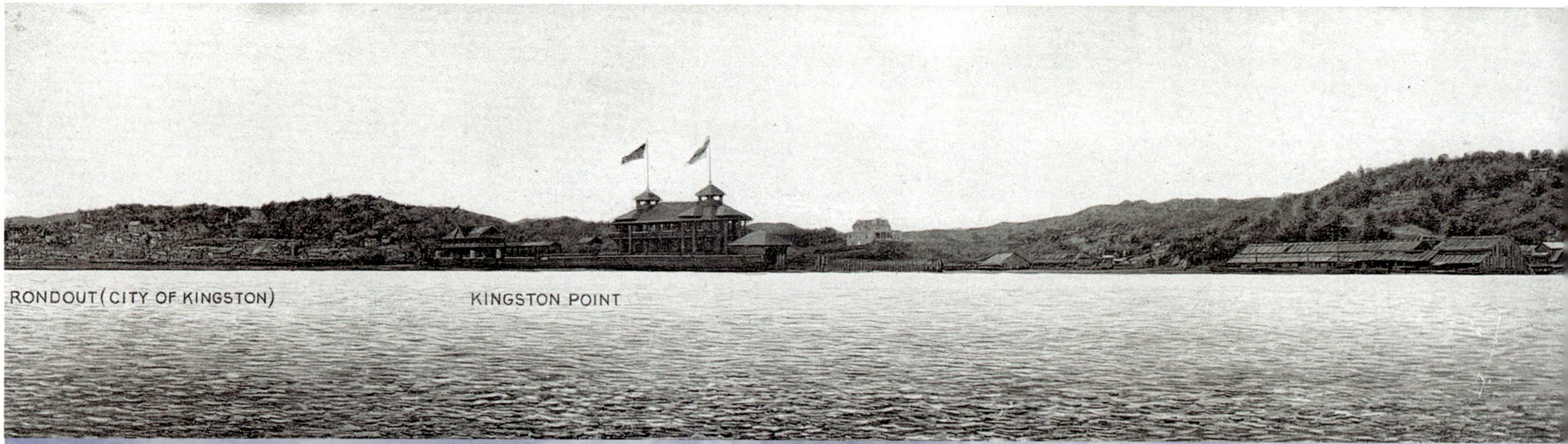

RONDOUT (CITY OF KINGSTON)

KINGSTON POINT

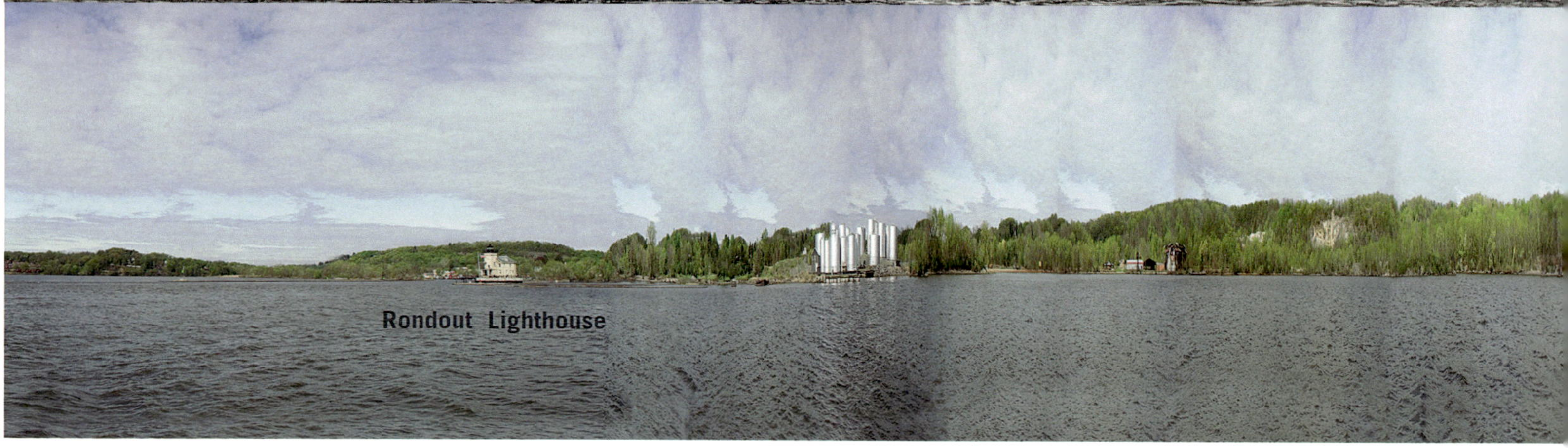

Rondout Lighthouse

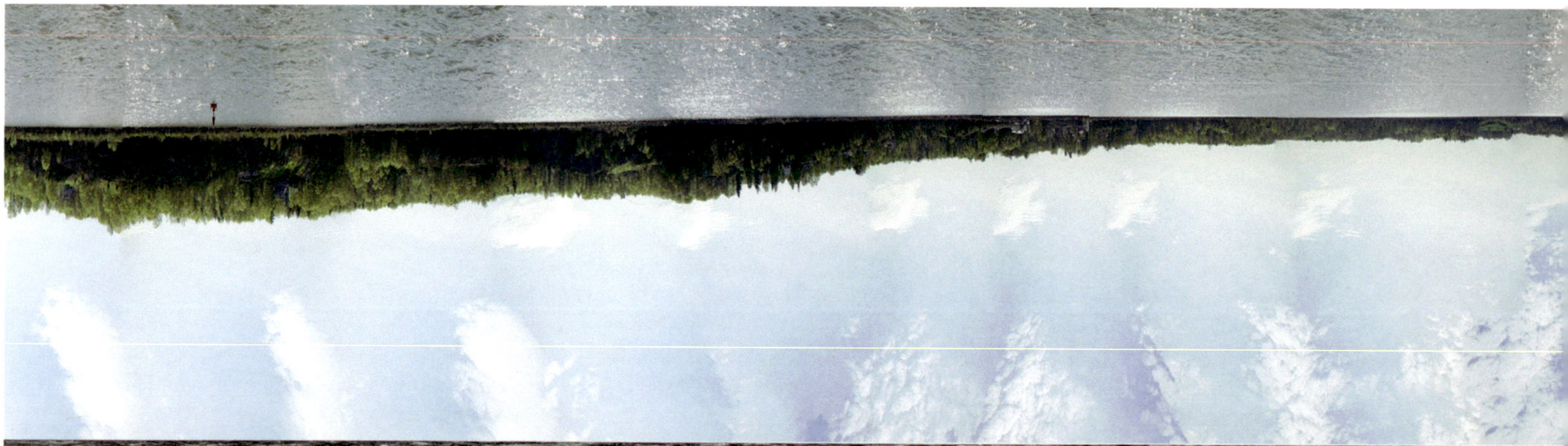

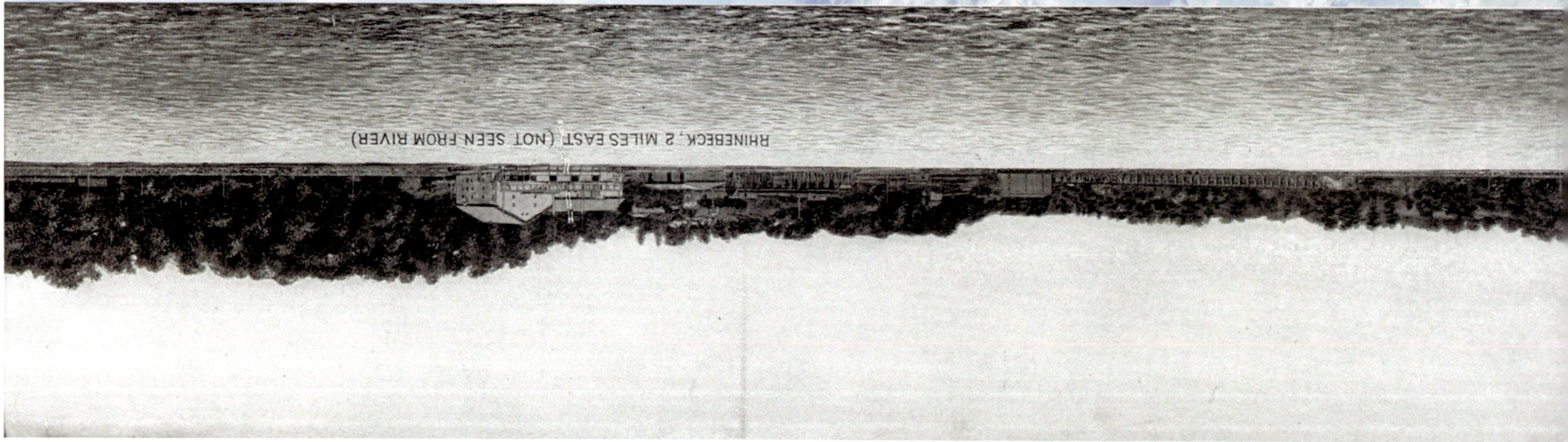

RHINEBECK, 2 MILES EAST (NOT SEEN FROM RIVER)

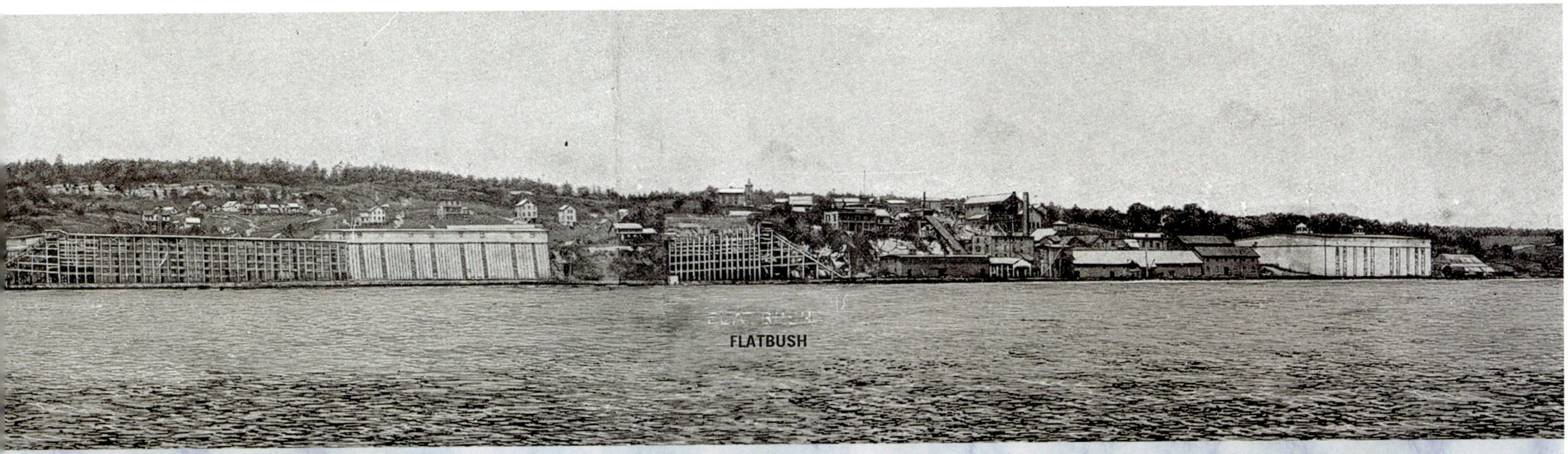

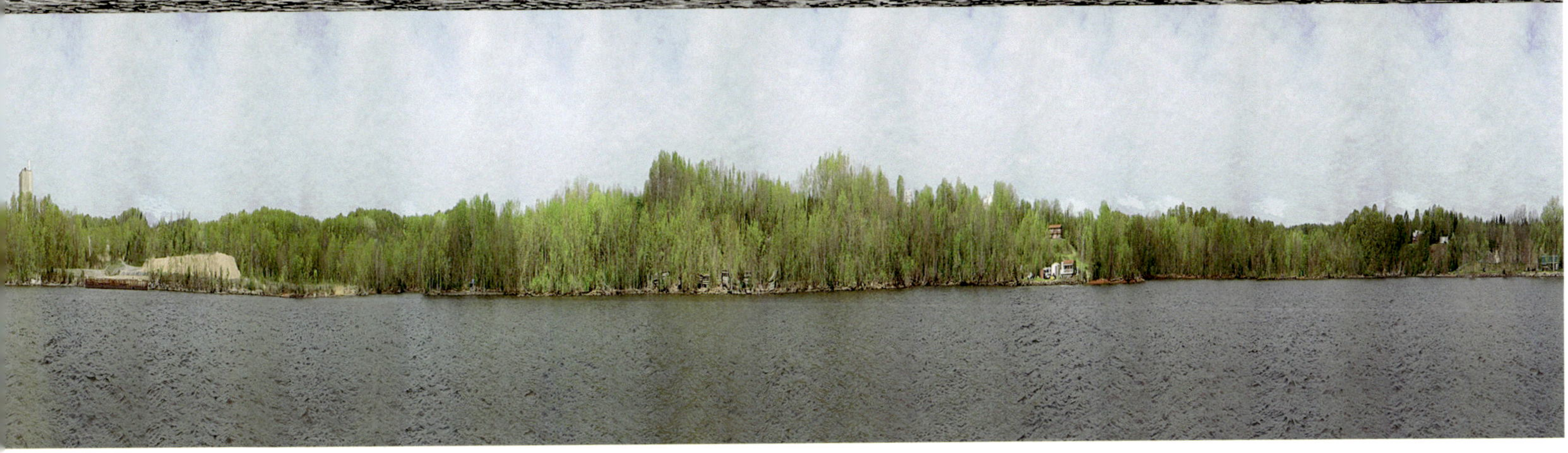

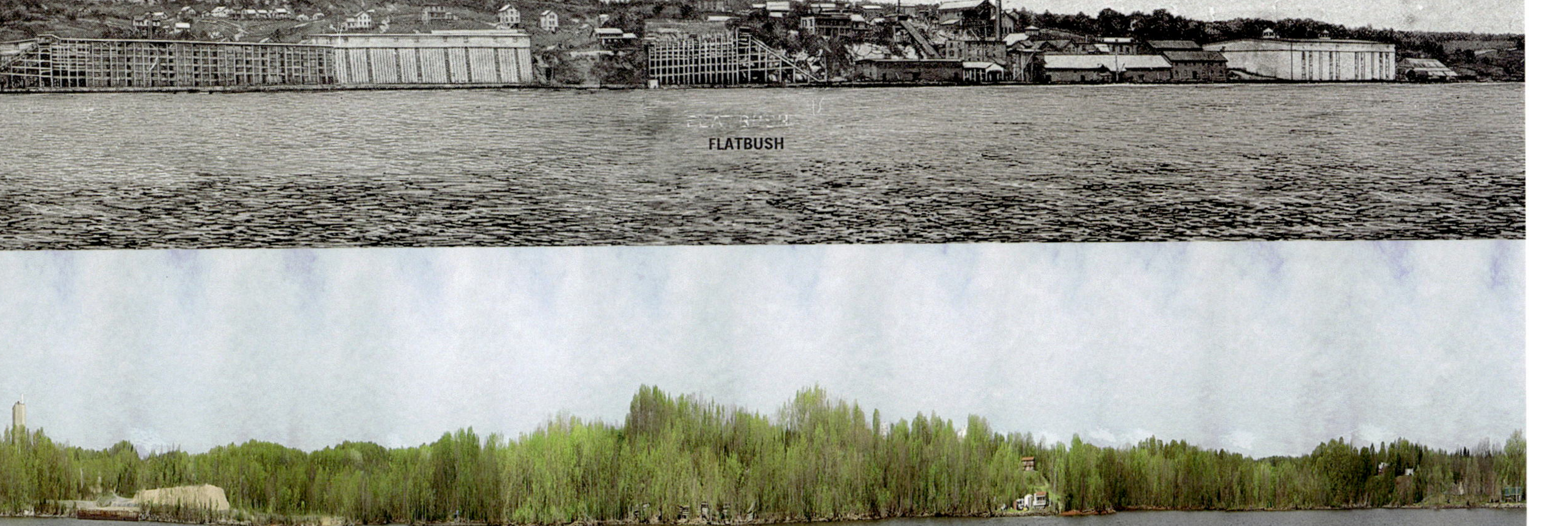

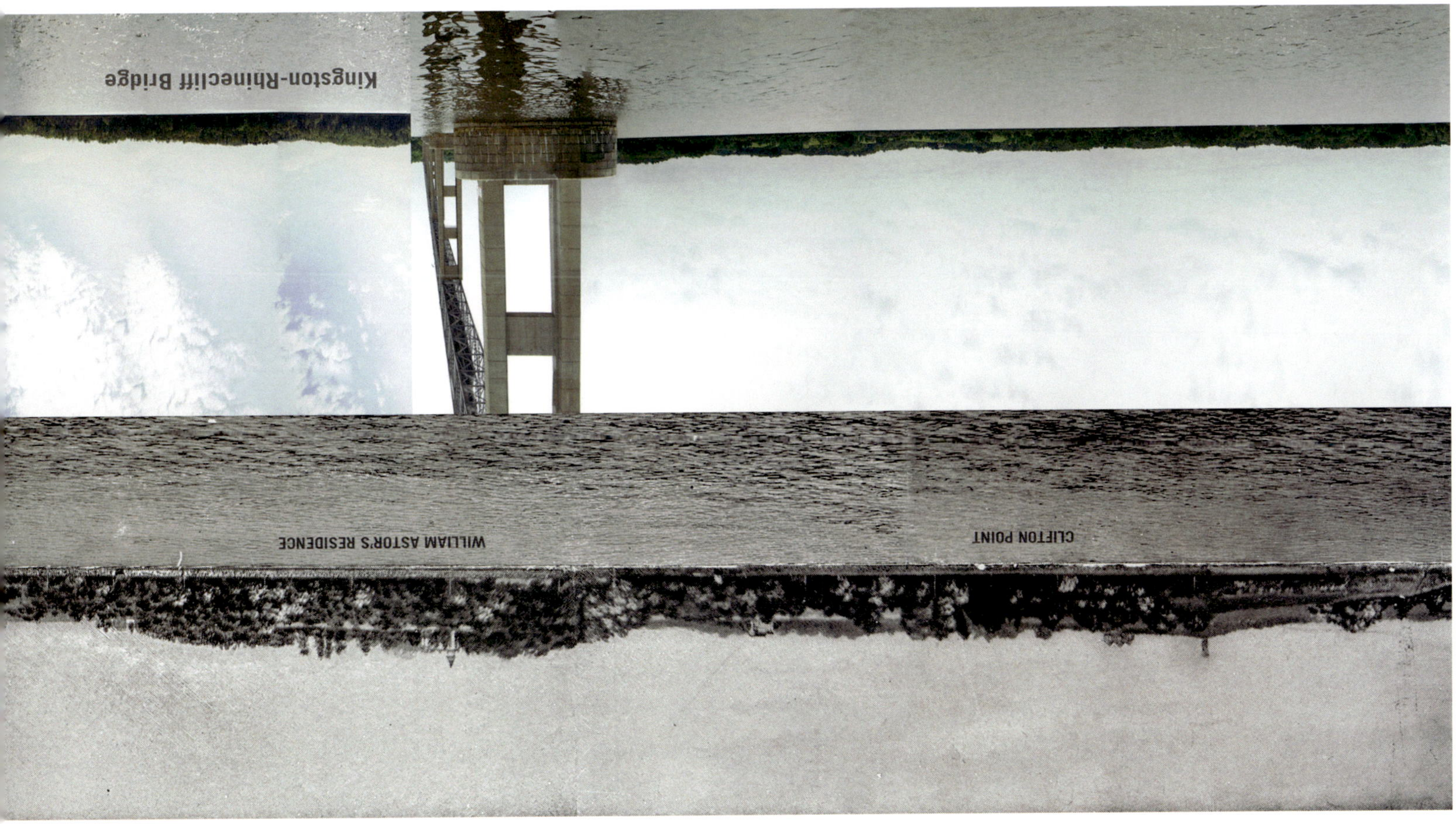

Kingston-Rhinecliff Bridge

WILLIAM ASTOR'S RESIDENCE

CLIFTON POINT

TURKEY POINT

Kingston-Rhinecliff Bridge

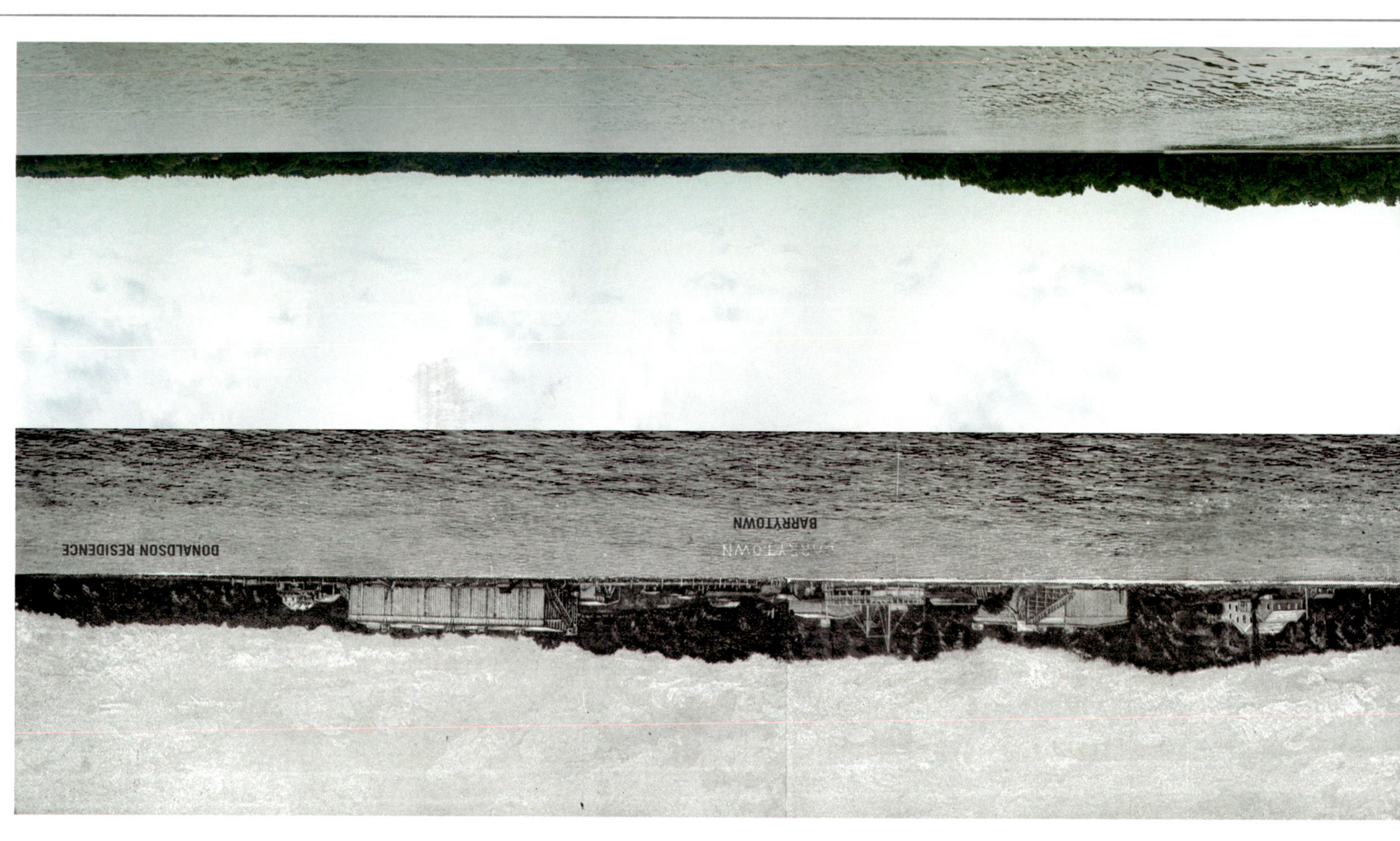

East Bank

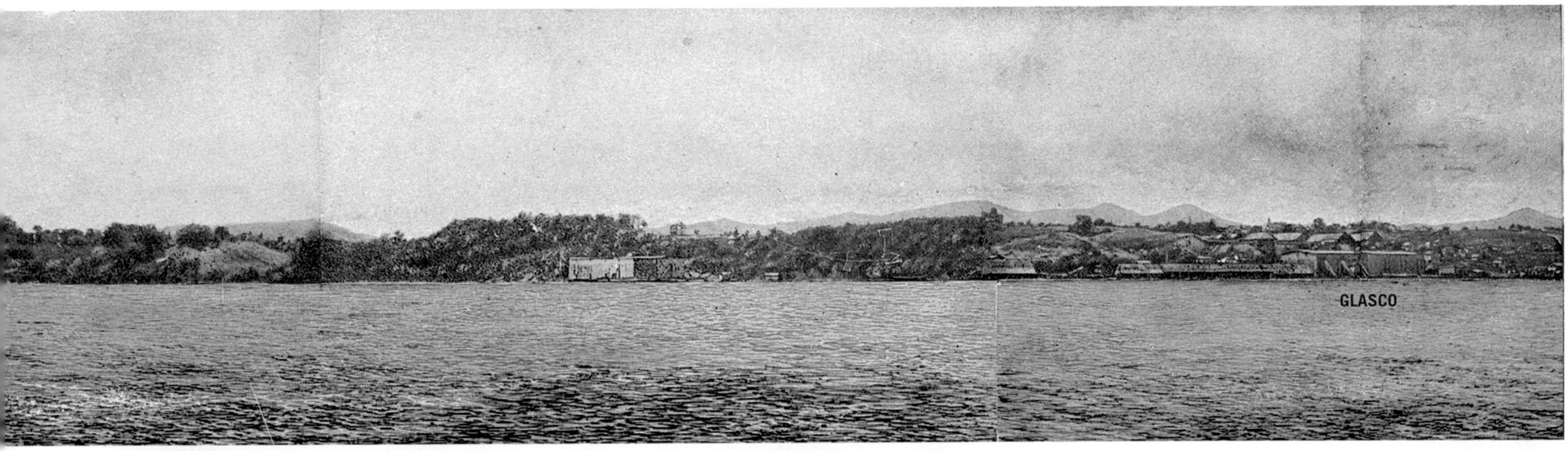

GLASCO

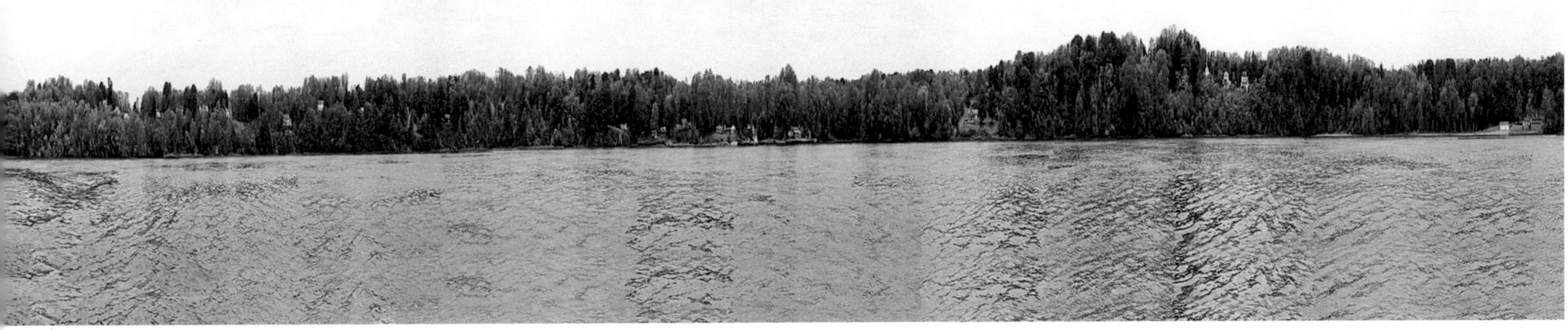

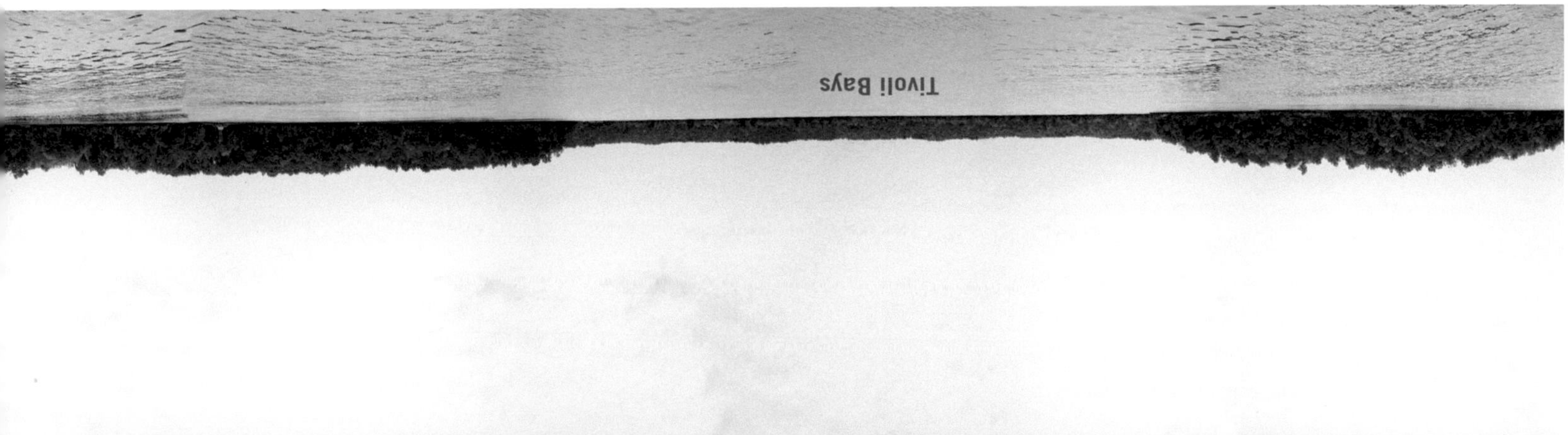

Tivoli Bays

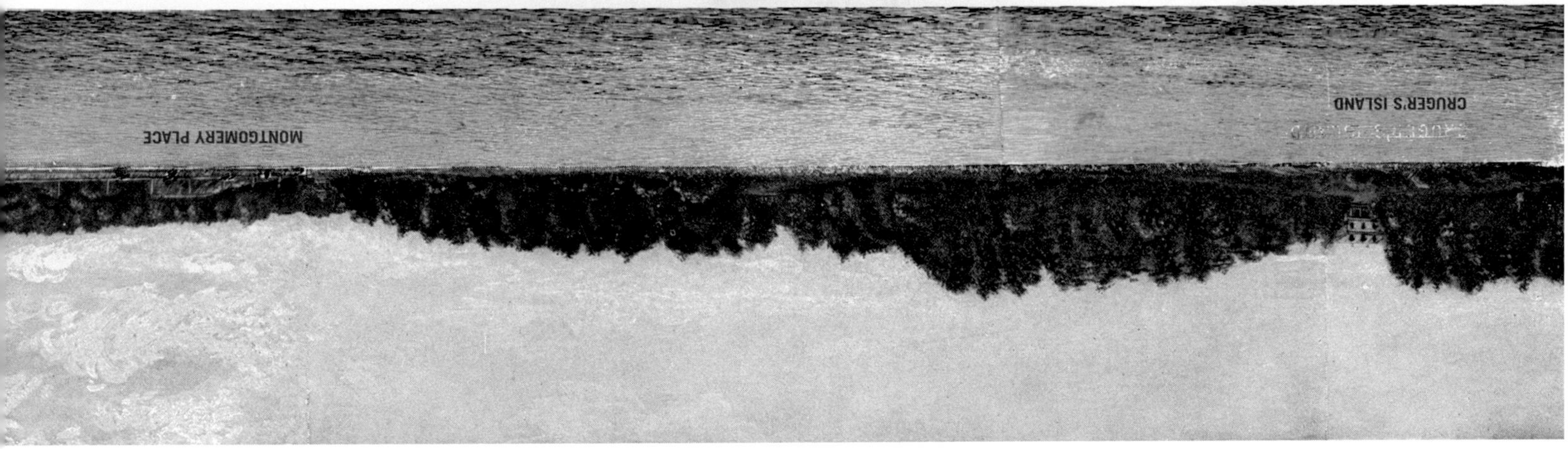

CRUGER'S ISLAND

MONTGOMERY PLACE

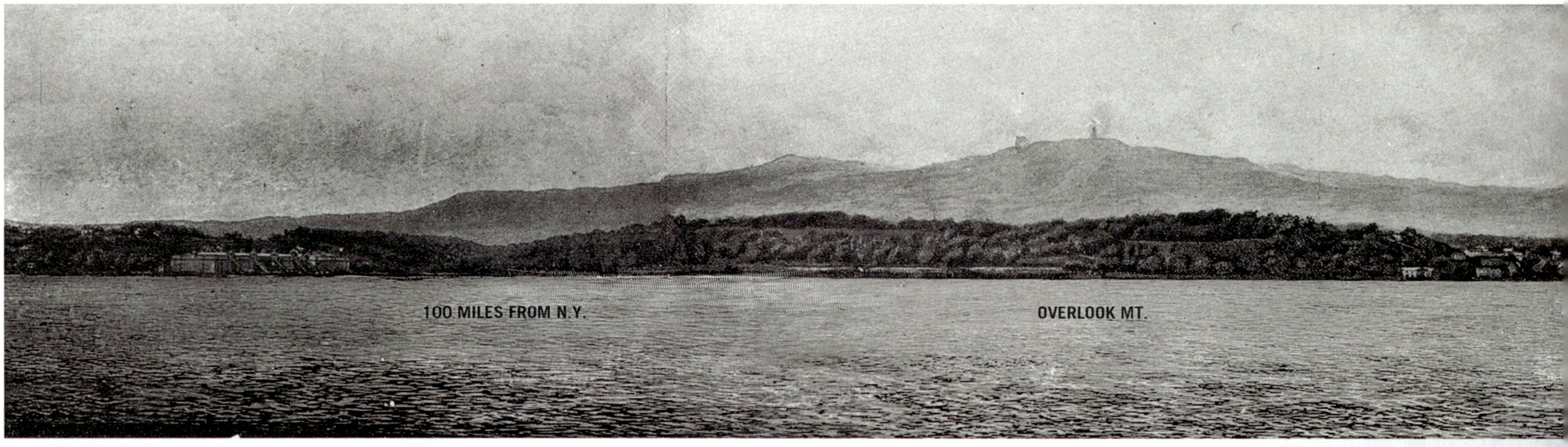

100 MILES FROM N.Y.

OVERLOOK MT.

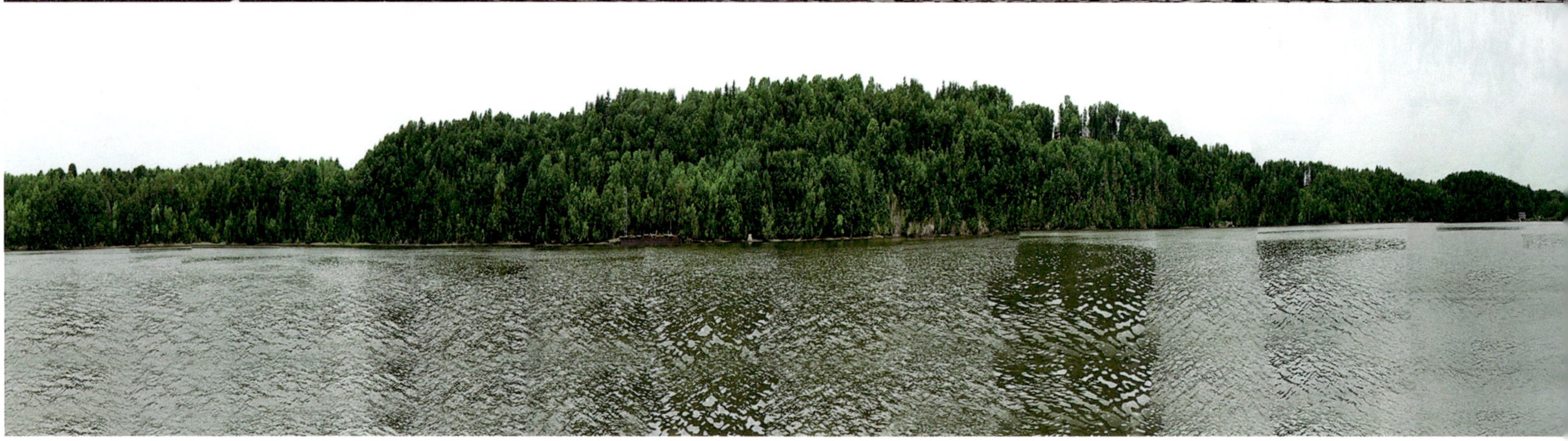

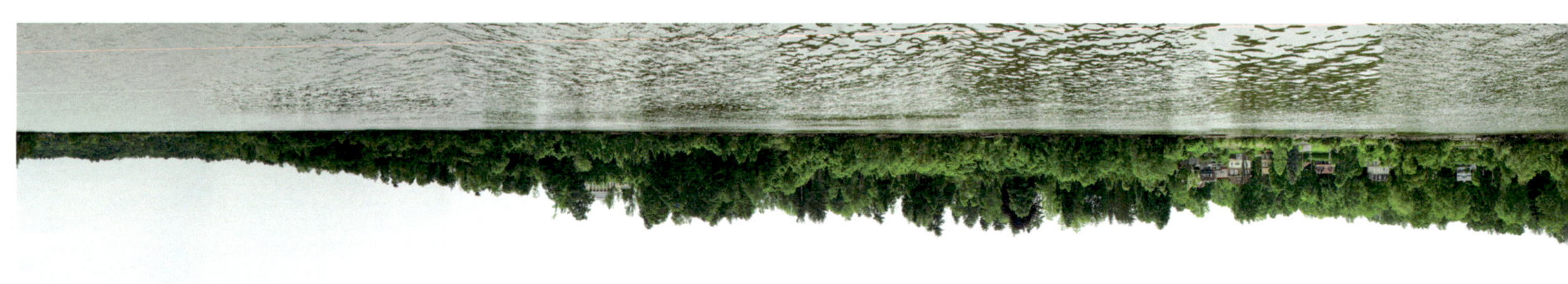

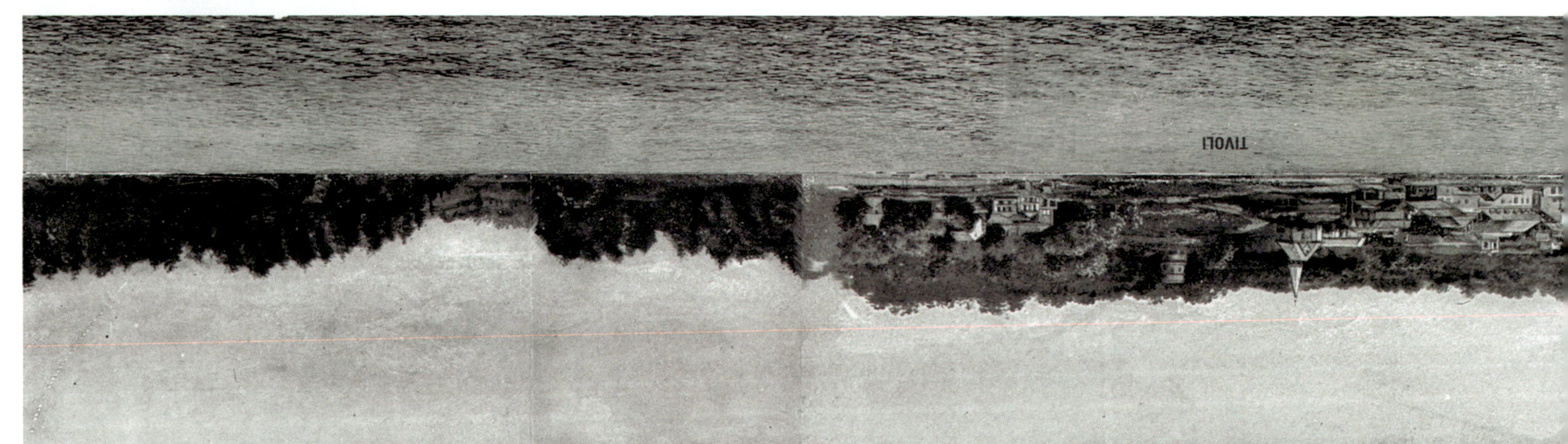

East Bank

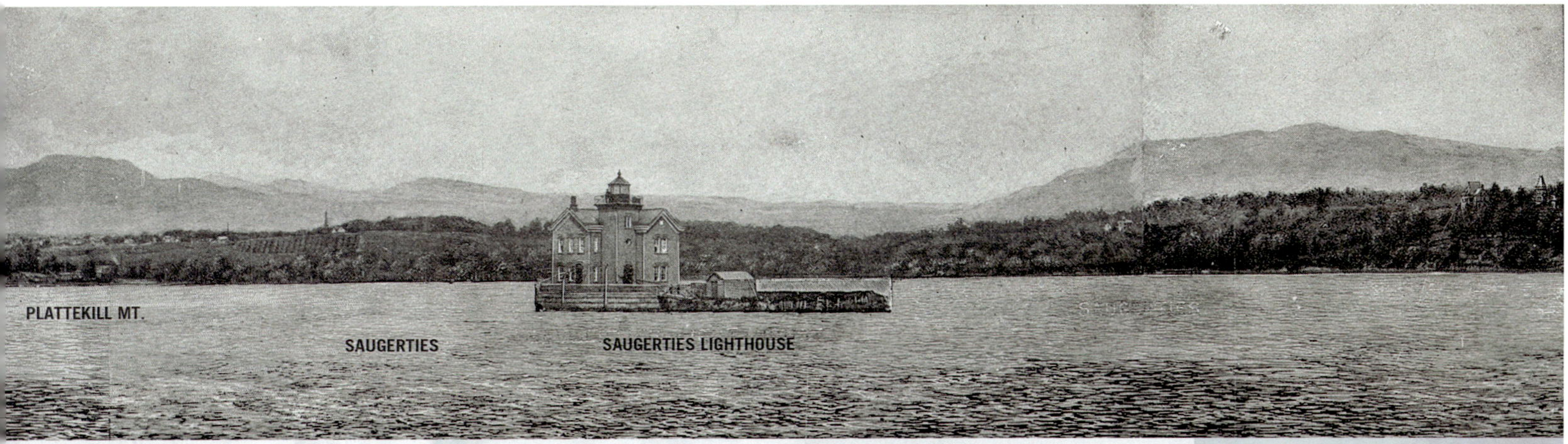

PLATTEKILL MT.

SAUGERTIES

SAUGERTIES LIGHTHOUSE

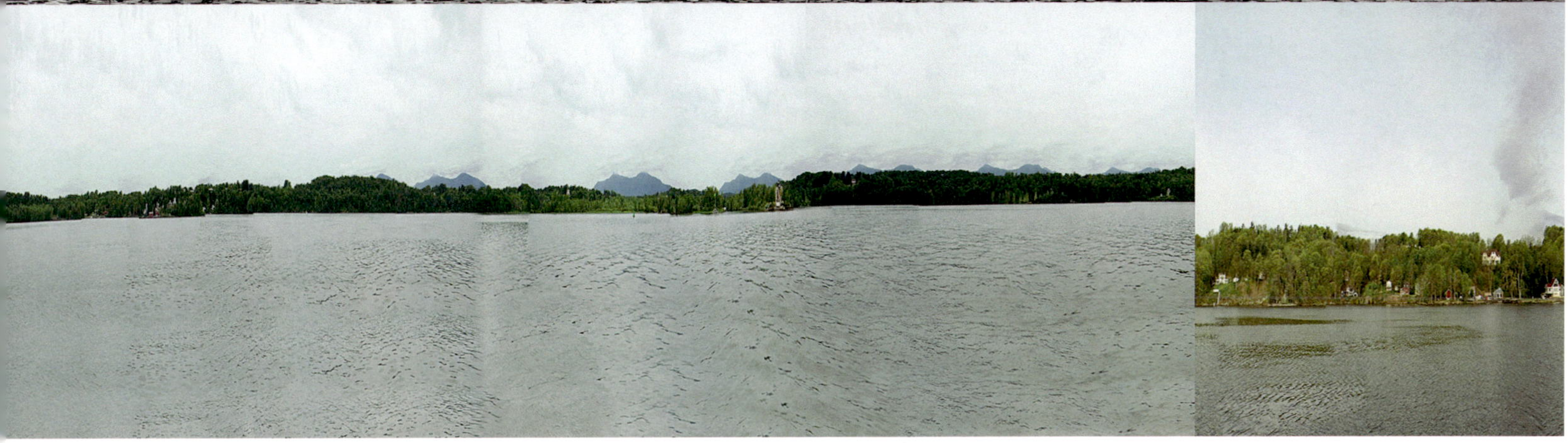

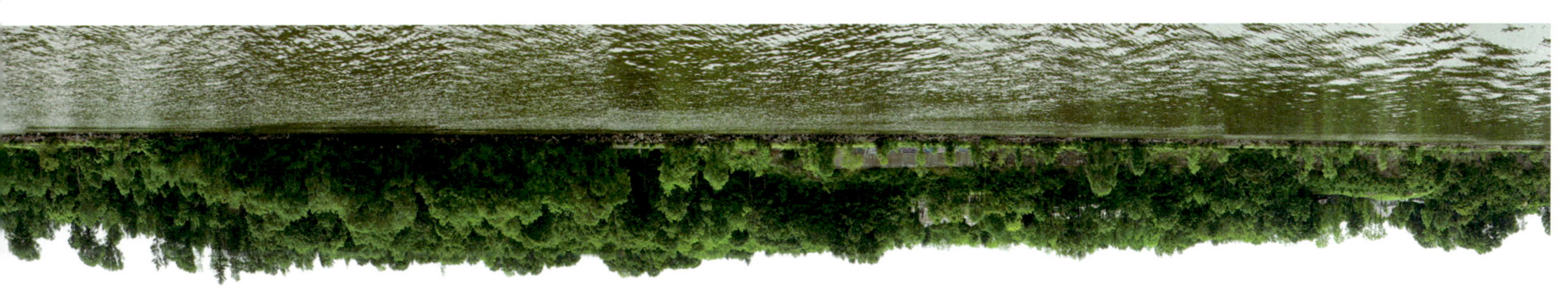

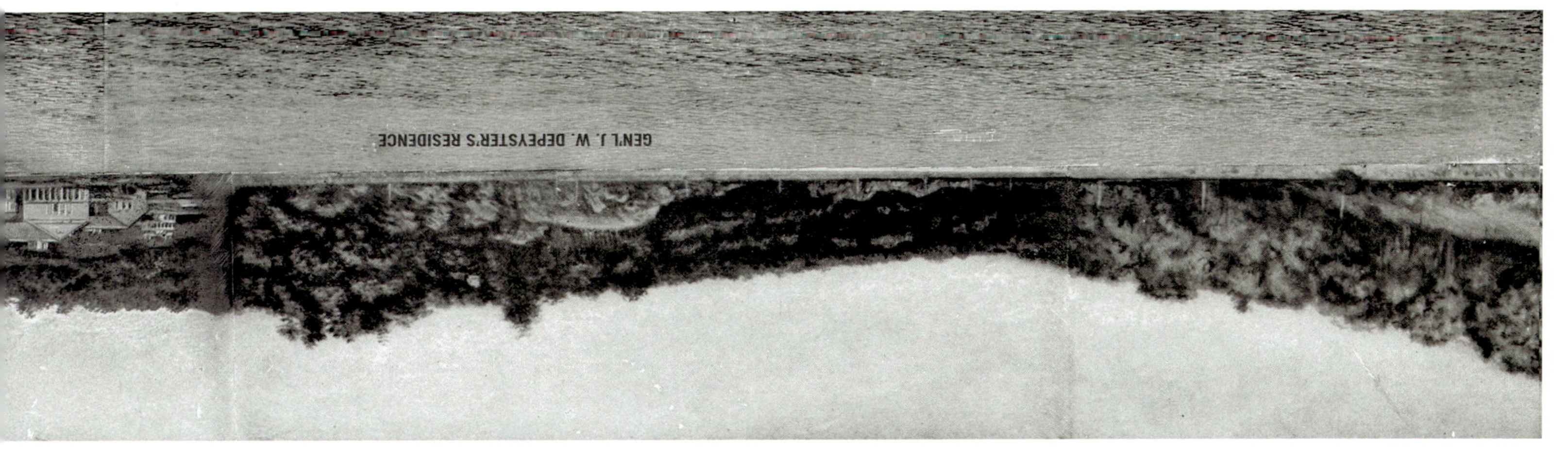

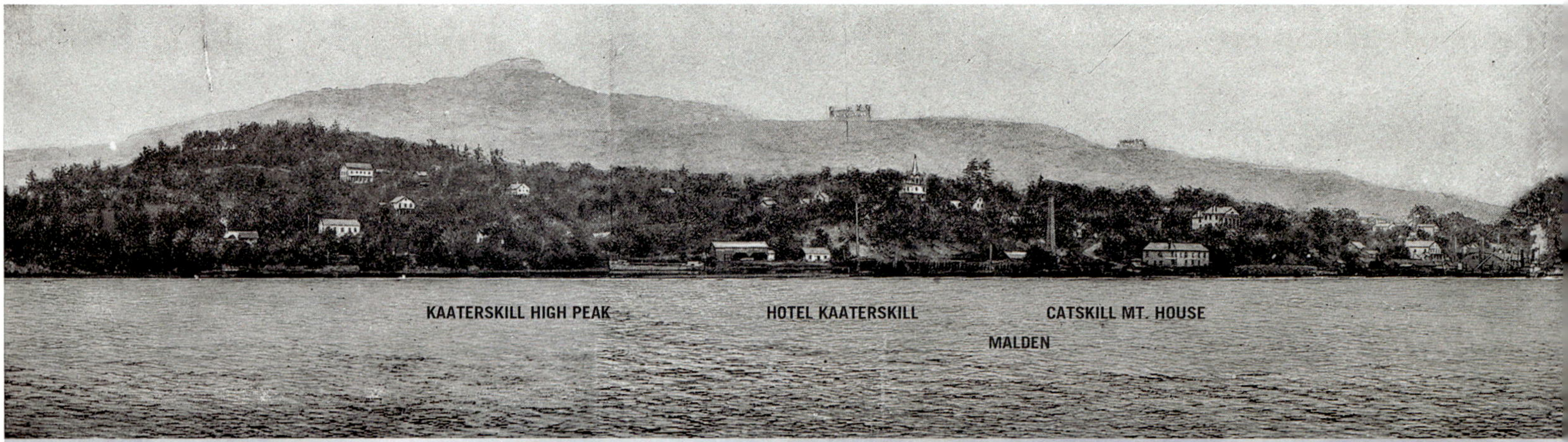

KAATERSKILL HIGH PEAK

HOTEL KAATERSKILL

CATSKILL MT. HOUSE

MALDEN

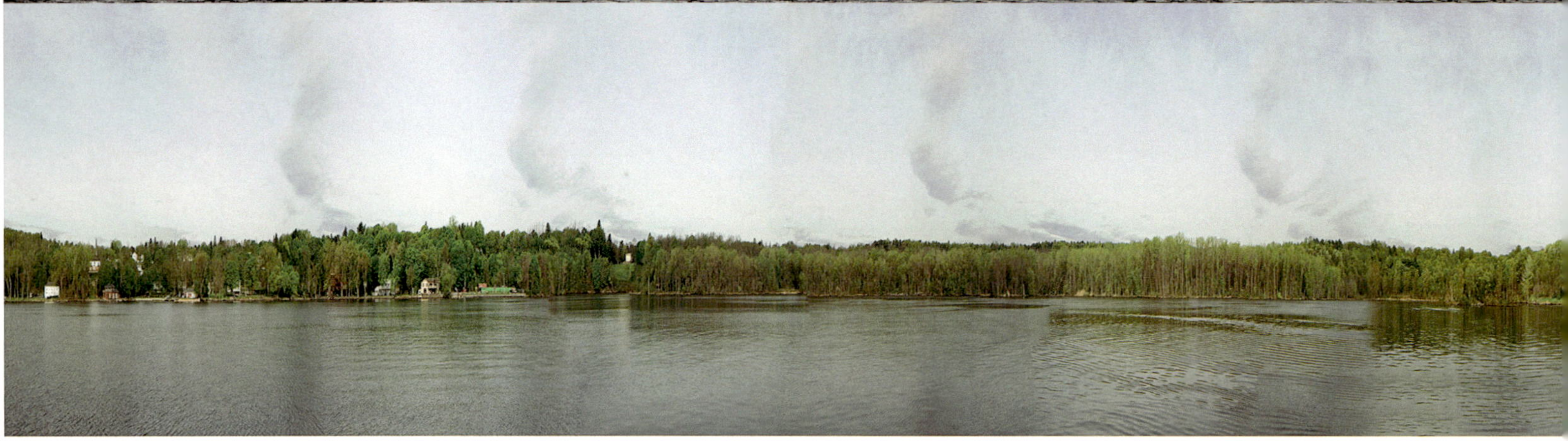

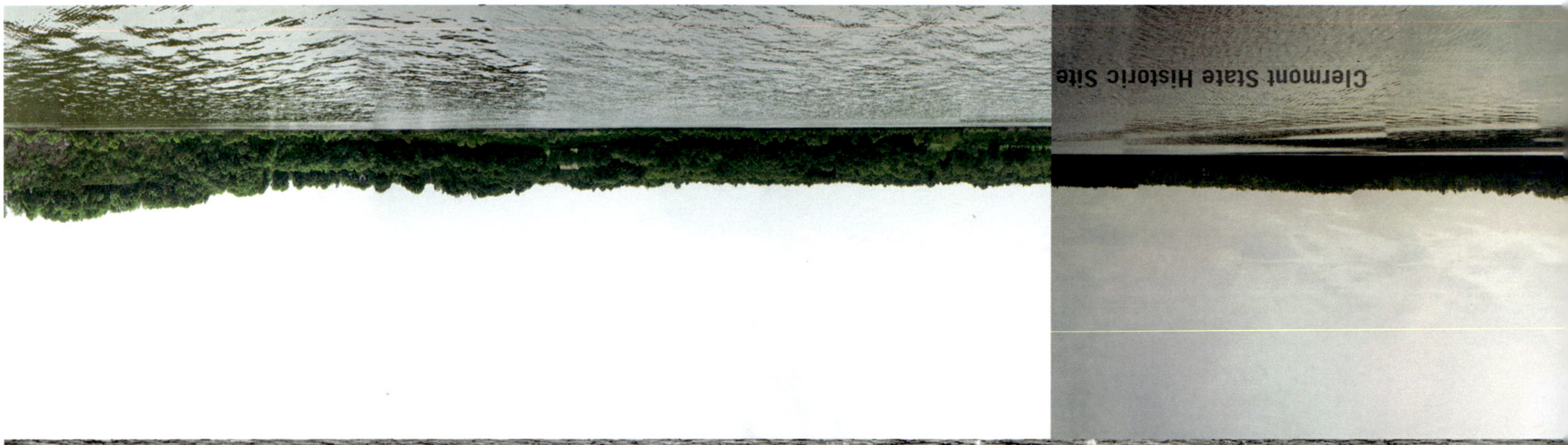

Clermont State Historic Site

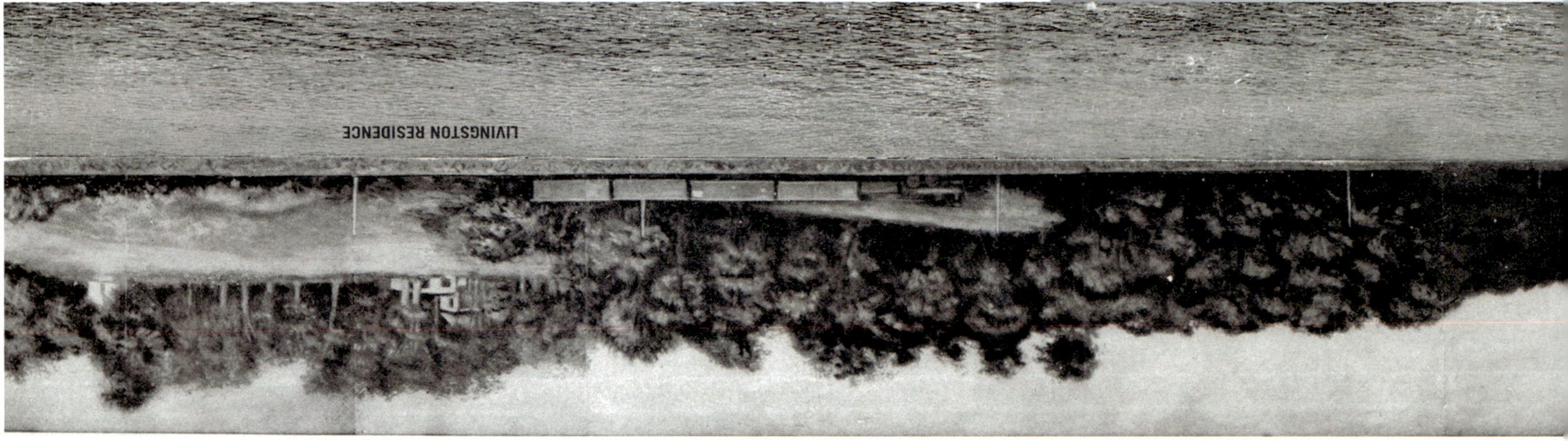

LIVINGSTON RESIDENCE

East Bank

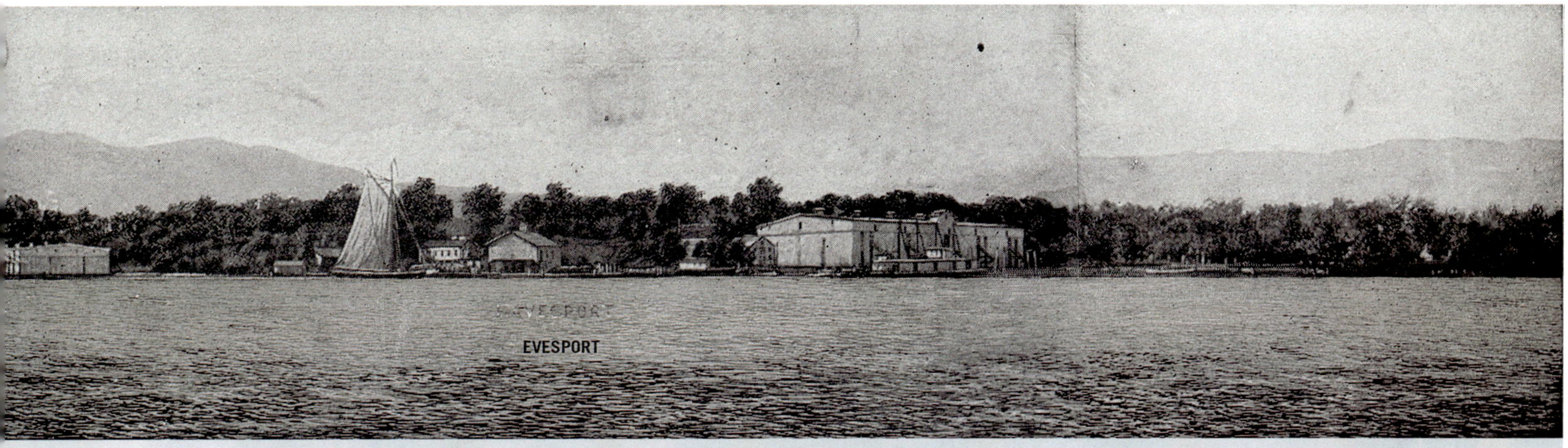

EVESPORT

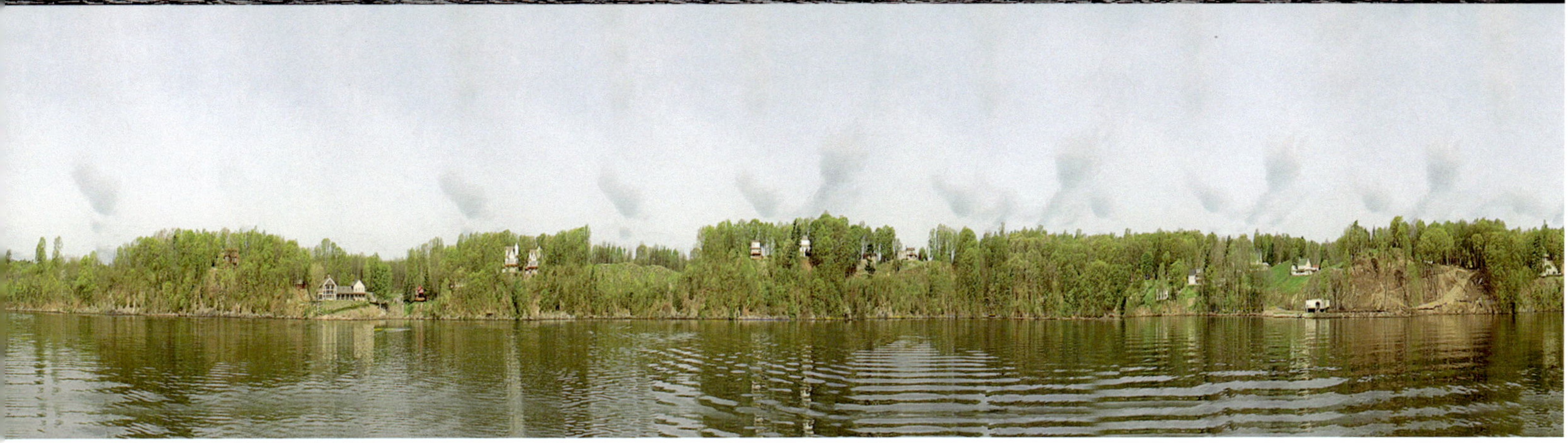

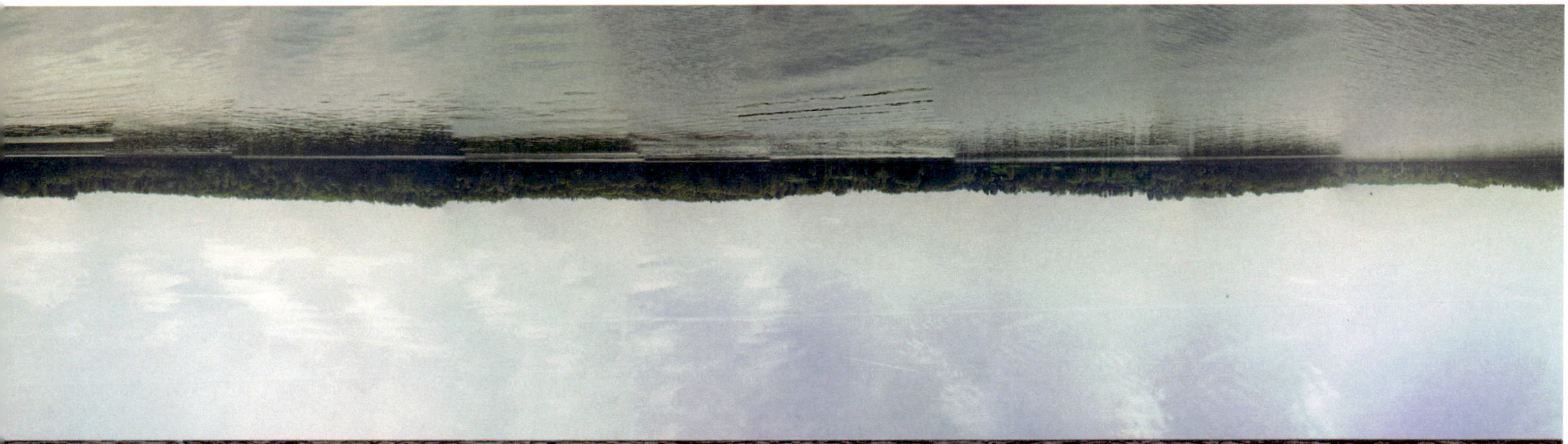

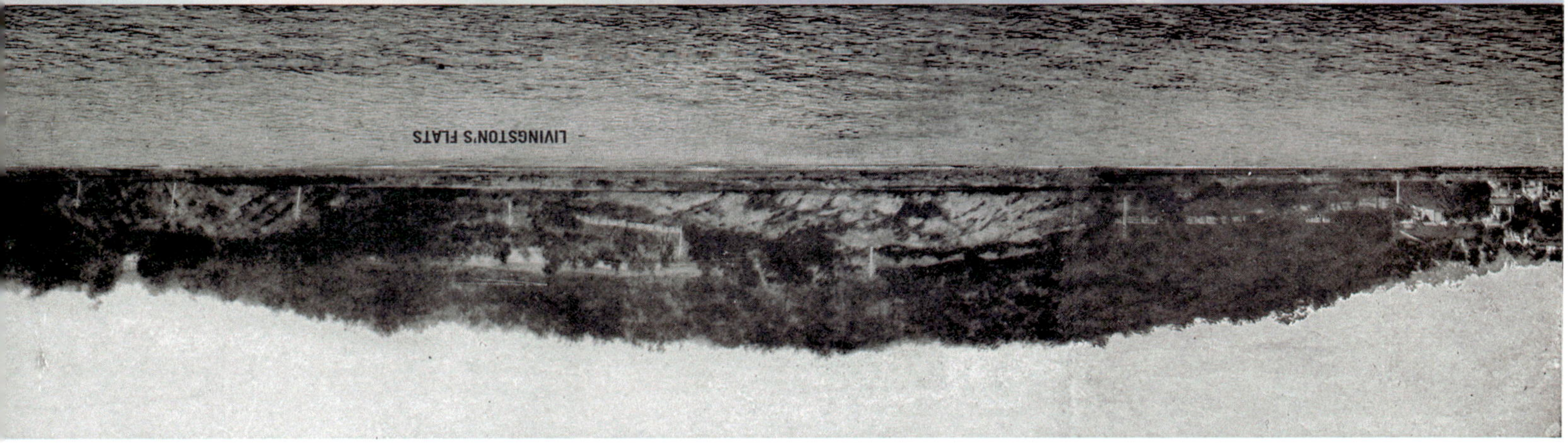

LIVINGSTON'S FLATS

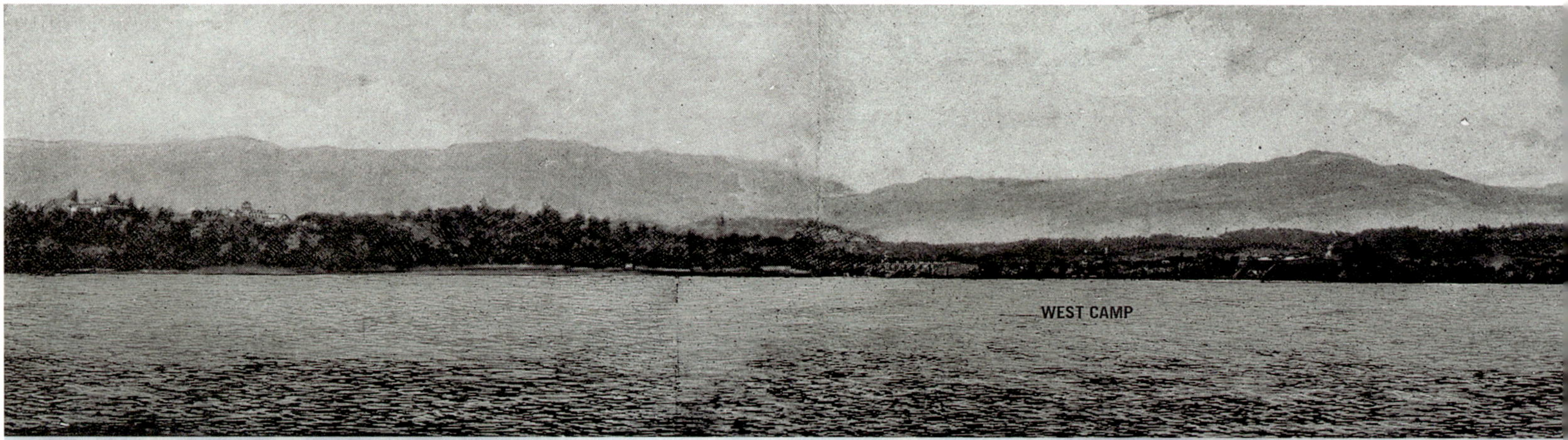

WEST CAMP

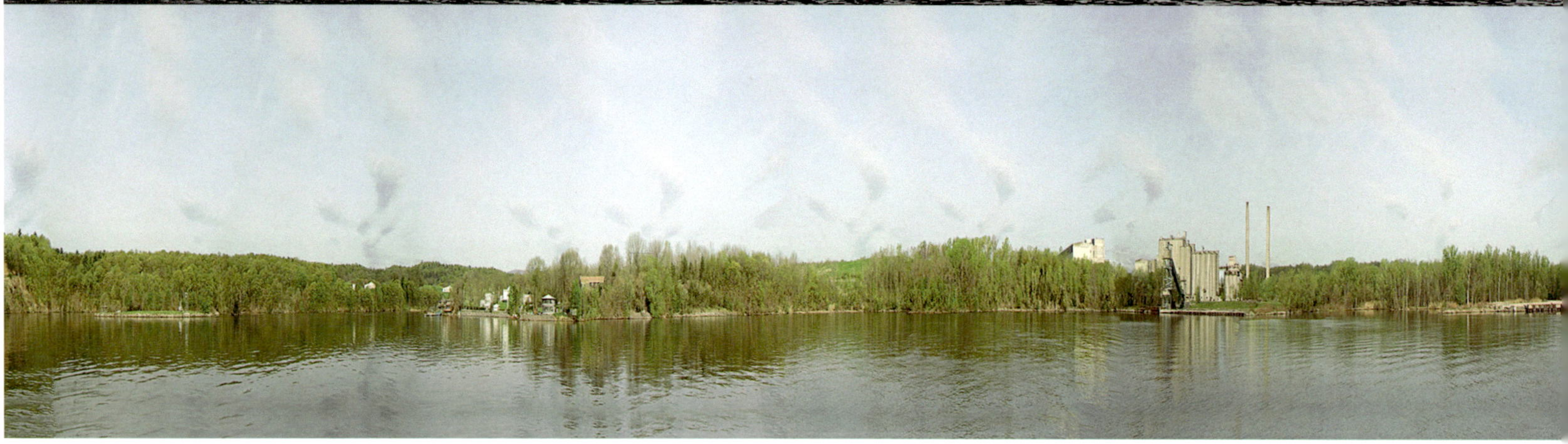

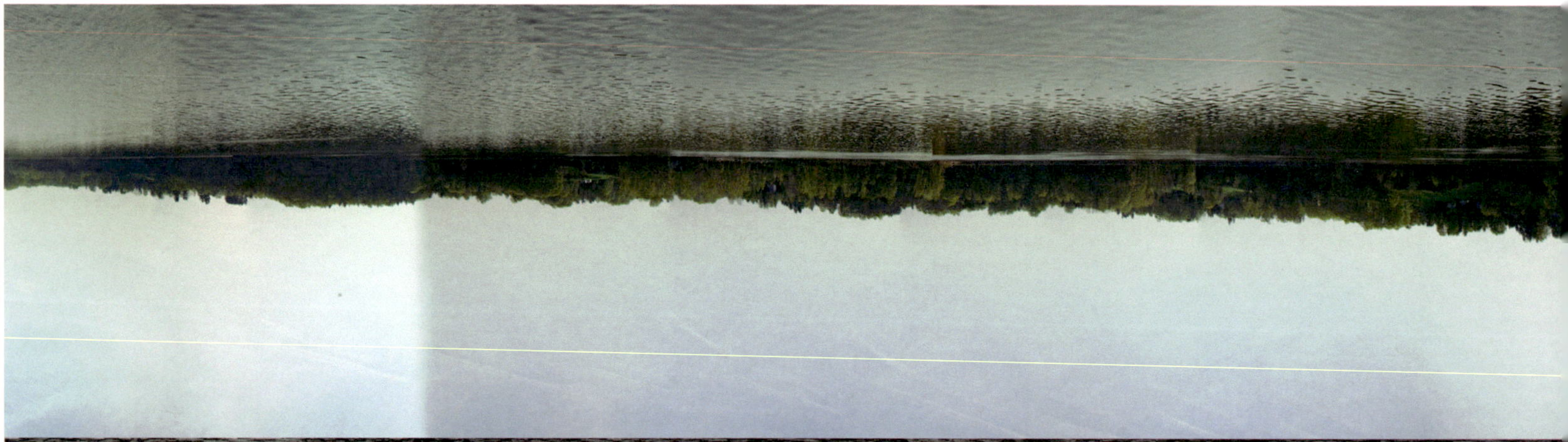

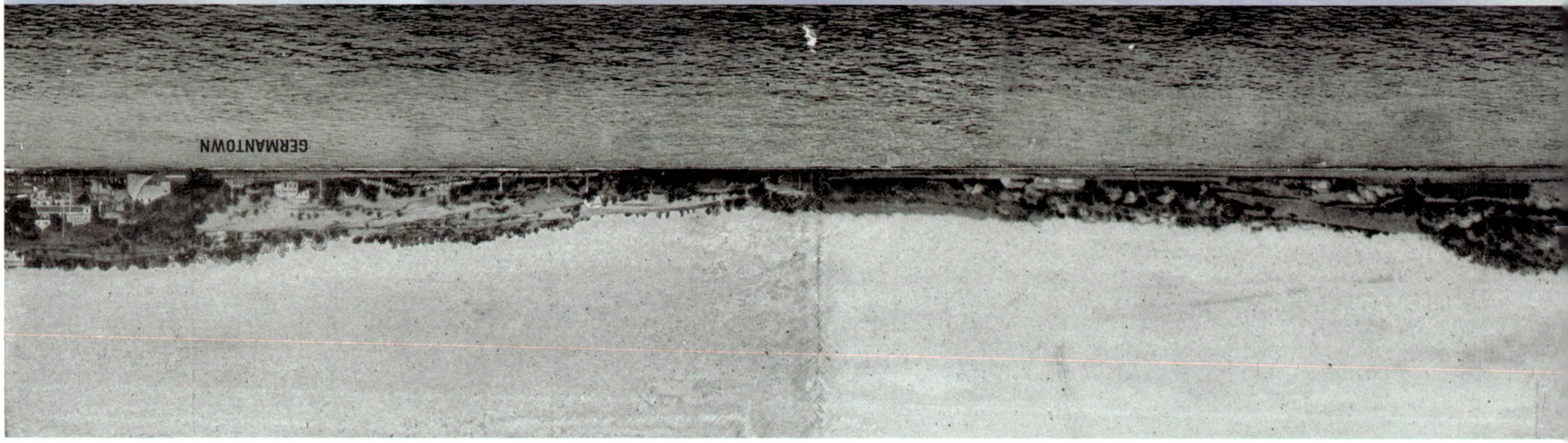

GERMANTOWN

East Bank

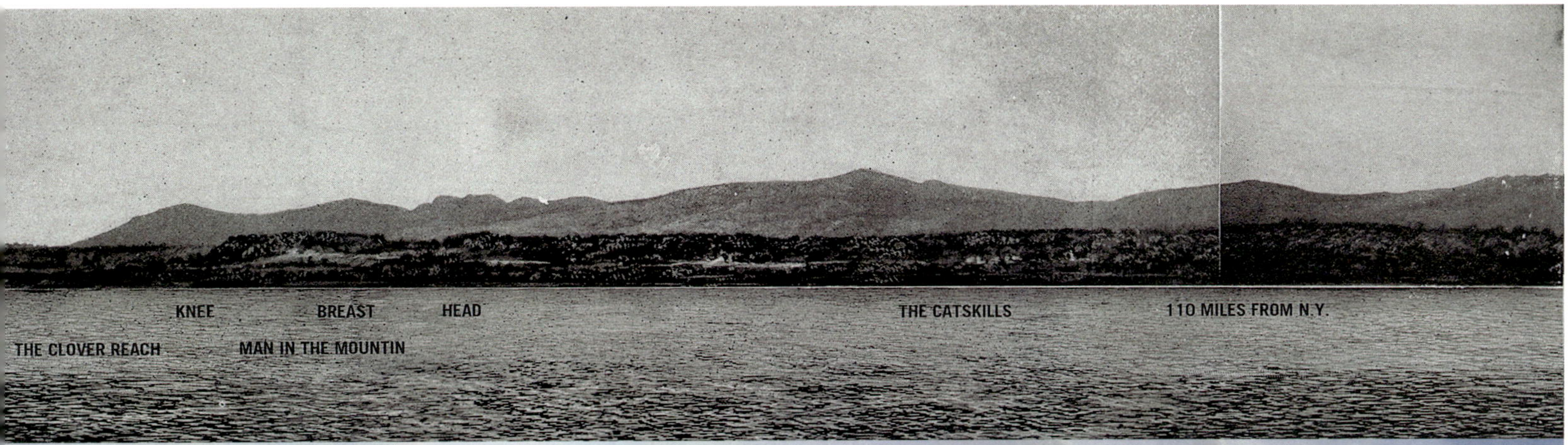

KNEE
BREAST
HEAD
THE CATSKILLS
110 MILES FROM N.Y.
THE CLOVER REACH
MAN IN THE MOUNTIN

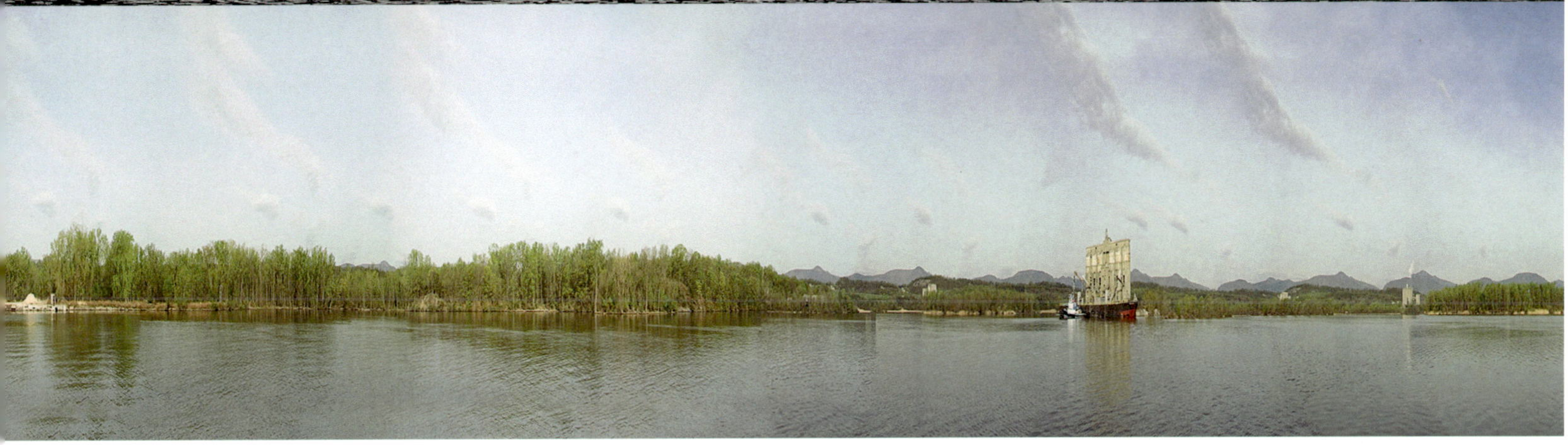

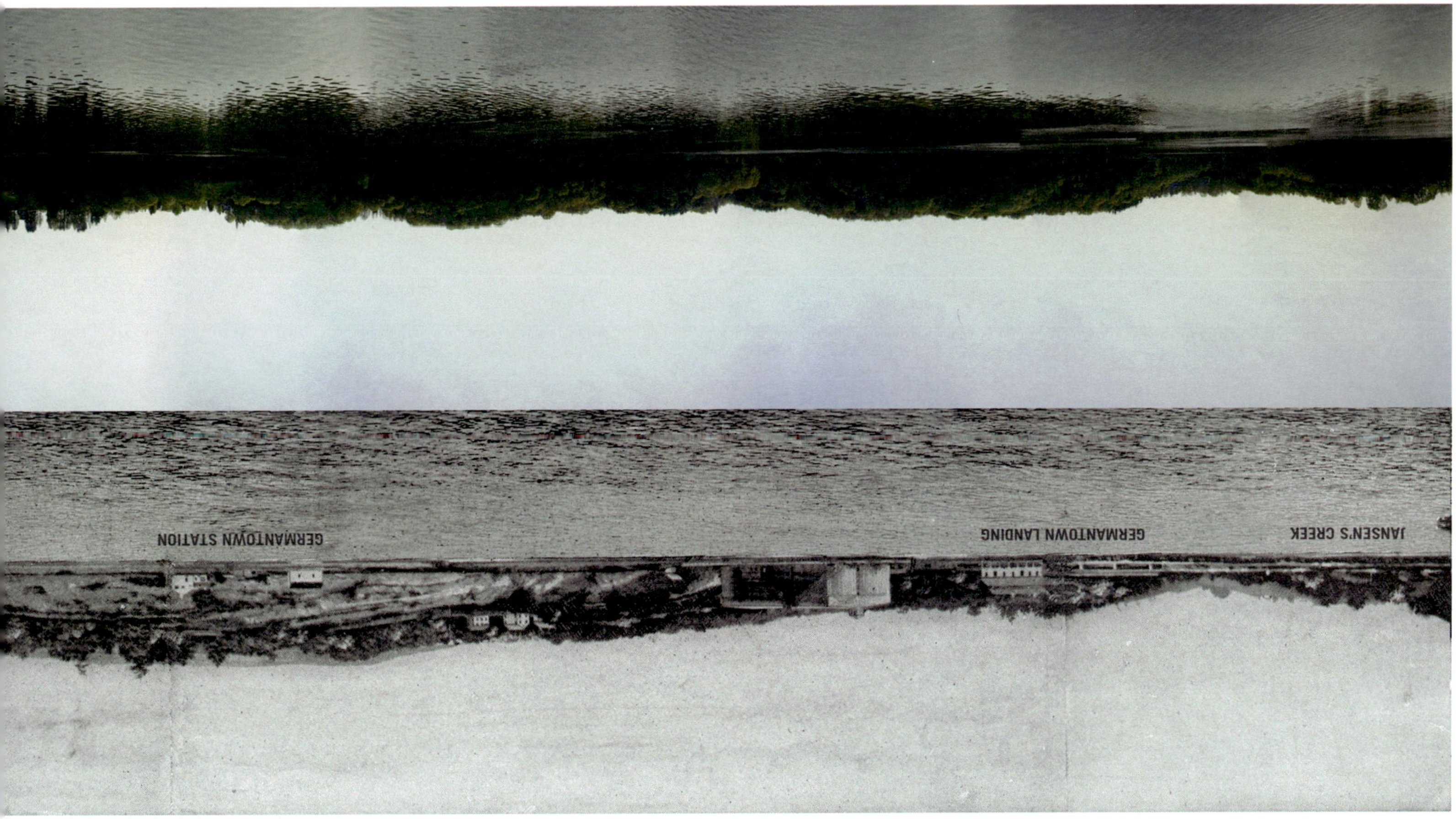

JANSEN'S CREEK
GERMANTOWN LANDING
GERMANTOWN STATION

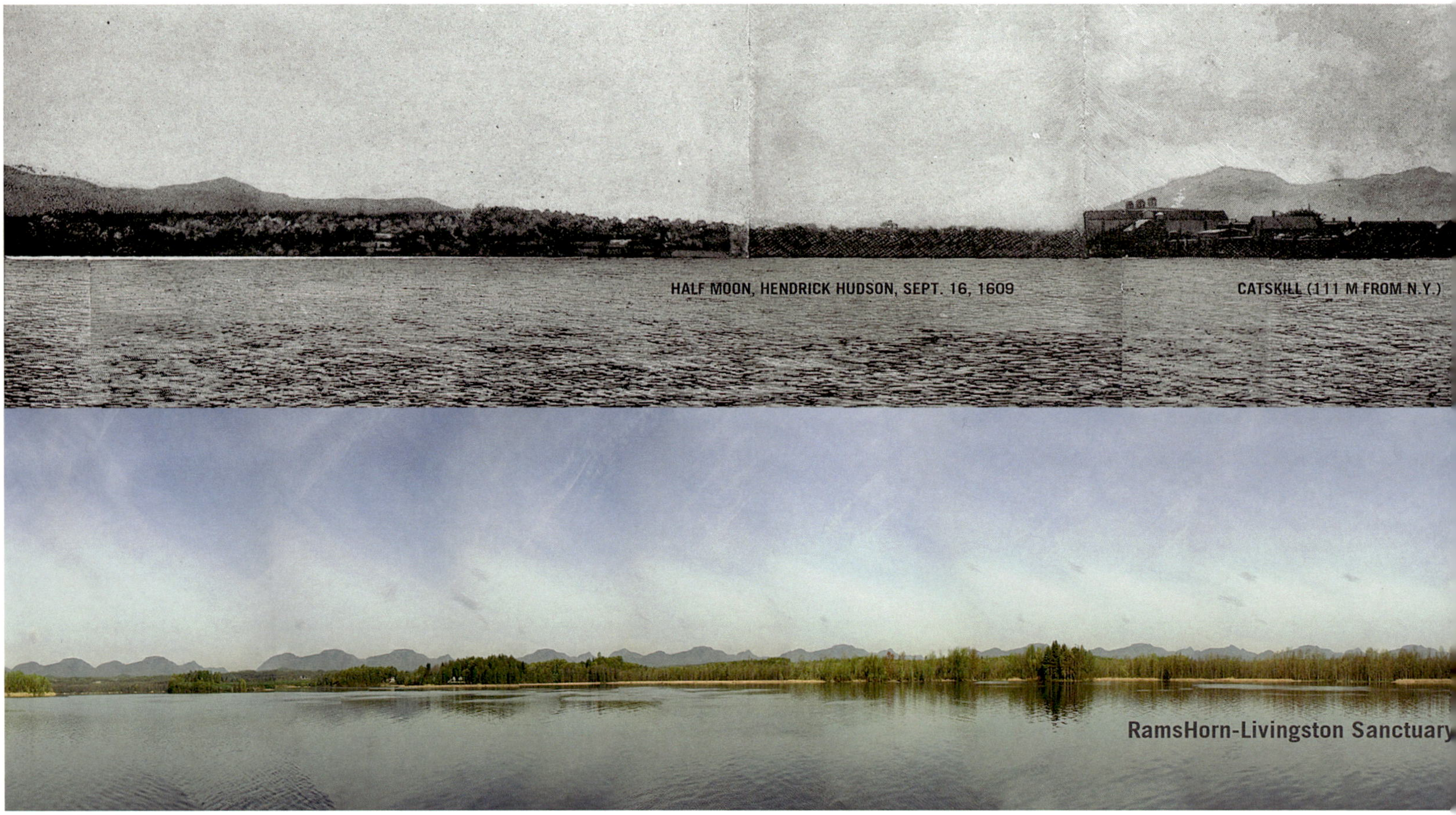

HALF MOON, HENDRICK HUDSON, SEPT. 16, 1609

CATSKILL (111 M FROM N.Y.)

RamsHorn-Livingston Sanctuary

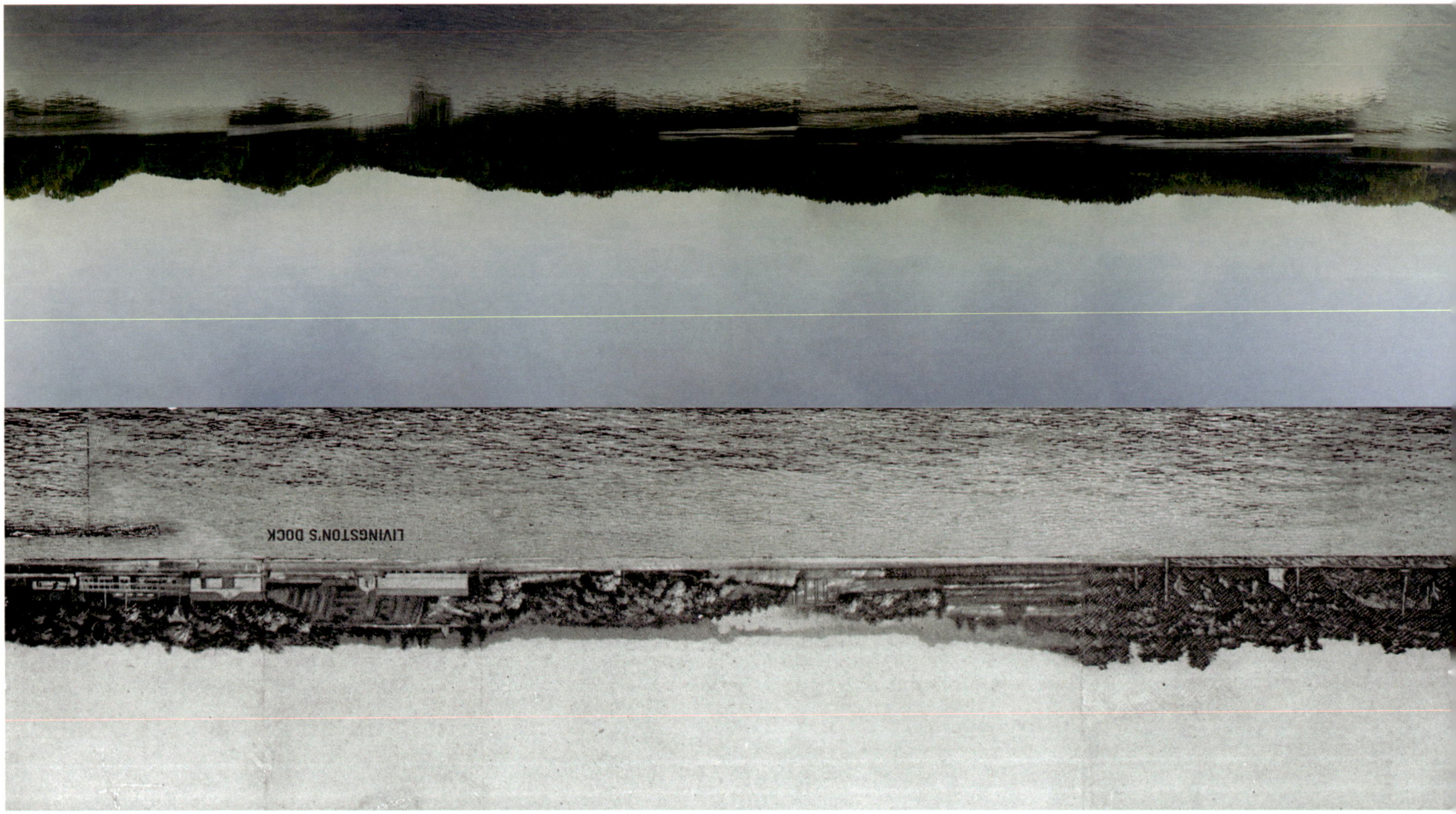

LIVINGSTON'S DOCK

East Bank

PROSPECT PARK HOTEL

Catskill Point Park

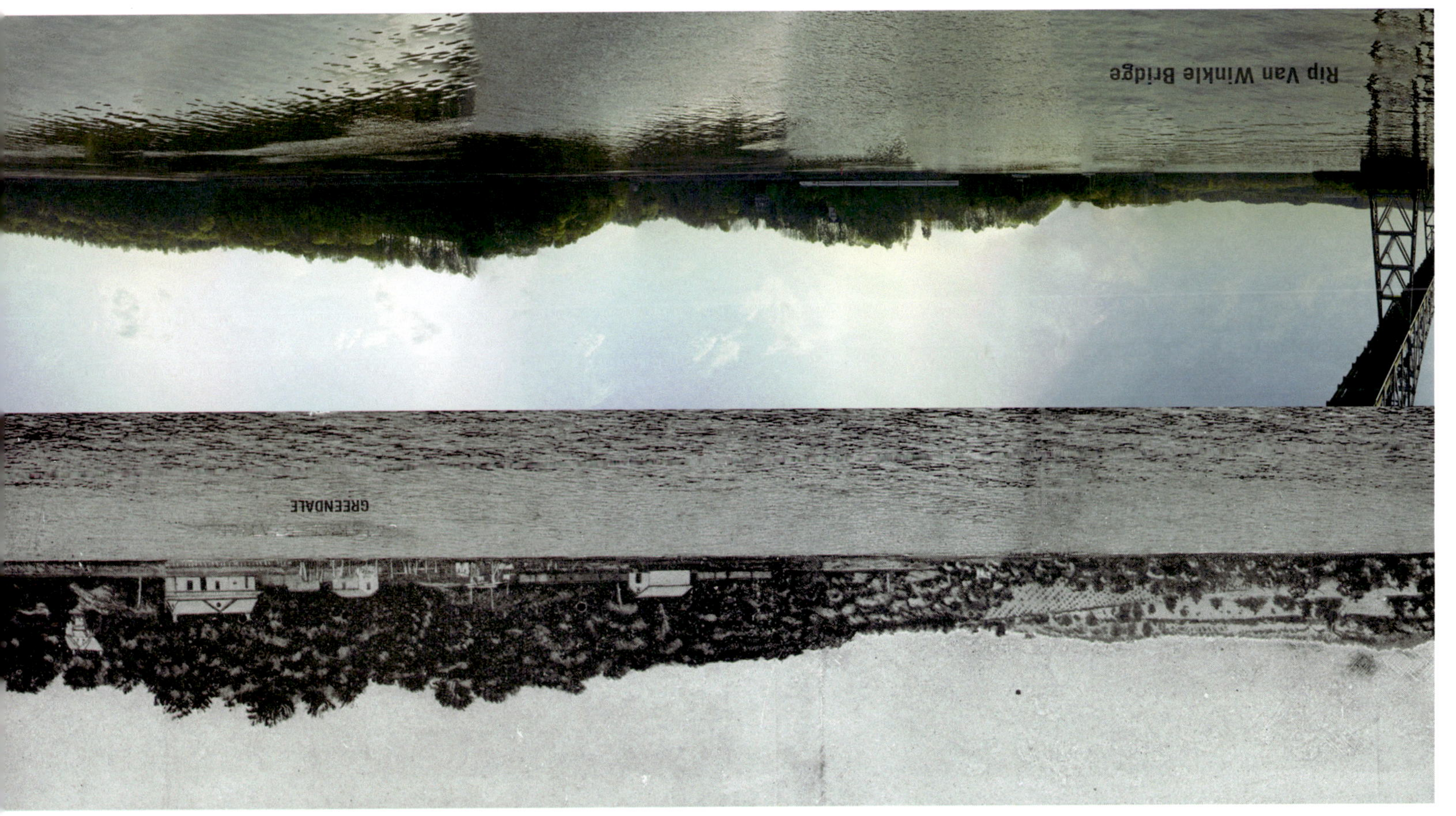

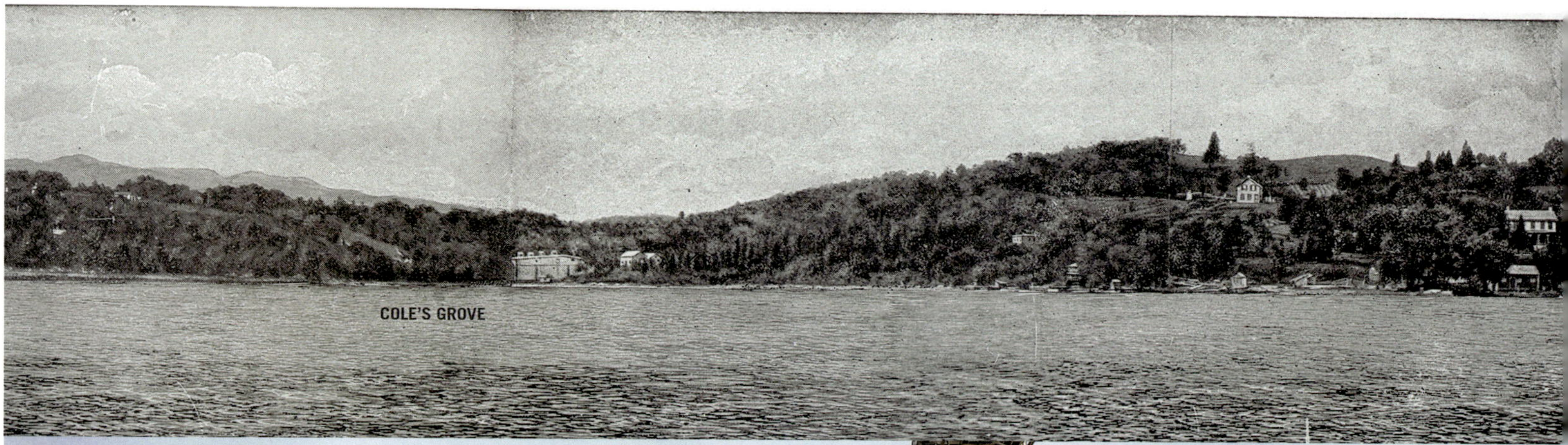

COLE'S GROVE

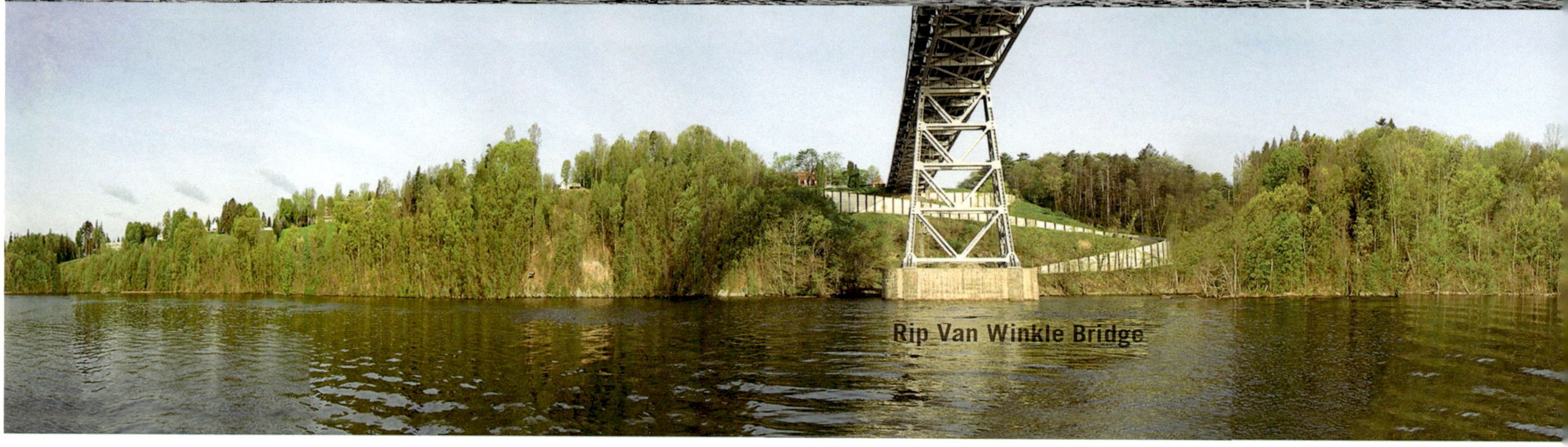

Rip Van Winkle Bridge

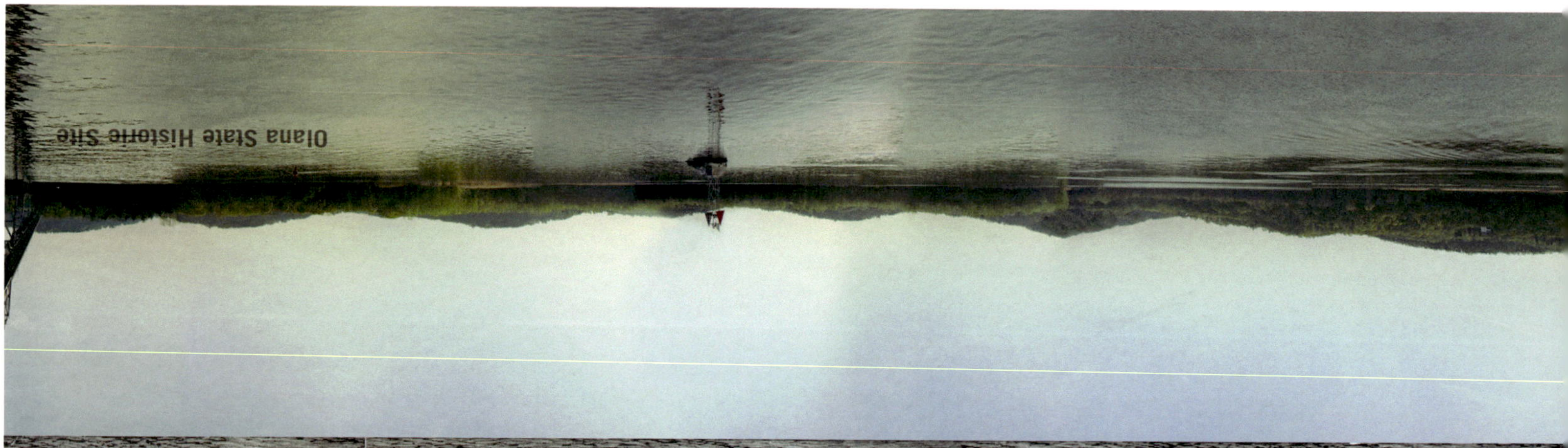

Olana State Historic Site

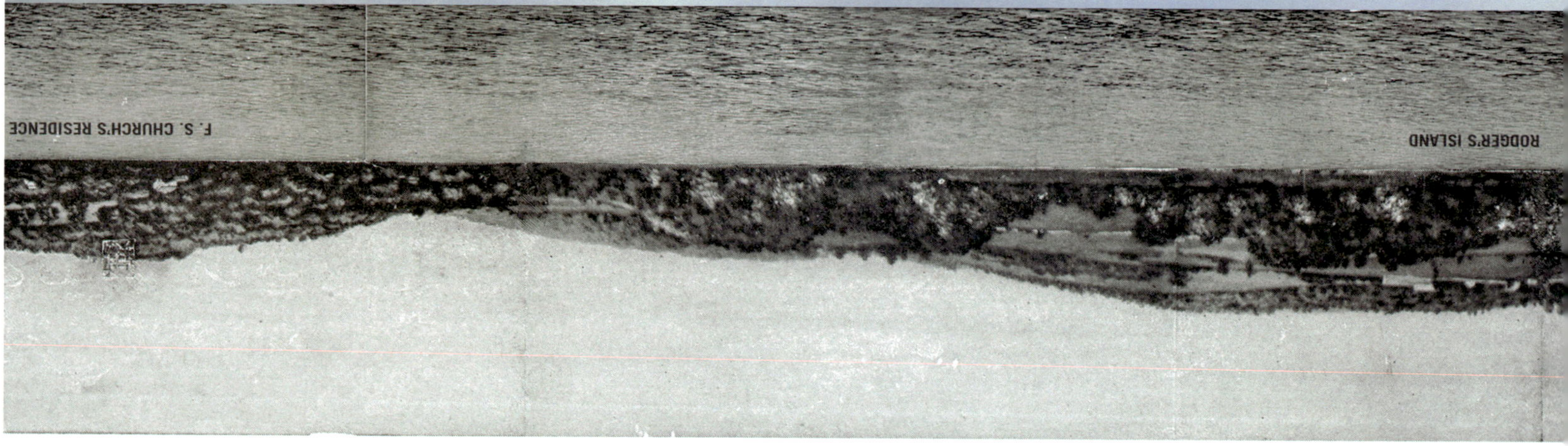

F. S. CHURCH'S RESIDENCE

RODGER'S ISLAND

East Bank

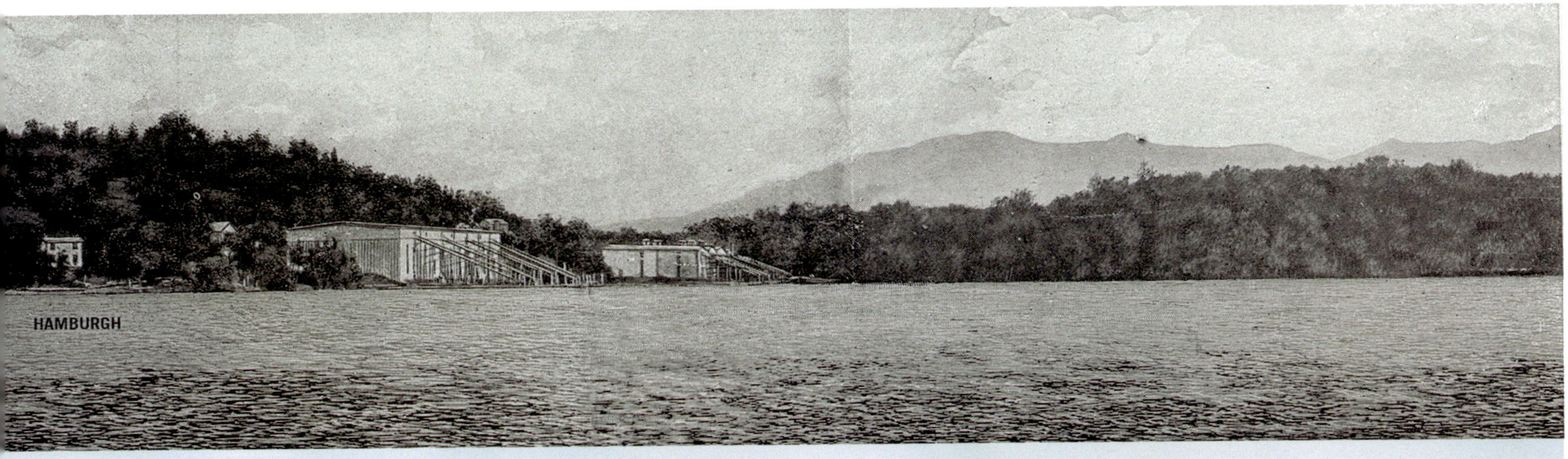

HAMBURGH

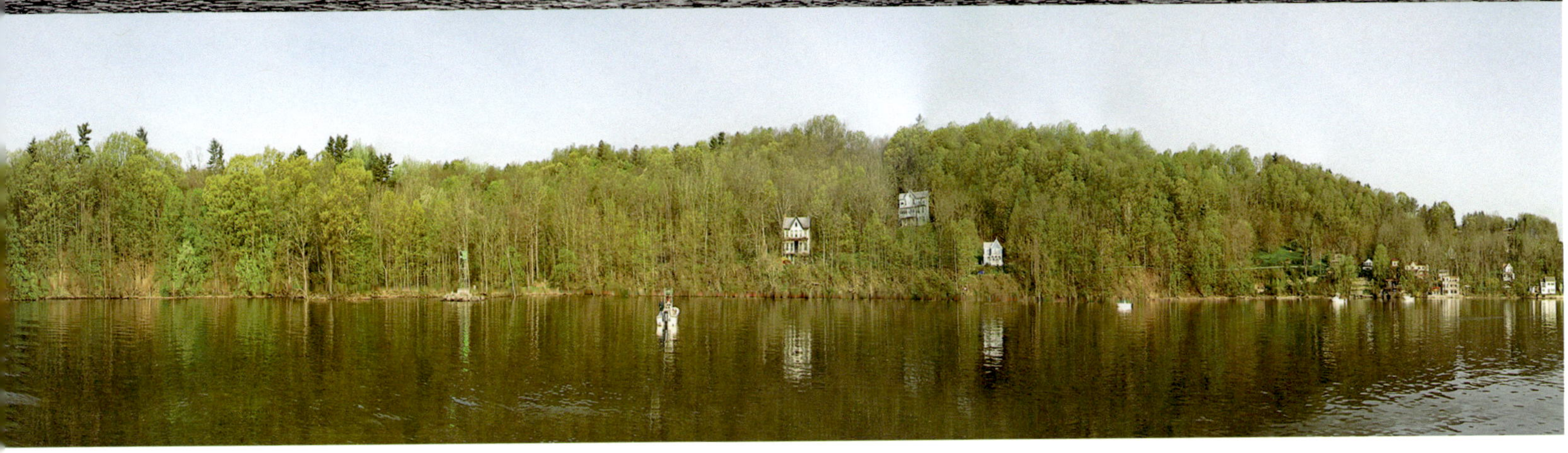

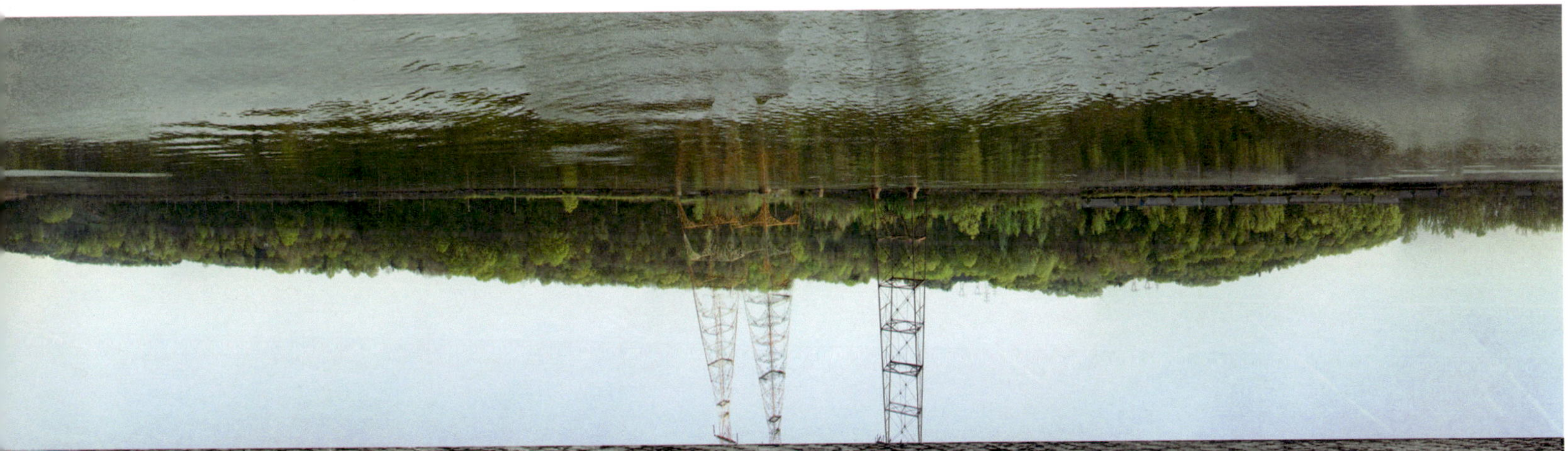

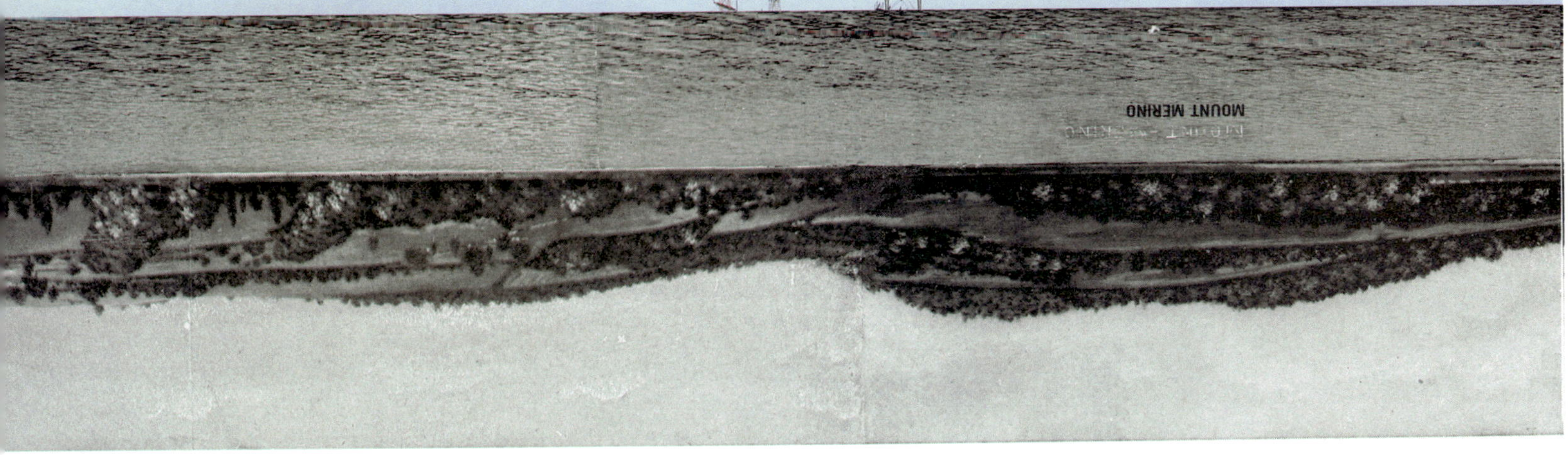

MOUNT MERINO

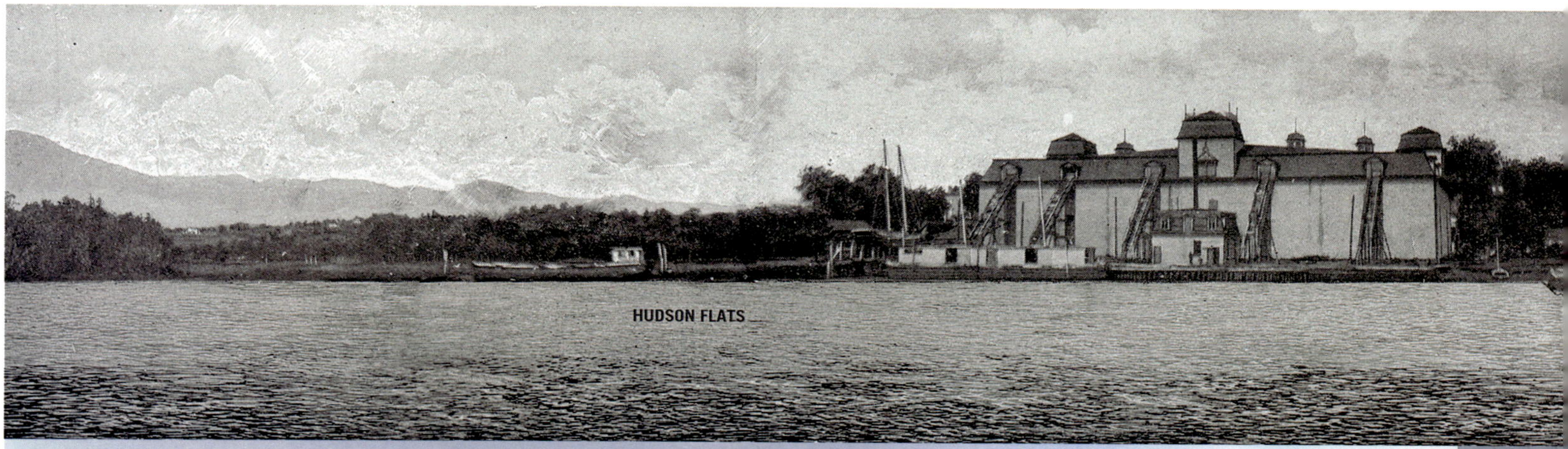

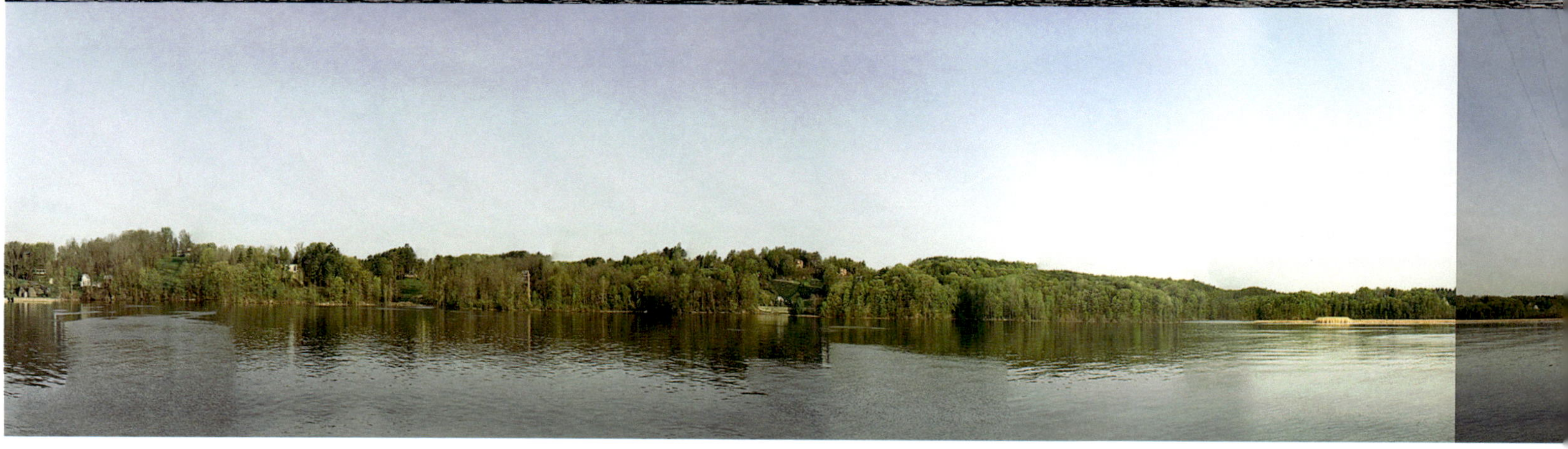

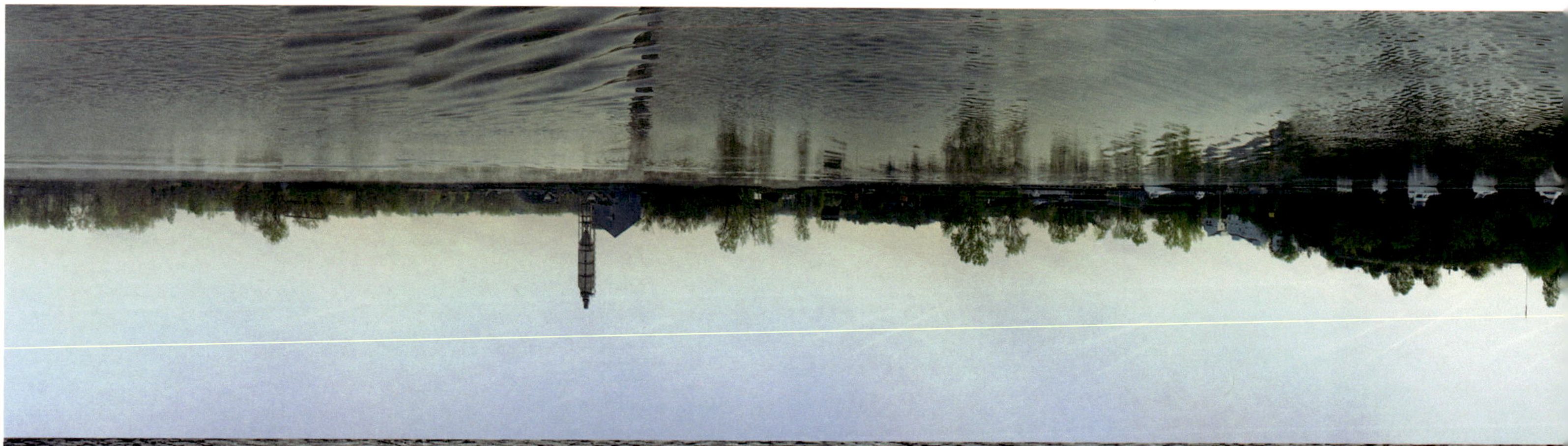

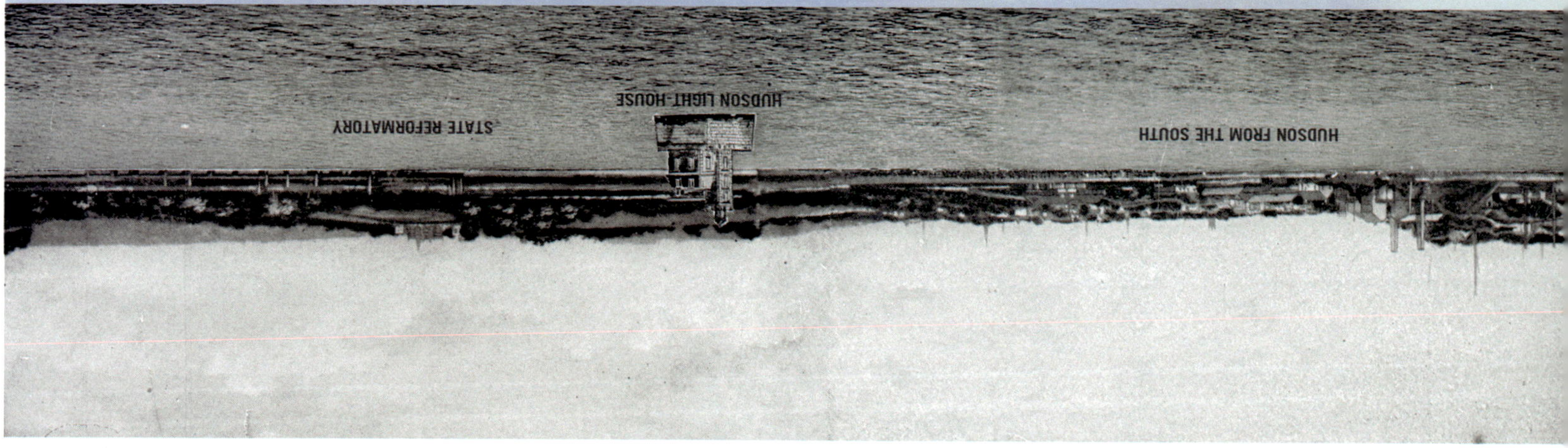

HUDSON FROM THE SOUTH

HUDSON LIGHT-HOUSE

STATE REFORMATORY

HUDSON FLATS

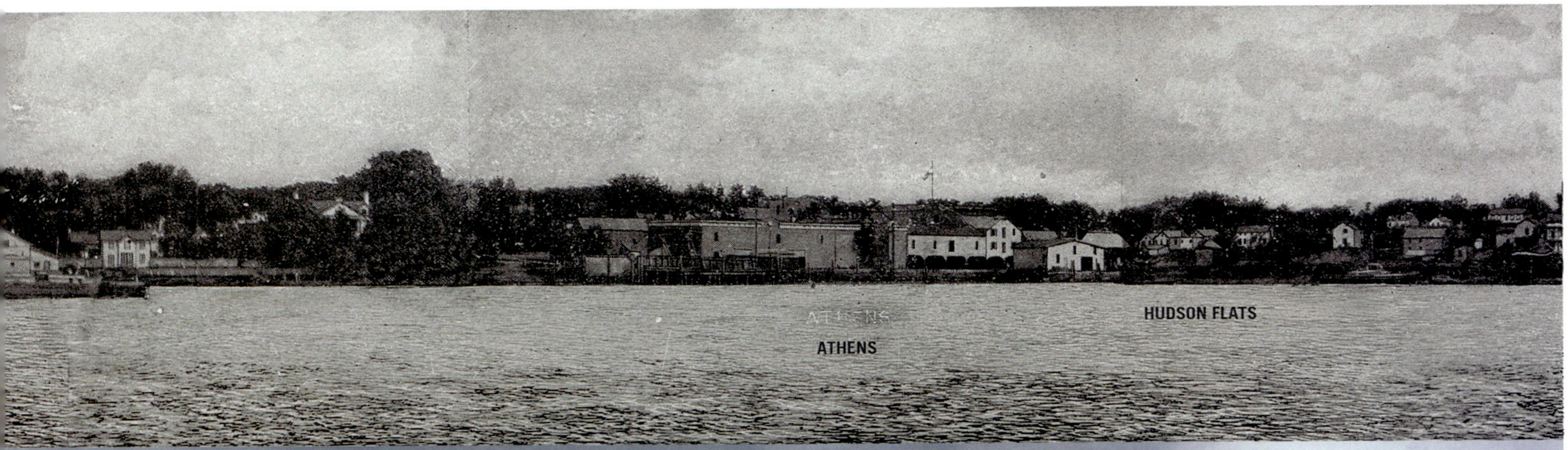

HUDSON FLATS

ATHENS

Hudson-Athens Lighthouse

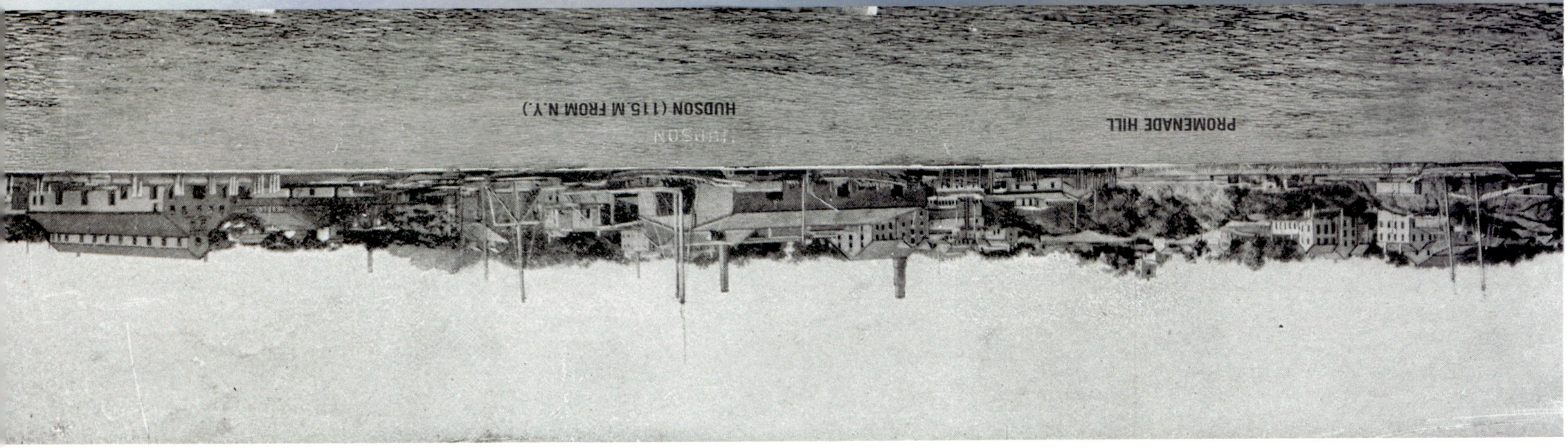

HUDSON (115 M FROM N.Y.)

PROMENADE HILL

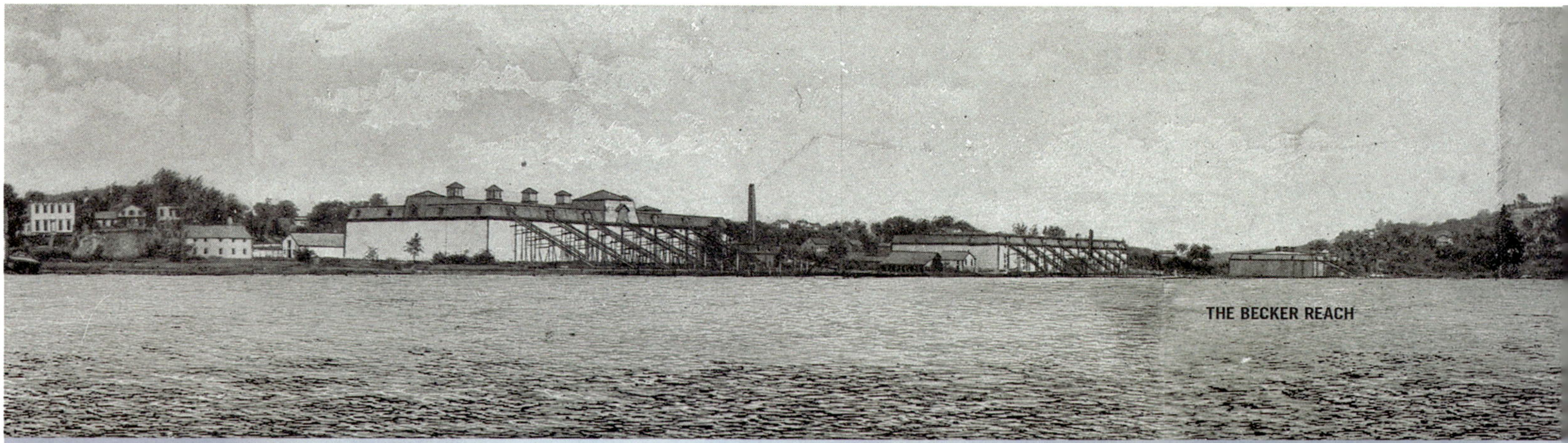

THE BECKER REACH

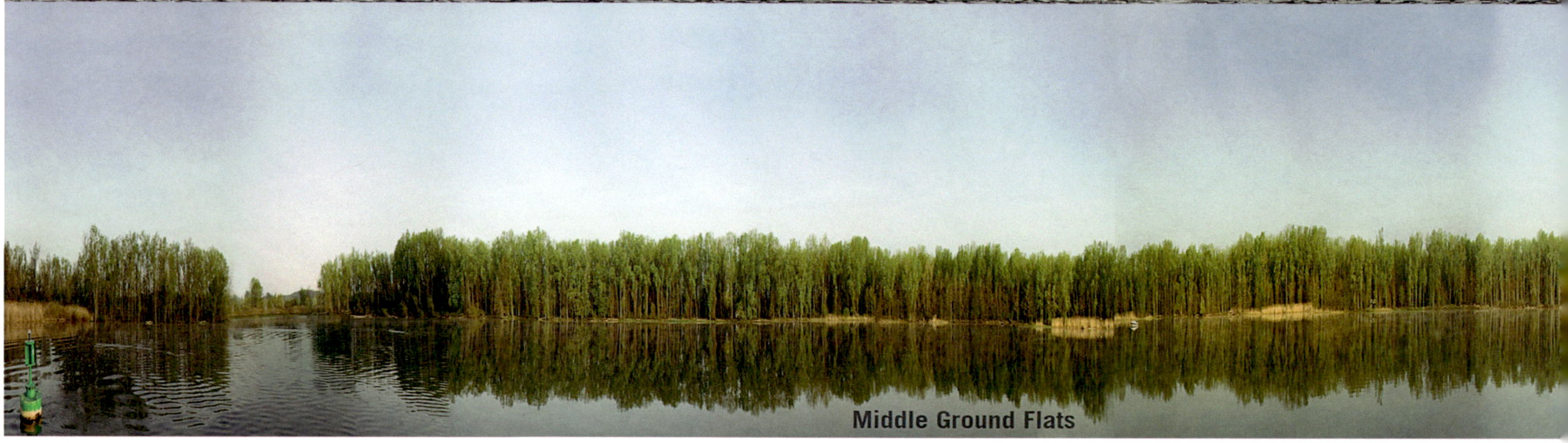

Middle Ground Flats

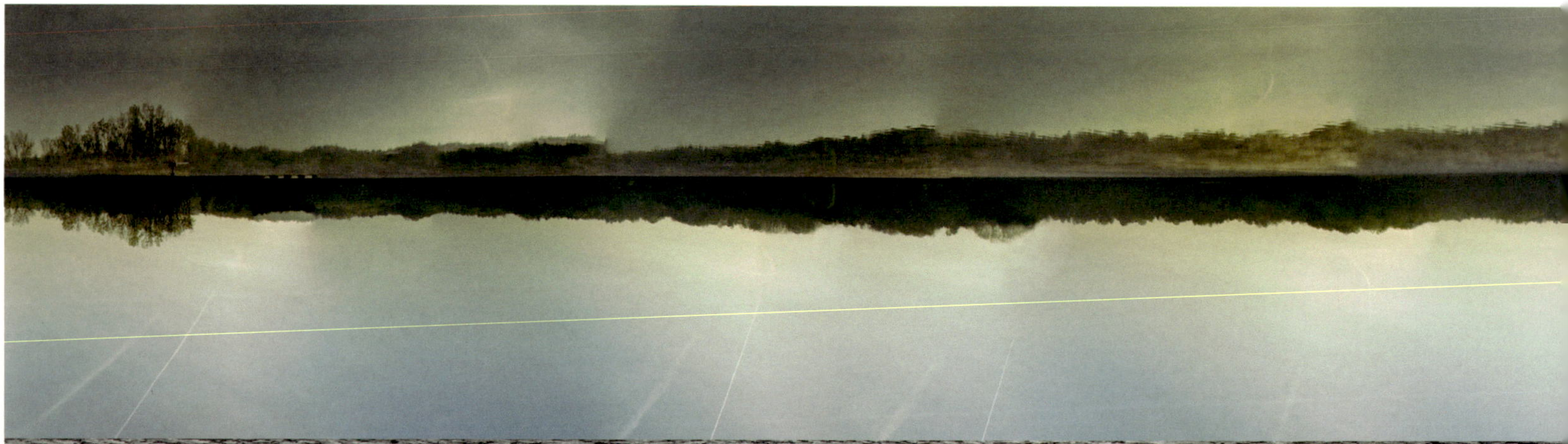

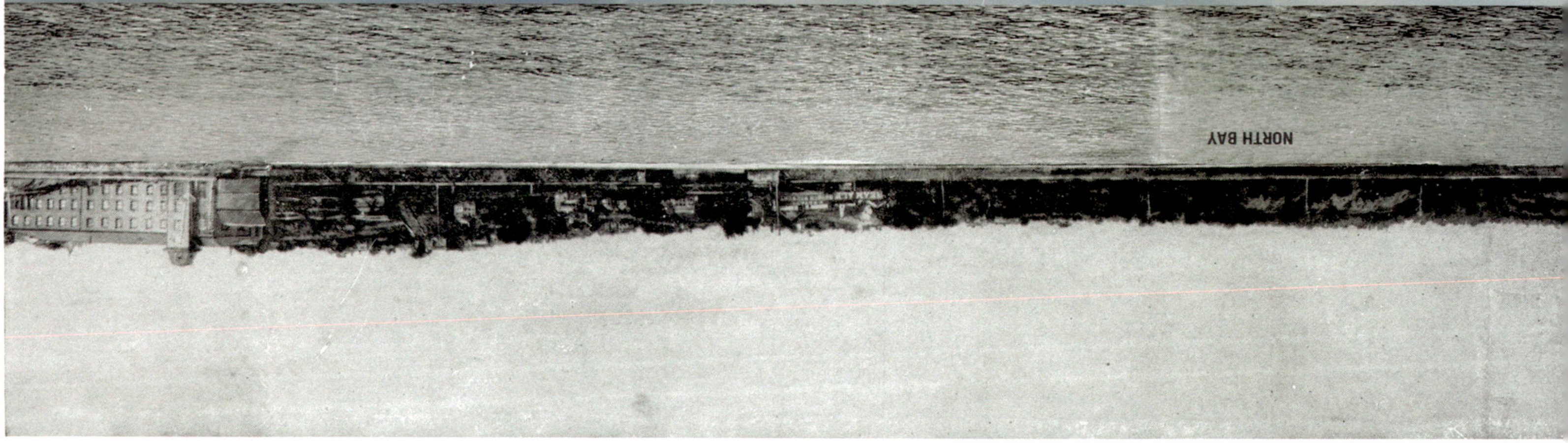

NORTH BAY

East Bank

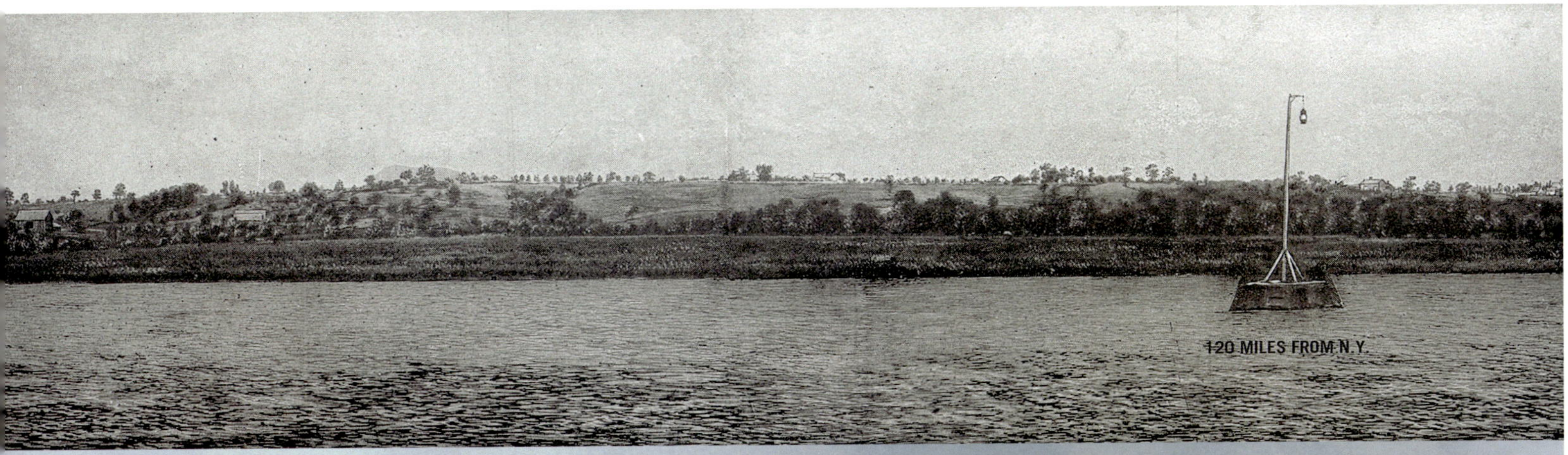

120 MILES FROM N.Y.

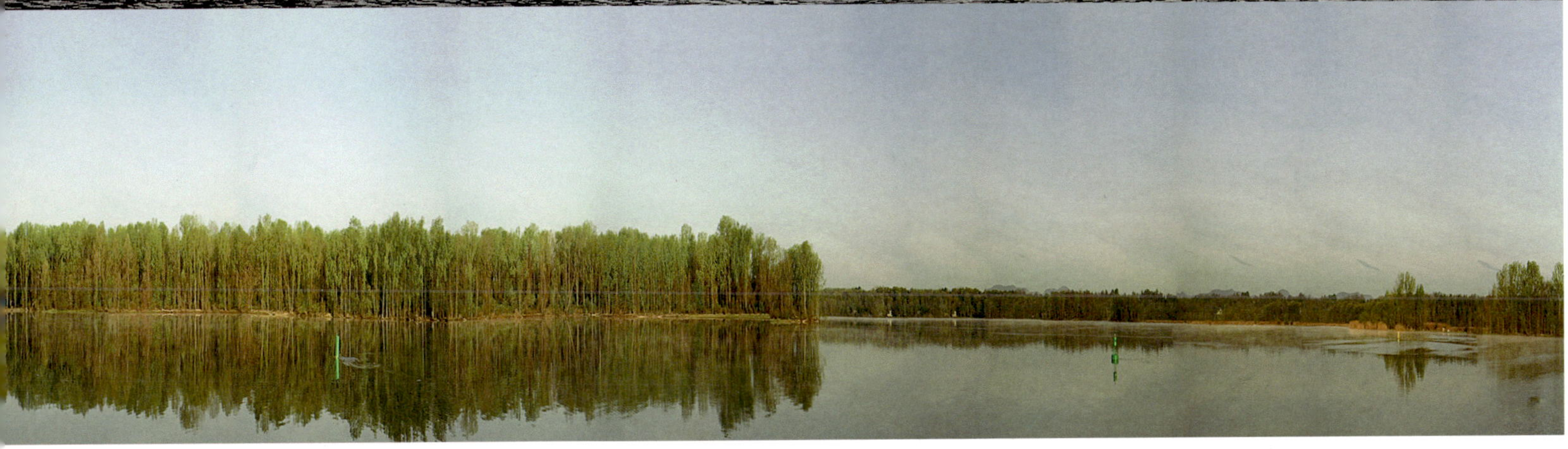

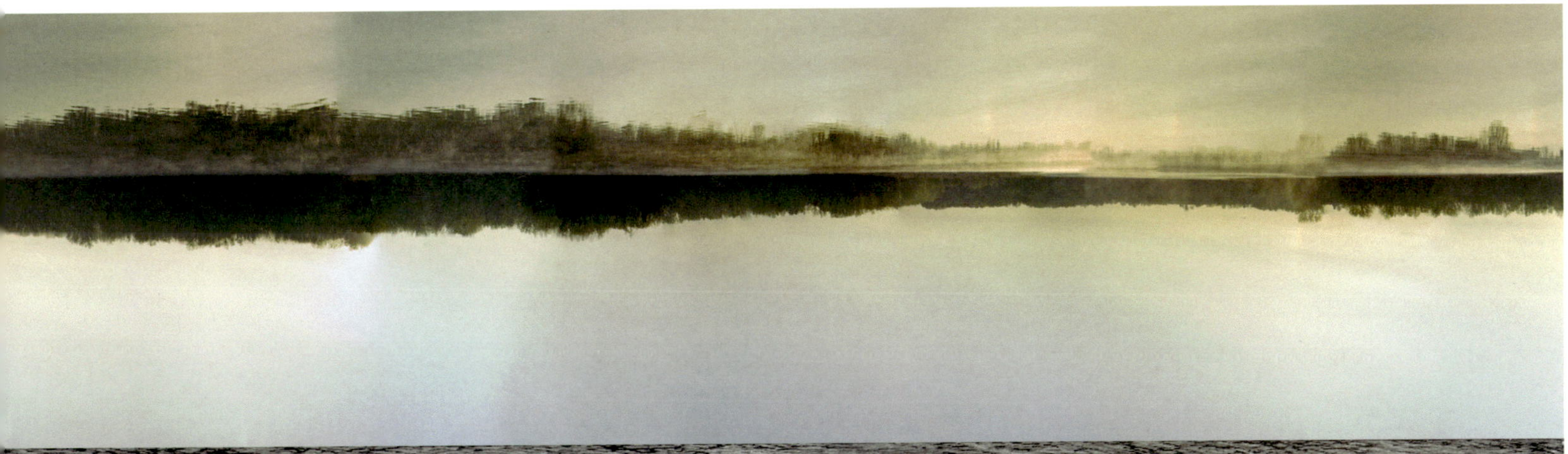

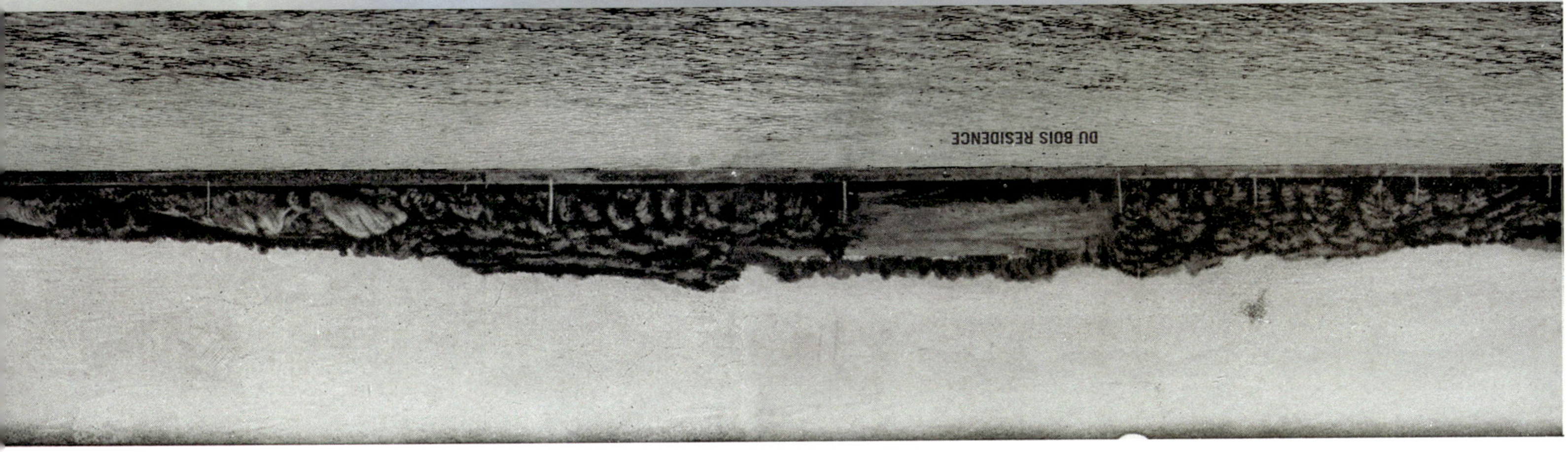

DU BOIS RESIDENCE

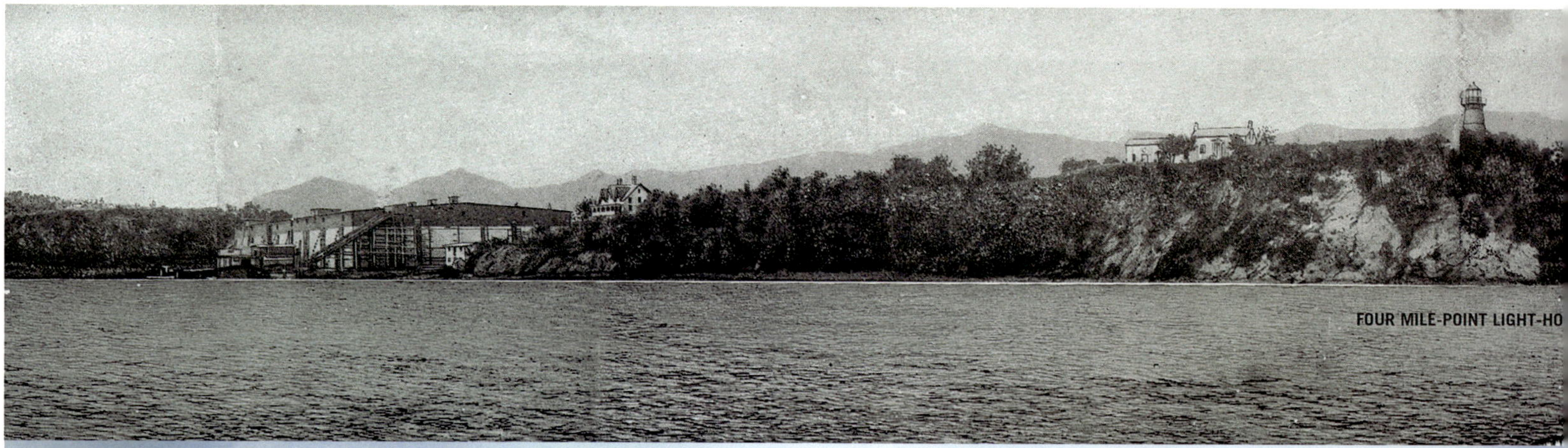

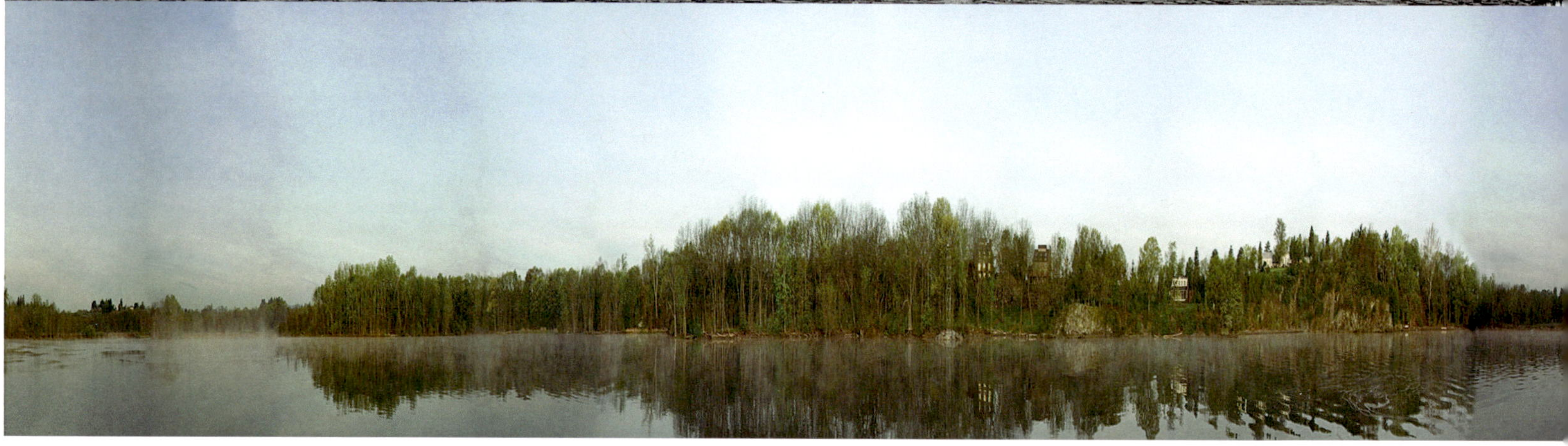

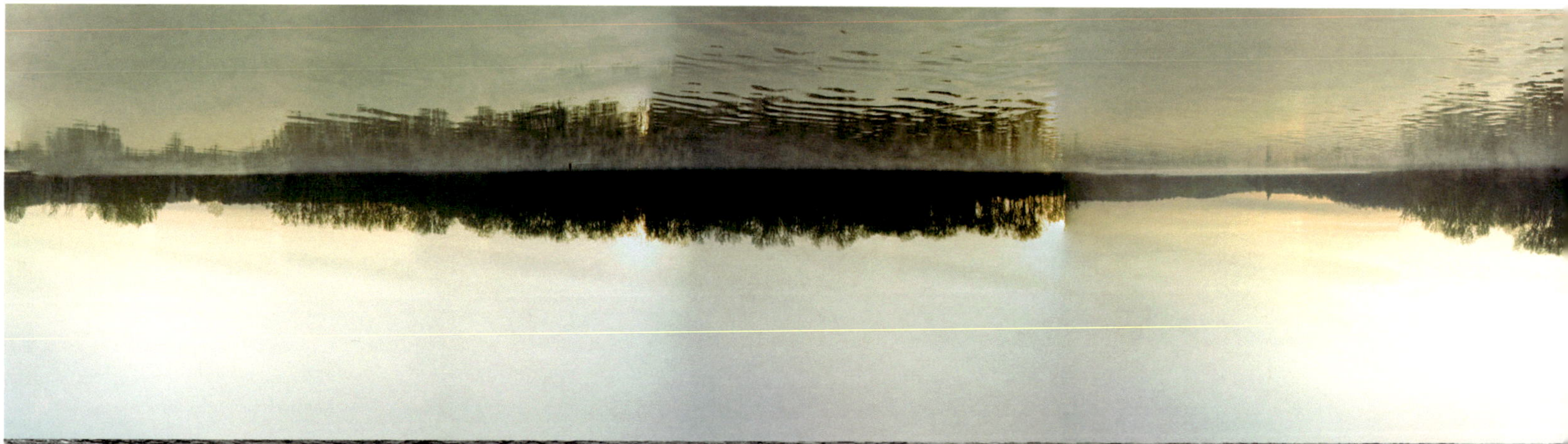

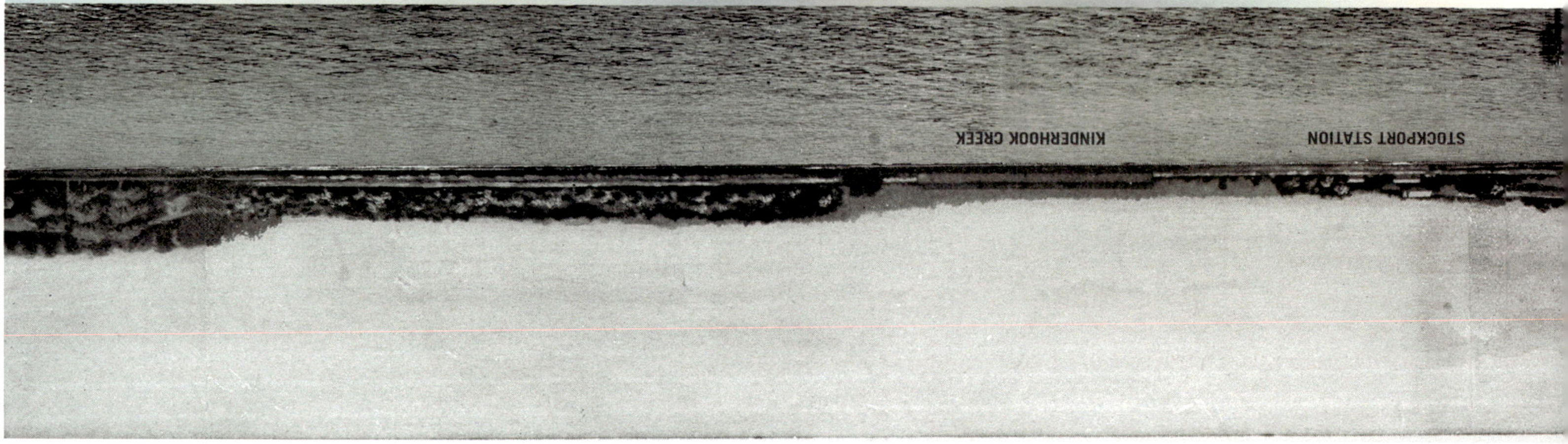

STOCKPORT STATION

KINDERHOOK CREEK

FOUR MILE-POINT LIGHT-HO

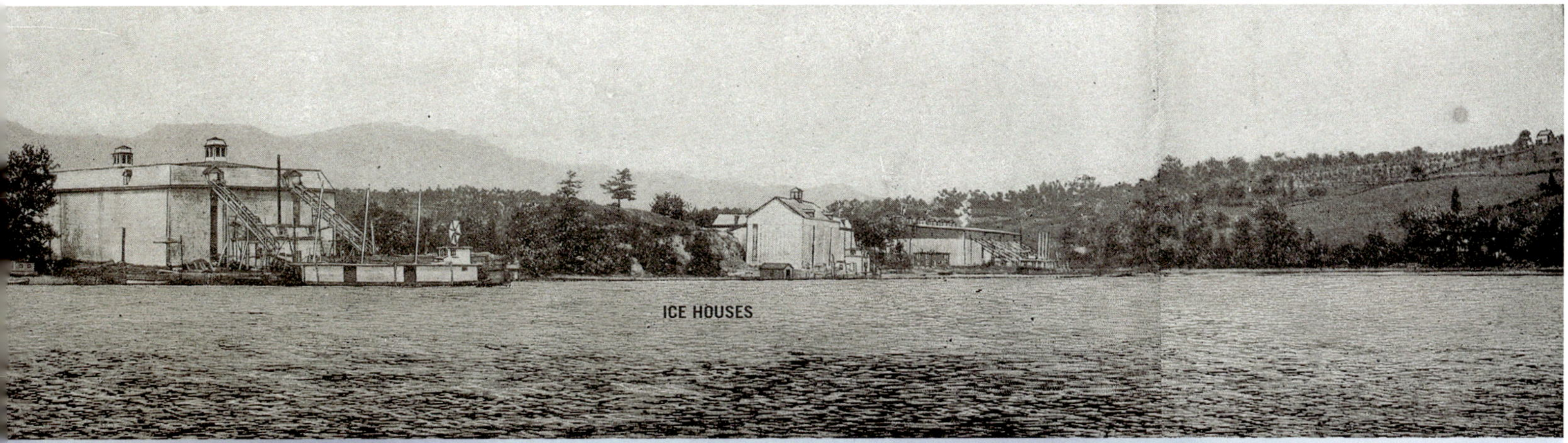

ICE HOUSES

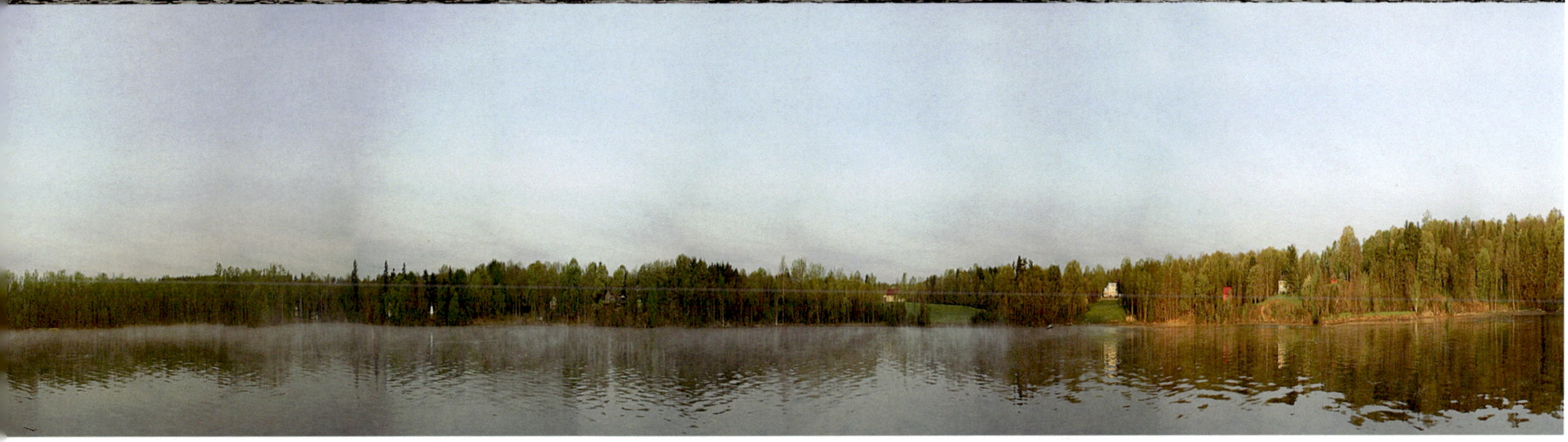

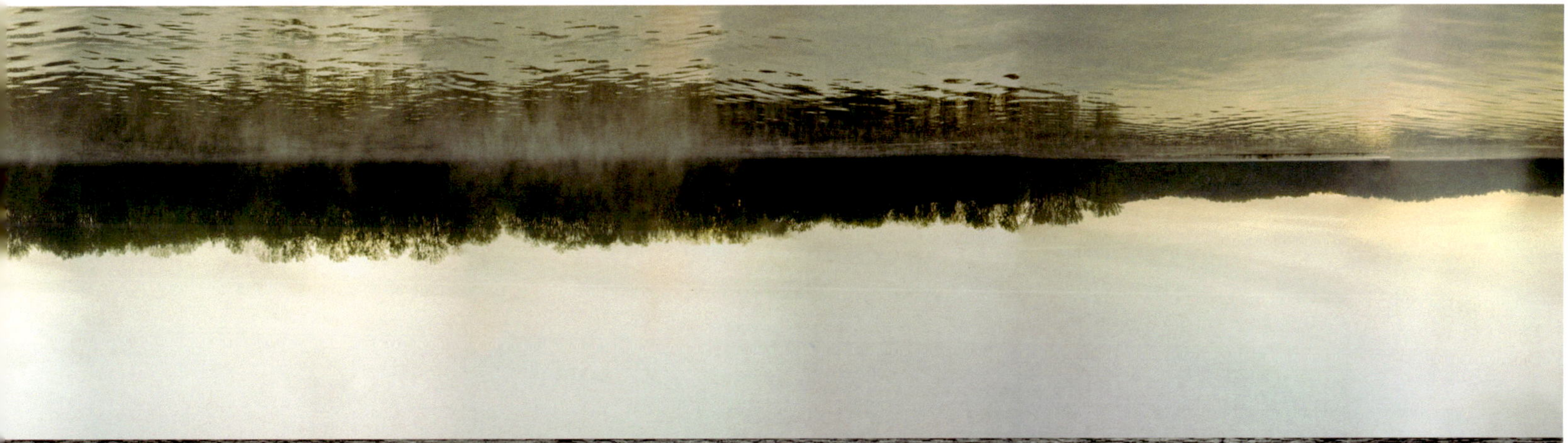

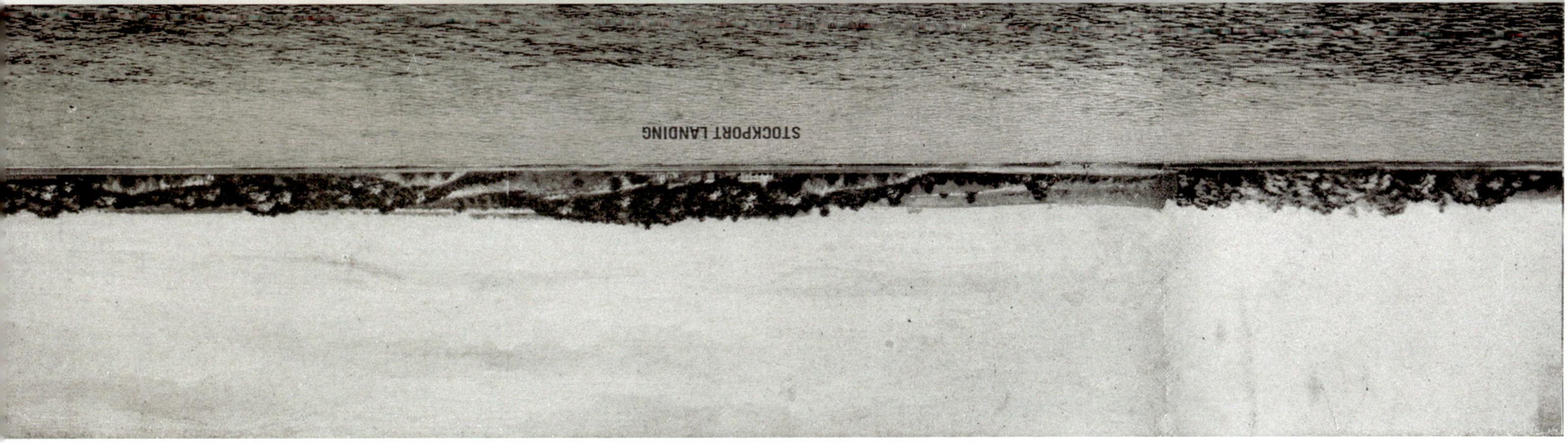

STOCKPORT LANDING

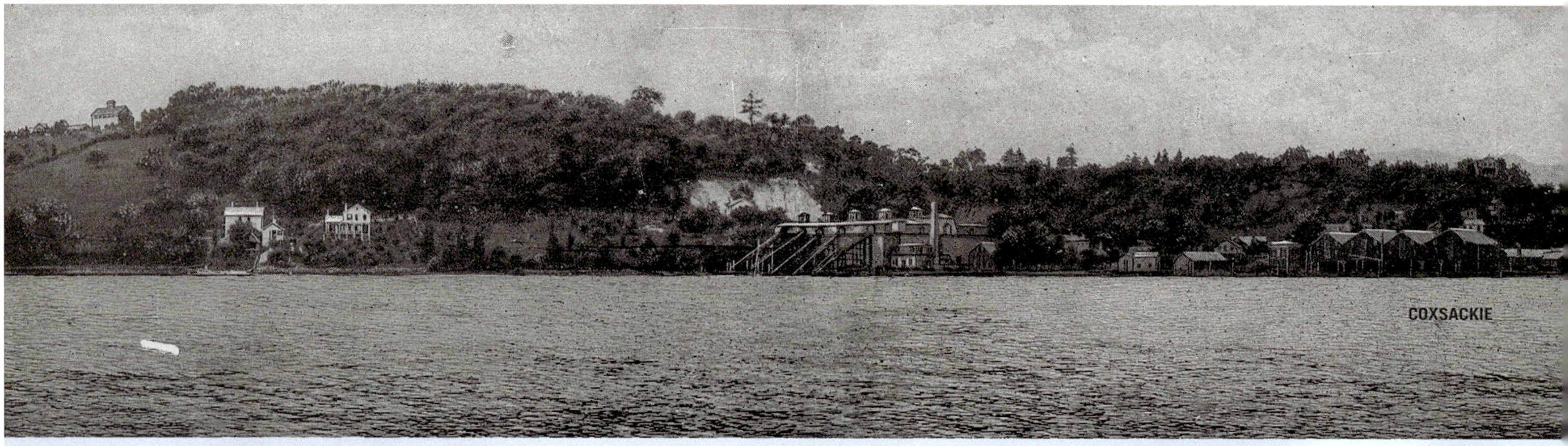

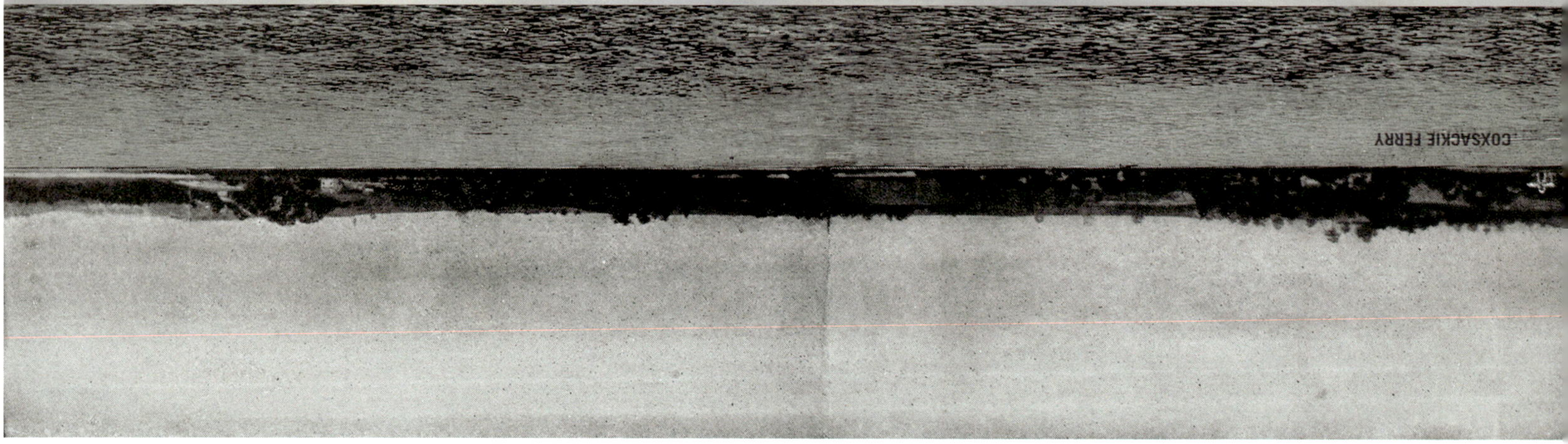

COXSACKIE FERRY

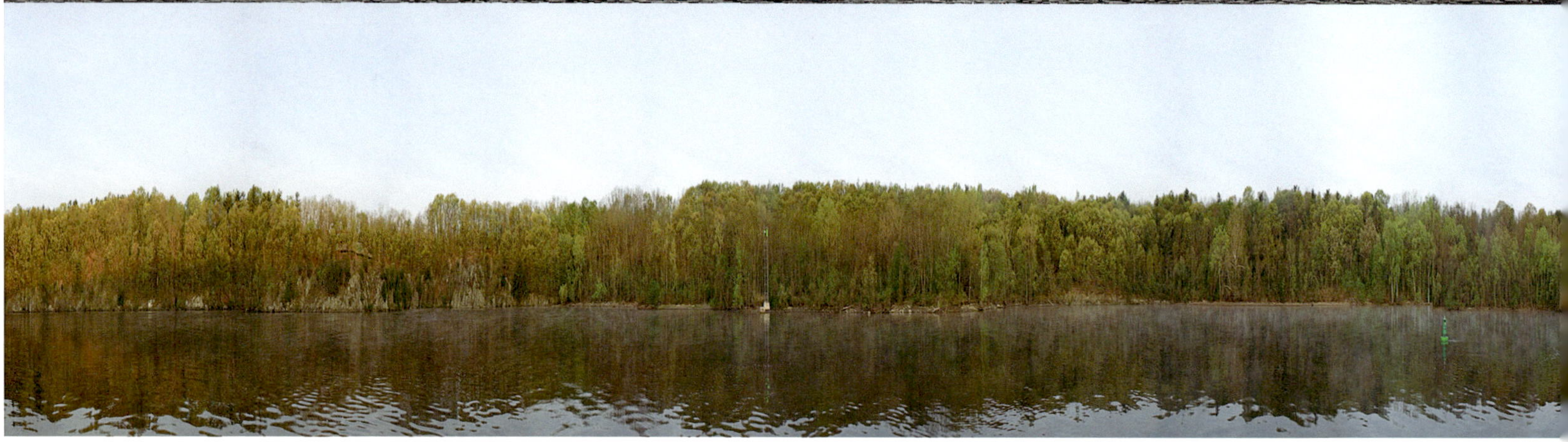

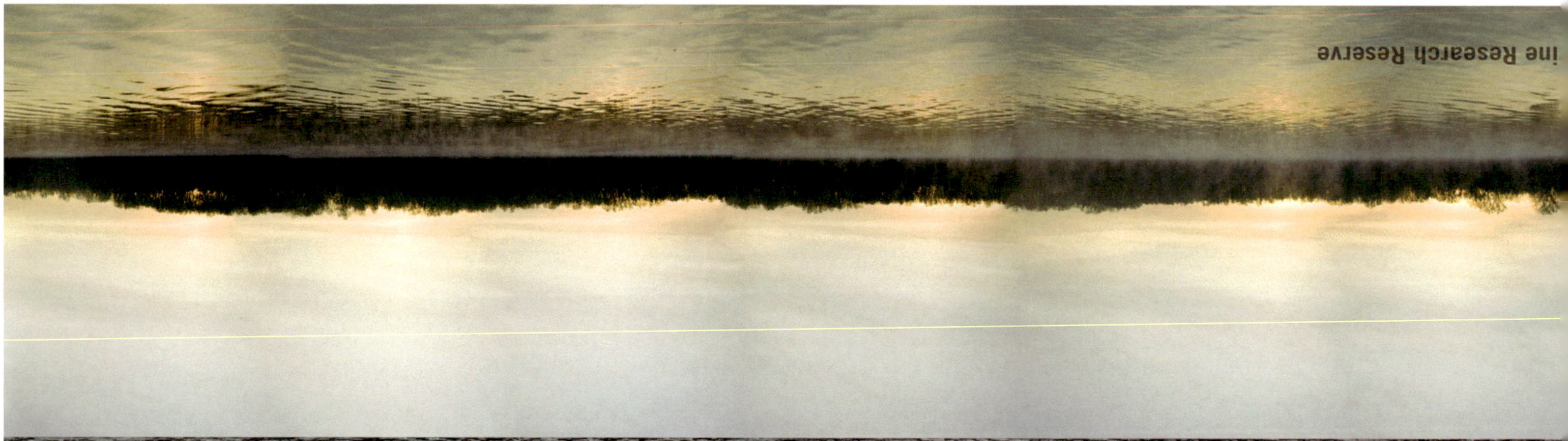

ine Research Reserve

COXSACKIE

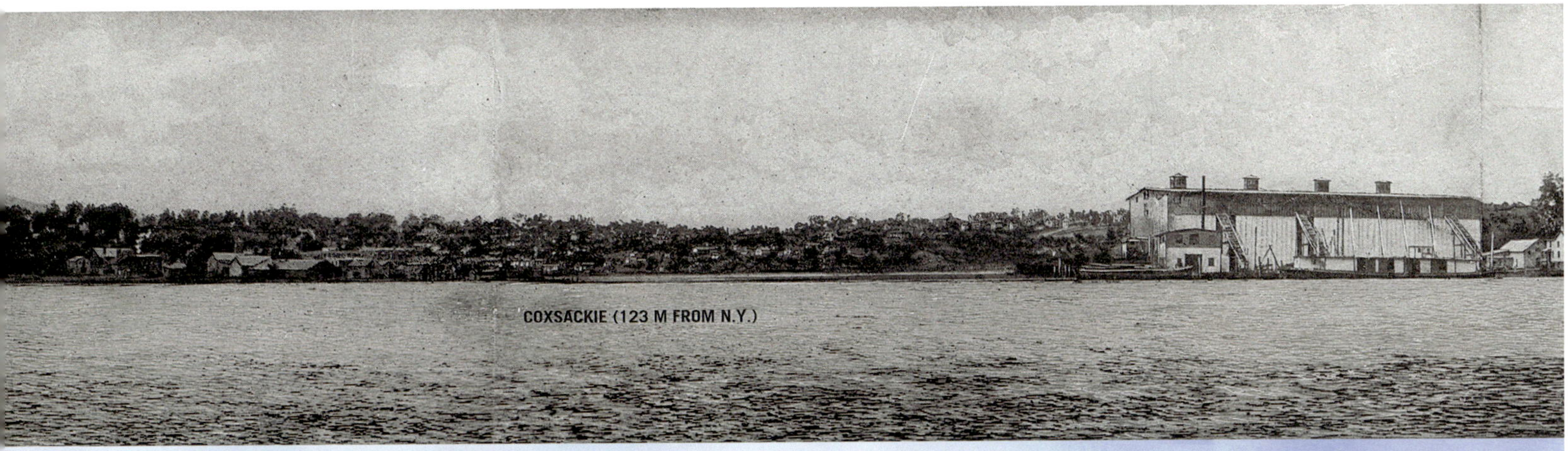

COXSACKIE (123 M FROM N.Y.)

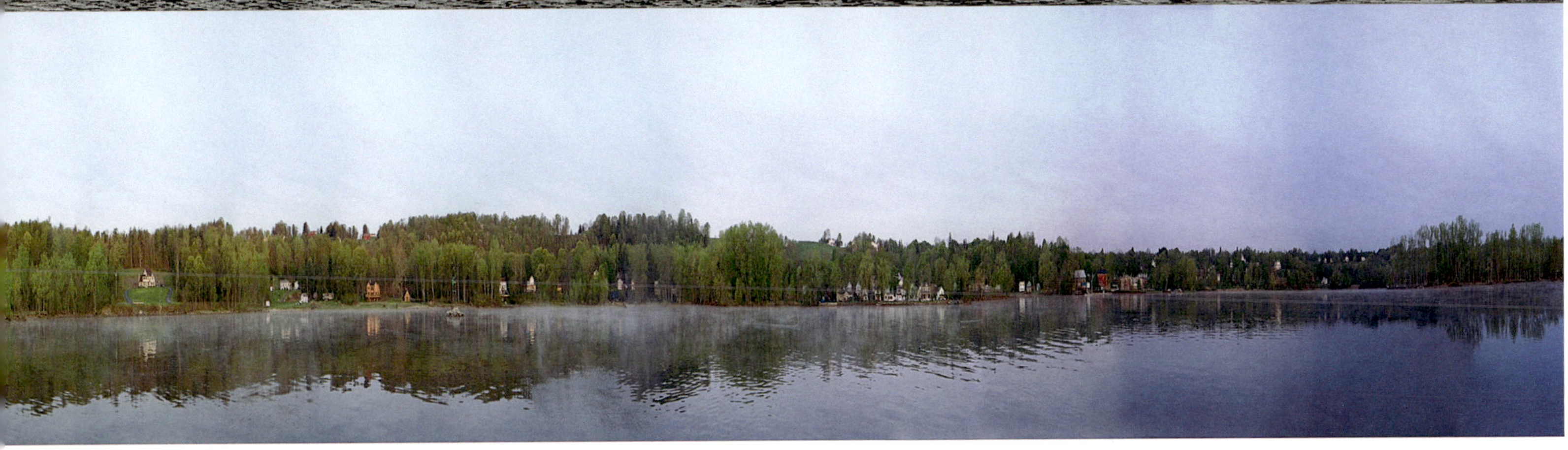

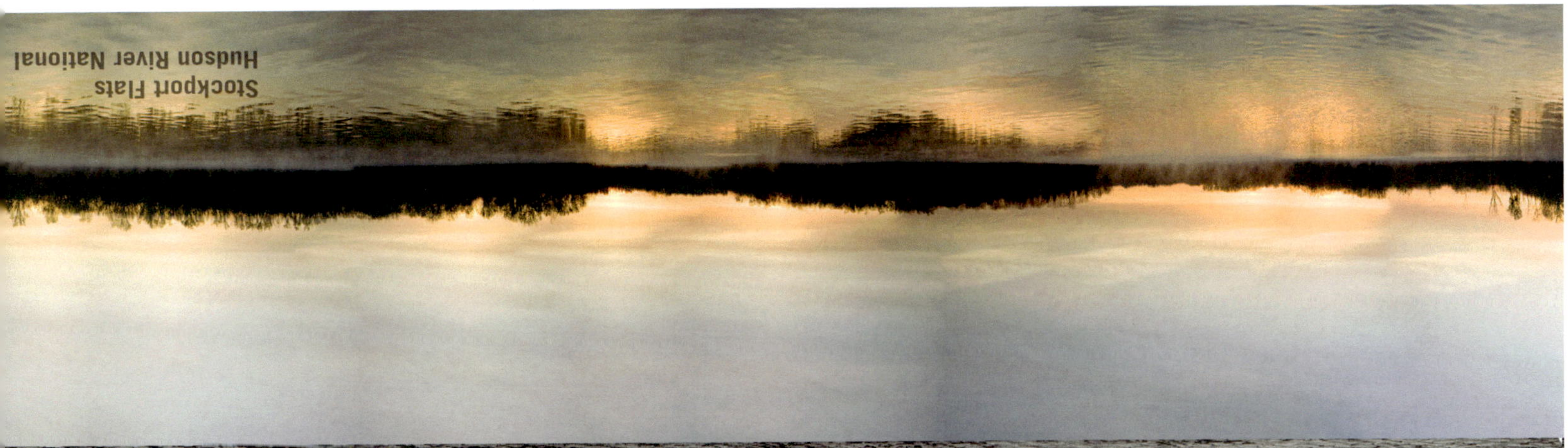

Stockport Flats
Hudson River National

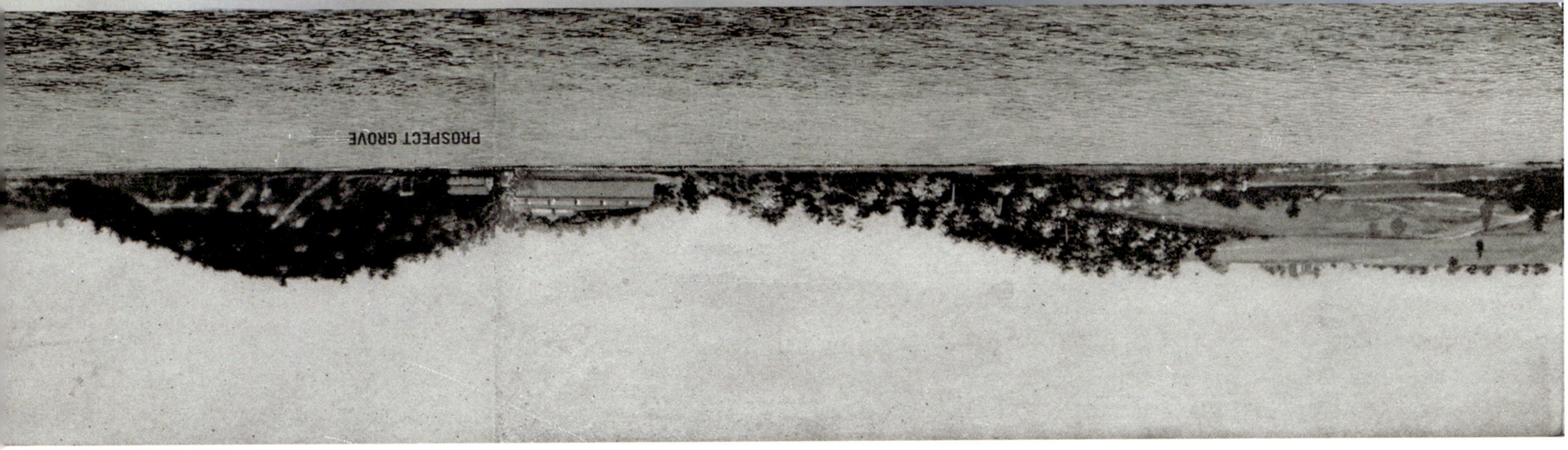

PROSPECT GROVE

COXSACKIE LIGHT-HOUS

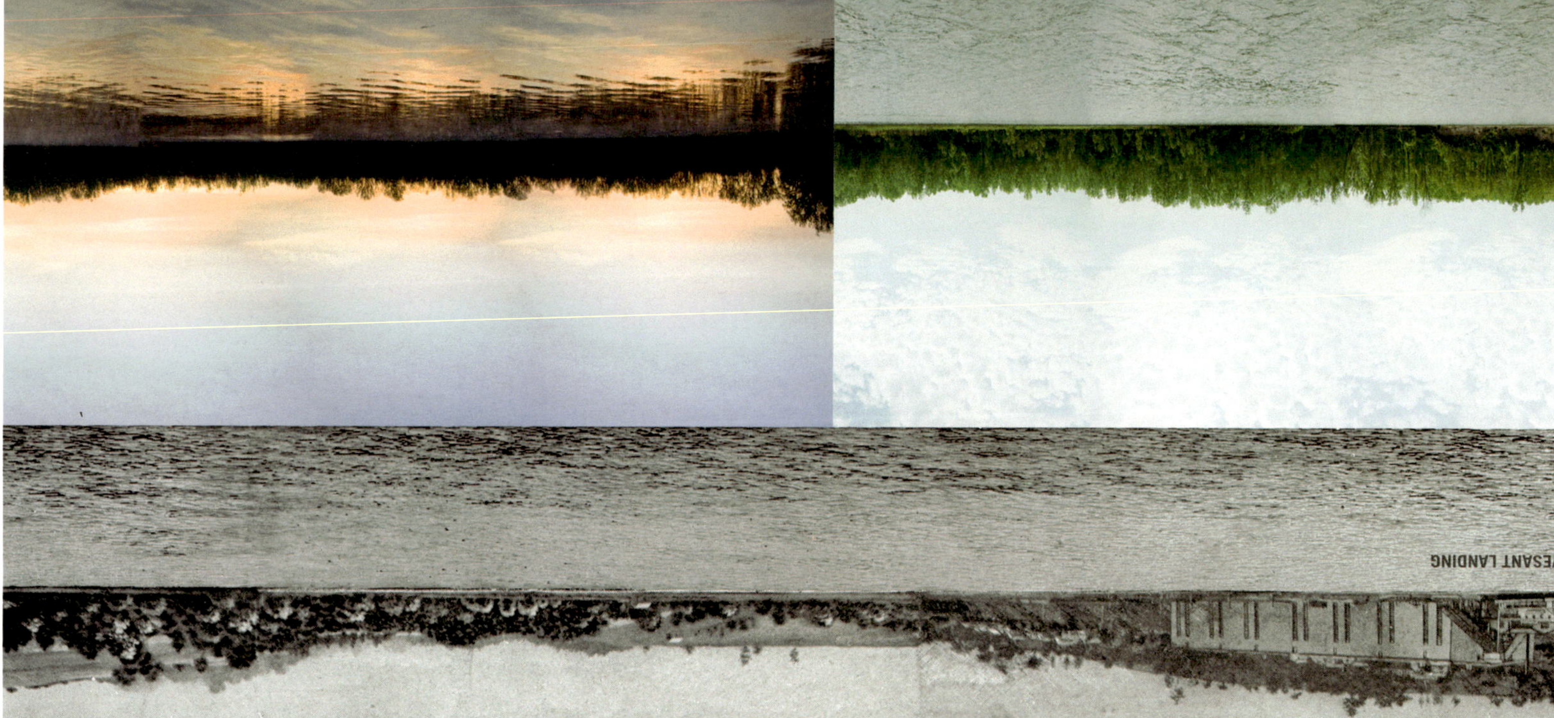

East Bank

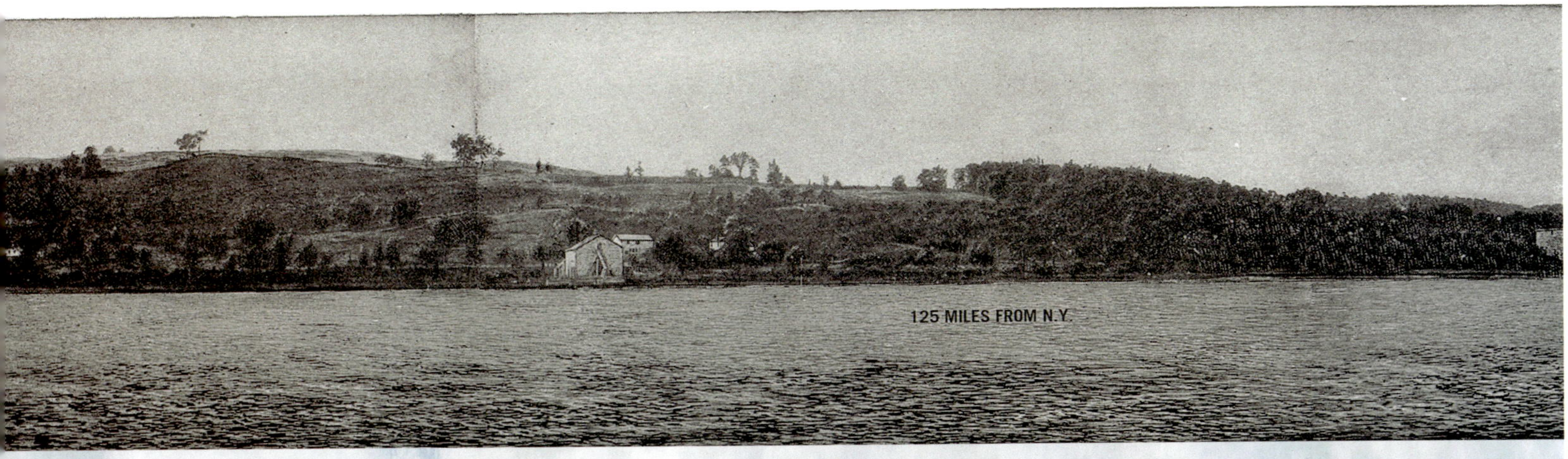

125 MILES FROM N.Y.

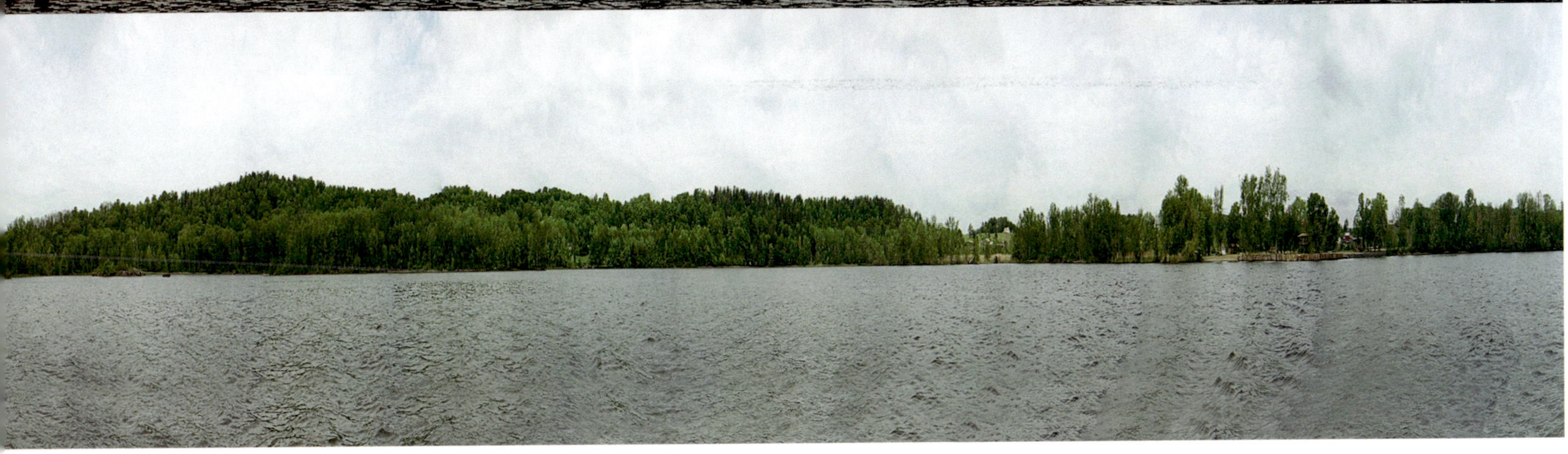

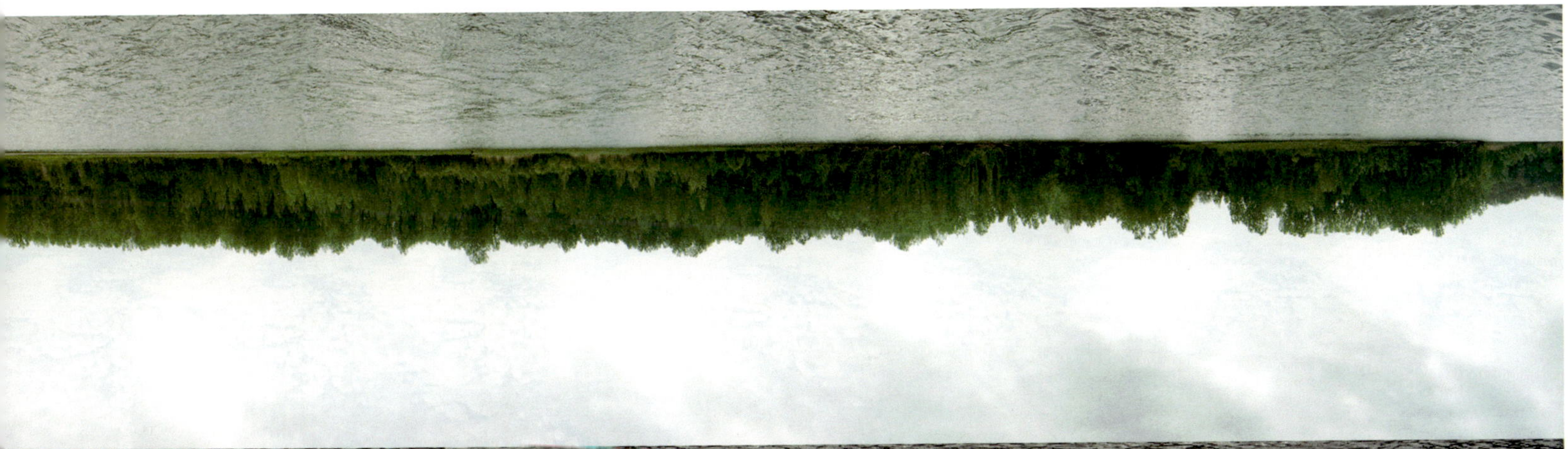

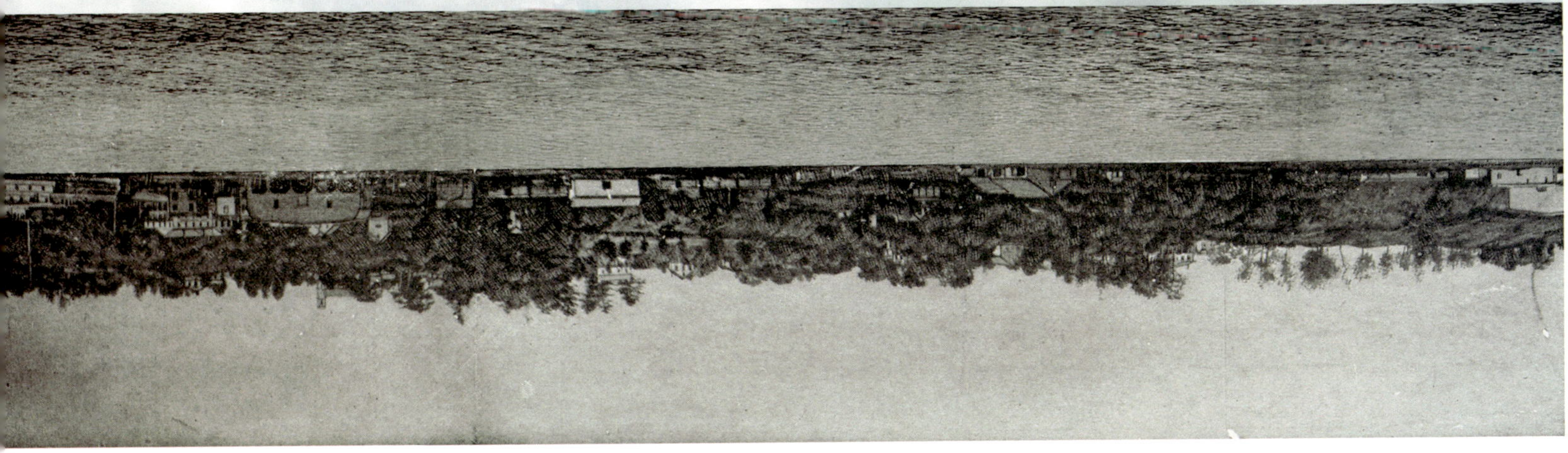

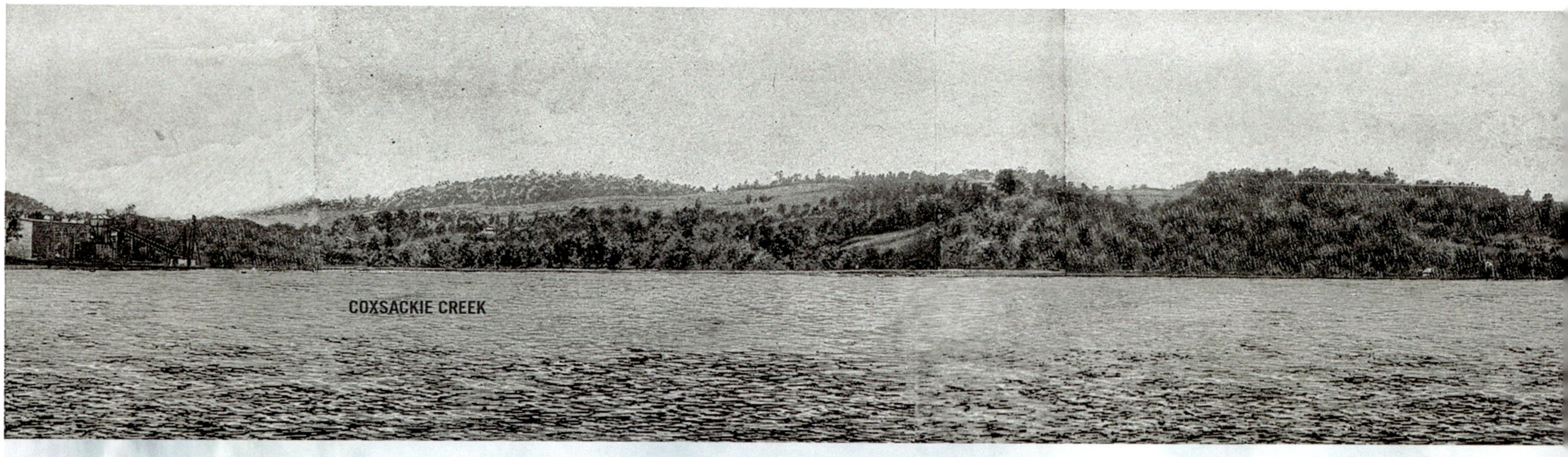

COXSACKIE CREEK

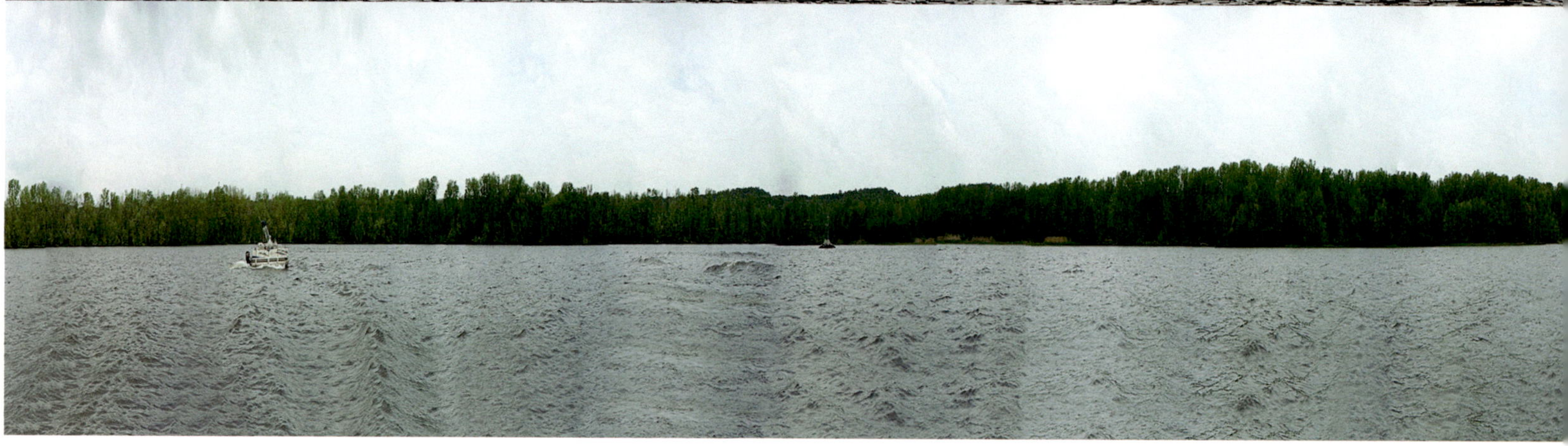

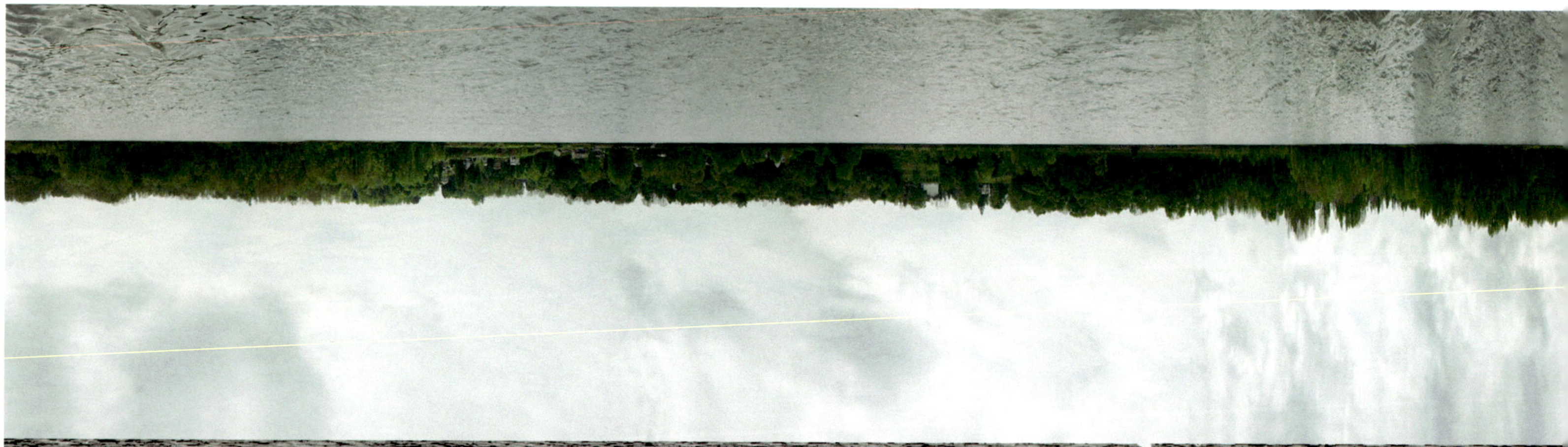

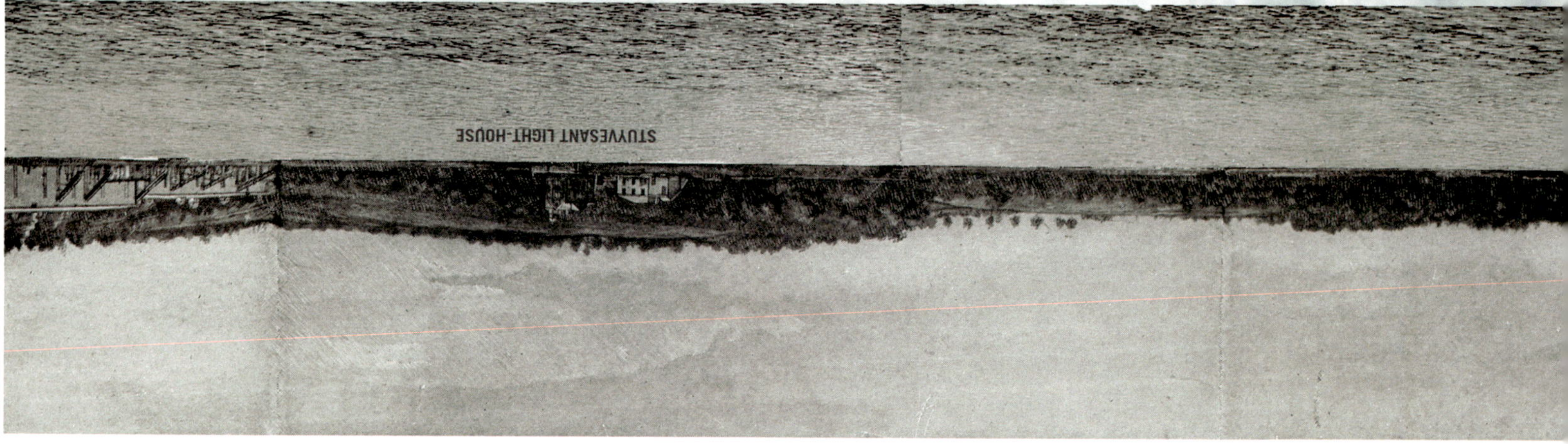

STUYVESANT LIGHT-HOUSE

East Bank

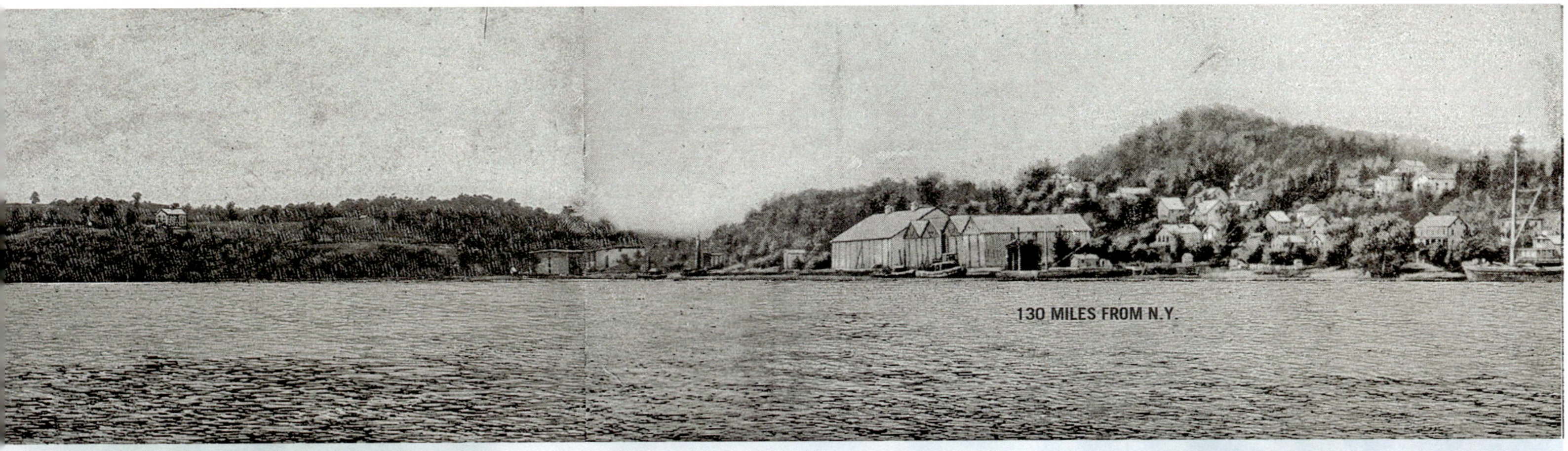

130 MILES FROM N.Y.

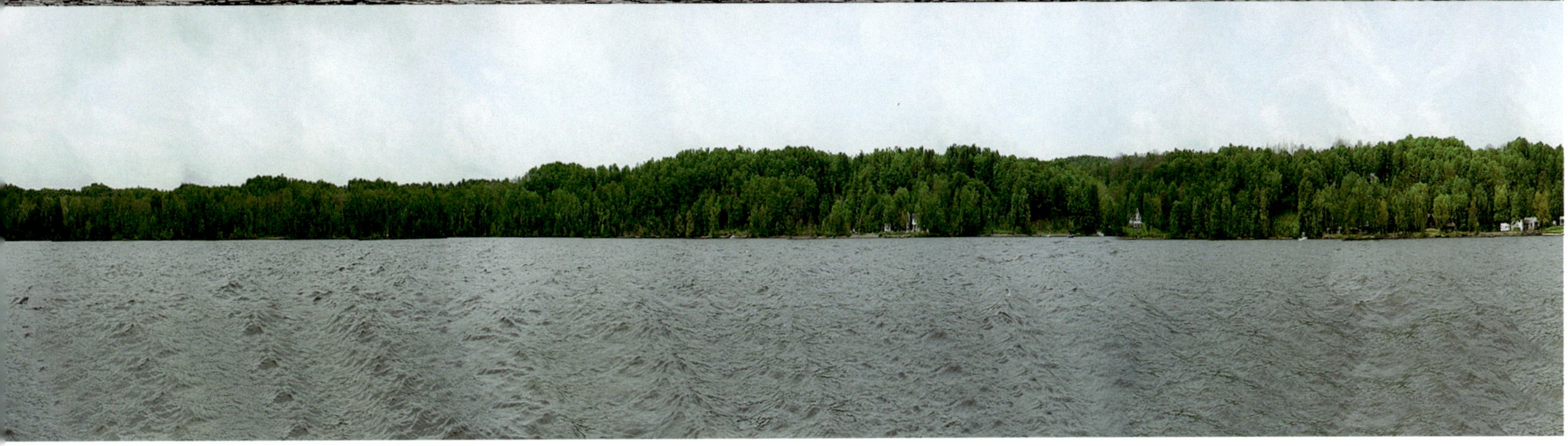

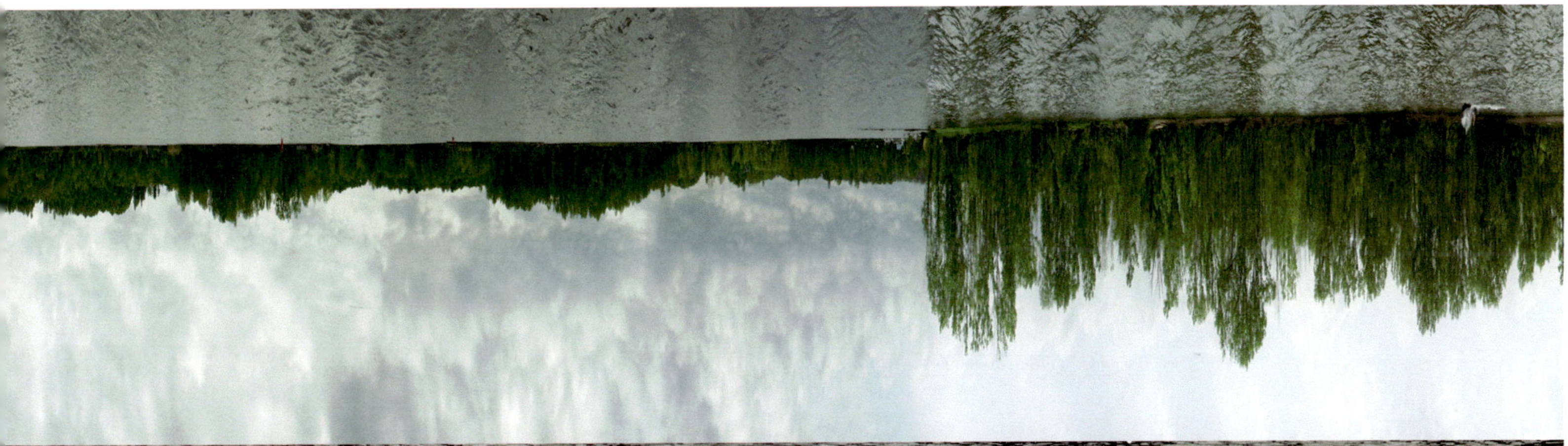

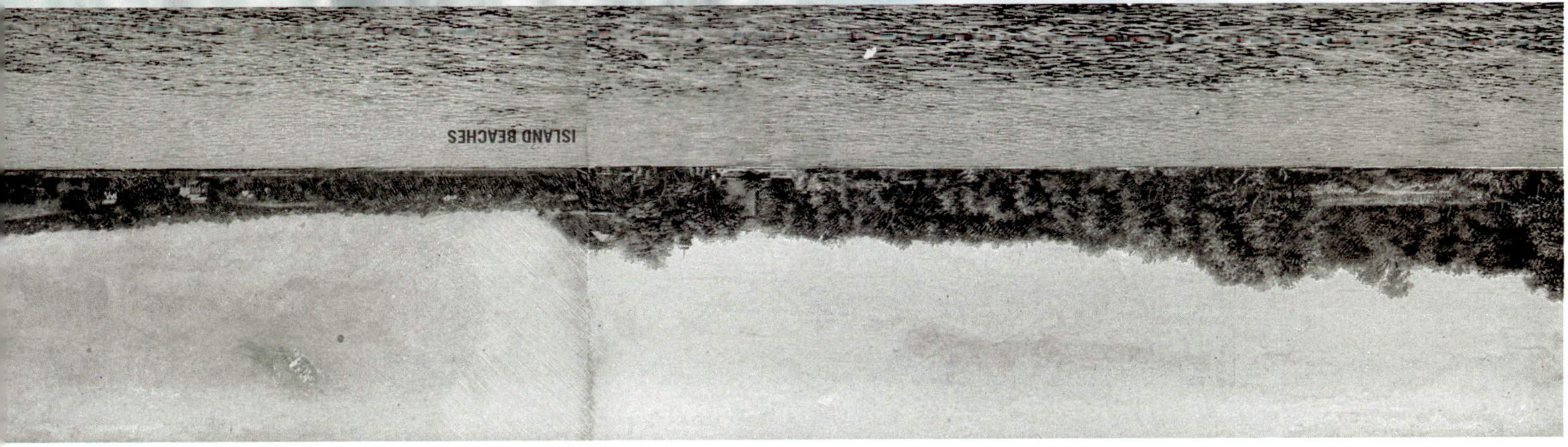

ISLAND BEACHES

NEW BALTIMORE (131 M FROM N.Y.)

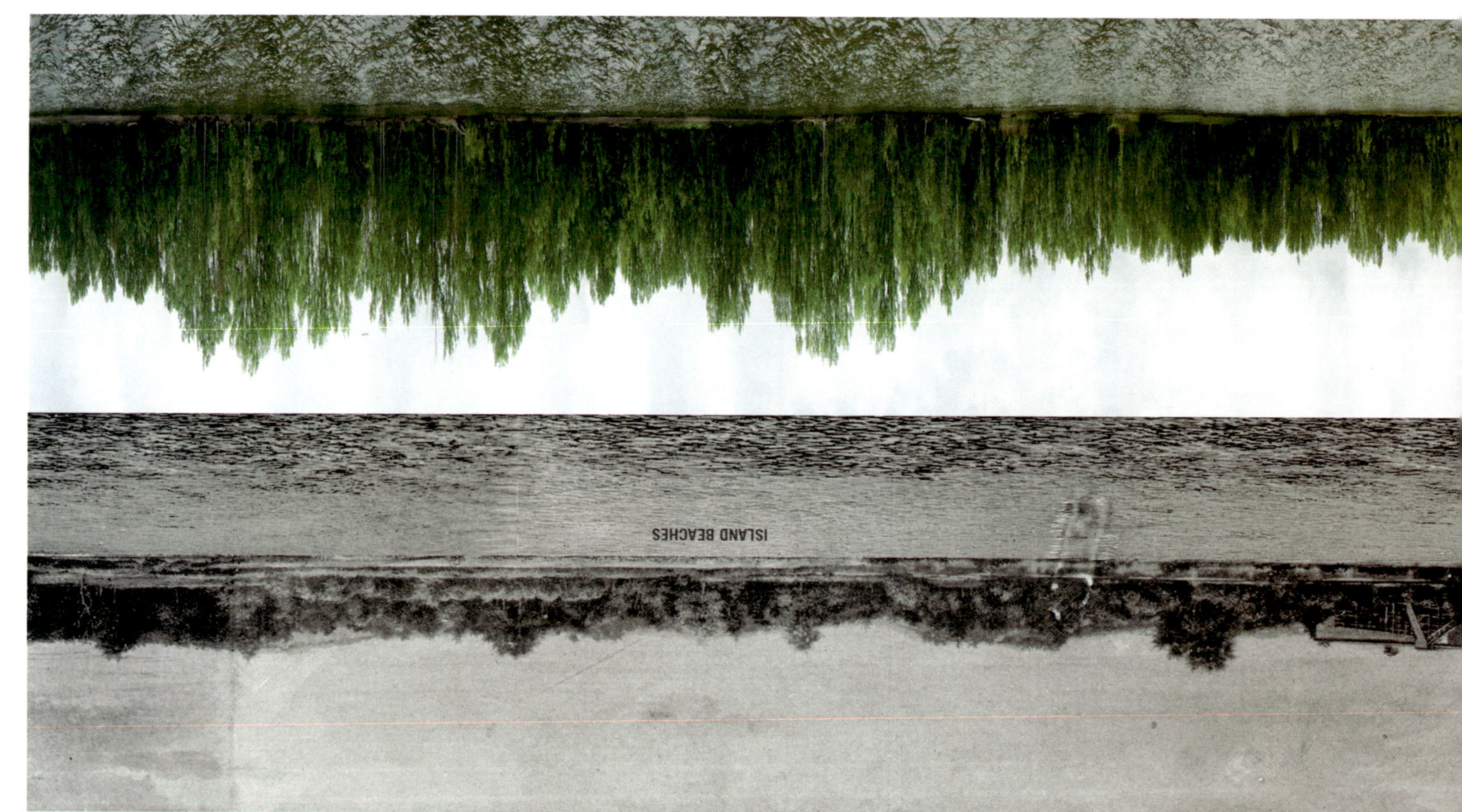

East Bank

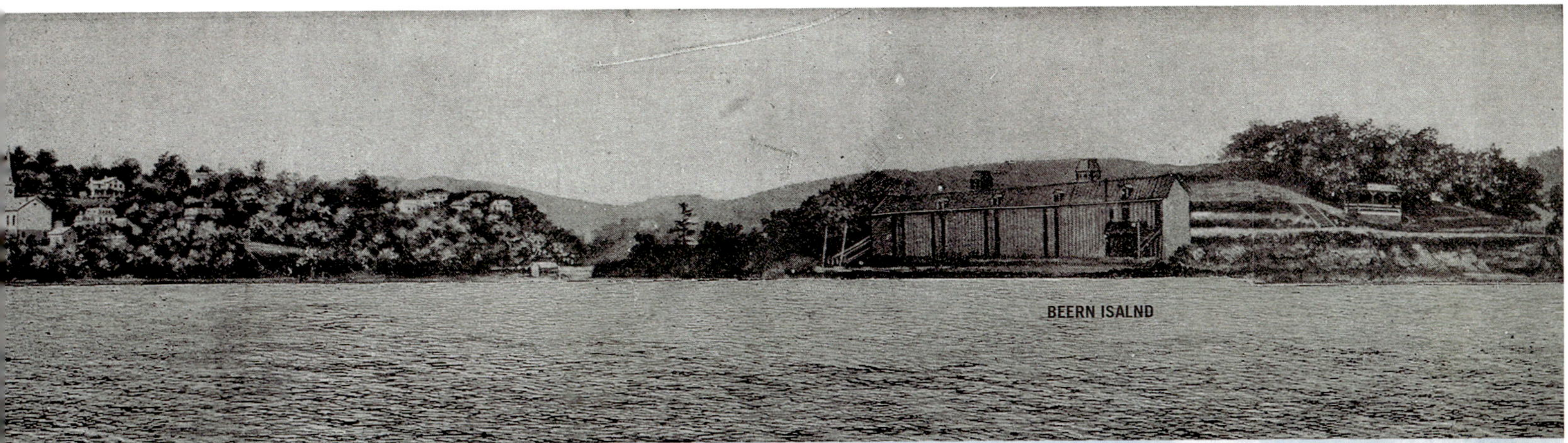

BEERN ISALND

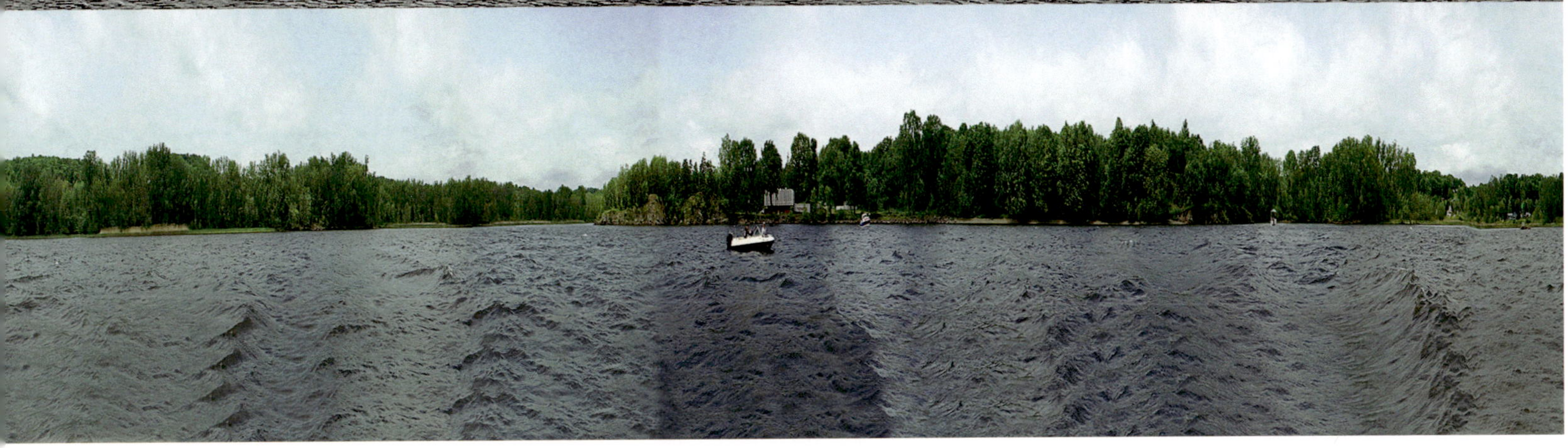

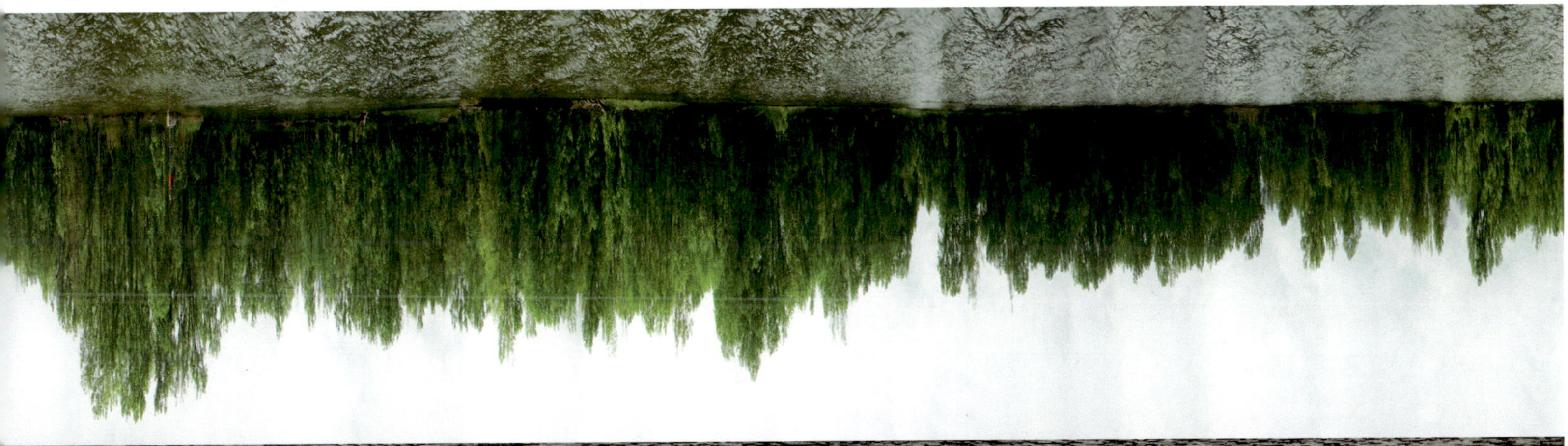

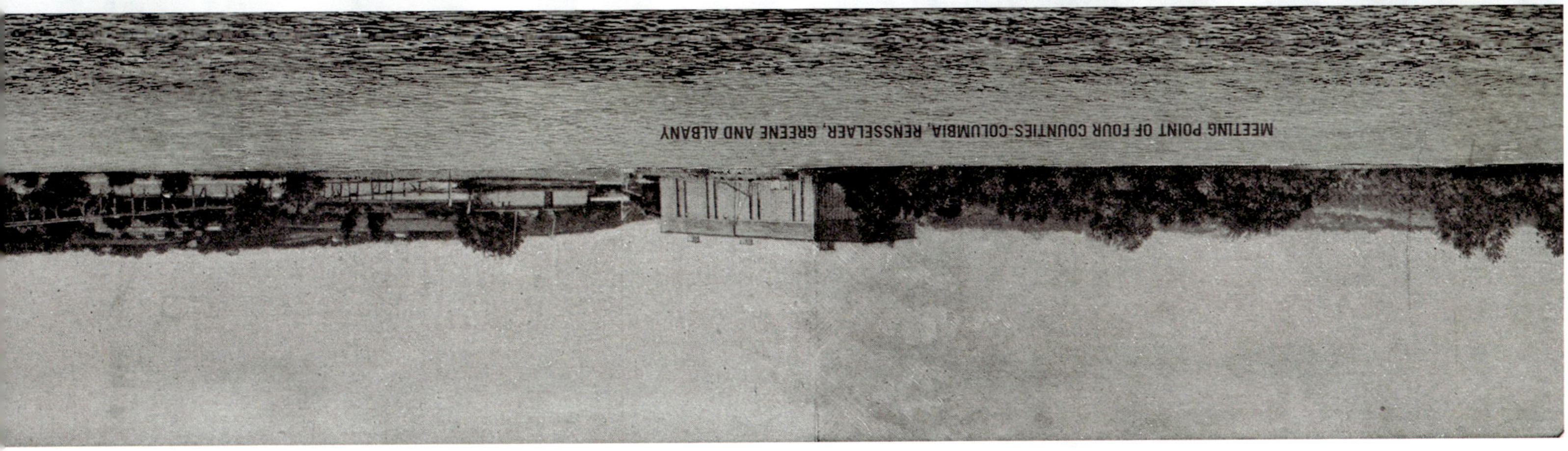

MEETING POINT OF FOUR COUNTIES-COLUMBIA, RENSSELAER, GREENE AND ALBANY

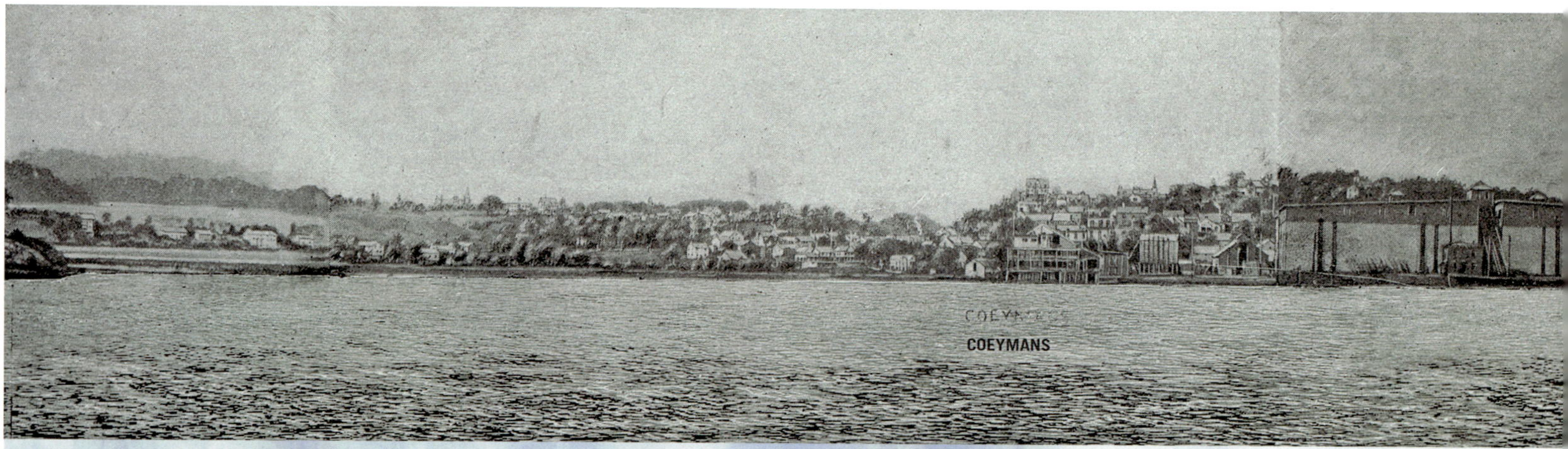

COEYMANS

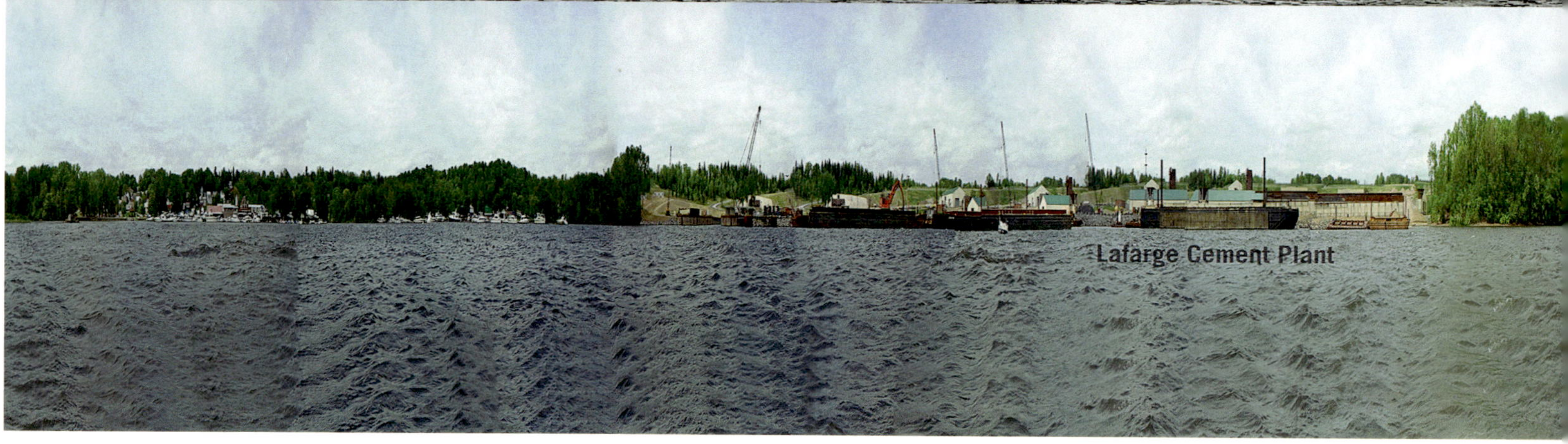

Lafarge Cement Plant

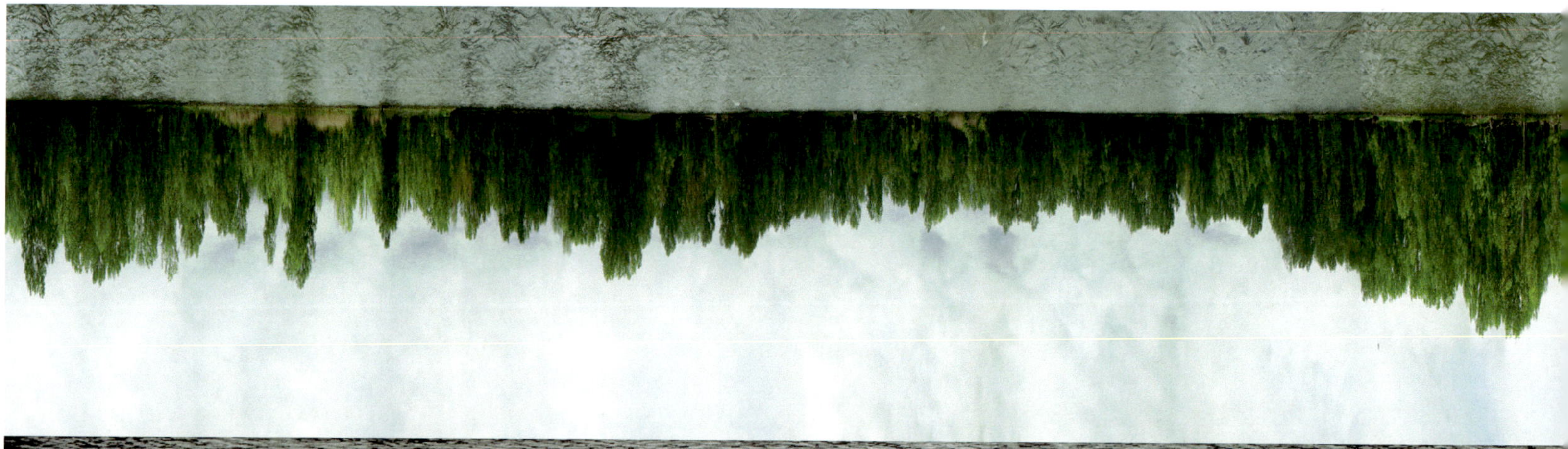

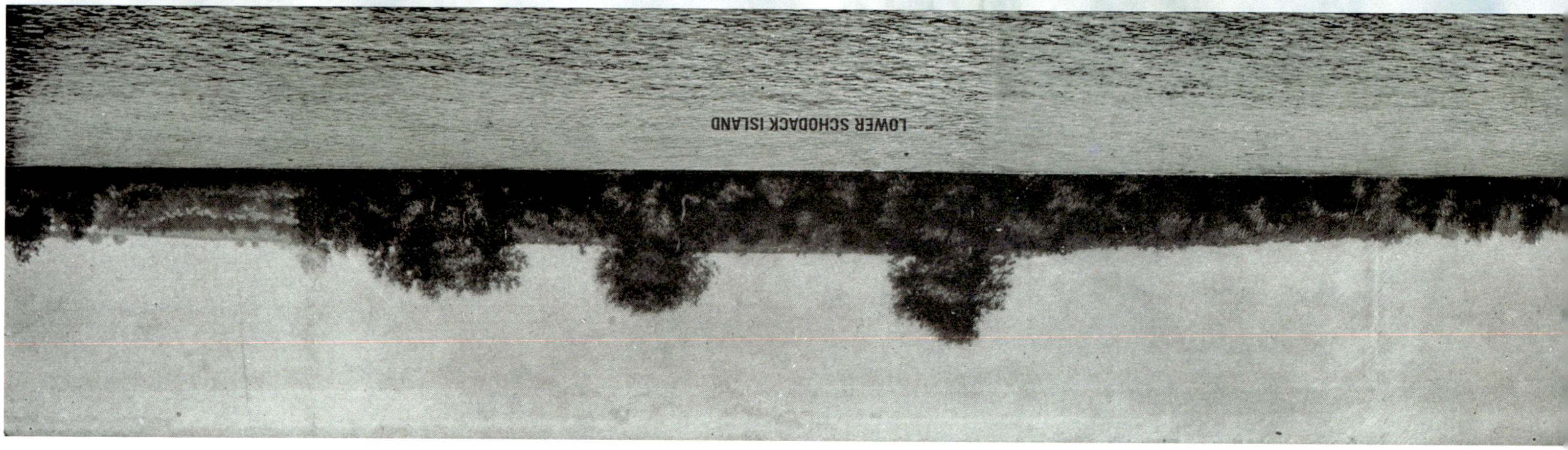

LOWER SCHODACK ISLAND

East Bank

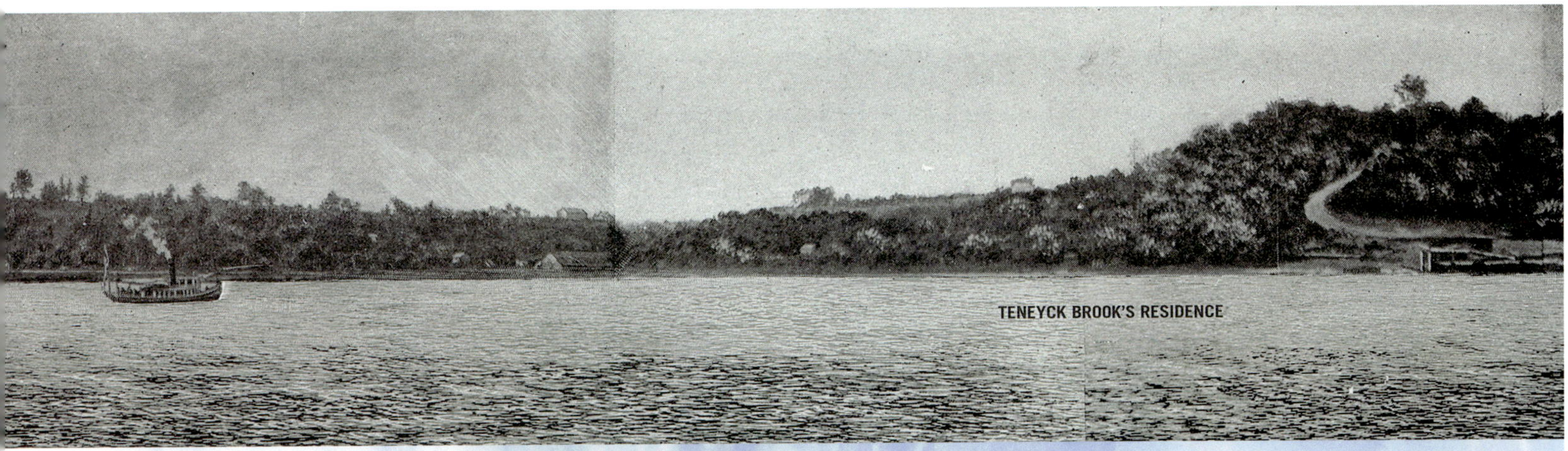

TENEYCK BROOK'S RESIDENCE

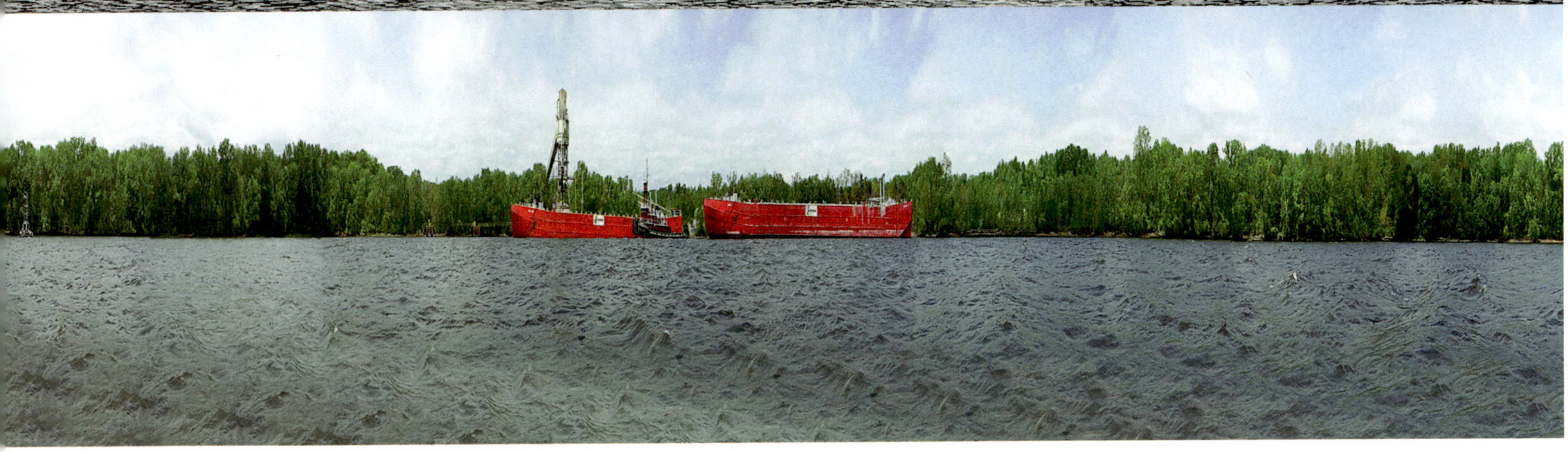

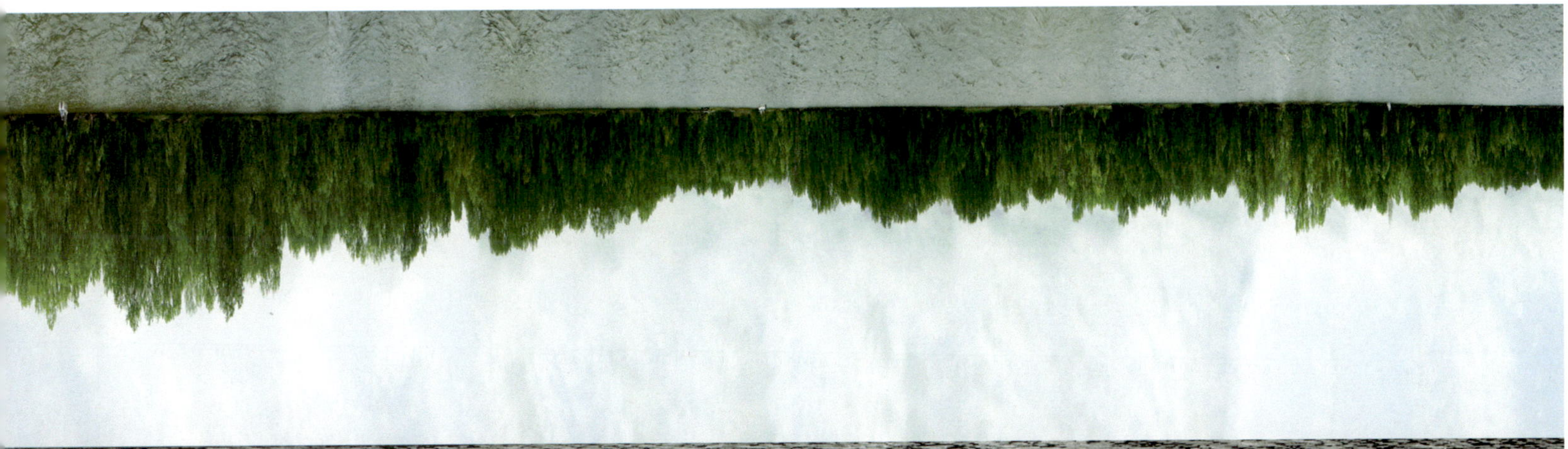

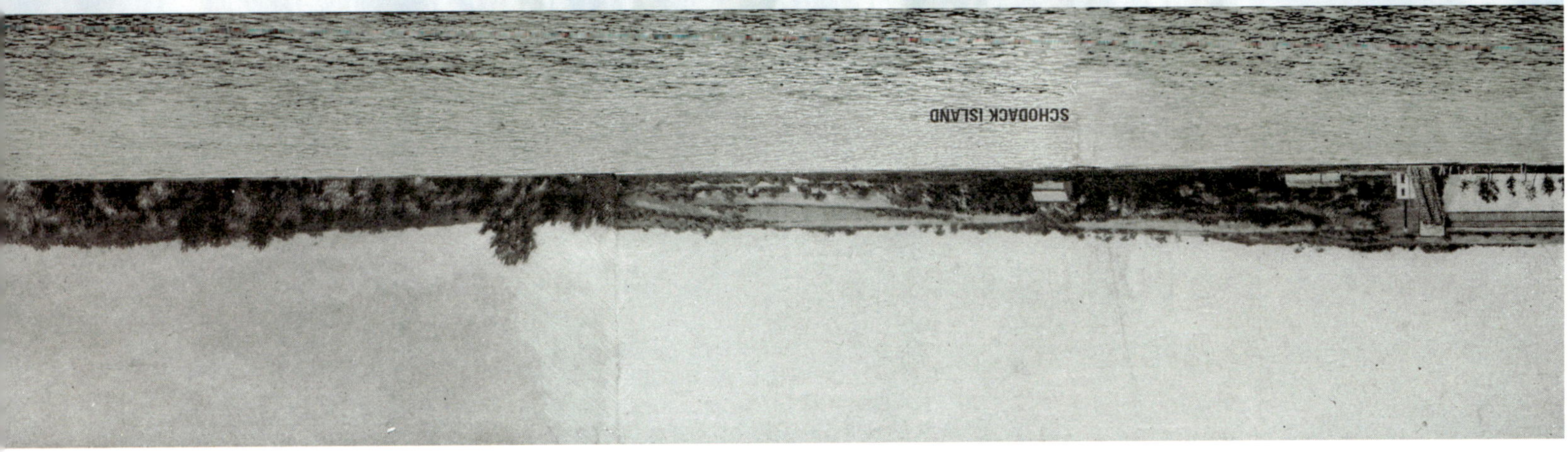

SCHODACK ISLAND

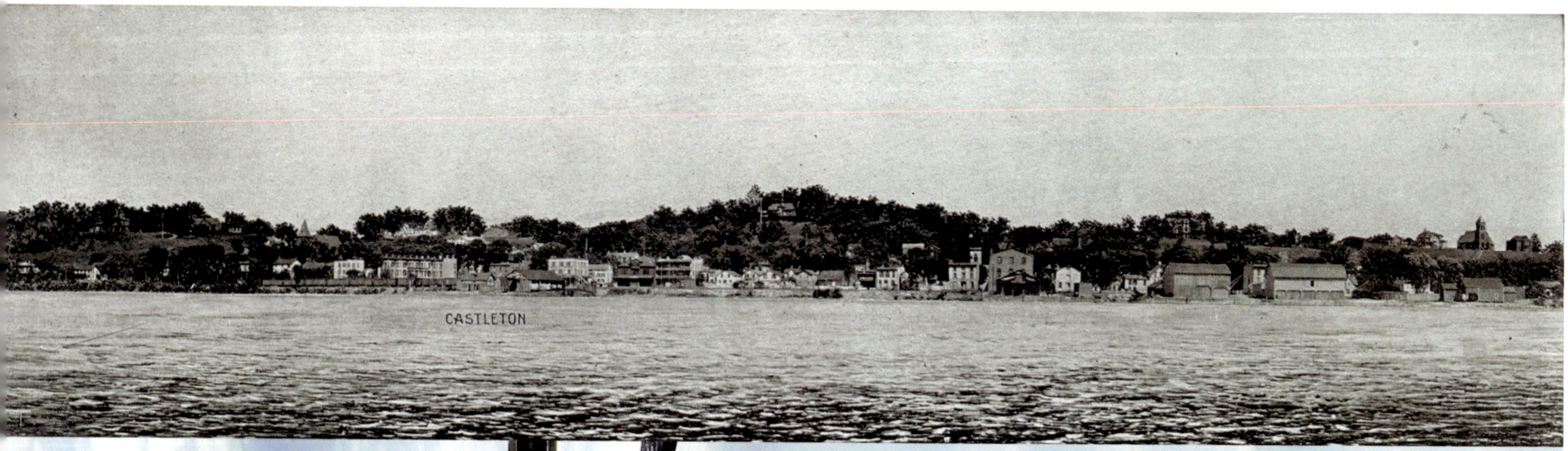

CASTLETON

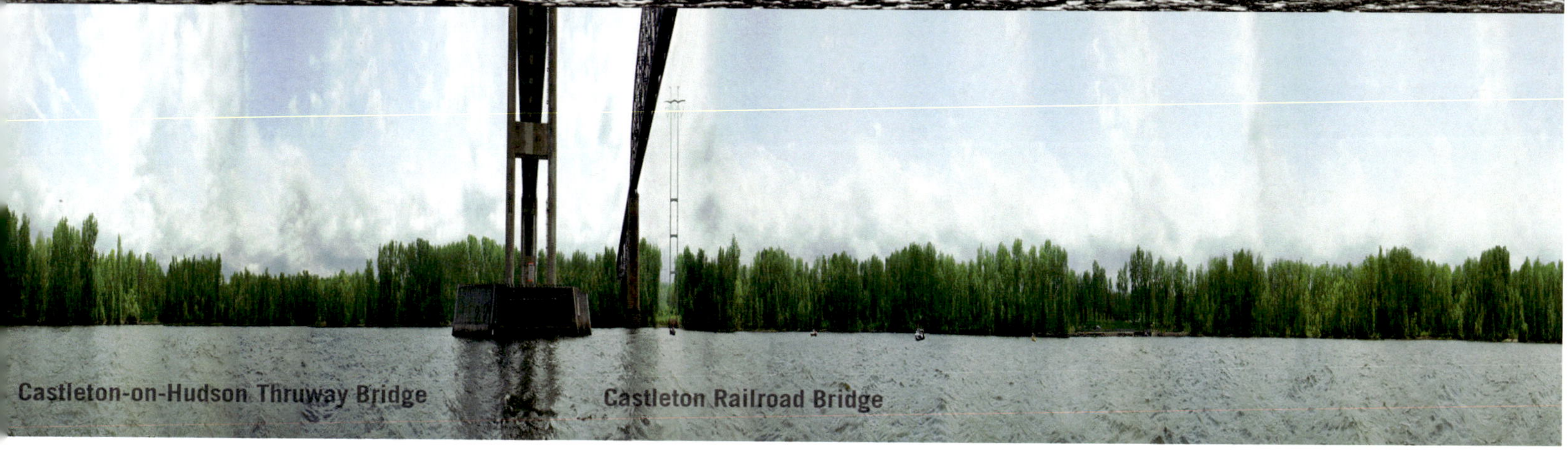

Castleton-on-Hudson Thruway Bridge

Castleton Railroad Bridge

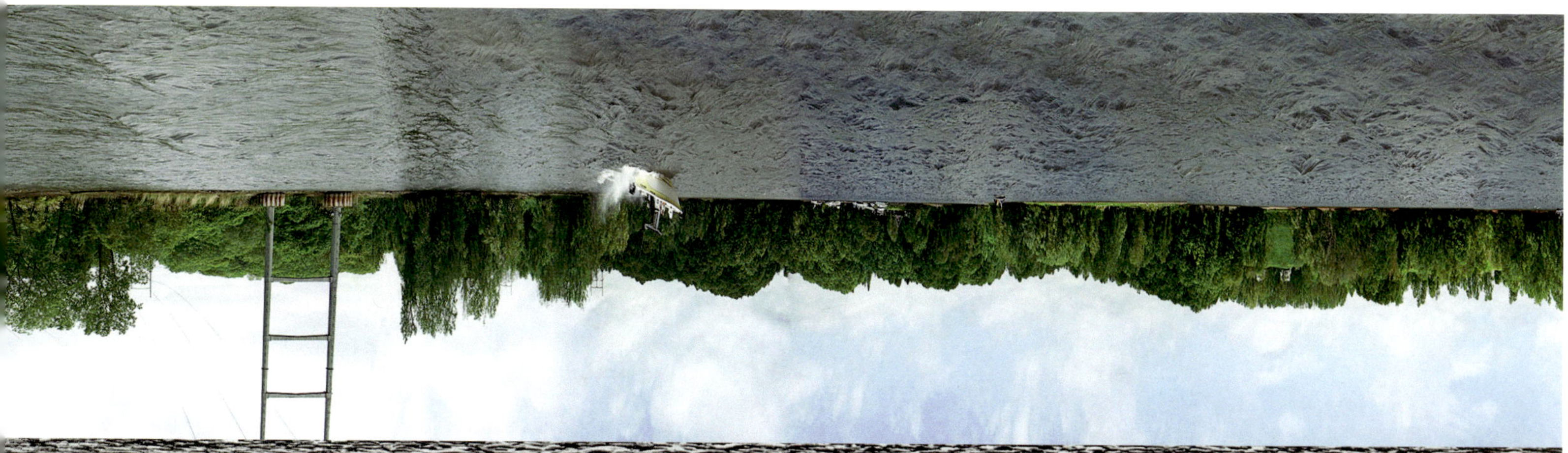

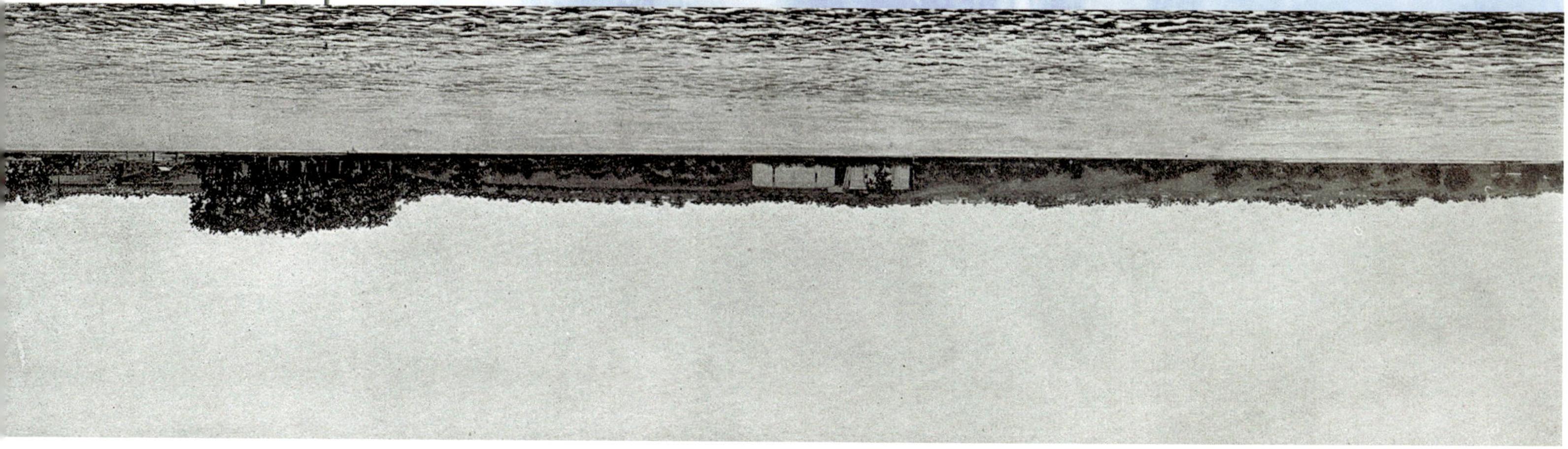

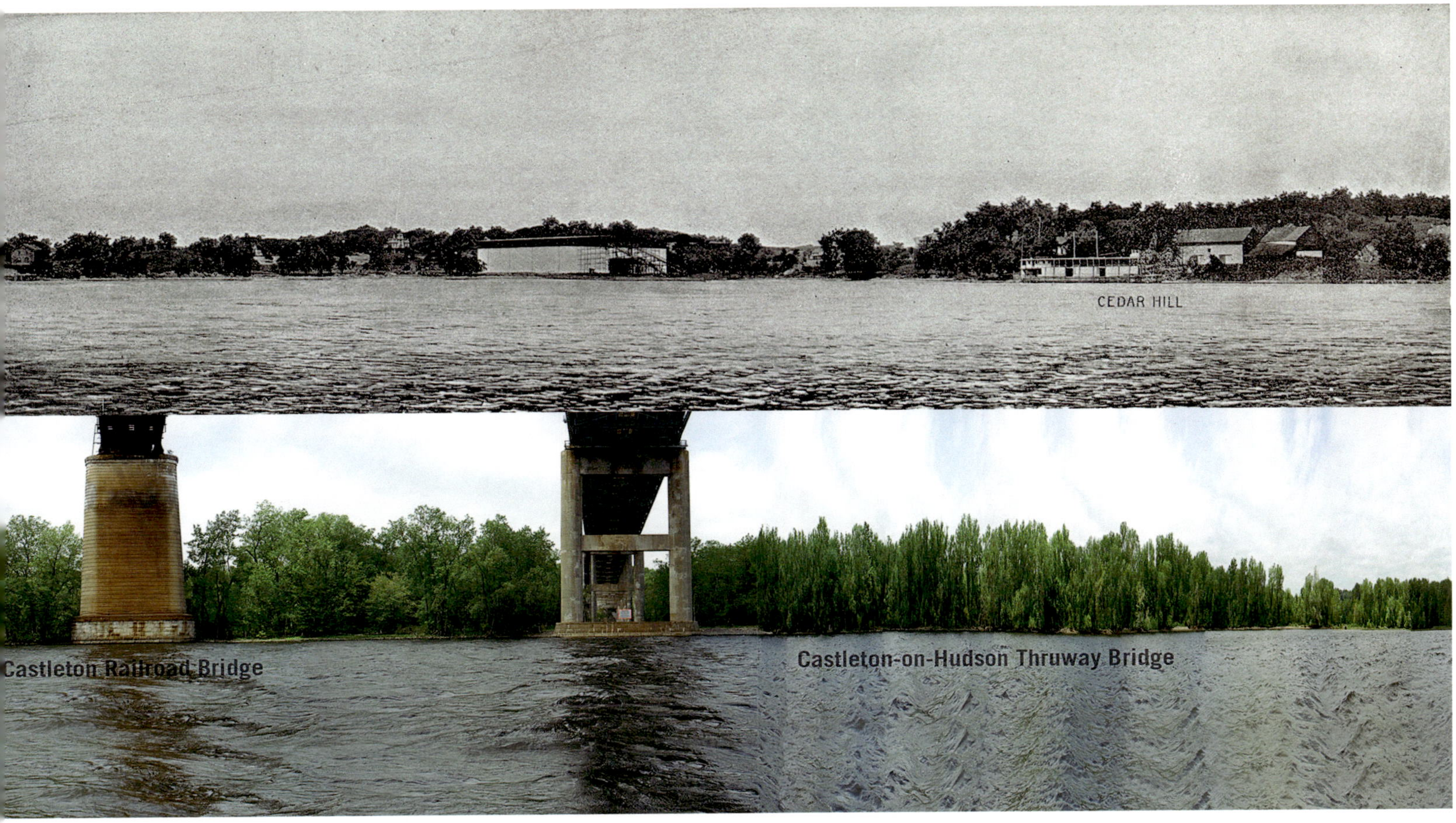

CEDAR HILL

Castleton Railroad Bridge

Castleton-on-Hudson Thruway Bridge

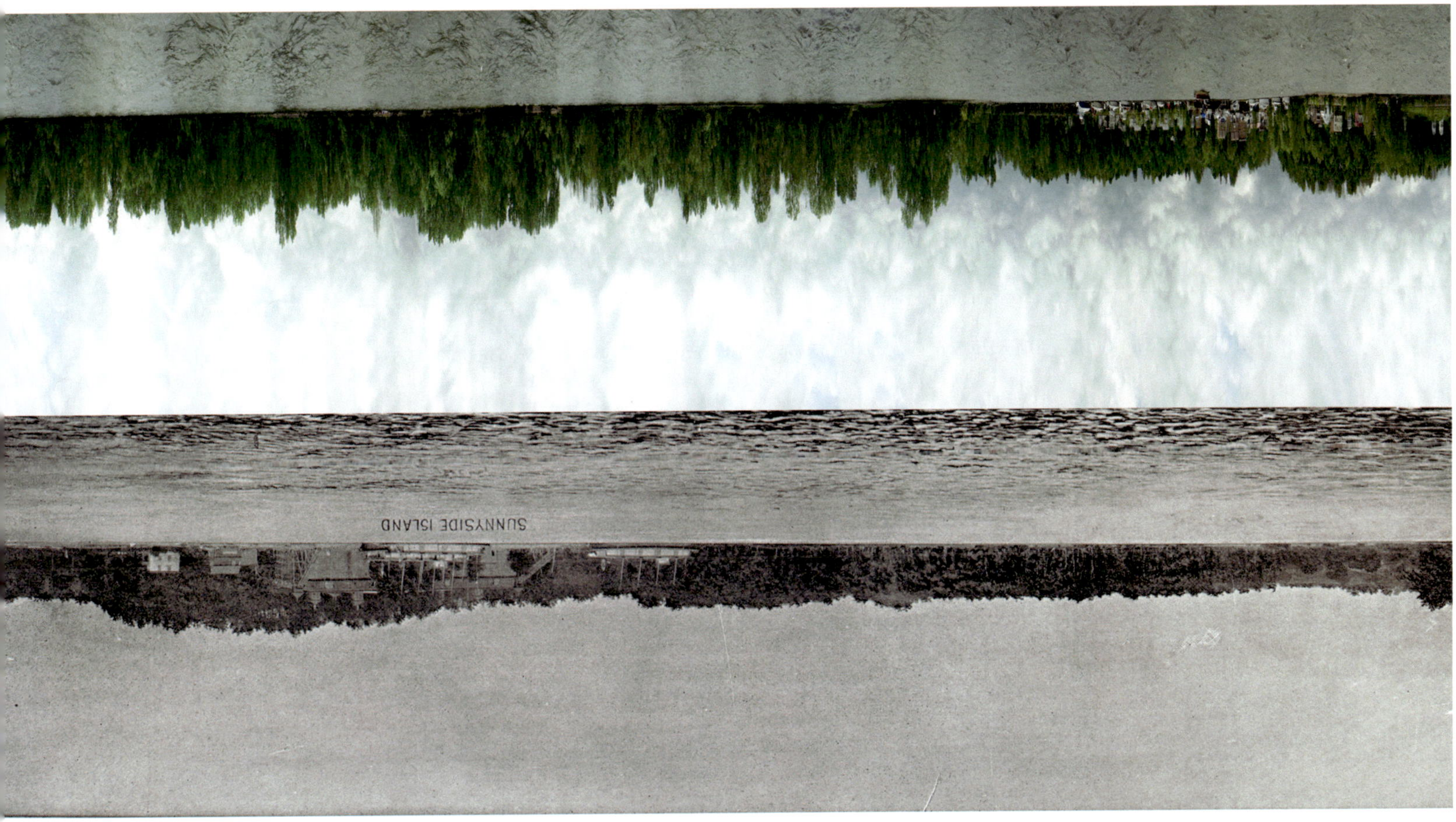

SUNNYSIDE ISLAND

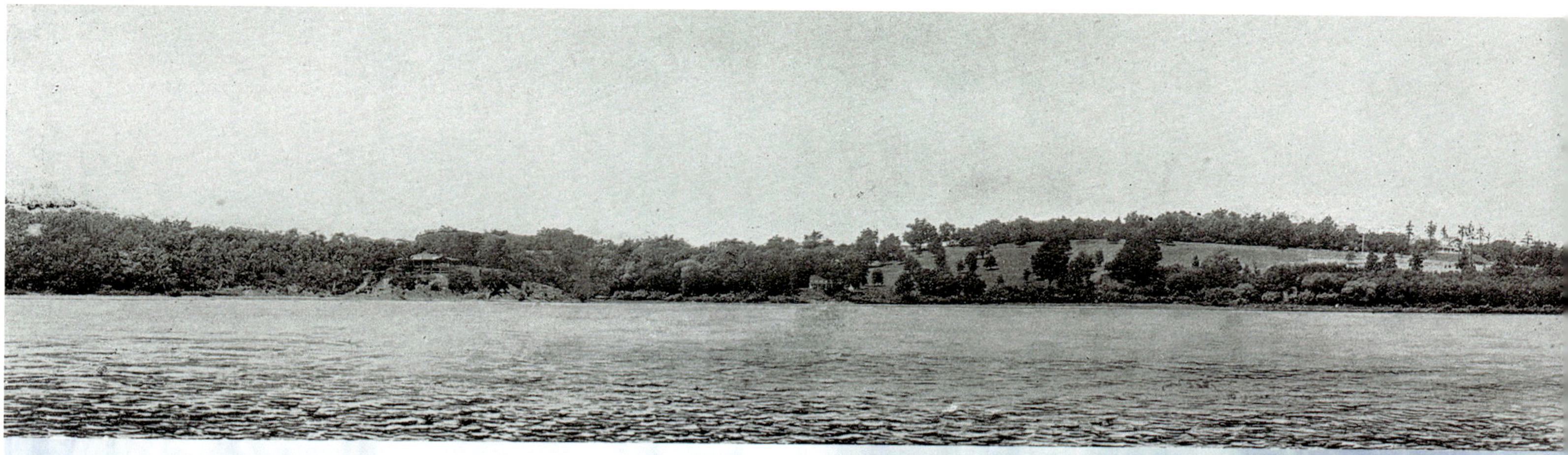

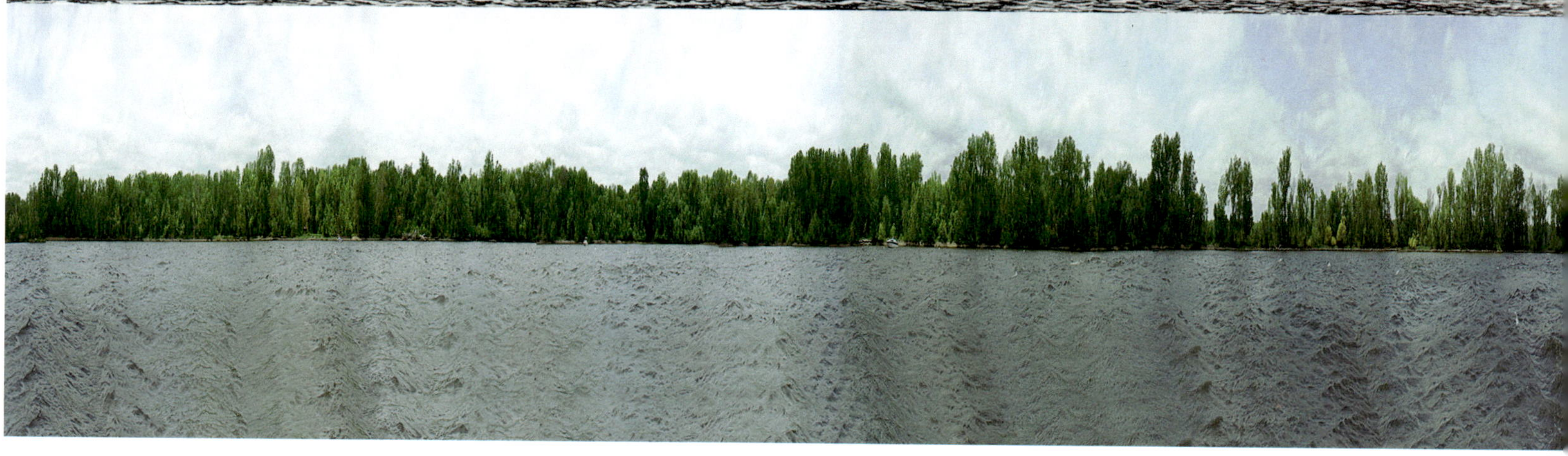

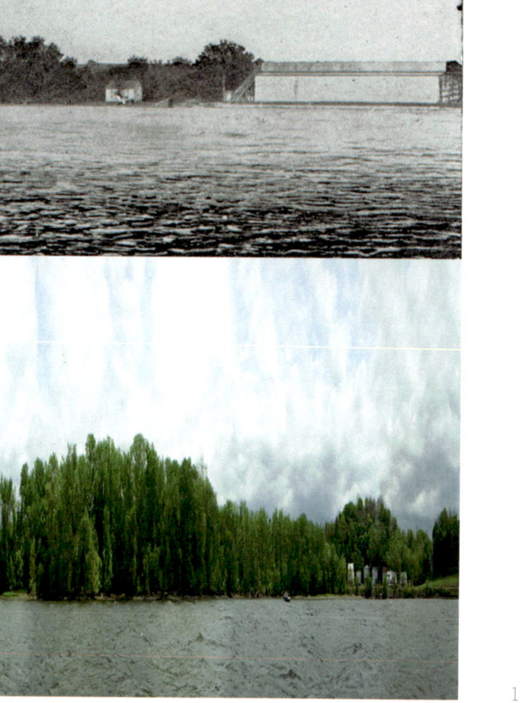

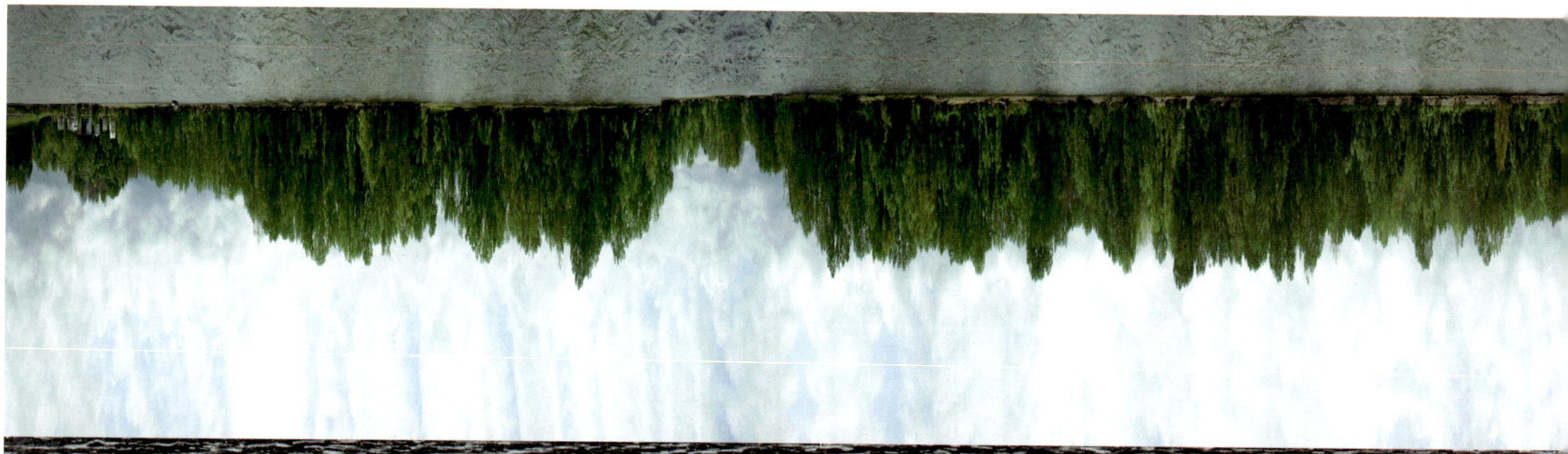

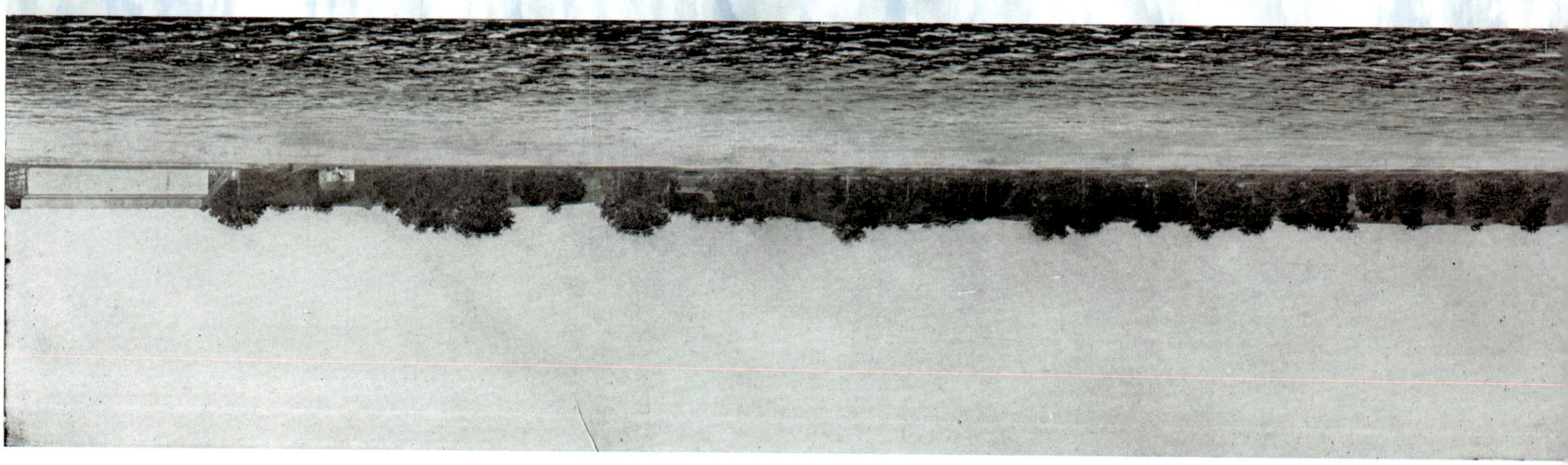

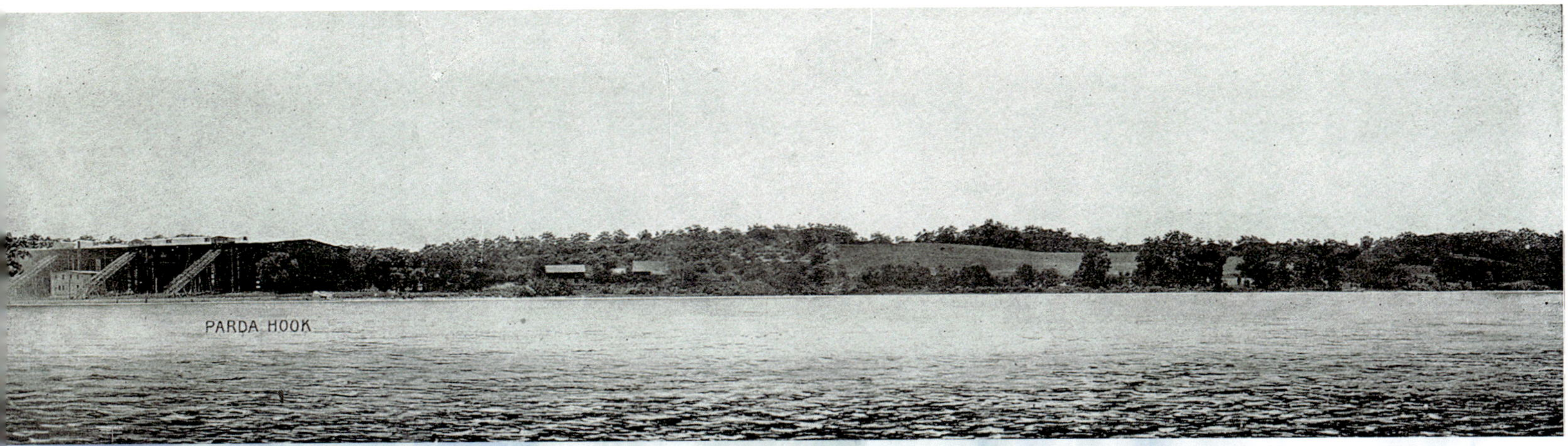

PARDA HOOK

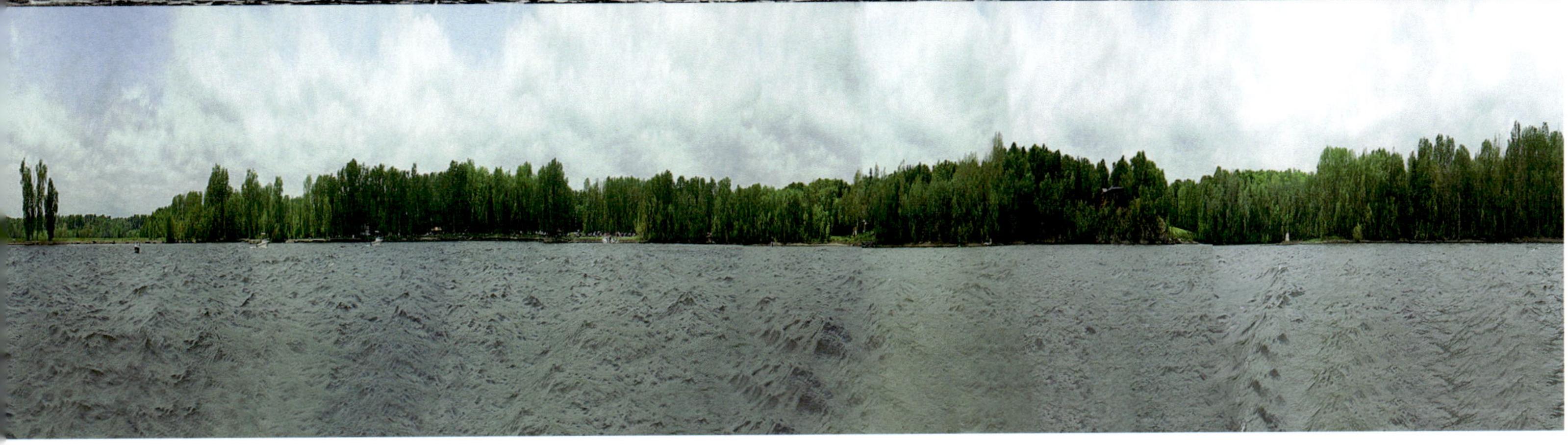

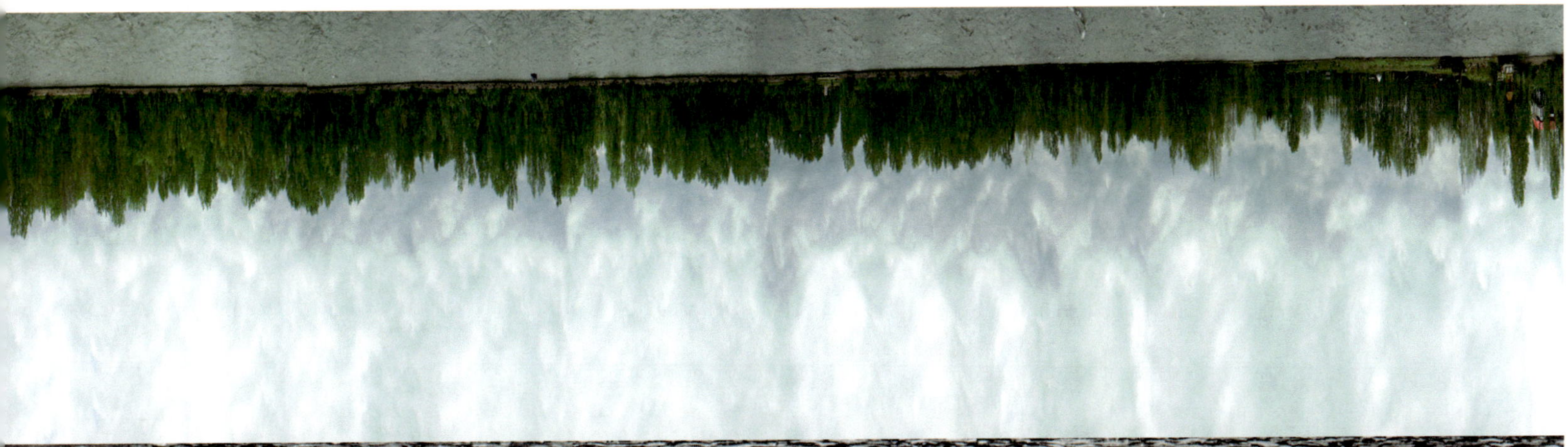

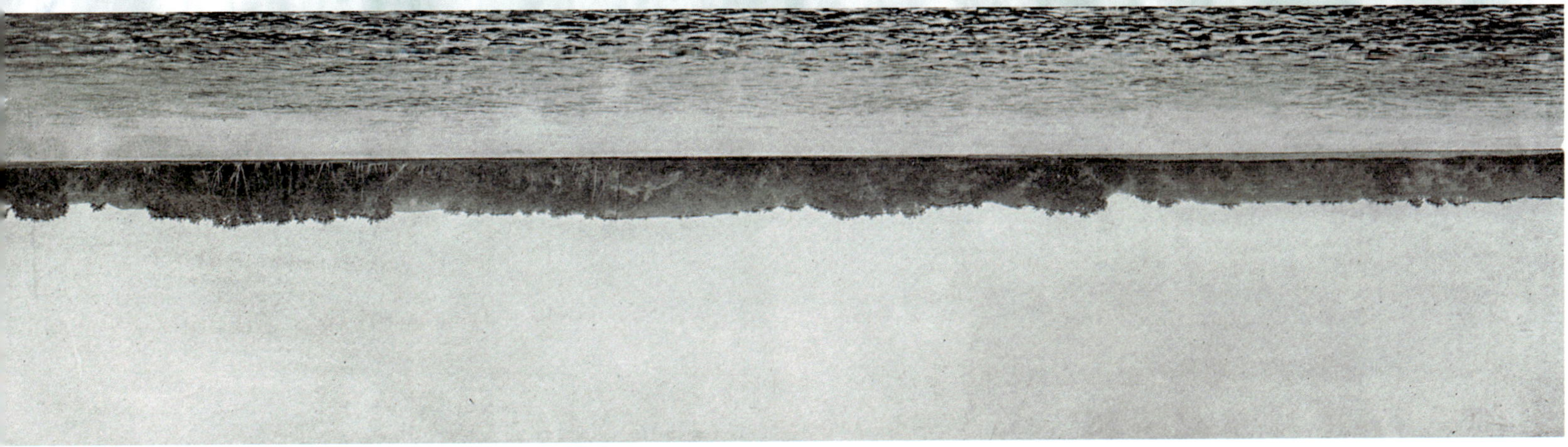

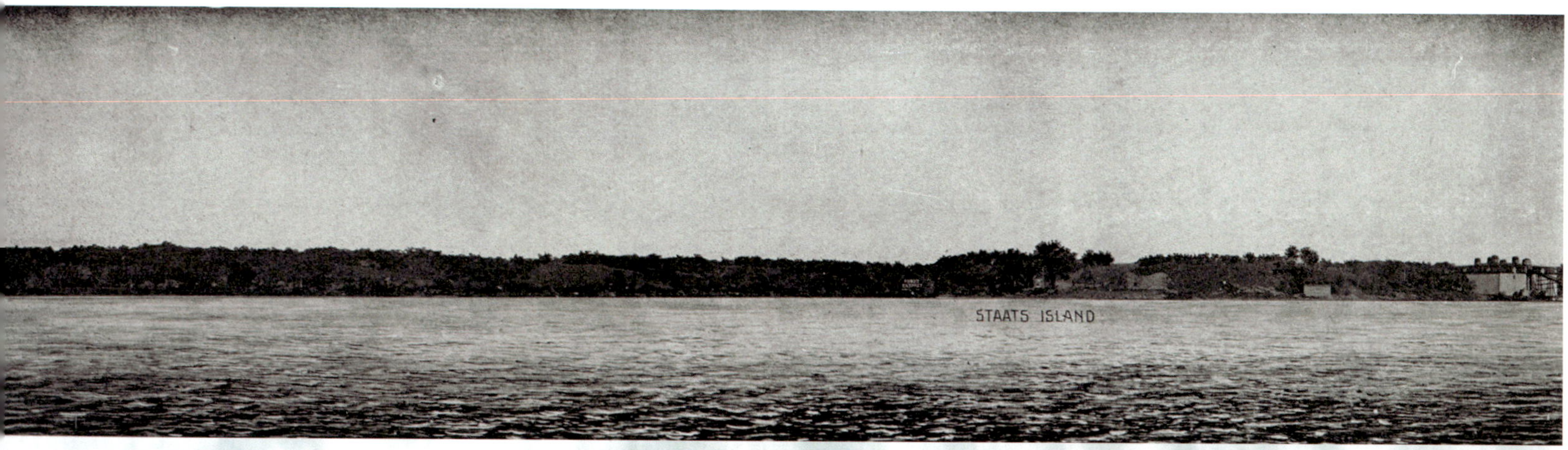

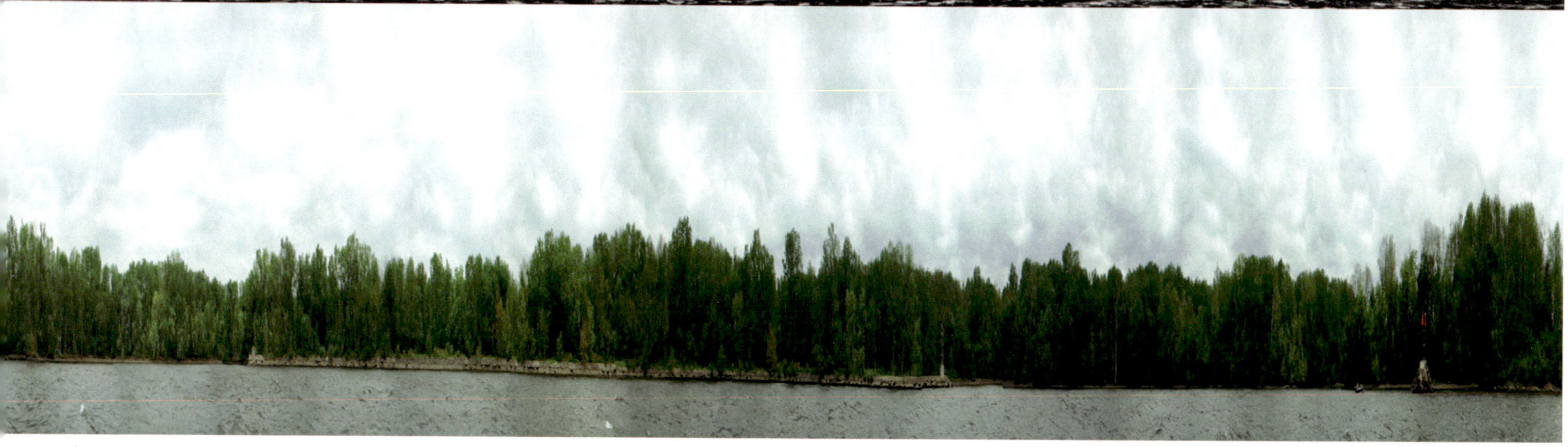

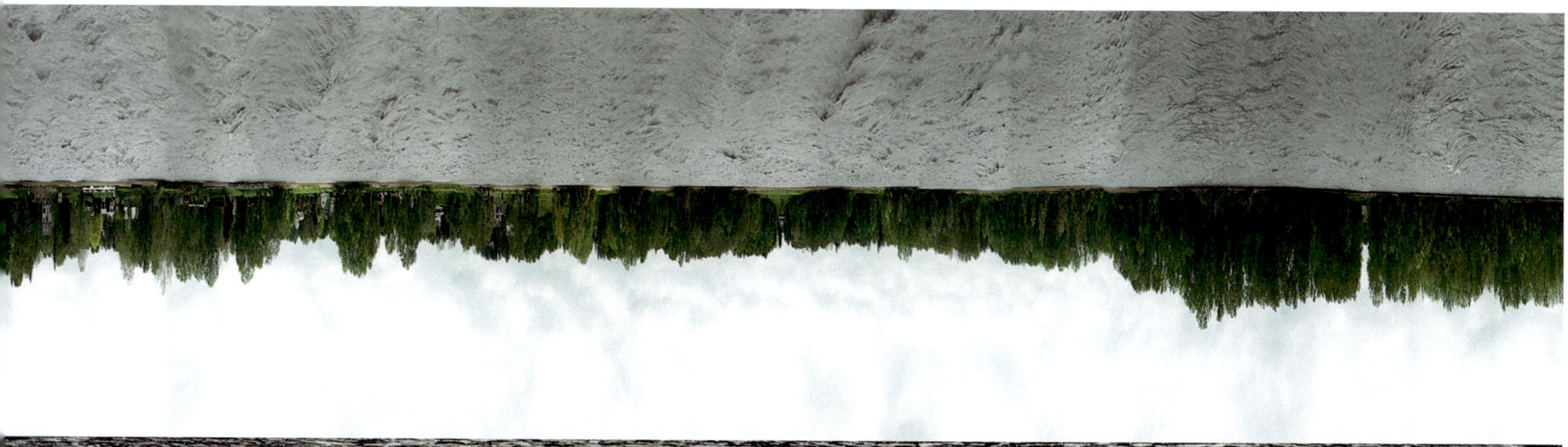

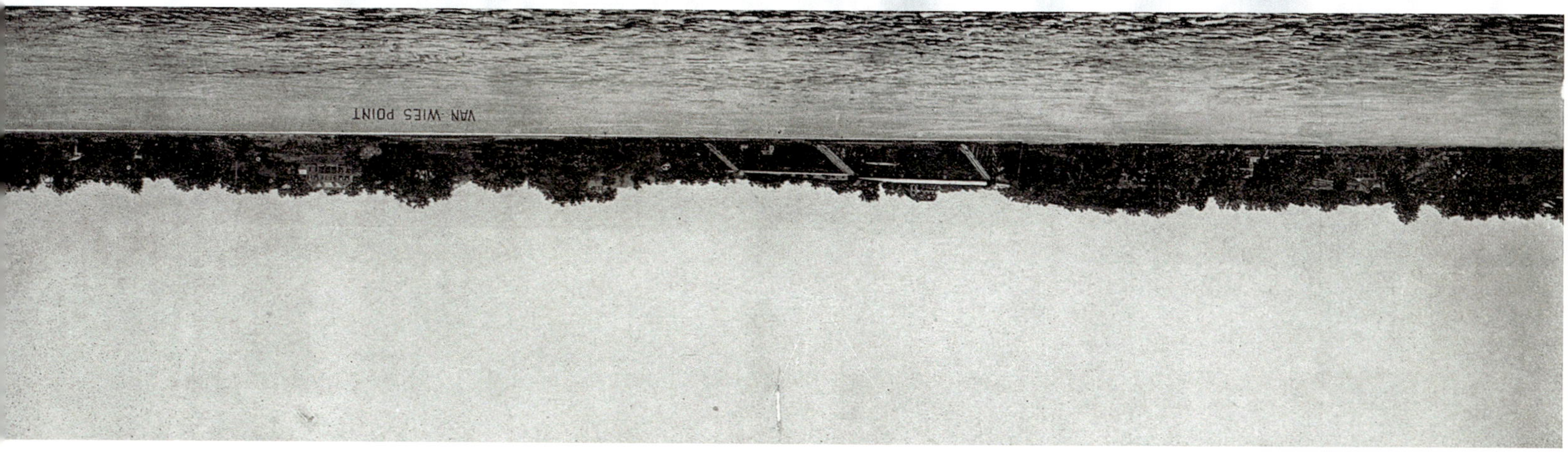

VAN WIES POINT

STAATS ISLAND

East Bank

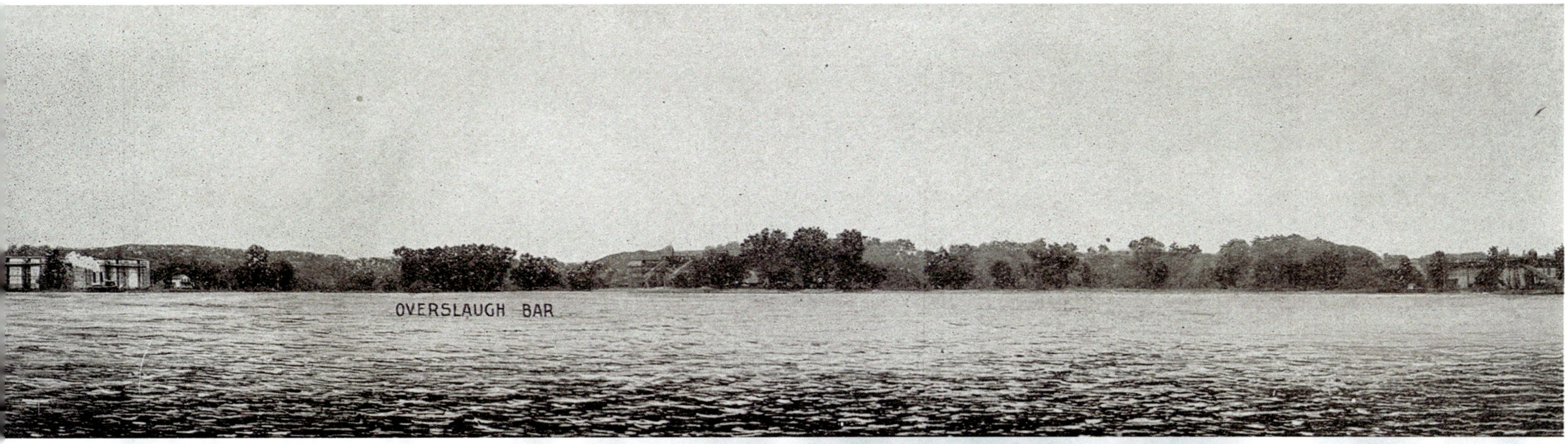

OVERSLAUGH BAR

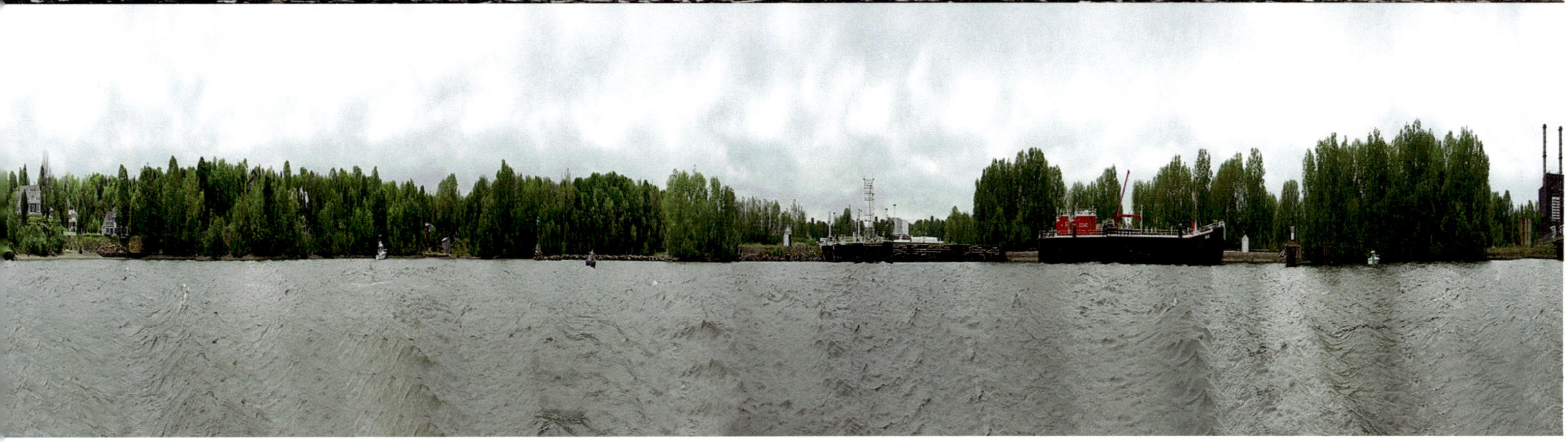

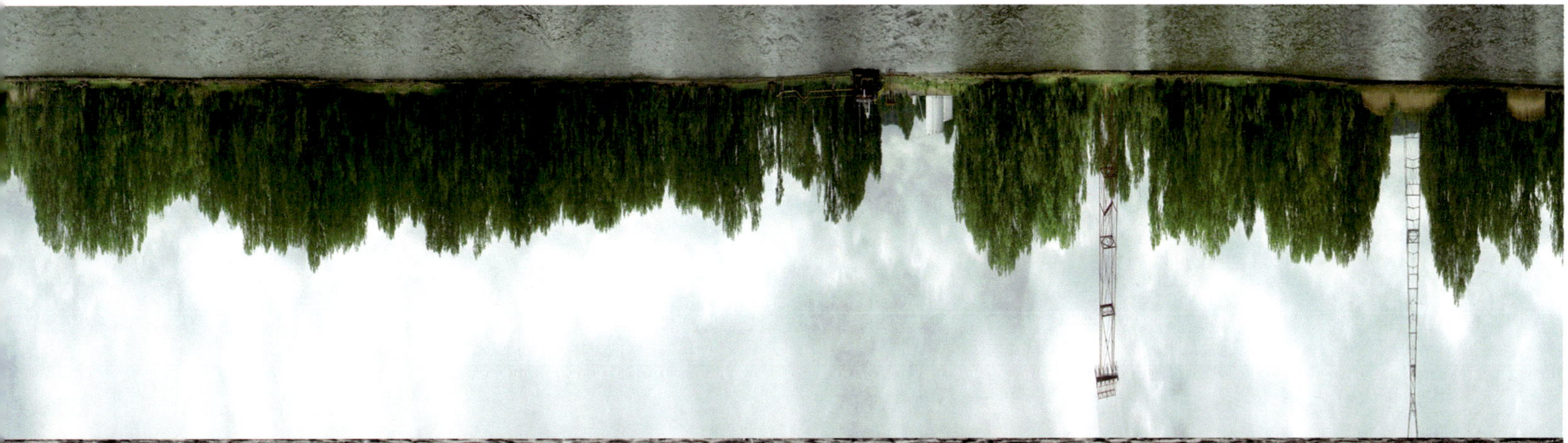

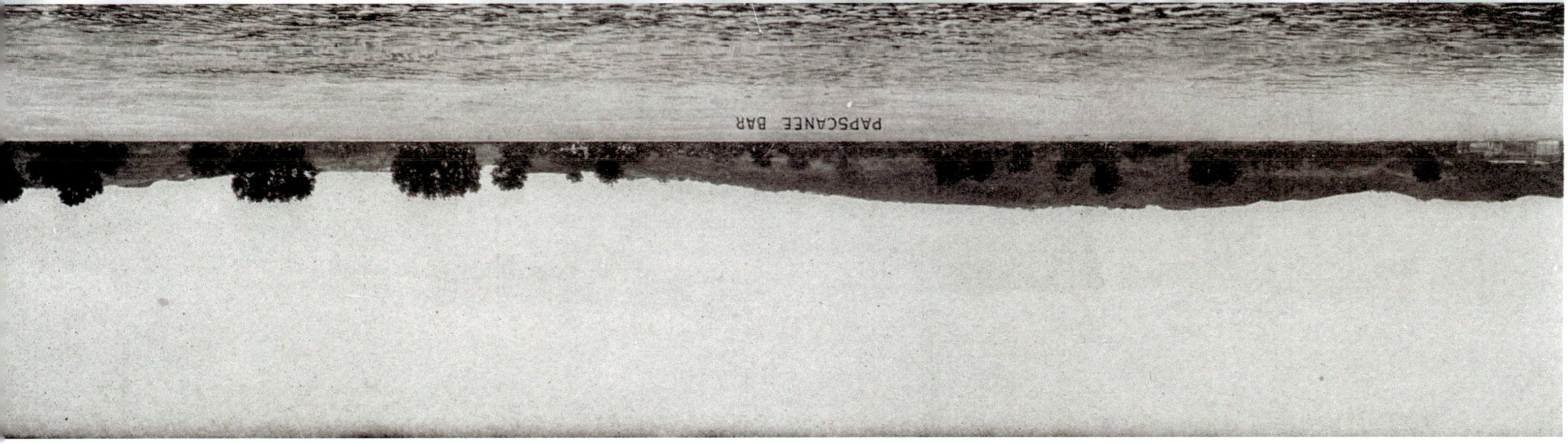

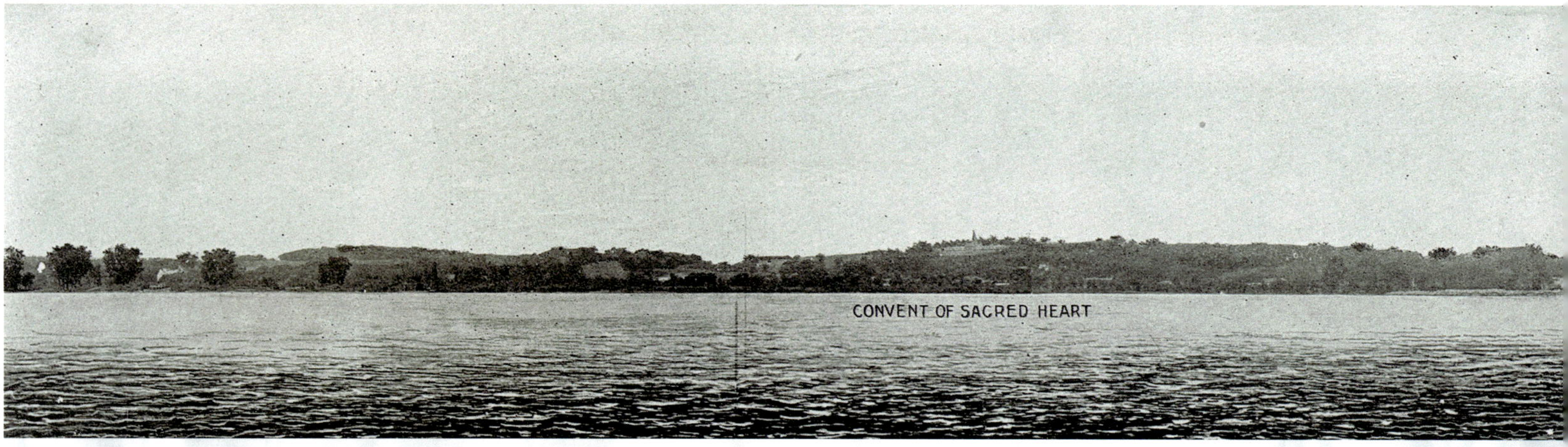

CONVENT OF SACRED HEART

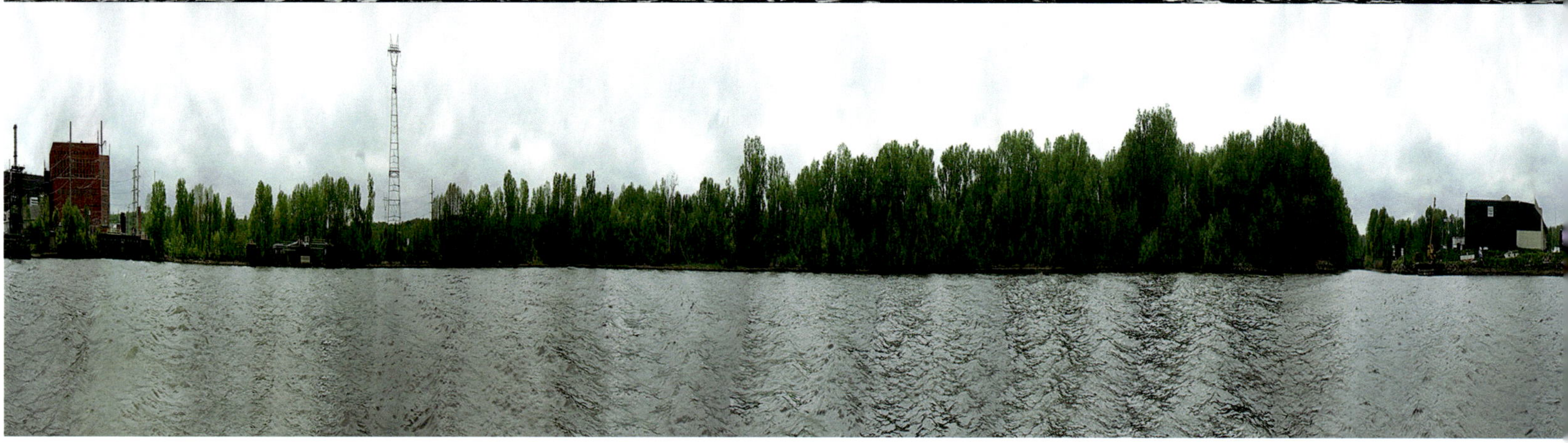

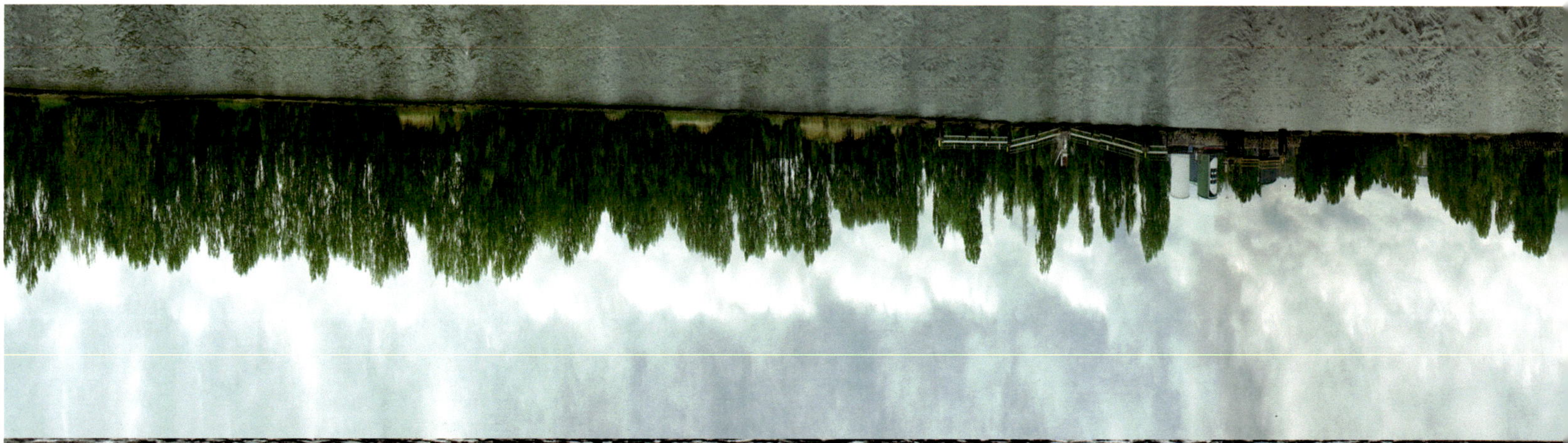

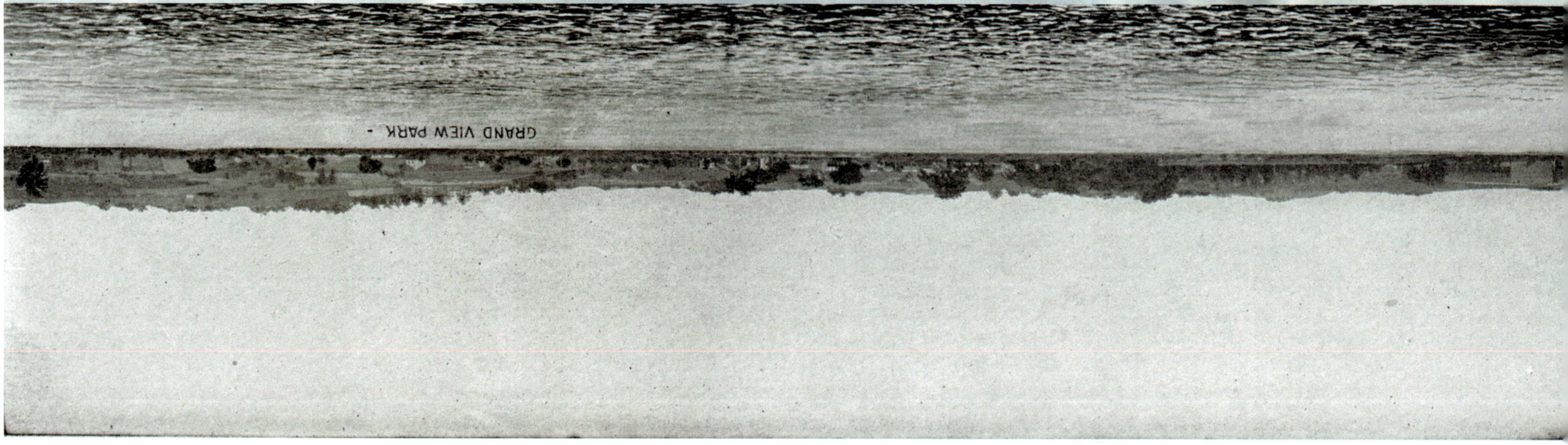

GRAND VIEW PARK -

East Bank

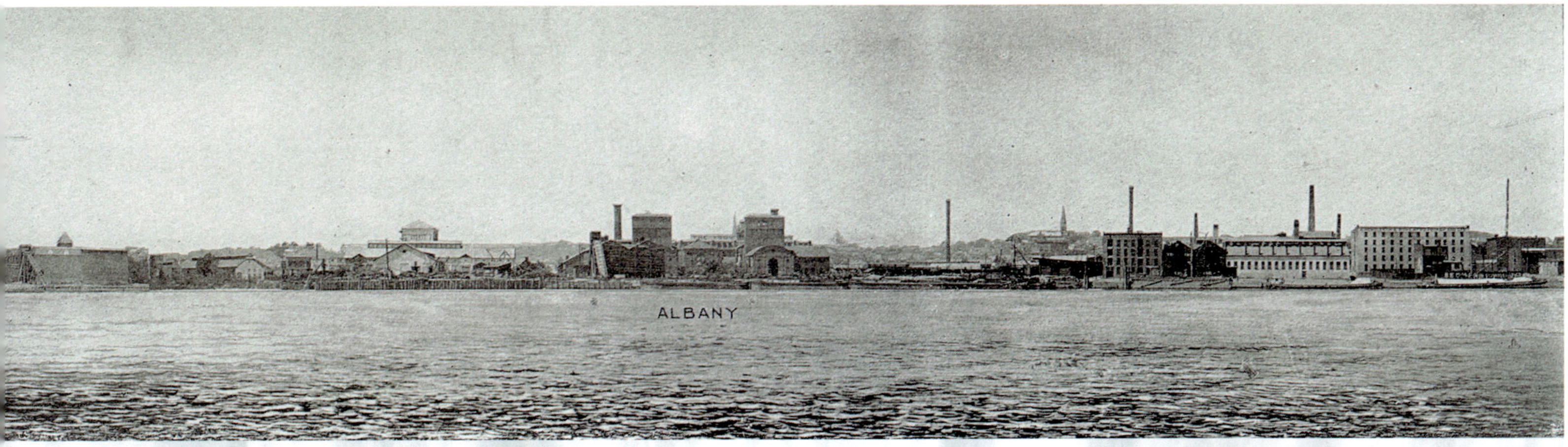

ALBANY

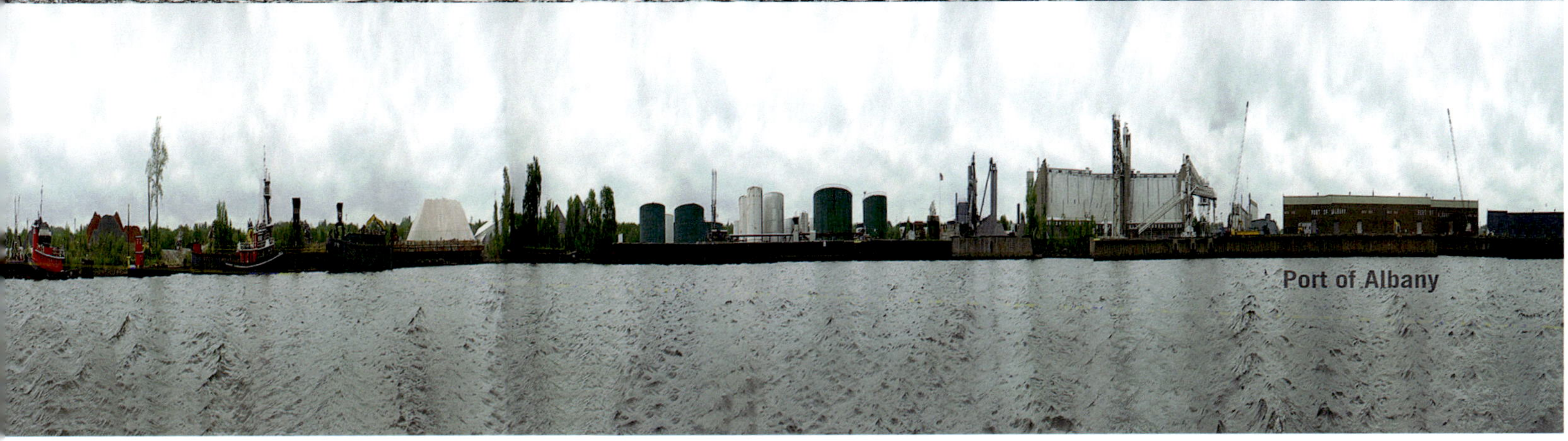

Port of Albany

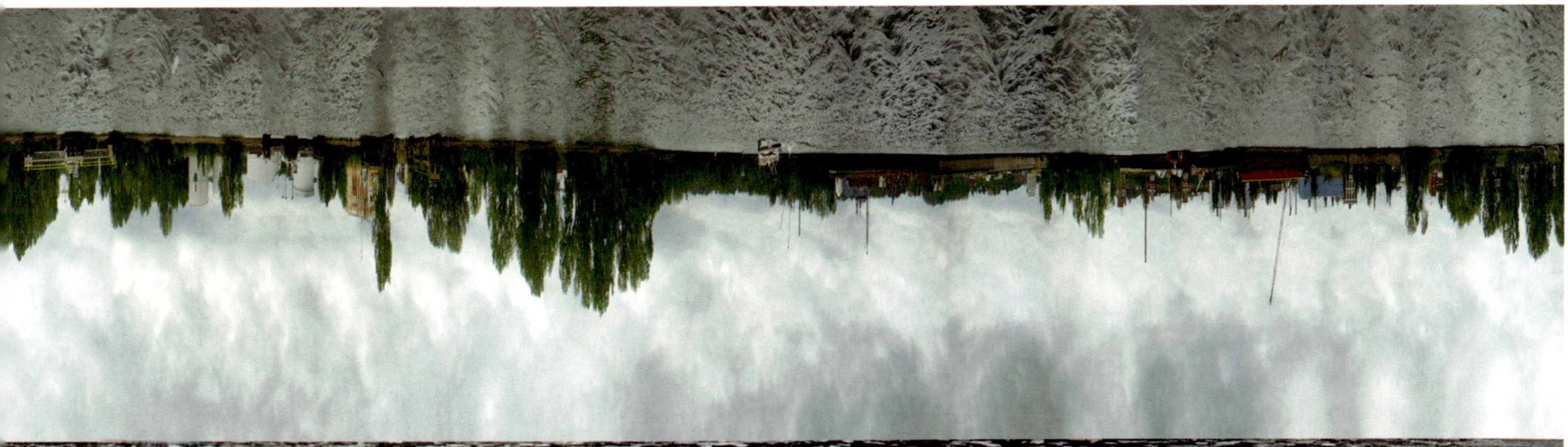

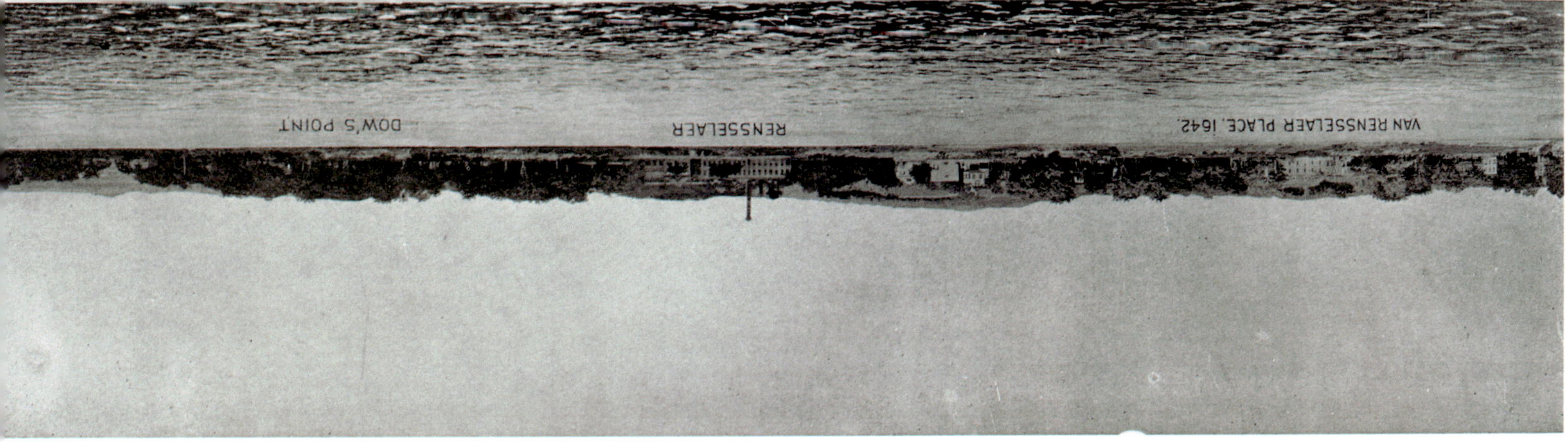

DOW'S POINT

RENSSELAER

VAN RENSSELAER PLACE, 1642.

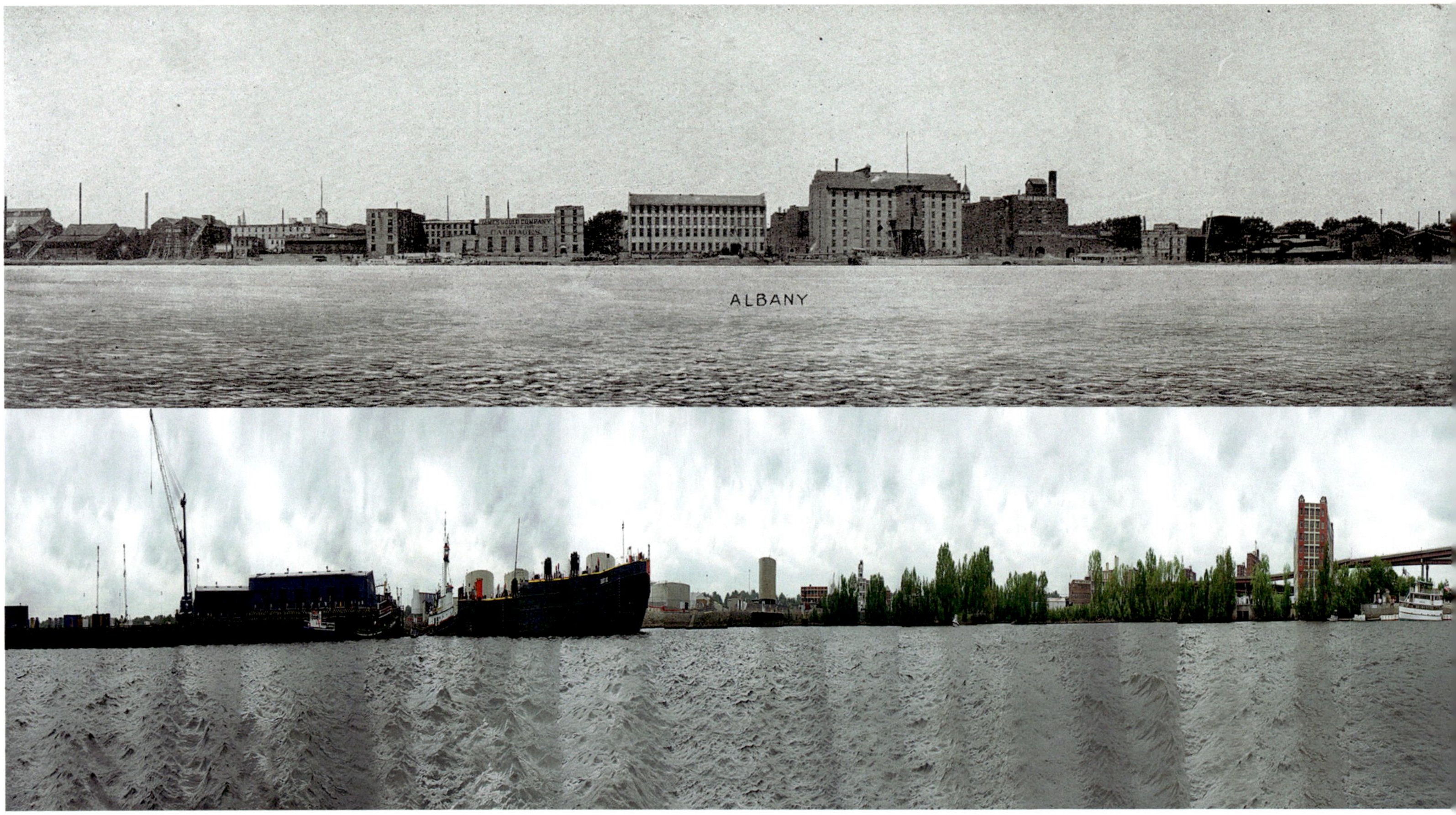

ALBANY

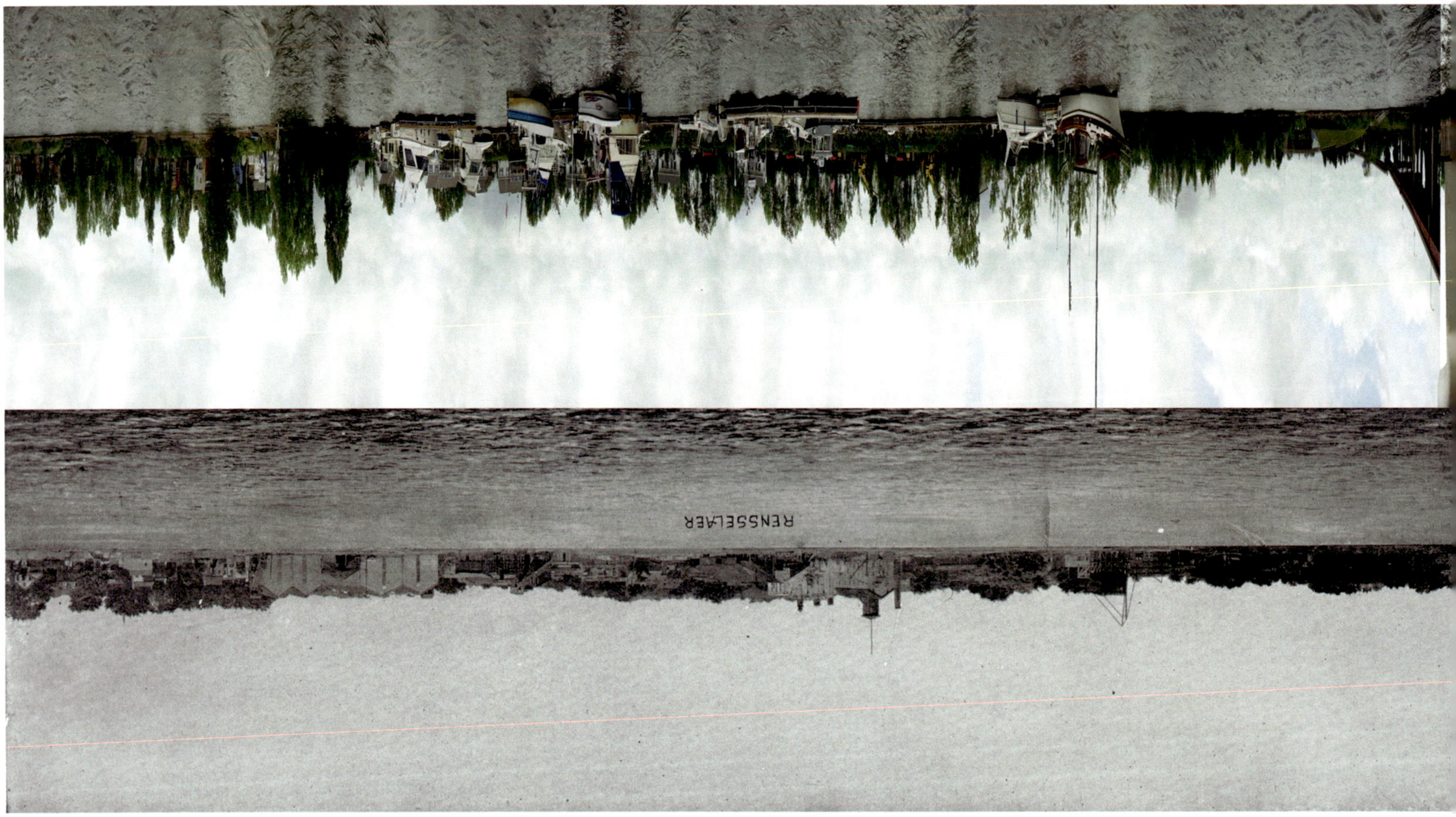

RENSSELAER

East Bank

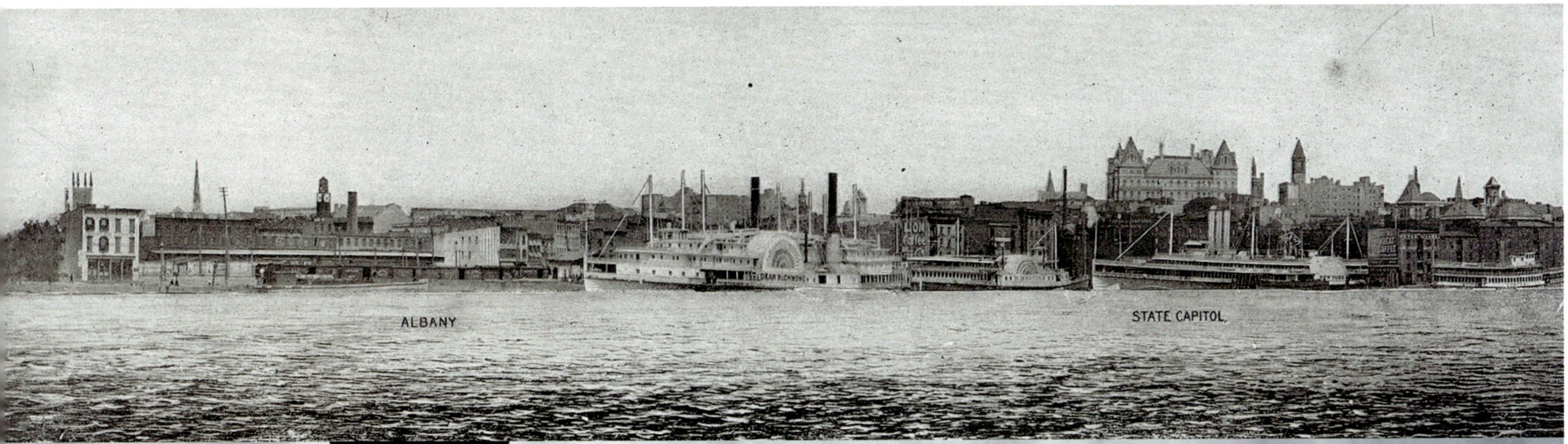

ALBANY
STATE CAPITOL

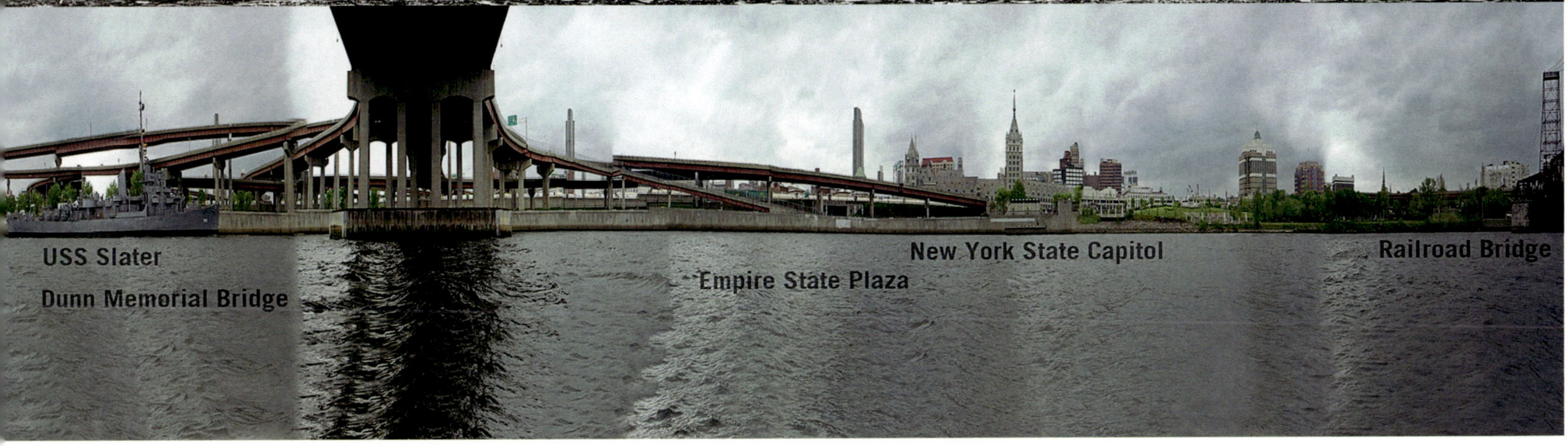

USS Slater
Dunn Memorial Bridge
Empire State Plaza
New York State Capitol
Railroad Bridge

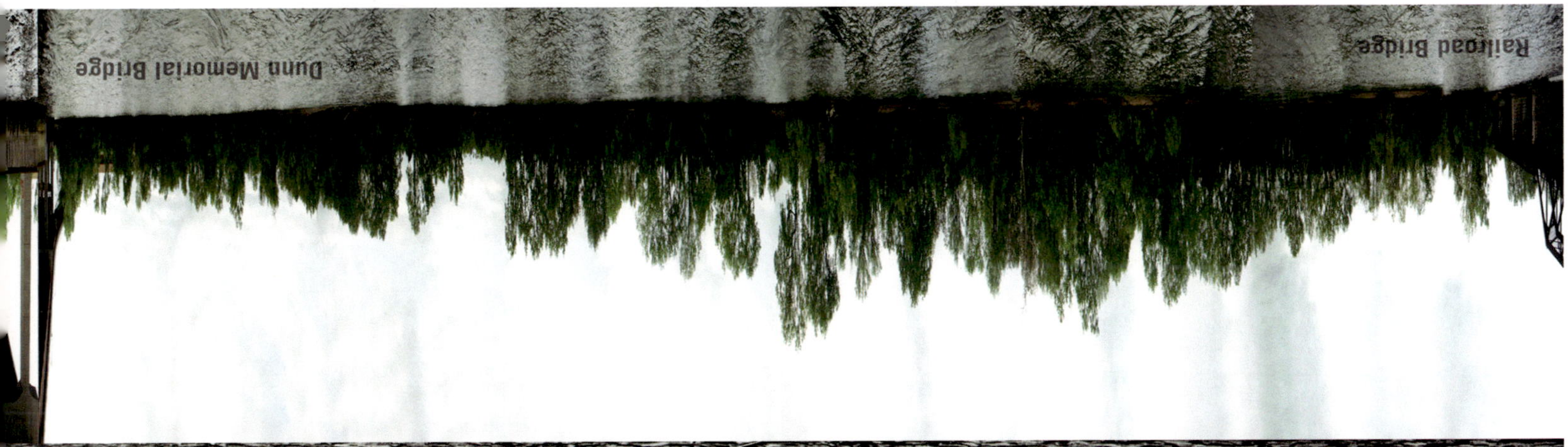

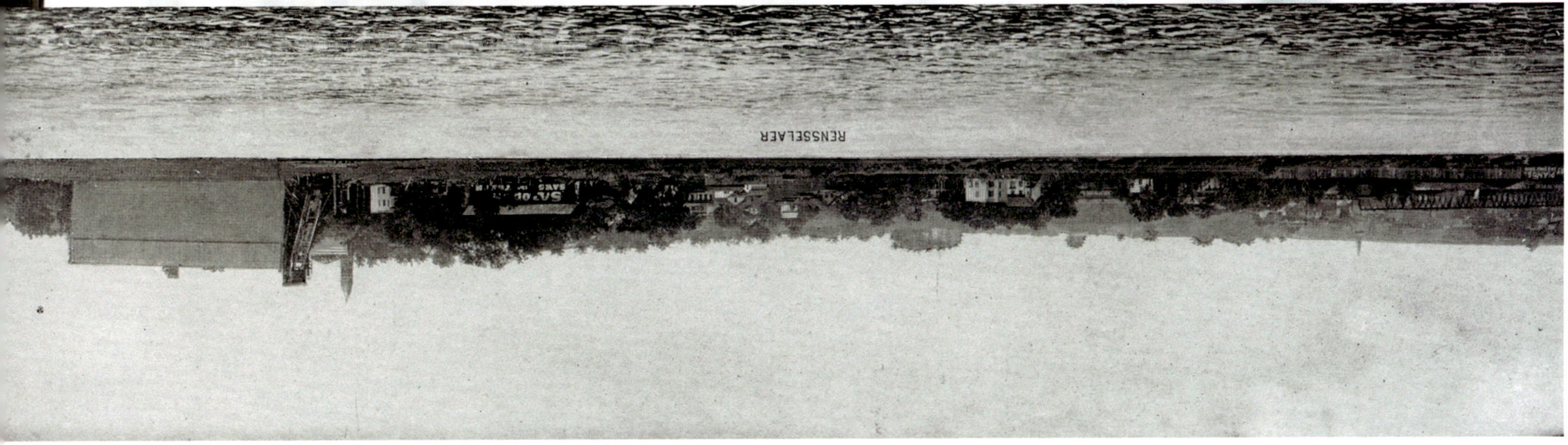

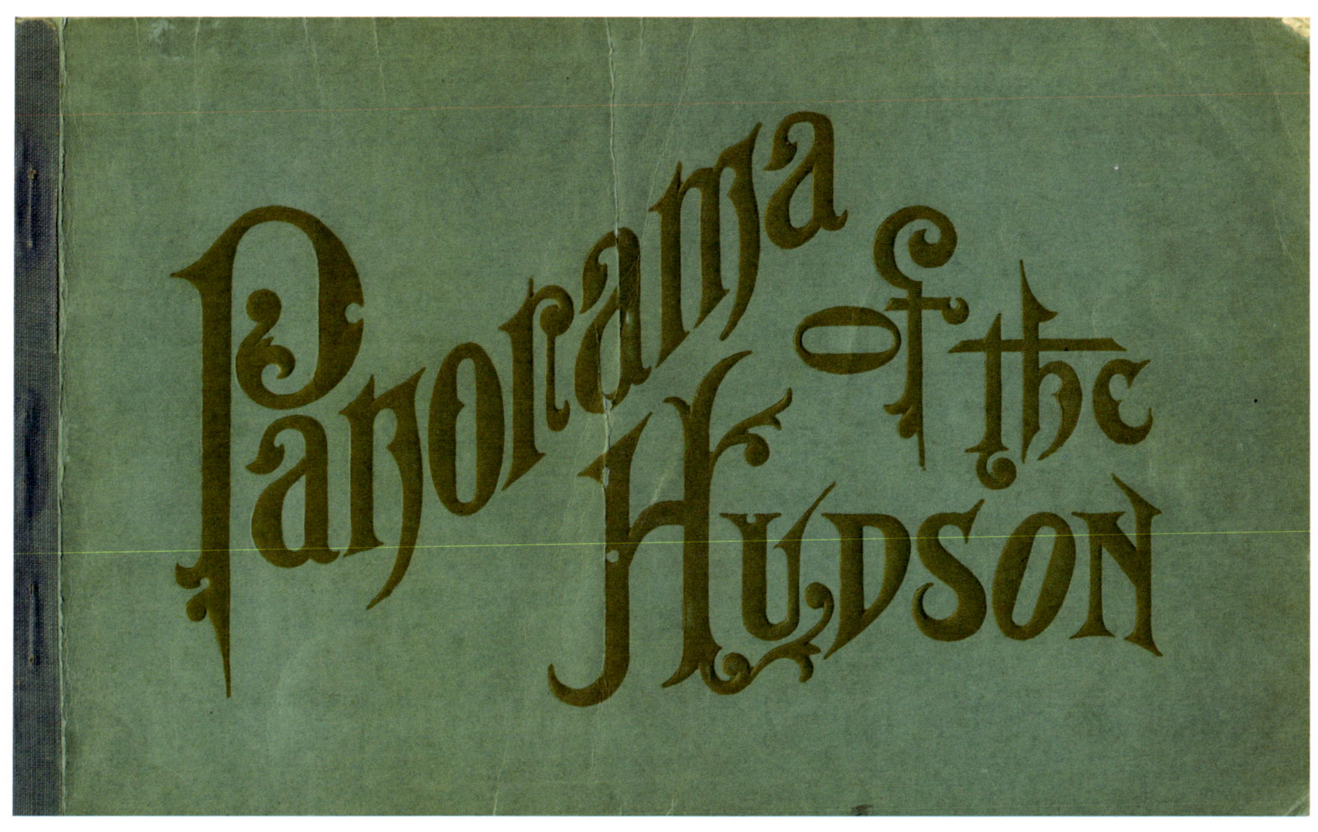

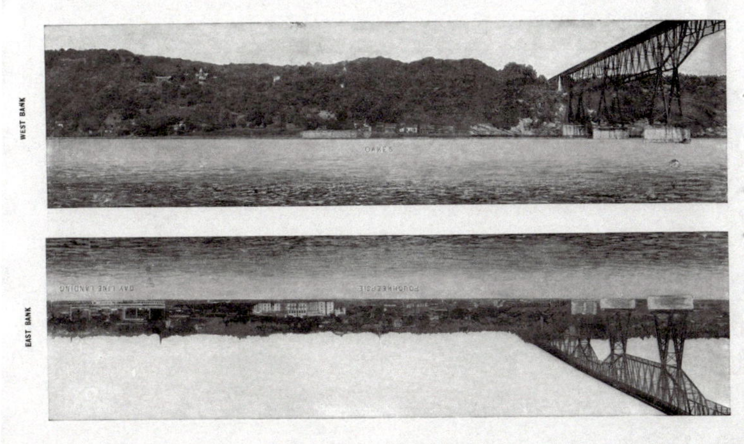

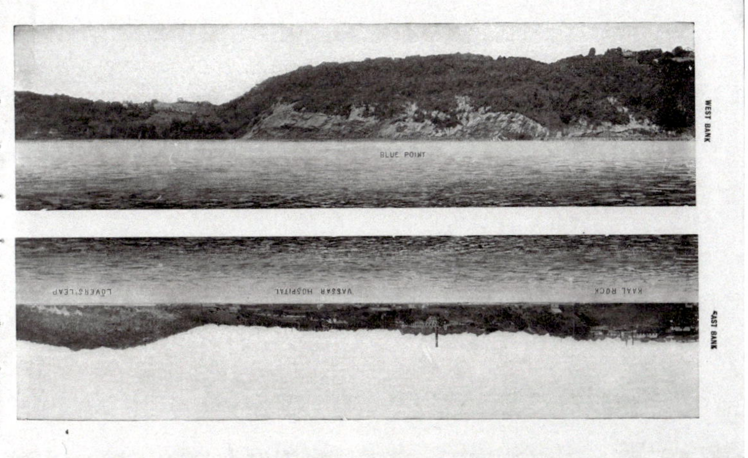

Opposite, the orginal colophon page text. Top, cover from the original publication, copyright 1910.
Above, a sample spread from the original publication (not to scale).

NEW EDITION
PRICE ONE DOLLAR
SOLD ON HUDSON RIVER DAY LINE STEAMERS FOR 50 CENTS

BRYANT UNION PUBLISHING CO.
81 FULTON STREET
NEW YORK

PRINTED BY THE A.V. HAIGHT COMPANY

SENT POSTPAID ON RECEIPT OF PRICE

PANORAMA OF THE HUDSON

SHOWING BOTH SIDES OF THE RIVER
FROM NEW YORK TO ALBANY

AS SEEN FROM THE DECK OF THE HUDSON RIVER DAY LINE STEAMERS

FIRST PHOTO-PANORAMA OF ANY RIVER EVER PUBLISHED

ONE HUNDRED AND FIFTY MILES OF CONTINUOUS SCENERY ACCURATELY REPRESENTED FROM EIGHT HUNDRED CONSECUTIVE PHOTOGRAPHS

FROM THE CAPITOL TO THE METROPOLIS THE HUDSON VARIES IN WIDTH FROM A HALF MILE TO FOUR MILES AND A HALF; BUT THE RIVER REMAINS UNIFORM IN THESE PAGES AS MOST CONVENIENT FOR A BOOK OF REFERENCE OR TOURIST GUIDE

Title page from the original 1910 publication.